BROKEN PROMISES

D0775394

E.P.L. - MNI

BROKEN PROMISES

A HISTORY OF CONSCRIPTION
IN CANADA

by

J. L. Granatstein
and
J. M. Hitsman

TORONTO
OXFORD UNIVERSITY PRESS
1977

© Oxford University Press
(Canadian Branch) 1977

Cover design by FRED HUFFMAN

ISBN -0-19-540258-8

1 2 3 4-0 9 8 7

Printed in Canada by
WEBCOM LIMITED

Contents

In memory of Mac Hitsman

Preface

No single issue has divided Canadians so sharply as conscription for overseas military service in time of war. In 1917 and again in 1942 and 1944, the question of conscription split the country down the middle. Political parties either collapsed or tore apart as old and tried loyalties fell to pieces under the stress of war. Rioting and widespread evasion of the law followed the passing of conscription measures. And the cry of race swept through the nation, overshadowing the supposed military necessity that, it was claimed, made conscription essential. Compulsory military service seemed to be one issue that Canadian politicians could not readily handle.

Conscription always seemed to be imposed on one segment of the population by the other. In neither war did French Canada want or accept conscription; in both wars, insofar as it can be determined, most English Canadians did. This fundamental divergence in opinion roused fears in both the majority and minority segments of the population. The problem was compounded because Canadian territory was never threatened in a sustained, direct fashion in either world war. This relative safety naturally deflated the potential military ardour of those who would have been prepared to defend their native land against invasion, and it led to the claim that imperial ends, not national ones, were being served by Canada's participation in the fighting. 'Que devons-nous à l'Angleterre?', Henri Bourassa's question in the Great War, was one that many, probably most, French Canadians and many Canadians of neither British nor French origin asked in 1917 and 1944.

Probably a great many English Canadians asked it as well. Certainly the answer did not include the lives of their sons.

Conscription was no new phenomenon when it first impinged directly on Canadians in 1917. The concept had existed for 300 years in Canada, sporadically implemented and laxly enforced, with predictably unsatisfactory results. Its history was more a folk memory than a clearly perceived past, but even these vague recollections probably helped shape the Canadian response in 1917. European immigrants, many of whom had come to Canada precisely because they wanted their children to escape military service in the old country, brought more recent experience of conscription and a sharp dislike for it. In turn, memories of the great schism of 1917 shaped policy and the public response during the interwar years and during the Second World War. That second wartime experience again helped to determine government actions and planning during the Cold War years. The past held us prisoner.

Why? Why was conscription such a shibboleth to Canadians in Quebec, such a potent weapon in the hands of politicians? Was it ever a military necessity in 1917, 1942, and 1944? Who decided and why? How did Mackenzie King handle conscription so successfully in the Second World War? And how could the question of conscription be raised after 1945 by a French-speaking prime minister? These are some of the questions that this book poses.

This study was conceived in the mid-1960s by J. M. Hitsman, with whom I then worked at the Directorate of History in the Department of National Defence. We agreed to collaborate in writing a book on conscription, and Mac Hitsman completed his drafts shortly before his death on 11 February 1970. My own chapters and the work of revision, I regret to say, took much longer.

Mac Hitsman was in the terminal stages of a painful and paralyzing illness when he wrote his sections of this book. How he managed to function so well in the face of such disabilities was an amazement to me and one sign of his very great fortitude. Charles Stacey, with whom Mac worked for many years, said in an obituary note in the *Canadian Historical Review* that Hitsman's friends will remember him best for his courage and resolution in overcoming physical miseries that would have reduced most men to complete inaction. In his case, Colonel Stacey said, 'the well-worn phrase rings true: he was an example to us all.' He was indeed, and he taught me a great deal and not only about history.

Many people have assisted in the preparation of this book. I am grateful to my colleagues in the Department of History at York University and particularly to Peter Oliver, Viv Nelles, Chris Armstrong, Paul Stevens, and Ramsay Cook; to Desmond Morton; to Norman Hillmer; to Charles Stacey who will disagree with much of it; to Mr Henry Borden and Professor Craig Brown for permission to make use of the Borden Diaries; to those individuals who permitted me to see manuscript collections under their control; to the helpful staff at the Public Archives of Canada; and to Ian Wilson, late of the Queen's University archives. Mr and Mrs Ted Hitsman assisted greatly. The research on which this book is based was funded by the Canada Council, that great aid to Canadian scholarship.

Three acknowledgements remain. Ms Tilly Crawley of Oxford University Press did the editing on this book. Editing can mean many different things, but in this case, as in every other dealing I have had with her over a ten-year period, editing means what it should always and so rarely does. Mrs Martha Dzioba of OUP checked and rechecked the references and the text for consistency and style and greatly improved both. She and Ms Crawley are responsible for everything but the errors, which are mine alone. Finally my wife Elaine, and my children, Carole and Michael, have assisted in many ways and I am grateful to them. May they never be conscripted for anyone's war.

JLG

One

THE BEGINNINGS

Conscription has been and remains an unhappy word. No farmer, labourer, or student, no husband, father, or brother, will ever be pleased to be taken from his family or livelihood, exposed to dangers and discomforts far from home, and then, if he has survived the vicissitudes of war, demobilized with little compensation. Conscription disrupted the whole fabric of society, slowing industry and agriculture, upsetting life in a thousand major and minor ways. Whether the power of the state to compel men to perform military service was exercised by a colonial governor or by the democratically elected representatives of a free people made no difference to its effects.

But in other ways the question of who imposed conscription was likely to assume substantial importance. To fight and die for the interests of the *ancien régime* or the first British Empire was one thing; to assume the same risks in the interests of your own country may have been another. Some argue forcefully that Canadian interests were at stake in the Great War, the Second World War, and the Cold War years; others claim with equal or greater conviction that only the interests of the imperial power were at risk. But few will suggest that in the years before 1914 anything other than the prestige and might of the metropolitan power were at stake. Perhaps that is why military service seemed so unattractive.

I

As early as Frontenac's day there were complaints from the habitants that they were called up for military service while regular soldiers, hired out by their officers as civilian labourers, remained in safety. 'It is very aggravating for the poor habitants of this country', wrote the Intendant Jean Bochart de Champigny, 'to find themselves continually ordered out for war when the majority of soldiers are not; they have never yet refused to march, but they, as well as their families, are reduced to such a miserable state, I believe it to be urgent that they be employed in some other manner. . . . '[1] There in essence was the problem—danger, hardship to one's family, injustice. Nothing would change when Britain took New France in the Seven Years' War. The first Captain-General and Governor-in-Chief of the new Province of Quebec, General James Murray, was given 'full power & Authority to Levy, Arm, Muster, Command and Employ all persons whatsoever, residing within our said province, and as occasion shall serve them to march, Embark or Transport from one place to another for the resisting and withstanding of all enemies . . . both at land and at sea; and to Transport such Forces to any of our Plantations in America. . . . '[2] Clearly the Governor had the power to employ the habitants on military ventures anywhere in America, and in 1763-4 he ordered the mustering of 300 *Canadiens* for service during the emergency caused by Pontiac's conspiracy. Murray had expected that enough volunteers would be found for the task,[3] but ten men from parishes above Quebec had to be conscripted. As it turned out, however, additional volunteers came forward from the Montreal region, and the unlucky ten were released; nonetheless the first case of conscription for a British war had taken place.

Ten years later conscription was again a possibility as Quebec faced invasion from the rebellious *Bastonnais*, the New Englanders. Short of British regulars and worried that the French had lost their 'ancient habits of obedience and discipline',[4] Carleton, the new Governor, feared that the habitants would not be 'pleased at being suddenly, and without Preparation embodied into a Militia, and marched from their Families, Lands, and Habitations to remote Provinces, and all the Horrors of War, which they have already experienced.'[5] He was right. Not even the proclamation of martial law could force the *Canadiens* to serve in the militia in any numbers or to any effect. Companies refused their summons, unpopular officers were assaulted, and some *miliciens* armed themselves and resisted efforts to enrol them. The *Canadien* had no reason to feel loyalty to a regime that had so recently conquered New France, no more than he had any desire to assist the hated New Englanders. Most wanted nothing more nor less than peace—and the chance to sell provisions to both sides at cash prices.[6]

The experiences of 1775 did not prevent Carleton from pressing a militia ordinance through the Legislative Council in 1777. All physically fit males between 16 and 60 were declared liable for service within the parish in which they resided, and four days each year were set aside for drill. In the event of war or emergency, the Governor had the power to draft any number of men he believed necessary.[7] But to pass a law and to enforce it were very different things, and there was little to be gained by the British in completely antagonizing a restive population.

In Nova Scotia too there was difficulty in mobilizing the militia, for similar reasons. Settlers there also wanted to be left alone, and when the Governor tried to summon one-fifth of the males for service he was greeted by angry petitions protesting that Nova Scotians did not want to fight against their New England brethren. In consequence the Governor had to agree in January 1776 that the militia could remain at home unless there was an actual invasion of the colony, an eventuality that fortunately did not occur.[8]

In Quebec there were regular attempts in the 1780s and 1790s to secure the co-operation of the *Canadiens* in planning for the defence of the colony, but all foundered on a stubborn reluctance to have anything to do with the military. The result, as the Governor of Lower Canada was forced to report in 1799, was that his militia of 28,264 French-Canadian and 1,376 English-speaking officers and rank and file had 'not one effective man',[9] a state of affairs that was the norm throughout British America, not the exception. Two years earlier, for example, the Duke of Kent, while military commander in Nova Scotia, had called up militia to work on fortifications with disillusioning results. Enlisting the men had bad effects on their families, he said, and 'the laws by which they were governed when embodied, are so totally inefficient that it is next to an impossibility to enforce any kind of control or subordination. . . . ' The average regular soldier, in His Grace's estimation, did three times the work of a militiaman.[10]

The war scare of 1807 between Britain and the United States produced yet another attempt to call up the militia in the Canadas and Nova Scotia. In Lower Canada 10,000 men, selected by ballot, were instructed to hold themselves in readiness. Most did, but there were a few instances of 'misbehaviour and insubordination' in the area of Montreal.[11] Again, however, even when the populace co-operated, little was effected. Colonel Isaac Brock complained that 'The men thus selected for service being scattered along an extensive line of four or five hundred miles, unarmed and totally unacquainted with everything military, without officers capable of giving them instruction, considerable time would naturally be required before the necessary degree of order and discipline could be introduced among them.'[12] The situation was no better in Upper Canada. Lieutenant-Governor Gore reported in 1808 that large numbers of Americans, with their 'ideas of equality and insubordination',[13] made the militia unwieldy and ineffective.

The loyalty and utility of the militia would be soon tested by the War of 1812. If the Canadas were to be defended, every measure would have to be taken, and this included conscription. In April 1812 a new Militia Act was passed, empowering the selection of 2,000 males by ballot for 90-day terms of training in each of two successive summers.[14] The process of selection was still in hand when the war broke out, and although there was again some difficulty in the Montreal area,[15] including an incident when regulars fired on a crowd attempting to free conscripts, in general the militia did its duty, probably because the militiamen did not have to face very much actual fighting. Most of them served on the *corvée*, hauling troops and supplies up the St Lawrence from Montreal to Kingston, a dull, hard, but vital role. In Upper Canada, where Loyalist stock accounted for only one-sixth of the population, and another one-fifth came from the United Kingdom, the authorities thought it might not be prudent to arm more than a third of the estimated 11,000 militia. But even those 'loyal' militia were not a force to be relied upon. The Captain-General and Governor-in-Chief, Sir George Prevost, noted in 1813 'the frequent desertion of even the well disposed . . . to their farms for the purpose of getting seed into the ground. . . . ' The militia could be important in subsidiary roles behind the lines; certainly it had little value as a fighting force.[16]

The coming of peace saw the militia return to its once-yearly drinking affairs and farcical musters. But when the rebellions of 1837 occurred, men flocked to the colours. In Lower Canada the recruits were almost entirely English-speaking; in Upper Canada a refusal to muster must have seemed almost enough to brand a man as a traitor.[17] And yet Lord Durham reported in 1839 on the Canadas, 'The militia . . . is completely disorganized. A muster of that force, would in some districts, be the occasion for quarrels between the races, and in the greater part of the country the attempting to arm or employ it would be merely arming the enemies of the government.'[18]

The true enemies of the militia were apathy and unconcern. In 1848 only six men turned out for the annual muster in Toronto and not even corporals' guards could be mounted in other parts of the Canadas. Not until 1855 and a new Militia Act were measures taken. The liability of men to be called for compulsory service was maintained through a nominal enrolment in the sedentary militia; but authorization was now given for the creation of volunteer units, up to 5,000 strong, who would do ten days' training each year in uniforms to be provided at the volunteers' own expense. The result was that in 1857 the sedentary militia, almost all the fit men in the Canadas, numbered 235,000, while 6,000 men trained in the volunteer units. Between 1856 and 1864, no annual musters at all took place.[19]

When relations between Britain and the United States deteriorated in the early 1860s as a consequence of the Civil War, the defences of Canada again became a focus of attention. A Militia Commission, named in January 1862, reported that Canada needed a force of 50,000 men. The Commission, headed by John A. Macdonald, proposed to secure this force by expanding the volunteer units in the urban areas and by raising battalions in the countryside. If enough volunteers could not be secured, then men would be called to serve by ballot or by conscription. The costs for this scheme were $1.1 million, a tenth of the provincial revenue. But when the Macdonald-Cartier government moved to implement the Commission's recommendations and introduced a bill into the legislature to this effect, the measure was defeated, thanks to the opposition of the Reformers and to the desertion of the government by a substantial number of French-Canadian members.[20] The new government of Sandfield Macdonald and Louis Sicotte informed the Governor General that it could not approve of compul-- sory service in peacetime, and argued that the voluntary movement was the proper outlet through which the 'military spirit of the people must find vent. . . . ' The citizenry could be relied upon in times of war, but it was 'not desirable to excite discontent among them, by any premature attempts to exact compulsory service',[21] a Council minute maintained correctly.

After its re-election the next year, the Macdonald-Sicotte government passed two Militia Acts, one authorizing an increase in the volunteer militia to 35,000, the other prescribing a careful nominal enrolment of the sedentary militia.[22] But once again, although 80,000 men were balloted for service, none were trained. And the Fenian scares that preceded Confederation and helped secure it revealed the shoddy nature of the arrangements for the volunteer militia. There was no administrative organization to speak of, and many of the 15,000-odd troops on duty went hungry and ill-supplied, unless they were fortunate enough to be able to draw from the areas in which they were billeted. Moreover municipalities had to provide for their volunteers' dependants as there were no proper pay arrangements.[23] One good lesson was drawn from the affair, however. A Council minute of 21 June 1866 maintained with a mix of good sense and wishful thinking that 'recent experience has shown the efficiency of the Volunteer Force and that it is obviously better to accept the willing services of such men than to resort to the conscription provided by the Militia Act.'[24]

II

Then came Confederation. The British North America Act declared that the Parliament of Canada should have exclusive legislative authority for the 'Militia, Military and Naval Service, and Defence', and the Dominion's first Militia Act received royal assent on 22 May 1868. For practical reasons the wording of many sections of this Act was similar to the militia legislation of the Province of Canada, and indeed the same officer who had been Adjutant-General in the Canadas before Confederation continued in this post for the Dominion after Confederation.

The sedentary militia of the former separate colonies now became the reserve militia, in which all physically fit males between the ages of 18 and 60 were liable for service unless exempted or disqualified by law. The active militia consisted of the volunteers and a regular militia of men between 18 and 40 who would either volunteer or be balloted for service whenever called upon, as well as a marine militia composed of professional sailors. The Militia Act authorized annual paid drill for a maximum of 40,000 men of the active militia, and the annual musters of the reserve militia were done away with.

Exemption from service in the militia automatically applied to all judges, clergymen, professors, staff of penitentiaries and lunatic asylums, the physically unfit, and to the only sons of widows. Half-pay and retired British officers, sailors, pilots, and school teachers were enrolled, but would only be called upon to serve in case of actual invasion. Why professors were treated differently than teachers is unclear. And with some liberality the exemption of Quakers, Mennonites, Tunkers, and other males recognized as sincere conscientious objectors would be authorized by regulations prescribed by the Governor in Council.

Less clear was Section 61 of the Militia Act, which in vague, general terms restored the liability of militiamen for compulsory overseas service:

> Her Majesty may call out the Militia or any part thereof for actual service, either within or without the Dominion, at any time, whenever it appears advisable to do so by reason of war, invasion or

insurrection, or danger of any of them; and the Militiamen, when so called out for actual service, shall continue to serve for at least one year from the date of their being called out for actual service, if required to do so, or for any longer period which Her Majesty may appoint.[25]

Yet in 1884, when the question arose whether Canada could or should send troops to the Egyptian Sudan, Prime Minister John A. Macdonald told the Governor General's Military Secretary, Lord Melgund, that 'no Government in Canada could possibly officially take Canadian Regiments as such . . . to assist the old country; he considered any such action would be quite outside the meaning of the Act.'[26] When the Act of 1868 was being drafted, it seems, Macdonald and his colleagues had been thinking only of employing militia abroad on offensive operations directed at the United States.

The volunteer militia authorized by the 1868 Act seemed to meet the limited needs of the country. In 1869 there were 43,541 officers and men enrolled, and Colonel Patrick Robertson-Ross, a British officer, the Adjutant-General of the Militia and as such its commander, was generally pleased. 'The existing force,' he reported in 1870, 'has been raised, and is still maintained entirely by voluntary enrolment . . . [while] more than the quota required annually for training has been furnished. . . . ' But Robertson-Ross did have fears for the future:

> It should be borne in mind, however, that by continuing to rely upon voluntary enrolement [sic] for the maintenance of the active force (which however convenient to the country at large, and suitable in time of peace, when a comparatively small force is required, and no strain put upon the country), yet many evils caused by a voluntary system are perpetuated.

> 1st. The equal burden of military service in defence of the country is not properly shared by its young men, and this burden still continues 'to fall on the willing few,' a matter of frequent complaint.

> 2nd. In the event of foreign war, the system of voluntary enrolment would be found quite insufficient. The necessary large number of men then required would have to be obtained through the instrumentality of the Reserve Militia by means of the ballot.

> On military considerations, therefore, also those of justice and fairness, all that seems necessary to perfect that portion of the military organization of Canada relating to the mode of obtaining men, would be the observance of that system in time of peace, which

would become necessary in time of war; thus, when such an emergency arose, no alteration of system at a critical moment would become necessary, but simply an expansion of an existing system.[27]

Most of the arguments in favour of conscription, arguments that would be heard intermittently for the next hundred years, had been sketched out by the Adjutant-General in his report.

In succeeding years Robertson-Ross returned to his theme. Very few units of the volunteer militia were at full strength, he pointed out, and his officers believed that the deficiencies could only be met by the ballot. Rank-and-file volunteers similarly objected that it was unfair that they should bear the entire burden of defending Canada. By transforming volunteers into regular militia and by installing a measure of legal compulsion, employers of the 'Scrooge' variety would be deterred from threatening to dismiss employees who went off to attend militia summer camp. In 1871, therefore, Robertson-Ross again offered homilies in favour of compulsion:

> Experience proves that the strongest national military organization is that one which is founded upon the principle of obligatory service; the people of Canada wisely recognized this fact in the Dominion Militia Act; doubtless the same wisdom and feelings of patriotism with which they were actuated in framing the law will induce them to carry out its provisions, whenever they find that necessity has arisen.[28]

That would be a long time, as the Adjutant-General well knew. The Macdonald government and its successors would not resort to compulsion in time of peace, particularly as the numbers turning out for the annual drill were about all the government expected—and about all it was prepared to pay for. Furthermore the restoration of Anglo-American harmony after the Treaty of Washington in 1871 removed the overt American threat, at least for the time being.

The first real test of the volunteer system came in the Riel Rebellion of 1885. The Canadian force—the first and only independent Canadian expedition in our history—took its men from among the most efficient units of the volunteer militia, and the call-up was handled with informality and despatch. The Minister of Militia, for example, asked a captain in the Governor General's Foot Guards of Ottawa how long it would take to mobilize a company for service. The reply—less than 24 hours—proved correct.[29] The Canadian force did its work expeditiously and creditably; significantly, French-Canadian militiamen served in the force without complaint. Rebellion was rebellion, whoever caused it.[30]

That there were any French-Canadian militia at all was in some ways surprising. Certainly Ottawa had done nothing to encourage *Québécois* to feel that they had a place in the militia. There was a continuing shortage of competent French-speaking officers, words of command were ordinarily given in English (and then explained in French, a procedure that would have made drill or battle into a shambles), and the whole ethos of the force was militantly Anglo-Saxon. When, for example, in the late 1870s some *Québécois* made an attempt to form a unit that would wear the dress of Zouaves, the response from Ottawa was to delay and then to refuse this un-British request—Canadian military dress was not foreign as was the Algerian-based Zouave outfit. Canadian military dress quite properly included such native outfits as kilts, trews, busbies, and the like. No one seemed to realize the contradiction; no one seemed to care about the insult.[31]

The result of such unthinking prejudice was that French Canadians stayed away from the militia in droves. At the first enrolment in 1868, French-speaking Quebec produced only slightly more than half of the 12,600 volunteers from the Province of Quebec despite the vast numerical superiority of French-speaking citizens. Those *Québécois* who did join up often came for the wrong reasons. There seemed to be a higher proportion of political appointees among the French-speaking officers, and the quest for patronage was, perhaps, hotter in Quebec than elsewhere. And too many illiterates and ne'er-do-wells, otherwise public charges on the municipalities, tended to find their way to training schools over the winter, a clear saving to the local tax rolls. Liberal politicians and their press complained bitterly, and when the rebellion of 1885 produced a sudden wealth of funds and a potential flow of honours and awards, their complaints increased quickly.[32] But so too did pride in the military performance of the French-Canadian troopers during the short North-West campaign. The *Canadiens* acquitted themselves well, performing their duties with at least as much skill as their English-speaking compatriots.

The execution of Riel changed matters somewhat. The anger of Quebec at this vengeful political murder of the Métis leader was deep indeed, and the political ripples took years to die away. In 1886 Honoré Mercier led Quebec *nationalistes* to victory in the provincial elections, helped in part by the after-effects of Riel's execution as well as a host of additional factors. And in 1888 he was scoring points by attacking what he saw as the resurgent imperialism of English-speaking Canadians and their brethren in the United Kingdom, an imperialism that might try 'to impose upon us a political regime which through conscription could scatter our sons from the icefields of the North Pole to the burning sands of the Sahara; an odious regime which would condemn us to pay an arbitrary tax of blood and money and tear our sons from us, in order to cast them into remote and bloody wars which we could neither prevent nor stop.'[33]

Unfortunately some Canadians were thinking along similar, if less pejorative, lines. The Imperial Federation League, particularly active in Toronto, believed fervently that Canadians should participate in British wars.[34] Others reasoned that by sharing in the burdens and responsibilities of Empire, Canadians could best develop and nurture their own nationalism. And as Canada was certain some day to be the greatest, most populous, and most powerful part of the Empire, inevitably this nation would become the heart of the Empire, its directing force.*[35]

The agitation that engulfed the country at the time of the Boer War has to be seen in this light. Many English Canadians believed that Prime Minister Sir Wilfrid Laurier had compromised the Dominion into the worst of all possible positions. Canada under Laurier rejected the possibility of standing aloof; similarly it refused to arm, equip, and pay its own troops and have them commanded by Canadian officers. The adopted middle position—that troops should be sent but that the British should be responsible for their pay and maintenance and for command arrangements—was the worst of all choices to Canadian imperialist-nationalists. Canada had abdicated its responsibilities and had acted in a colonialist fashion, they argued. The nationally responsible course was to have a force paid, equipped, and commanded by Canadians.

Perhaps it would have been, but whether there was much desire to fight in South Africa is another question. In proportion to population, for example, Canada contributed substantially fewer men than did the Australian colonies and New Zealand. And although British-born males made up only 7 per cent of the population of Canada, just under 30 per cent of the Canadian contingent had been born in the United Kingdom.

---

*A perfect example of this attitude is found in an analysis by an unnamed Briton, written sometime before 1914: ' . . . inside the Empire there is a future for Canada. . . . Canadians admit that Canada can never catch up to America. So, the demon of ambition whispered the answer. "Why not become the moving spirit of Empire? Then you'll have a bigger future than the United States. At any rate you will be one of the great world powers of the future." If few Canadians have put it to themselves exactly like this, most of them have looked ahead and seen as big a destiny for their country, within the Empire as they could hope for without. As one Westerner said to me, "If the Empire is the biggest thing, Canada will take it." ' (Scottish Record Office, Edinburgh, Lothian Papers, file GD 40/17/14, 'The Situation in Canada', n.d.)

Most important, perhaps, was Quebec's virtual indifference to the war. Of the 7,368 Canadians who went off to the Boer War, no more than 3 per cent were French-speaking.*[36] Perhaps it was the colonial character of the Canadian force that disturbed both French- and English-speaking Canadians; more likely, however, few had anything more than a vicarious interest in events in Africa.

The military and the politicians, however, had been disturbed by the disasters that befell British arms in the first year of the Boer War, and cries for reform arose in Canada as elsewhere in the Empire. In 1904 the Militia Act was substantially amended by the Laurier government, and larger numbers of troops were soon going to summer training camp each year. The new Act also created a Militia Council and removed the requirement that a British officer had to be the General Officer Commanding the Canadian militia. There was some criticism of this cutting of a link with the British army, but the Minister of Militia diffused the criticism by securing a British regular, Colonel Percy Lake, to serve as the first Chief of the General Staff.[37] At the same time the Militia Act of 1904 defined the liability of troops for service overseas: 'The Governor in Council may place the Militia, or any part thereof, on active service anywhere in Canada, and also beyond Canada, for the defence thereof, at any time when it appears advisable to do so by reason of emergency.'[38] There was no explicit reference to conscription, and there is no evidence to suggest that the Laurier government even con-

---

*A study of the armed forces prepared for the Royal Commission on Bilingualism and Biculturalism broke down Permanent Force officer appointments by language group for 1899, the year of the Boer War, and 1912:

	1899		1912	
	Eng.	Fr.	Eng.	Fr.
Maj.-Gen.	—	—	—	—
Brig. Gen.	—	—	3	1
Col	1	—	9	3
Lt Col	14	4	27	3
Maj.	11	3	52	5
Capt.	13	4	68	12
Lt	12	1	67	3
	51	12	227	27

As well, few officers of French-Canadian background graduated from the Royal Military College: to 1900, only 10 of 255 graduates since the College's opening in 1876 were French Canadians. (Royal Commission on Bilingualism and Biculturalism, 'Armed Forces Historical Study' (mimeo, n.d.), part II, pp. 23, 31.)

sidered the question at this time. Why should it? Not even Great Britain had compulsory service.

But in the United Kingdom the National Service League was, in fact, pressing for peacetime conscription. And wherever Mother England led, Canadians were certain to be only a few paces behind. The Canadian Defence League was founded in Toronto in 1909 as 'a non-political association to urge the importance to Canada of universal physical and naval or military training'. Its objects, expressed in pamphlets widely distributed throughout English Canada, were to arouse interest in national defence, to press for the 'adoption of the principle of patriotic, unpaid, or universal naval or military training, in the belief that such training conduces to the industrial, physical and moral elevation of the whole people', and 'to aid in securing the systematic physical and military training of all youths between the ages of fourteen and eighteen'.[39] The board of the League was full of notables, but nothing availed against public indifference. Only one major public meeting was held under its auspices, and by 1913 the organization was in an advanced state of decay.[40] Its impact had been minimal, but it was not alone in pressing for compulsory service.

The Minister of Militia in the Borden government after 1911 was Sam Hughes. An Ontario imperialist and nationalist, Hughes was a ceaseless advocate of better prepared Canadian forces, a proponent of the militia, and a bitter opponent of regular soldiers whom he saw as stultified and snobbish. To Hughes compulsory service offered a chance to inculcate moral values into the youth of the nation, and in 1912 he even advocated linking his department with the Women's Christian Temperance Union. The militia, Hughes argued,

> upbuilds manhood, defends homes and loved ones, supplies teachers and instructors all over Canada for cadet corps, Boy Scouts, physical training, training school teachers, schools of military instruction, and at times for police, upbuilds youth mentally, morally, and physically, instills a spirit of obedience, discipline, patriotism, veneration and love for principle, preserves the spirit of liberty and independence and keeps the old flag flying to the breeze, and trains the boys to be an asset to the nation.[41]

The men 'who croak about militarism', Hughes argued on another occasion, 'have not the faintest conception of what militarism really is. They sneer at the volunteers as men hired by the country for militia purposes. They do not realize that the militia is upholding the manhood of the nation....' Every boy in Canada, Hughes urged, should have military training,[42] a cry that the Governor General, the Duke of Connaught, cheerfully endorsed.[43]

But people did sneer, denouncing the super-patriots as zealous fools. In 1912 the Toronto *Globe*, for example, jeered at the Canadian Defence League as a group of militarists, and the Liberal newspaper opposed military training. It would be better, it maintained, to have universal agricultural training.[44] Others took similar approaches, denouncing those who wanted to heat up Canada's military spirit.[45] In Quebec in particular anti-militarism was strong, and the conscription bogey was manipulated with substantial effect.

The *casus belli* was the Naval Bill proposed by the Laurier government in 1910*, a bill that proposed to create a small Canadian navy that could be placed at the disposal of the Admiralty in the event of war, but a bill that *Le Devoir*, the newspaper run by the great *nationaliste* leader Henri Bourassa, saw as bringing Canada to 'le bord de l'abîme'.[46] Why did Canada need a navy?, critics asked, unless it was to draw Canada into Britain's wars. It was, said F. D. Monk, the Conservative leader in Quebec, 'l'imperialisme pur et simple. J'y suis absolument opposé.'[47] Inevitably the Naval Bill was seen as leading to conscription. Bourassa painted the darkest picture, foreseeing a time when mothers would be asked for their sons 'non pas pour defendre le pays natal, mais pour se battre sur toutes les terres et toutes les mers du monde en faveur du drapeau anglais'. Several months later grieving parents would learn that their sons had been slaughtered by 'un boulet japonais ou une balle allemande'. Laurier, Bourassa added darkly, 'n'a pas d'enfant'.[48] Inevitably Laurier had to respond, and in a speech on 10 October 1910 he stated unequivocally that service in the navy would be 'purement voluntaire, rien de compulsoire'.[49] Three days later the Prime Minister announced that a by-election would be held in Drummond-Arthabaska, a seat he had himself once held. The battle would be joined.

By-elections, unlike general elections, can be fought around an issue, and the issue in this by-election was the Naval Bill and the related but spurious question of conscription. When Laurier spoke in the constituency, for example, he stressed again and again that the Bill did not

---

*Elsewhere in the country there was opposition to the Naval Bill and in general to expenditures on armaments. On the Prairies, for example, *The Grain Growers' Guide* led the fight. In December 1913 the *Guide* ran a poll that found a huge majority against naval armament and for efforts 'toward the establishment of universal peace and disarmament'. See Donald Page, 'The Development of a Western Canadian Peace Movement', in S. Trofimenkoff, ed., *The Twenties in Western Canada* (Ottawa, 1972), pp. 76-8.

call for or require conscription; the *nationalistes* and their allies reiterated with equal force that it would.[50] The anti-government candidate naturally portrayed himself as the peace candidate, and his literature asked the voters 'Are you in favour of peace or war?'[51] Another *nationaliste* pamphlet portrayed the scene when 'the volunteers shall have sunk . . . in their old warships and when the law demands the mother of the family after she has sacrificed her eldest son, that she give up also her husband and her last child. . . . '[52] Equally as important as these rhetorical flights, the Liberal organization in the constituency was slack and over-confident while the *nationalistes* were well financed, well organized, and eager for the chance to humiliate Laurier on his own ground. The result was a narrow *nationaliste* victory, a staggering defeat for Laurier, and a triumph of unscrupulous propaganda over a credulous electorate. It was also an indication of the unpopularity of militarism, defence expenditures, and conscription in French Canada, no doubt of that.

The next year, in the general election, English Canadians exercised themselves in denouncing or supporting reciprocity in trade with the United States and in attacking Laurier as a man who would sever the imperial tie; French Canadians to a substantial extent fought about the navy—and conscription. Bourassa, now closely linked to the Conservatives, made the Naval Bill the centre piece of his attack against Laurier Liberalism, and denounced the Prime Minister as a *vendu* who invariably followed London's dictates. The Naval Bill had been adopted at the demand of the British government, he said, and although the bill did not explicitly make reference to conscription, the course of events was clear. If you had the ships you had to man them; if you could not man them with volunteers, then conscription would be necessary.[53] To Laurier these were lies, simply lies. 'I told the people repeatedly that the bill did not involve conscription,' Laurier recalled six years later, 'and that moreover it was against conscription. The result was that we lost heavily in Quebec. When we went into the campaign we had 50 against 15, after the elections they had 28 and we 37.'[54] The *nationalistes* and the Conservatives had eaten heavily into Liberal strength in Quebec and helped secure Laurier's defeat. In the process the efficacy of conscription as a political weapon had been irrefutably demonstrated.

What was so disillusioning to French Canadians and to *nationaliste* voters in particular was that Borden was even more imperialist than Laurier had been. Laurier had wanted a Canadian navy; Borden proposed to give Britain $35 million to build three battleships or battlecruisers of the most modern type. To French Canadians this was as bad or worse, and a great debate within the Cabinet developed. Borden's

Quebec ministers were largely *nationalistes,* men who had been elected in part through their denunciations of Laurier's naval policy. Now Borden proposed to humiliate them, an indication in their eyes and, they feared, the eyes of their voters of how little weight Borden put on their advice. Frederick Monk, the leading *Québécois* in the Cabinet, pressed for a referendum and when Borden refused to consider it—'It would probably be fatal to us in the English Provinces,' he wrote in his diary—Monk resigned. Borden was unmoved, and when the debate in the House of Commons showed no sign of concluding, he forced the bill's passage with the first use of closure.[55] Robert Borden was a determined man, but the Senate, filled with Liberals after Laurier's 15-year tenure of office, could not be controlled, and the contribution of dreadnoughts died in the upper chamber in May 1913.

The naval question had gone a substantial distance towards destroying Laurier in Quebec in 1911. The same question, differently constituted, had clearly undercut whatever support Borden had in the province. The battle lines were clearly drawn, and the coming of war in August 1914 would provide the opportunity for a test of strength between Robert Borden and Quebec.

NOTES

1 W. J. Eccles, *Frontenac, The Courtier Governor* (Toronto, 1959), pp. 218-19.

2 Adam Shortt and Arthur Doughty, eds, *Documents Relating to the Constitutional History of Canada 1759-1791* (Ottawa, 1918), I, 39.

3 *Ibid.,* 177. See Hilda Neatby, *Quebec: The Revolutionary Age 1760-1791* (Toronto, 1966), pp. 10ff. for the story of the conspiracy.

4 *Ibid.,* p. 144.

5 Clements Library, University of Michigan, Gage Papers, Carleton to Gage, 4 Feb. 1775.

6 J. M. Hitsman, *Safeguarding Canada 1763-1871* (Toronto, 1968), pp. 29ff.

7 17 Geo. III, Cap. VIII.

8 Public Archives of Canada [PAC], Nova Scotia, B/16, Minutes of Executive Council 21, 27 Nov. 1775; Nova Scotia, A/95, Legge to Dartmouth, 21 Jan. 1776; Nova Scotia, B/17, Minutes of Executive Council, 8 Jan. 1776.

9 PAC, Colonial Office Records, CO 42/113, Milnes to Portland, 25 Oct. 1799.

10 Nova Scotia, A/126, Kent to Portland, 7 Nov. 1797.

11 *Quebec Gazette,* 10 Sept. 1807.

12 F. B. Tupper, *The Life and Correspondence of Major-General Sir Isaac Brock* (London, 1847), p. 65.

13 CO 42/136, Gore to Craig, 5 Jan. 1808.

14 J. M. Hitsman, *The Incredible War of 1812* (Toronto, 1965), p. 35.

15   CO 42/147, Prevost to Liverpool, 6 July 1812.

16   CO 42/150, Prevost to Bathurst, 26 May 1813.

17   PAC, War Office Records, WO 43/72, Paid Corps in Upper Canada During the Winter, 1837-8.

18   Sir C. P. Lucas, ed., *Lord Durham's Report on the Affairs of British North America* (London, 1912), II, 53.

19   O. D. Skelton, *Life and Times of Sir Alexander Tilloch Galt* (Toronto, 1920), pp. 337-8; George F. G. Stanley, *Canada's Soldiers* (Toronto, 1974), pp. 209ff. There is a good account of the pre-Confederation Canadian militia in George T. Denison, *Soldiering in Canada* (Toronto, 1900). Cf. David Gagan, *The Denison Family of Toronto, 1792-1925* (Toronto, 1973), pp. 26ff.

20   See Donald Creighton, *John A. Macdonald*, Vol. I: *The Young Politician* (Toronto, 1966), pp. 325, 329ff.; Elisabeth Batt, *Monck, Governor General 1861-1868: A Biography* (Toronto, 1976), pp. 43ff.; Charles Stacey, *Canada and the British Army 1846-1871* (Toronto, 1963), pp. 130ff.

21   Minutes of Executive Council, 28 Oct. 1862, in Sessional Paper No. 15, Province of Canada, 1863; *ibid.*, Newcastle to Monck, 20 Dec. 1862; Hitsman, *Safeguarding Canada*, p. 175.

22   27 Vic., Cap. III; 27 Vic., Cap. II.

23   Maj. G. T. Denison, *The Fenian Raid on Fort Erie*... (Toronto, 1866). Cf. C. P. Stacey, 'Fenian Troubles and Canadian Military Development', *Canadian Historical Association Report 1935*, 33; Stacey, *British Army*, pp. 190ff.

24   CO 42/655, Report of a Committee of Executive Council, 21 June 1866.

25   31 Vic., Cap. XL. See also D. P. Morton, *Ministers and Generals* (Toronto, 1970), pp. 6-7; Stacey, *British Army*, p. 200.

26   C. P. Stacey, 'Canada and the Nile Expedition of 1884-85', *Canadian Historical Review*, XXXIII (December, 1952), 329-30.

27   *Report on the State of the Militia of the Dominion of Canada for the Year 1870*, p. 12. Cf. D. P. Morton, 'The Militia Lobby in Parliament...' in Adrian Preston and Peter Dennis, eds, *Swords and Covenants: Essays in Honour of the Royal Military College of Canada, 1876-1976* (London, 1976), p. 78.

28   *Report on the state of the Militia... 1871*, p. 61. The best description of the Canadian volunteer militia, its role, and the attitudes of some of its members is in D. P. Morton, *The Canadian General: Sir William Otter* (Toronto, 1974), chapters 2-4. For Cartier's views, see Joseph Tassé, *Discours de Sir Georges Cartier, Barronet* (Montréal, 1893), pp. 707-10.

29   *North West Rebellion 1885 Recollections and Items from the Diary of Captain A. Hamlyn Todd*... (copy in Directorate of History, National Defence Headquarters, Ottawa).

30   On the rebellion, see D. P. Morton, *The Last War Drum* (Toronto, 1972).

31   See especially D. P. Morton, 'French Canada and the Canadian Militia, 1868-1914', *Social History* (1969), 32ff. Very useful is Jean-Yves Gravel, *L'Armée au Québec (1868-1900) Un Portrait social* (Montréal, 1974).

32   Morton, 'French Canada', 32ff.

33   Mason Wade, *The French Canadians* (Toronto, 1955), p. 416.

34   R. A. Preston, *Canada and 'Imperial Defense'* (Durham, 1967), pp. 108-11.

35   See Carl Berger, *The Sense of Power* (Toronto, 1970).

36 Carman Miller, 'A Preliminary Analysis of the Socio-Economic Composition of Canada's South African War Contingents', *Social History*, no. 16 (November, 1975), 221-2.

37 Morton, *Ministers and Generals*, pp. 193-4.

38 4 Edw. VII, Cap. 23.

39 Leaflet in PAC, Fotheringham Papers, Vol. 5, folder 26.

40 See *ibid.* for details on the decline.

41 Toronto *Globe*, 17 Mar. 1912.

42 Toronto *Mail*, 14 Feb. 1914.

43 *Ibid.*, 2 Feb. 1912.

44 Toronto *Globe*, 28 Dec. 1912.

45 Copy of letter in Belleville *Daily Intelligencer*, 5 Mar. 1914, found in PAC, W. M. Ponton Papers, Vol. 7.

46 *Le Devoir*, 13 janv. 1910.

47 H. B. Neatby, 'Laurier and a Liberal Quebec', Ph.D. thesis, University of Toronto, 1956, 313.

48 *Le Devoir*, 10 sept. 1910; Robert Rumilly, *Histoire de la province de Québec* (Montréal, 1945), XV, 132-4.

49 A. DeCelles, *Discours de Sir Wilfrid Laurier, 1889-1919* (Montreal, 1920), I, 143-202.

50 *La Presse*, 19, 21 oct. 1910.

51 See House of Commons *Debates*, 23 Nov. 1910; O. D. Skelton, *Life and Letters of Sir Wilfrid Laurier* (Toronto, 1921), II, 130.

52 Toronto *Globe*, 17 Nov. 1910.

53 Rumilly, *op. cit.*, XVI, 81.

54 PAC, Sir Wilfrid Laurier Papers, Laurier to H. Dewart, 29 May 1917, ff. 195738-40.

55 R. C. Brown, *Robert Laird Borden*, Vol. I: *1854-1914* (Toronto 1975), pp. 237 ff. See also PAC, Robert Borden Papers, Memo 7, Apr. 1937, ff. 153573ff. in which Borden reflected on his reasoning over the Naval Bill.

Two

THE GREAT WAR: MANPOWER PROBLEMS 1914-1917

'To maintain in strength and efficiency so large a force [in France] (in round numbers 50,000 men),' the Chief of the General Staff wrote to a friend in July 1915, 'is as much, I believe, as we ought to undertake. . . . who shall say how long the war will last?' Major-General W. G. Gwatkin, sensible old soldier that he was, added that 'It would be a mistake, I think, to go on adding to the number of regiments, batteries, and battalions at the front.[1] It would be better to concentrate efforts on the raising and training of reinforcements, the supply of remounts, the upkeep of transport, the replenishment of war material and, especially, the output of arms and ammunition.'[2] Wise words from the officer responsible for the military efficiency of Canada's soldiers, but not words that would be heeded. By the end of 1916 the strength of the Canadian Expeditionary Force in France would be more than double that recommended by Gwatkin. Those policies would have severe consequences on Canada's war efforts and on the political harmony of the Dominion.

I

The outbreak of war in August 1914 had found Canada, although relatively unready for war, better prepared militarily than only a few years before. The dynamic Sam Hughes, the Minister of Militia and Defence, had built armouries across the land in profusion, reorganized the army command, and trained both officers and men to a far higher standard than had prevailed at the turn of the century. The strength of the partly trained, partly equipped Active Militia was 59,000 officers and men, and on the day war was declared, 4 August, there was little difficulty in producing approximately 10,000 uniformed, armed, and more-or-less trained men for guard duties and coast defence.

The Minister turned largely to the Militia a few days later when orders were issued to raise a contingent for overseas service. Eventually some 36,267 men would form the first contingent of the Canadian Expeditionary Force, which sailed for England between 29 September 1914 and 31 March 1915. And although there are some variations in the data, it is inescapable that most of the men in this first draft were not Canadian natives, but British-born immigrants.[3]

Nationality [Place of Birth]	Total All Ranks
Canadian	9,635
French Canadian	1,245
English	15,232
Scots	5,440
Irish	2,176
Welsh	363
American	130
Russian	36
Others	2,010
	36,267

Of the privates and non-commissioned officers, less than 30 per cent were Canadian-born. Only the officers, of whom there were 1,811 in the first contingent, were largely Canadian, almost 70 per cent born on this side of the Atlantic.*[4]

The ethnic composition of the contingent was reflected in its battalions, of course. Two-thirds of the Black Watch, raised in Montreal, were British-born, although only four of the regiment's officers had not been born in Canada.[5] The 73rd Battalion, also raised in Montreal under Black Watch auspices in September 1915, was largely Scottish-

---

*Not surprisingly perhaps, given the ethnic composition of the contingent, more troops were Church of England than any other denomination. There were 4,626 Catholics, along with 8,704 Presbyterians, 1,351 Baptists, 2,539 Methodists, 47 Jews, and 1,813 others. (A. F. Duguid, *Official History of the Canadian Forces in the Great War 1914-1919*, Vol. I, *Appendices and Maps* (Ottawa, 1938), p. 58.) This was 'the kind of stuff we want in our army', Sam Hughes had told Ralph Connor, the novelist, 'good solid Presbyterian churchmen. . . . clean-living religious men . . . good clean fighting men and we will knock hell out of those square heads.' (C. W. Gordon, *Postscript to Adventure: The Autobiography of Ralph Connor* (New York, 1938), p. 212.)

born.[6] The Loyal Edmonton Regiment (49th Battalion), raised in 1915, had a strength of 35 officers and 975 men—754 British-born and only 208 Canadians.[7] Indeed similar enlistment figures dominated the Canadian picture for at least a year and a half after the start of the fighting. Brigadier-General James Mason, a septuagenarian militia crony of Sam Hughes', told the Senate in March 1916 that although there were three times as many Canadian-born men of military age as British-born, the latter group to the end of 1915 had produced 63 per cent of all enlistments; the Canadian-born had mustered only 30 per cent.[8] It is difficult today to be quite as precise as General Mason was, but the census data from 1911 show that out of a population of 7.2 million, 804,324 were born in Britain while 5,619,682 were born in Canada.[9] Even when every allowance is made, even when one considers that the British immigrants included large numbers of single men, even when one adds in the special factors of familial ties with and closeness to Britain, the disproportion in numbers cannot easily be explained away, except to say that Canadians had initially little evident desire to go overseas to fight for King and Empire.[10]

By the end of the war, after heroic recruiting measures and after the imposition of conscription, the imbalance between Canadian- and British-born in the Canadian Expeditionary Force had been partially redressed.[11]

Place of Birth	Number Enlisted
England	156,677
Scotland	47,432
Ireland	19,342
Wales	4,723
Other British Possessions	9,431
Canada	318,705
Foreign Countries	59,509
Not Stated	3,817
	619,636

In all, 51 per cent of the Canadian Expeditionary Force was born in Canada.

If English Canadians at first felt the call from the Mother Country weakly or not at all, how much more was this true for French Canadians. We have seen earlier that the Canadian militia had been structured to be unattractive to French Canadians. Sam Hughes had done nothing during the first three years of his tenure of office to change this; indeed it is fair to say that he was oblivious to the *amour propre* of French Canada. Senior officers of *Canadien* extraction were retired or transferred to English-speaking areas of the country. And often Hughes, an Orangeman, forbade militia units in Quebec from participating in religious processions, which galled faithful *Québécois* mightily and infuriated the militia soldiers. Equally important, Hughes' regime was possibly even more patronage-ridden than that of any of his predecessors, a state of affairs that led to wholesale replacements of Liberal officers by good Tories. This did nothing to improve the quality and military ability of the Quebec regiments. As Professor Desmond Morton noted:

> In 1870 there had been fifteen French Canadian infantry battalions and sixty-four comparable English-speaking units. In 1914 there were now eighty-five English-speaking battalions and still only fifteen French. . . . Since 1899 a militia staff course had been training officers for senior appointments in time of war. By 1913 there were fifty-eight graduates; only seven were French-speaking. In 1912 one of the four brigadier-generals and three of the twelve full colonels in the Canadian permanent force were French Canadian—but only 27 of a total of 254 officers. It was in the middle ranks, where wartime advancement would come, that French Canadian representation was weakest.[12]

Even had the war been universally popular in Quebec, even if the government had managed the war and recruiting with exquisite sensibility, there would likely have been difficulties in Quebec.

There were difficulties aplenty. In the first few days of the war enthusiasm in Montreal and Quebec equalled that in Toronto* or Vancouver. Crowds gathered to sing and cheer outside newspaper offices, and there were spontaneous parades through the streets.[13] Even Henri Bourassa, the leader of the *nationalistes*, who when travelling abroad in the summer of 1914 had narrowly escaped internment in Germany, was not unmoved by the emotion of those summer days. But the euphoria of August 1914 quickly subsided and French Canadians settled back to let the war run its course, as did most of their English-speaking compatriots.

The government's dealings with the first contingent did not help matters. There were enough French-speaking soldiers gathered at the new camp at Valcartier in the late summer of 1914 to form a French-

---

*Toronto enthusiasm was very intense. 'If you have not given a machine gun yet,' the Toronto *Globe* reported on 8 August 1914,' you had better hurry up. . . . Everybody's doing it, doctors, lawyers, bankers, Freemasons, Varsity students. . . . The Ministerial Association of Toronto, in solemn session, decided to give an extra good gun.'

Canadian battalion, a gesture that might have been of decisive importance to Quebec opinion. Instead Hughes chose to put his French-speaking volunteers into two different units, one a mixed English-French Montreal unit, the other a hodge-podge of *Québécois*, New Brunswickers, and Prince Edward Islanders. And by the time the first contingent got to France as the First Canadian Division, there was only one solitary company of French-speaking soldiers in it, one forty-eighth of the Division's infantry.[14]

A great opportunity had been lost, an opportunity that some had seen. In the first days of the war, for example, Austen Chamberlain, one of the leading figures on the Opposition front benches at Westminster, had suggested to Sir George Perley, in charge of the Canadian High Commission in London, that a unit to be called the Royal Montreal Regiment should be raised from French Canadians. The British politician thought this might help with sentiment in Quebec and in France, a well-meaning suggestion. Perley's advice, conveyed when he forwarded the suggestion to Ottawa, was that it would be unwise to 'accentuate different races as all are Canadians'.[15] The sentiment was splendidly unrealistic, for French Canadians could not easily feel at home in Sam Hughes' English-speaking army. Nor did other Canadians take quite the same tolerant view, and from the first there were complaints that Quebec was not doing its share. People were asking where were the French Canadians for the front, the historian William Wood wrote to the Premier of Quebec, Sir Lomer Gouin, on 7 September 1914. The answer, Wood suggested, was 'Bourassassm [sic]'.[16] And Laurier, hearing similar complaints, told one of his close colleagues that English Canadians were in no position to reproach French Canada: 'parmi les voluntaires jusqu'ici inscrits,' he noted on 14 August, 'il n'y a que 18% de canadiens soit anglais soit français; les autres 82% sont des "English-born" ou "foreign-born".'[17]

This would become a constant refrain from French Canadians replying to increasingly sharp comments from Toronto, Winnipeg, and Vancouver. Naturally enough, Henri Bourassa entered the fray, the one *Québécois* certain to provoke deep hostility in the rest of the nation. 'If English Canada is to be credited with all the English-speaking soldiers gone from Canada, then French Canada has the right to count to her credit all the Frenchmen and Belgians, residents of Canada, who have joined their colours or enlisted in their native lands,' Bourassa wrote in *The Duty of Canada at the Present Hour*. 'They are Canadians, just as much as the newcomers from the British Isles.'[18] True enough, but even in 1914 few would listen.

Fewer still would listen as the war dragged on and French Canada's disinterest in it seemed to increase. The war would be over soon, after all. Everyone believed this.[19] It was not Canada's war, despite the efforts of Sir Robert Borden's government in Ottawa to make it appear so; it was Britain's war, France's war, Europe's war. What did we owe to them? Loyalty, yes, but not military service in a war that did not really involve Canada. 'The French-Canadian,' O. D. Skelton wrote in 1921 in his biography of Laurier, 'was a Canadian, and a Canadian only, perhaps not always an all-Canada man, but certainly none-but-Canada.'[20] In addition, and most important perhaps, relations between French and English Canadians were at a low point in 1914. Three years earlier Laurier had been driven from office on the grounds that he, as a *Québécois*, was disloyal to Empire and sought reciprocity to further his continentalist ends. Then in 1912 and after came the Ontario Bilingual Schools Question; as French Canadians across the country perceived it, the provincial government was trying to eliminate the French language in Ontario by destroying it in the schools. 'What community,' the leading Montreal newspaper, *La Presse*, asked in a pamphlet published in 1916, 'would not be disgusted if it had to stand for what Quebec stands for from Ontario?'[21] Matters were not helped at all by simultaneous efforts to re-open the Manitoba Schools Question, ostensibly settled by Laurier after his accession to power in 1896.

There was some truth in the complaints from Quebec. Certainly the English-language press did nothing to encourage *Québécois* to enlist. Every opportunity to downgrade the province's effort was avidly seized. *La Presse*'s pamphlet presented a sampling of these attacks:

> The story of the French-Canadian battalions includes a great disgrace. They enlist in retail and desert in wholesale. (*The Sentinel*, August 21, 1915).

> It is true, we believe, that the French ecclesiastics oppose recruiting in Quebec. . . . Since the war began they have written only another chapter in the long conspiracy to dominate Canada. (Toronto *News*, August 19, 1915).

> Valcartier, or rather the very name of Valcartier, is an impediment to recruiting in this city and province. . . . The rumour that Toronto and Ontario recruits are to be marooned at VALCARTIER ALL SUMMER should be promptly and authoritatively denied. (Toronto *Telegram*, March 3, 1915).[22]

Insults and counter-insults, the schools questions, and a host of other grievances, major and minor, combined to produce a certain sullenness towards the war.

This was reflected in the recruiting statistics. While there are no hard and fast figures on the number of French Canadians who enlisted in the Canadian Expeditionary Force, there is little doubt that the numbers were disproportionately low. In the first contingent there were reportedly 1,245 French-speaking soldiers. Early in 1916 Brigadier-General Mason told the Senate that 12,000 had enlisted, a guess based on numbers in French-Canadian battalions and on French names in other battalions.[23] Sessional Paper 143B, the official source if no more reliable, which was laid before Parliament on 14 June 1917, gave the available data up to 30 April 1917:[24]

French Canadian soldiers commanded by officers speaking the French language serving with units organized in the Province of Quebec	5,443
Soldiers speaking the French language commanded by officers speaking the English language, belonging to units organized in the Province of Quebec	1,536
Soldiers speaking the French language serving in units organized in other Provinces of Canada	5,904
[Men in the first contingent speaking the French language]	1,217
The total of Canadian soldiers speaking the French language from all parts of Canada who have proceeded overseas is	14,100

According to the same source, there were by April 1917 125,245 native-born English-speaking Canadians in the CEF and 155,095 British subjects born outside Canada. However the figures were interpreted, Quebec had not done its 'share' in the war and had not borne its burden of sacrifice, and this was the dominant theme behind the conscription crisis of 1917.[25] Why?

Quebec apologists referred to the usual litany of sins stemming from years of Anglo-Canadian bigotry, all old stuff, but then they added some new demographic justifications. For one, French Canadians tended to marry earlier than English Canadians, thus creating difficulties in the way of those who might otherwise have volunteered. According to La Presse, Quebec's single male population between 17 and 45 years of age numbered only 151,038 or 29 per cent of the male population over 20 years of age. In Ontario by contrast, 36.5 per cent of men over 20 were single. In addition Quebec was more heavily rural than Ontario, a factor of some importance as the urban areas all across the country provided far more recruits than the countryside.[26] In Quebec, *La Presse* calculated, there were only 610,000 urban French Canadians while in Ontario there were 1,328,499 city dwellers. For all these reasons, therefore, Quebec had recruited fewer men and, if this was not justifiable, under the circumstances it was at least understandable. Indeed it was.[27]

But these justifications notwithstanding, the recruiting problems in Quebec seemed insoluble. In the early fall of 1914, for example, a substantial group of prominent Quebec business and political leaders began to organize to ensure that French Canada would receive its due representation among the men of the second overseas contingent. Arthur Mignault, a wealthy Montreal physician, offered $50,000 to meet the costs involved in raising a French-Canadian battalion, and on 25 September he led a delegation to call on Prime Minister Borden to seek official sanction. Authority was soon given to raise the 22nd Battalion, and a recruiting campaign featuring mass rallies and speeches by men such as Sir Wilfrid Laurier got under way. 'This is a voluntary sacrifice,' Laurier said in one speech on 15 October in Montreal. 'Great Britain accepts with gratitude what we do for her, but she does not set any obligation upon us. Once more I repeat Canada is a free country. If some Canadians were frightened by the monster of conscription in the past,' the old Liberal leader said, harking back to 1911, 'they must now recognize that this monster was a myth.'[28] Nonetheless there was no flood of recruits. At the end of October the 22nd was short between 400 and 500 men, and even as late as March 1915 the regiment lacked 100 soldiers and was forced to secure a draft from another incomplete Quebec unit to reach its full strength.[29]

The recruiting experience was worse still with the 41st Battalion, the second French-speaking infantry battalion to be authorized and one in which Dr Mignault also had a hand.* Founded in February 1915, the 41st was an unmitigated disaster. Successive commanding officers were caught with their hands full of regimental funds, officers sold goods to their men, and the flow of recruits, naturally enough in such circumstances, was a bare trickle. In the fall of 1915 the unit was shipped to England notwithstanding its ill discipline, its drunken officers, and its low state of training. Matters were no better in Great Britain, with murder being added to the list of crimes committed by the unit's

---

*Mignault's biography (written by himself?) in *Who's Who and Why 1921* (Toronto, 1921, p. 422) argues that the 22nd was 'raised to full strength in less than a month' while the 41st battalion 'recruited to full strength in a few weeks.'

officers. The 41st did not find its way to France, and its surviving officers and men were used as reinforcements. A sad story. Desmond Morton, the 41st's chronicler, blames the prewar Militia Department because 'too few officers or politicians had been concerned about the failure of a key national institution ... to attract support from able and representative French Canadians.' The consequences for recruiting, for the war effort, and for political peace in Canada would be severe.[30]

The wartime Department of Militia shared some of the blame as well. In Montreal a Protestant clergyman had charge of all recruiting after August 1916, an eventuality that produced dismal results. This was not, as it is usually portrayed, yet another example of Sam Hughes' Orange-tinted anti-Catholicism. His District Officer Commanding (an English-speaking Major-General) had sought a Roman Catholic priest to share the task of recruiting together with a Protestant minister, in itself a revelatory comment on the attitudes of the day. But when no suitable curé could be found, the Methodist minister blossomed forth as an acting major in charge of the key Montreal district.[31]

There were other reasons, too. The lacklustre Quebec politicians serving in Borden's cabinet in Ottawa—the Nantels, Coderres, Pelletiers, and Casgrains—were all nationalistes of the 1911 genre, all men who had denounced Laurier's navy and portrayed it as a ruse to force conscription on an unwilling Quebec. How could such men now ask their compatriots to fight in a British war? This was a problem because Hughes' recruiting system largely depended on prominent men stepping forward to raise a battalion. The Mignaults were few and far between in a Quebec where social pressures rapidly developed to discourage recruiting. Nonetheless by the summer of 1916 there were 11 battalions recruiting in the province for overseas. But by this time the Canadian corps in France was effectively complete with its four divisions, each of 12 infantry battalions, and no further full units would reach France. This was the final blow to recruiting in Quebec, where a few zealots continued to strive towards the goal of a Francophone brigade of four battalions. No commander in the field would willingly break up tested formations to insert raw and sometimes ill-disciplined troops into the front line. However understandable this was, it was yet another blow to patriotic Canadiens—and a still further diminution of the posts for senior officers open to French Canadians.[32] And yet despite it all, the chief concern of Tories was to ensure that no blame for events should fall on them. 'I think it most important,' Arthur Meighen, the Solicitor General, a hard and unsympathetic viewer of French Canada and increasingly one of Borden's key advisers, told his

Prime Minister, 'that we take every means to prevent the impression gaining ground that the failure of recruiting in Quebec is any fault of ours.'[33]

Where should the blame be placed? Many Tories accused Sir Wilfrid Laurier of doing nothing for the war effort, an unjust charge. The old chief had made countless recruiting speeches—'If I were young enough myself, I, too, would be in the firing line'[34]—and many of his senior colleagues had worked hard for the cause as well.[35] An easier target was Henri Bourassa, always suspect in English-Canadian eyes and now becoming the *bête-noire* to Toronto and those who shared the Queen City's attitudes. With great force and great effect, Bourassa carried the attack against the Ontario government's policy on bilingual schools and linked this issue to the war. 'The French temperament,' wrote Colquhoun, the biographer of Sir John Willison, 'is prone to listen with credulity to the shouting of agitators',[36] and none was listened to more eagerly than Bourassa.

'Une vague de fanatisme impérialiste soulève le Canada,' Abbé Lionel Groulx recollected of this period,[37] and only Bourassa seemed willing to fight against it totally, to defend French Canada's interests. Worse, in Bourassa's view, the blind imperialists of Toronto could not even discern their own true interests. 'The anti-Nationalist programme of our politicians remains within the circle of the Colonial servitude system which they have inaugurated,' he wrote in *Le Devoir* early in January 1916. 'Before the war is over,' Bourassa added with a terrible prophetic accuracy, 'Canada will have tasted all its harsh and fruitless bitterness, its consequences will last long after the struggle is past and seriously hinder the progress of the country.'[38] This was bad enough, but Bourassa also attacked British policies with a ferocity that English Canadians employed only against the Hun or the French Canadians. The British were embarked on a career of 'rapine and cupidity' and British colonial policy was a 'tyranny'. The Jingos had control of England, and they were bleeding Canada dry because Canadians were too foolish even to realize that they were being used.[39] To many, such remarks in wartime came close to treason.

Only a few in French Canada apparently perceived Bourassa in this light.[40] Occasionally the diehard *bleu* or *rouge* press hit out at the *nationaliste* leader, who was assailing both old parties with equal vehemence, but not until July 1916 was a genuine challenge launched by a French Canadian in the form of an open letter in the Montreal *Gazette* and other papers. The author was Talbot Papineau, an officer in the Princess Patricia's Canadian Light Infantry in France, a cousin of Bourassa and a descendant of Louis-Joseph Papineau. Papineau wrote in English and took his famous cousin to task. What would have happened had the Canadian government adopted Bourassa's position on the war? 'Either the Allies would have been defeated or they would not have been defeated. In the former case Canada would have been called upon either to surrender unconditionally to German domination or to have attempted a resistance to German arms.' That was a dubious assumption, as was Papineau's assertion that Canadian nationalism was being forged in the fires of France: 'There ... her citizens are being knit together into a new existence because when men stand side by side and endure a soldier's life and face together a soldier's death, they are united in bonds as strong as the closest of blood-ties.' That ideal, today almost mythologized into fact, was a noble one, but if it existed at the front it did not flourish at all in Canada, where the two races fought each other with unparalleled vehemence.

Bourassa's reply was equally blunt and forthright, and he easily won the war of words. 'I find,' he said, 'that Canada, a nation of America, has another mission to accomplish than to bind herself to the fate of European nations and of despoiling empires. . . . ' Turning to Canada, Bourassa denounced the 'backward and truly Prussian policy of the administrators in Ontario and Manitoba. . . . To speak of defending French civilization in Europe while harrying it in America seems to us an absurd inconsistency.'[41]

If those who had published Papineau's letter had hoped that he would turn the tide in Quebec, they were wrong; nothing, it seemed, could do that by the summer of 1916. Even Cardinal Bégin, the senior cleric in the province, could not be persuaded of the urgency of the situation. In a letter to Sir Charles Fitzpatrick, the Chief Justice of Canada and a former Liberal Justice Minister, Bégin spoke of the need for men to work at constructive projects and to do 'les travaux urgents de la campagne'; he complained about the mis-employment of Quebec infantry shipped to Bermuda to release a British regiment for service at the front; he protested about the schools question, adding that many of his flock wondered 'Pourquoi se tuer et se faire tuer pour des gens qui veulent nous étrangler et nous traiter comme des parias . . . ?'; and above all Bégin warned against conscription, which, he seemed to believe, would mean 'une guerre civile, une revolution'.[42] Some of the Cardinal's archbishops were more sympathetic to the war's aims, most notably Archbishop Bruchési of Montreal,[43] but there seemed little to justify Abbé Lionel Groulx's later comment that he could not understand 'la ferveur belliqueuse des chefs religieux, ces bulletins par trop ressemblants à ceux des chefs d'armée, et ces dénunciations véhémentes de l'ennemi'.[44] Cardinal Bégin did tell his priests not to oppose recruiting in late summer of 1916,[45] but that was too little too late from the government's point of view. The *curés*, the key figures in the province, were firm in their opposition to or lukewarmness about the war by that time.

Quebec's attitude to the war seemed unshakeable. Nothing could move the *Canadiens*—neither the importation of French priests to preach for the war;[46] nor bringing over French army officers with distinguished records at the front;[47] nor appointing a French Canadian as Director of French Canadian Recruiting. This last expedient was tried in late November 1916 when Arthur Mignault, the man who had provided the money to raise the 22nd Battalion, and now a colonel, was named to investigate 'the whole situation, with such powers as may be necessary . . . to re-organize the recruiting of French Canadians in Canada'.[48] Mignault chose an advisory board of distinguished French Canadians,[49] but perhaps because of the sweeping nature of his mandate, he soon created a flood of enemies in Ottawa. 'Colonel Mignault is not altogether satisfactory,' the Adjutant-General told the Deputy Minister of Militia and Defence less than two months after the Colonel's appointment, 'and is, I think, increasing the number of Recruiting Officers beyond what is necessary or advisable. . . . He seems to have no one to control him. . . . '[50] By February 1917 Mignault and his men were full of their own grievances, and it seems clear that more time was devoted to fighting Ottawa headquarters than to recruiting. In March Mignault was effectively eliminated when recruiting was put in the hands of Lieutenant-Colonel P.-E. Blondin, one of Borden's Cabinet ministers, assisted by Major-General F. L. Lessard.[51] Unfortunately Blondin was not a strong man either, and his recruiting efforts, most notably a major drive in May 1917, produced less than 100 recruits.[52]

The lack of success of all methods was so pronounced as to lend some credibility even to the explanations of F.-X. Lemieux, the Chief Justice of the Quebec Superior Court and the president of the Quebec Anti-alcoholic League. Writing to the Prime Minister in January 1917, Lemieux argued that recruiting had failed because temperance-minded *Québécois* were shocked at reports of drunkenness in army camps. 'Surely such examples were hardly of a nature to place recruiting in a favourable light in the estimate of fathers and mothers of families. Enlistment appeared to them fraught with danger for the morals of their sons; it seemed to them a school of drunkenness and depravity rather than a course in physical training. . . . ' In such circumstances could parents be blamed for not encouraging their boys to enlist? If prohibition was imposed, the Judge said, he would undertake a recruiting campaign.[53] Prohibition would not come until December 1917, after conscription had been imposed. Not even temperance zeal could have produced many volunteers by that point.

II

Recruiting in English Canada had its problems as well. The enthusiasm of the first days of the war had helped to produce large numbers of volunteers although, as we have seen, the British-born enlisted in far greater numbers than did native Canadians. In part, at least, this rush of enthusiastic volunteers was a reflection of the difficult employment situation in the country. The winter of 1913-14 had been 'the worst for the labouring classes',[54] and a drought in the summer of 1914 had had serious effects on the Prairie wheat crops. The beginning of the war, with its attendant financial panic and the almost instinctive cutbacks in public works by all levels of government, worsened matters,[55] and Borden's Minister of Labour was forced to admit to a friend that 'I could not name a place where any considerable number of men could find employment, except, perhaps as workers on the land.... '[56]

So serious did unemployment become that in the summer of 1915 a scheme was devised to export munitions workers to Britain, where jobs existed. Other workers were shipped to north Russia to build railways or to England to work in the mines.[57] The crisis in the employment situation co-existed, of course, with the expansion of the army. In June 1915 the strength of the CEF was 100,247 officers and men, and it is significant that even the removal from the labour force of so many fit men did not markedly ease the unemployment problem.

But neither did unemployment appear greatly to assist recruiting in mid-1915. By the summer of that year, in fact, the first rumblings about difficulties in securing men for the army were being heard. A recruiter from Hamilton, Ontario noted that 'The first 100,000 came easily. We found other men were not coming.' Others pointed the finger at specific localities. The Toronto Globe felt rural Ontario and Quebec were lagging, while Saturday Night wanted the urban unemployed to be taken before farmers were removed from the land.[58] But significantly, there was no perceived shortage of men for the armed forces. How could there be a shortage when so many were unemployed? And with this evident surplus of manpower no one envisioned conscription as necessary or feasible. Sir Robert Borden seemed completely forthright when he told a Halifax audience in December 1914 that 'under the laws of Canada, our citizens may be called out to defend our own territory, but cannot be required to go beyond the seas except for the defence of Canada itself. There has not been, there will not be, compulsion or conscription.'[59]

Nonetheless the government began to take measures to make recruiting easier as 1915 wore on. In July the medical standard was lowered, the required height dropping by one inch to 5'2", and chest measurement decreasing by one-half inch to 33-4 inches. In the next month the requirement that a married man have the written permission of his wife before enlistment was waived. And in October the authorized strength of the Canadian army was set as 250,000.[60] In all 59,144 men had signed on in 1914 and 158,859 in 1915.[61]

There was some concern that the right type of men were not enlisting in the appropriate numbers. J. M. Macdonnell, a rising young employee of the National Trust, serving overseas with the artillery, wrote to the principal of Queen's University in February 1915 expressing the 'hope that there will be large recruiting among the students'. It was not that Macdonnell feared too few volunteers, 'only of the right sort of men'. Those who did not serve will 'miss what will probably develop them more than anything else in citizenship and in the belief in the righteousness and necessity of the British Empire.'[62] Macdonnell, however, was neither a snob nor a fool. He had a very clear idea of the reasons men did volunteer. 'Men enlisted not from the highest motives,' he wrote his father, 'but because they thought they would like it, because they were out of work, because they were drunk, because they were militiamen and had to save their face, some because of war's lure ... but being "in" they have quit themselves like men.'[63] That seemed realistic and sensible, a far cry from the high-flown patriotism that marked most recruiting efforts.

If there was criticism of a serious kind in this period, it was that the Borden regime was not doing enough. Opposition newspapers regularly demanded a greater effort, and Newton Rowell, the somewhat sanctimonious Ontario Liberal leader and a tireless crusader for Canada to strip itself to the last man for Britain, complained that the Dominion had not even enlisted 2 per cent of its men compared to the 10-12 per cent in Britain and France.[64] In the government, men like Sir Thomas White, the Minister of Finance, were extremely critical of those who demanded more. 'They are the men who vigorously opposed any increase in our military organization before the war broke out,' he wrote to Sir John Willison in Toronto, and the Minister called the carping critics 'hypocritical to the last degree . . . simply nauseating . . . '[65]

Politics aside, there was some point to White's rejoinders. The Chief of the General Staff, in a memorandum written shortly after the ceiling of the Canadian forces was raised to 250,000 men in October 1915, noted that soldiers had to be trained before they were sent to the front, that arms, equipment, and clothing had to be provided, and that 'there is a limit to our production'. In addition, General Gwatkin added sensibly, 'Reserves must be maintained. You cannot put every available man into the firing line at once. Casualties must be replaced. It takes 3,000 to place 1,000 infantrymen in the field and to maintain them there in numbers and efficiency for a year.' Other problems included shortages in shipping and in accommodation in England, particularly in the winter months, as well as the necessity of maintaining enough troops in Canada for home defence, especially in the West where many immigrants of dubious loyalty lived.[66]

Notwithstanding Gwatkin's sober comments, and notwithstanding the advice of some Conservative Members of Parliament,[67] Sir Robert Borden determined to raise the authorized strength of the army to 500,000 men. Ordinarily a cautious man, often accused by his supporters and opponents alike of lacking the requisite attributes of leadership, Borden seems to have decided on a dramatic gesture to symbolize Canada's devotion to the Empire and to the cause for which the Dominion was fighting. What could be more important than to raise the strength of the army to half a million men? Apparently after only cursory consultation with three of his ministers,[68] Borden told the Canadian people in a New Year's address of his bold step:

> On this the last day of the old year, the authorized forces of Canada number 250,000 and the number enlisted is rapidly approaching that limit. From tomorrow, the first day of the New Year, our authorized force will be 500,000. This announcement is made in token of Canada's unflinchable resolve to crown the justice of our cause with victory and with an abiding peace.[69]

This pledge—on the first day of the 1916 session of Parliament Laurier called it 'a large contract'—had been made without any clear idea whether the necessary men were available or of the means that might be needed to secure them.

Nor had Borden seemed to consider the manpower needs of industry and agriculture, a factor of some importance as war orders for munitions and foodstuffs had by the end of 1915 begun eating heavily into unemployment.[70] Borden himself usually tended to side in Cabinet with ministers like White who felt that consideration had to be given to the manpower needs of the home front, and at the end of January he told Sam Hughes that he wanted 'some systems which will interfere as little as possible with the agricultural and manufacturing interests of Canada.'[71] However sober Borden's afterthoughts were, his pledge soon had the character of a sacred promise that Canada had to redeem. This was evident in the press and in public statements; it also affected such men as General Gwatkin, who began a memorandum in January 1917 by stressing the government's undertaking. Fifteen years later John W. Dafoe wrote that the government 'engaged itself' to raise half a million men.[72]

Whether Borden's pledge was responsible or not, recruiting continued to go well in the first six months of 1916, with 29,295, 27,737, 34,913, 20,969, 15,359, and 10,619 enlisting from January to June respectively. In addition, by the end of June there were almost 150,000 men overseas, and the total that had enlisted thus far in the war was some 312,000 officers and men.[73]

This steady flow of men notwithstanding, opposition to the existing haphazard recruiting system was beginning to gain headway. In cities where patriotic intensity was high and where private recruiting leagues were well organized, systematic private censuses of manpower were taken in an effort to determine which men could best be spared for service.[74] One major element in focusing discontent was a memorandum prepared in March 1916 by Lieutenant-Colonel Lorne Mulloy, an instructor at the Royal Military College of Canada who, because of injuries suffered in the Boer War, was called 'the blind trooper'. Mulloy denounced the existing voluntary system as both wasteful and unreliable. Worse, voluntarism entailed the right to refuse to fight and this, Mulloy argued, undermined the basic principle of democracy: 'IN TIME OF WAR THE ELIGIBLE MALE CITIZEN MUST FIGHT.' The Colonel further argued that the voluntary system, 'while discriminating between men by drawing largely from the more efficient and those the country can least afford to spare, is nondiscriminating as between industries, drawing alike from the munitions plant and the distillery....' What was needed? To Mulloy the answer was plain: 'a re-classification of our industries and registration of our manpower. Some form of authoritative selection is necessary, not for the purpose of drag-netting the country for men to fight, but for the purpose of conserving our wealth-producing powers and putting into the field...the most effective force....'[75] Mulloy's message was national registration and selective conscription.

The same arguments were carried directly to the Prime Minister on 14 April 1916 when a large delegation representing recruiting leagues across the country came to protest the existing methods. The recruiters, private citizens all, demanded a national registration, the classification of industry, and 'some just and comprehensive system of draft'. S. F. Washington, representing the Hamilton Recruiting League, the initiator of the meeting and one of the more active leagues in the nation, began the audience:

> ... We have come to the conclusion, Sir, that the present system is a failure, and that if your promise to the British Government to back it up with the last dollar and the last man is to be carried out, some other system must be adopted.
>
> Sir Robert Borden—In what respect do you mean failure?
> Mr. Washington—This. We are getting the wrong men.
> Sir Robert Borden—You are not alluding to the number?
> Mr. Washington—Well, the number also. They are coming very slowly.
> Sir Robert Borden—Are you aware that in the month of March we enlisted 32,000 men ... ?
> Mr. Washington— ... I know that in my district the numbers are very small.

Another member of the delegation, Chief Justice T. G. Mathers of Manitoba, argued strenuously for conscription. The voluntary system was iniquitous, Mathers said, draining the country of 'its best blood', distributing the burden of sacrifice unequally. Yet another reason was the social pressure directed at men not in uniform:

> ... we have under the present system compulsion in its most obnoxious form. It is absurd to speak of enlistment at the present day as voluntary. In the cities of the West the man who is not in uniform is made to feel that he is a sort of social outcast. No man who joins the ranks today does so voluntarily. He does so because he can no longer resist the pressure of public opinion.

There was a great deal of truth in Mathers' argument, for those social pressures were becoming simply extraordinary. One eligible man wrote that he could not go 'to a public meeting ... walk down a street ... go to Sunday school ... or Church ... without being told I am a shirker.' And the recruiters were taking steps to put the message directly to such men. 'The average well dressed men seen at the dance halls and the skating rinks,' the Chief Recruiting Officer in Toronto told the *Globe*, 'are not coming to the Recruiting Depot,' so the recruiters would go to them. In Toronto, London, Winnipeg, and other cities, women organized to seek out men and to offer to do their jobs for them if only they would enlist. 'If mother didn't raise her boy to be a soldier,' the organizer of this Toronto scheme said, 'she didn't raise him to be the scorn of all things made either, and she should act accordingly.' Often these patriotic ladies could get carried away. Pierre van Paasen, a Dutch neutral and later a renowned journalist, was living in Toronto during the war. In his memoirs he recalled his experiences at the hands of one lady from the Queen City:

> One afternoon I was accosted on the rear platform of a streetcar by a woman, who was dressed in mourning. She told me that three of her sons had been killed at the front. She showed me their photographs. Suddenly she began to talk very loudly. 'Why aren't you in khaki?' she demanded. 'Why do you dare to stand there laughing at my misery? Why don't you go over and fight? Fight, avenge my boys!' she screamed. 'Madam,' I tried to calm her, 'I am not a Canadian.' That remark set her yelling at the top of her voice. She screamed that she, the mother of three heroes who had died for their king and country, had been insulted by a foreigner, a slacker, a German spy, a Red, and I don't know what else.
>
> I pulled the cord to bring the street car to a halt. I alighted. But the woman followed me off and she kept up her screaming about spies and Germans. A crowd gathered.... Somebody stopped me just at the moment when I thought of taking to my heels as the best way out of the predicament. I was immediately surrounded by a mob. A group of business men, who had managed to stay five thousand miles away from where the poppies grow, and who were at that moment emerging from the hotel, gallantly rushed to the woman's aid and forced me to submit, as she pinned a white feather through my coat into my flesh: the badge of white-livered cowardice. The last I saw of her was through a pair of badly battered eyes as she laughingly picked up some of the feathers which had dropped from her bag in the scuffle.
>
> ... The following day I enlisted.... [76]

All this amounted to powerful advocacy in support of a radical alteration in the methods of raising men. Borden was not unmoved and in his remarks closing the meeting with the recruiters he promised to think seriously about their complaints. 'I appreciate the considerations that have been urged upon us in this regard. There are perhaps, other considerations upon which you have not very fully dwelt, but which the Government must take into account before it comes to a final conclusion,' a reference to the problem of French Canada.[77]

Borden remained cautious. In a letter to a correspondent in Collingwood, Ontario a few days after this meeting, he alluded to conscription and pointed out one consideration that many overlooked: 'Until the end of this war we have no hope for immigration except from the western portions of the United States. American Real Estate men who are actively engaged against the effort of our Immigration Agents have eagerly seized upon the cry of conscription to render our efforts entirely nugatory.'[78] All that Borden would do to meet the recruiters' pressure was to ensure that skilled machinists and specialists were either discouraged or forbidden from enlisting, and in the summer of 1916 the government arranged leave for soliders willing to assist during the planting and harvesting seasons.[79]

This type of half-measure was insufficient for men—and women—[80] of the stripe of those who had formed the recruiting delegation. Disappointed with the Prime Minister's response to their requests for national registration and conscription, they had met again on the evening of 14 April to form the Canadian National Service League. The League would be open to all who endorsed the 'memorial' prepared by the Hamilton League, a statement calling for registration and the draft.[81] Selected as president was John M. Godfrey, the head of the Central Recruiting League of Military District No. 2, based in Toronto. A lawyer and a Liberal, Godfrey had helped organize Ontario's Peel County for recruiting with great success, and in November 1915 he had carried his methods to the rural districts around Toronto. Now as the head of the Canadian National Service League Godfrey would play a more prominent role in the nation.

In the course of a meeting with Sir George Foster, the Minister of Trade and Commerce, during the recruiting delegations' visit to Ottawa in April, Godfrey was made aware, apparently for the first time, of Quebec opposition to conscription and an expanded war effort. 'Sir George laid particular emphasis on the fact that the government would do nothing on account of the attitude of Quebec,' Godfrey wrote later. 'He led us to believe that . . . serious trouble would result if drastic measures were undertaken.'[82] In May Godfrey and two colleagues met with Sir Robert Borden again and discussed the Quebec situation:

Quebec seemed to be the stumbling block [Godfrey wrote of this meeting]. If anything were done there would be trouble there. We suggested that perhaps Quebec should not be brought under any advanced plan [such as registration], but that a campaign of education along the lines adopted in the second division [Military District No. 2] should first be proceeded with there. Discussion was very free and frank, and we were all of the opinion that we had made Sir Robert see what the situation was. He asked us not to proceed with our plan for compulsion.[83]

At this point Arthur Hawkes, a well-known journalist with the Toronto *Star* and one of the architects of the successful anti-reciprocity campaign of 1911, became involved with Godfrey's League. Seemingly knowledgeable about Quebec, Hawkes persuaded Godfrey that a meeting between prominent businessmen in French Canada and Ontario might produce useful results. Quebec, after all, 'had to be judged by the best men in it and not by its agitators and extremists,' Godfrey said. This was the genesis of the Bonne Entente movement.[84]

Godfrey's attempts to secure the co-operation of Sir Wilfrid Laurier failed, but the Bonne Ententists carried on nonetheless. A visit to Montreal produced a meeting with Paul-Emile Lamarche, a *nationaliste* Conservative who had just resigned from the House of Commons in protest against the Borden-Laurier argreement that extended the life of Parliament for a year beyond its normal term. These discussions were friendly but not productive. Lamarche argued that 'If you give us the right to volunteer you also give us the right to refuse.... Why do you complain?' A conversation with Austin Mosher, a Montreal *Gazette* reporter, was no more useful. Mosher, Godfrey noted later, 'claimed to be a great friend of the French Canadians. His position was that they were hopeless.... we should have a racial election. He hoped Laurier would sweep Quebec and not carry another seat in Canada. This is the only way of showing the French Canadian that he should behave himself.'[85] Fortunately perhaps, Godfrey and Hawkes did not take Mosher too seriously at this point. 'We now realize,' Godfrey wrote, 'that the best method of getting rid of interracial difficulties is by the process of psychoanalysis. The process cures nervous diseases between races just as it is effective with individuals. The Freudian philosophy can be employed with races....'[86]

Thus Godfrey had altered his views since his April visit with Borden. Now, rather than wanting to leave Quebec out of any registration scheme, he was coming to the conclusion that it would be possible to bring the French Canadians along. Indeed one leading English-speaking recruiter in Quebec wrote him that the province 'is ripe for National

Service... "That they would be ready to serve when all were called".'[87] This was encouraging; in August representatives of the Ontario Bonne Entente group met with some Quebec men, and there was even greater optimism. In a 'declaration of faith' all agreed to an 'unalterable belief that there is not now, nor ever will be in the future, any issue between the two races in Canada which cannot, and of right, should not be amicably and equitably settled, and in such a manner as to give satisfaction to the great majority of all concerned.'[88] A full-scale meeting was arranged for October.

There was a strong business component among the Ontario participants in Bonne Entente. Part of this was pure patriotism, no doubt, but part at least was because of the loss of business suffered by Ontario firms as a result of a Quebec boycott of Ontario goods, organized as a protest against the schools question and its handling. Perhaps Bonne Entente could resolve more than recruiting problems.

The Toronto Bonne Ententists pressed on. The October meeting in Montreal was a substantial success, with 48 Ontario businessmen making the trip and about 150 French Canadians participating. Godfrey in fact even persuaded a few New Brunswick participants not to press outright for conscription, an indication of his new belief that more could be gained with sugar than vinegar. And something was gained beyond goodwill. The Montreal Patriotic Fund was infused with new vigour and Montreal raised more money than Toronto; and a scheme to persuade workers to donate one day's pay every three months raised a further $800,000 from more than 100,000 participants.[89] Fortuitously, the dispute over the schools question was partially shelved, if not settled, by two decisions of the Judicial Committee of the Privy Council and by a moderate papal encyclical.[90] And a return visit to Ontario by a large, enthusiastic group of French Canadians in January 1917 gave further impetus to the accord between Quebec and Ontario. But that accord was based on a careful avoidance of contentious issues, most notably the war effort. The Quebec Bonne Entente men wanted to talk unity, not recruiting, and Godfrey and most of his friends deferred to them in this. Thus for Godfrey the gains were not particularly pronounced in the one area that really mattered.[91] Soon the Ontario Bonne Ententists would be taking a very different attitude.

III

Godfrey and his Canadian National Service League and the Bonne Entente movement served as well to keep up pressure on the Borden government. The Prime Minister had to respond and in August 1916 his government introduced major changes in recruiting procedures in an effort to end the unsystematic raising of men. A Director General of Recruiting was to be installed at Militia Headquarters, with Directors in each military district. To head the new effort Borden selected Sir Thomas Tait, a Montreal businessman, a former head of the Victoria state railways in Australia, and the present head of the Citizens' Recruiting League of Montreal. The Director General's task, Borden told Sir Thomas, was to obtain the largest number of recruits possible, having regard at the same time to the needs of agriculture, industry, and commerce. To this end the Director General should establish 'an authority which shall have the power and the duty of determining whether the services of any man of military age are more valuable to the State in his present occupation than in military duties . . . and either to permit or forbid his enlistment. . . . '[92] On 18 September 1916 Tait accepted the job, his title being altered in the interim to that of Director General of National Service.

Tait's first chore was to free National Service from the dead hand of Sam Hughes' Militia Department, one that he accomplished when the new organization was slipped out from under military control before the end of September. Henceforth National Service would be run by civilians.[93] Directors, all but one strong Conservatives, were appointed by the end of September, and from 9 to 12 October the National Service Board, consisting of Tait and his directors, was to meet in Ottawa. In preparation Tait was trying to gather information and advice and to select a staff. He wrote the Prime Minister to urge that as an example the civil service be employed to the best advantage and in accord with the principles of National Service.[94] He tried to discover Borden's intentions when he gave his pledge of half a million men in late December 1915.[95] And he appointed as Secretary of National Service one G. M. Murray, the Secretary of the Canadian Manufacturers' Association and editor of its journal.

The government balked at Murray. As the editor of *Industrial Canada* he had attacked the Borden administration for its patronage-ridden methods of issuing contracts, and just a month before he had blasted the Tories for their hesitancy in introducing a national registration. With some justice, therefore, Borden and his ministers felt Murray's to be an unwarranted appointment; with equal justice, Tait promptly resigned on 12 October.

The Director General's last act was to preside at the initial meeting of the National Service Board. The Board agreed to take an inventory of manpower, to issue certificates and badges to men who sought to volunteer but whose greatest service was adjudged to lie in continuing their civilian work, to urge the release of some serving men who should return to their old occupation, and to urge the registration of women to ensure that female labour was properly employed. The Board also recommended the formation of a bipartisan Parliamentary National Service Committee to urge—for the first time in the war—that all available men enlist in the forces or serve the country in the best possible way.[97]

This last, seemingly anodyne suggestion provoked a nasty squabble between Borden and Laurier. To Laurier, deeply troubled by the pressures that the war was placing on French-English relations and angered by what he perceived as the bungling incompetence of the Conservative government, Tait's resignation was just another example of the blind partisanship that had destroyed the war effort. The Director General had only been in office a few days, Laurier said, when 'finding himself baulked at his very first steps by this system which made everything subservient to private and party ends, he had to resign.' And on the next day 'as if nothing worth mentioning had happened,' Borden 'coolly asks me to join the organization of a Parliamentary Committee. I refused. I considered to accept that would have been sanctioning that condition of things which has become intolerable. . . . '[98] The issue was not particularly important except as an indication of the degree to which trust had collapsed between the Prime Minister and the Leader of the Opposition. To the public it served as yet another indication of the corruption of public life. To some it demonstrated that Laurier would do nothing for the war;[99] to others it confirmed that a Tory administration was a patronage administration. Tait's replacement by R. B. Bennett, the Conservative M.P. from Calgary, did nothing to weaken this conviction.

Bennett was an ambitious and vigorous man, eager to demonstrate that he could do any job well and merited a place in the Cabinet. But even Bennett was disturbed by the mess in National Service. 'I am confronted with a situation which I did not create,' he wrote to his old crony, Sir Max Aitken, in London, 'and have been charged with duties and responsibilities without having the option to say whether I would accept them or not.'[100] The chief task was the national registration. At the October meeting of the Board the Directors had unanimously agreed that the registration should be compulsory, but Borden, cautious and concerned about his government's position in Quebec, refused to accept this.[101] The best that could be done was to create an atmosphere that would ensure voluntary compliance, a task to which Bennett turned. In letters to M.P.s, newspaper editors, clergymen, labour leaders, and others he urged full support for the registration. The cards would be distributed through the post office, and people would fill in the answers to 24 questions and then return the card to Ottawa. Information was sought on health, dependants, citizenship, and special skills.[102] But without compulsion there was no effective way to ensure that a full return could be secured.

Indeed even before the cards were distributed in the first week of 1917, it was clear that there was substantial opposition to registration. Reports from Canadian Immigration agents in American cities suggested that substantial numbers of fit men were crossing the border to the United States because they feared registration would be a prelude to conscription.[103] Labour leaders and union locals protested, some demanding conscription of wealth, others calling for a referendum before any such measure as conscription was introduced.[104] Another critic was J. S. Woodsworth, already a leading pacifist. In a letter to the *Manitoba Free Press*, the director of the Prairie provinces' Bureau of Social Research objected to registration because the people had not been consulted and because conscription of material possessions should precede conscription of manpower. Woodsworth added that it was unclear just how men were to be transferred from unimportant jobs to military service. How would this be done? By intimidation? By blacklisting? And how could equal enforcement be secured, particularly among Mennonites and in Quebec?[105] French Canadians too were concerned, for the registration did seem a precursor of conscription. In an attempt to allay fears, Borden called on Archbishop Bruchési and Cardinal Bégin in early December and apparently satisfied them that the registration did not imply conscription. Other Conservative ministers followed the Prime Minister, one at least even telling the Archbishop that he would resign if the government adopted such a measure. As a result, the Archbishop supported the registration in a letter that was read in all the churches in the archdiocese of Montreal on 7 January 1917.[106]

In response to the criticism Borden issued an important statement in the form of a letter to leading figures in the Trades and Labour Congress. Borden flatly claimed that the National Service proposals 'are not connected with Conscription. Rather the idea was to make an appeal for voluntary National Service which would render unnecessary any resort to compulsion.' But the Prime Minister refused to make a blanket pledge against conscription: 'I hope that conscription may not be necessary but if it should prove the only effective method to preserve the existence of the State and of the institutions and liberties which we enjoy I should consider it necessary and I should not hesitate to act accordingly.'[107] Stated in such a way few could argue with Borden's comment. But in fact the Prime Minister had been thinking for some time of the increasing difficulty of finding the men the CEF needed and, in particular, of the problem of persuading French Canada to do its part. 'The vision of the French Canadian is very limited,' he wrote to a friend on 2 January 1916. '...It may be necessary to resort to compulsion. I hope not, but if the necessity arises I shall not hesitate to act accordingly.'[108] But for the moment the Prime Minister kept his own counsel.

Borden also undertook a national tour with Bennett, speaking in support of National Service and urging men to fill in the cards. In Edmonton on 13 December 1916 Bennett offered the view that it would be better if the burden of military service were shared unequally than that a civil war should result. The next week in Toronto he denounced conscription. It would divide Canada and destroy national unity.[109]

Perhaps these speeches helped to get the cards filled in. In all, close to 1.6 million cards reached Ottawa and as of 11 June 1917, when cards were still trickling in, the results were as follows:

Total received:	1,549,360
Complete:	1,342,755
Total military prospects:	475,363

Of the potential prospects, 36 per cent were engaged in occupations that were considered essential, leaving 286,976 men who might be considered fit for service. On the basis of the registration, therefore (and it was estimated that only 80 per cent of the male population had completed the cards), it seemed that there was still a pool of men in the country.[110]

Whether these men could be pried out of civilian life and put into the army was another question.* The National Service Board from February 1917 onwards sent lists of 'available military prospects' to the headquarters of each military district, while lists of skilled workers

---

*Recruiting had begun to slow down markedly in July 1916 when only 7,961 joined up, a far cry from the almost 34,000 of March 1916. From August to December 1916 between 5,000 and 6,500 enlisted each month, with roughly similar numbers coming forward in the first five months of 1917. The strength of the army, however, held constant at roughly 300,000 from June 1916 through to the end of December 1917. G. W. L. Nicholson, *Canadian Expeditionary Force, 1914-1919* (Ottawa, 1962) pp. 546-7.

went daily to the Director of Munitions Labour, an officer of the Board.[111] Each district headquarters then sent the lists to the cities and towns; there local methods of recruiting prevailed. In Guelph, Ontario, for example, a sweep was launched in April 1917 to round up the laggards:

> Three hundred and fifty of the young men of Guelph [the Toronto *Globe* reported on 10 April 1917] who signed the National Service cards several months ago received letters from the military authorities today that their services were required for overseas service, and asking them to report at once. . . .
>
> The receipt of these letters . . . made it very clear that this was the last call which would be made for voluntary service. . . .
>
> [A full report was made on every man.] If his reasons for not enlisting are unsatisfactory to the authorities there is not much doubt but that he will be compelled to join the colours. The citizens of Guelph regard this action on the part of the military authorities as a move in the right direction.

In an editorial the next day, however, the *Globe* objected. The social pressure exerted in Guelph 'overlooks the Government's pledge not to make the register the basis of any scheme of conscription.'[112]

So it did. But Borden's government was already beginning to move to compulsion, urged on by the National Service Board. In a letter in late April to Sir Edward Kemp, a Toronto industrialist who had become Sam Hughes' successor as Minister of Militia, Bennett advised that the Directors of National Service for Military Districts Nos 1 to 6 unanimously agreed 'that some form of compulsory military service should be imposed in Canada.' This seemed the only way of dealing with the 'large number of young men in the cities of Canada who have steadily refused to enlist and who are to no inconsiderable extent reaping advantages consequent upon the absence of those who have enlisted.'[113]

National Service, then, had served the purpose of demonstrating that men were available, men who could only be mustered for service by conscription. This had never been its public purpose, and Borden had pledged that that was not its intent. It is, however, difficult to escape the conclusion that National Service and its registration served in fact to justify conscription. The voluntary system seemed to have broken down, there were men available, and conscription would have to be employed to produce them.

IV

But before conscription would be feasible politically, the voluntary system must be seen clearly and incontrovertibly to have failed. This was the purpose behind the Canadian Defence Force, a short-lived and quickly forgotten force that the Borden government attempted to raise in the spring of 1917 in an attempt to provide men for home defence.

Home defence, unlikely as it may be considered, seemed a necessity to the government in the first two years of the war. Only 50 years earlier the Fenians had crossed into Canada, seeking to advance Irish purposes through depredations in Canada. Now the threat was primarily from German Americans, German sympathizers, or Irish extremists, all based in the neighbouring Republic. Another fear was of the hundreds of thousands of 'enemy' immigrants in Canada, particularly on the Prairies. The 1911 census showed 393,000 German immigrants in Canada and 130,000 immigrants from the Austrian Empire; fully 130,000 had immigrated since 1901. And in 1916 a Prairie census showed that 7.8 per cent of the Prairie population was born in enemy territory.[114] The fears may have been unrealistic, but they existed and hence were a political reality that the government had to face.*

From the opening days of the war, therefore, the Department of Militia and Defence mounted guards over various important strategic

---

*In addition to its concerns about potential unrest among immigrant groups in Canada, the government was worried about the implications of bringing male immigrants into the army. Proposals to raise a Polish battalion in 1916 were turned down, in part because of a story that a Danish-born New Zealander had deserted to the Germans and revealed information. (PAC, Borden Papers, Gwatkin to Christie, f. 16617.) There were also concerns about language difficulties, about the enemy alien status of some of the men, and about the extent to which Russians, Germans, Poles, and Austrians fraternized in Canada. (Ibid., Maj. Daly to Christie, n.d., f. 16618.) Japanese-Canadian proposals to form a unit received similarly short shrift (Ibid., docs on OC 194(1), ff. 16573ff.), and there were also concerns about Canadian Indians and Blacks. Sam Hughes worried that Indians might not receive the 'privileges of civilized warfare', while the Chief of the General Staff feared that Indians could not stand trench warfare and might fight among themselves. (PAC, Militia and Defence Records, docs on file HQ 593-1-7.) The government tried to encourage Black enlistment but ran into trouble with the CGS who argued that 'The civilized negroe [sic] is vain and imitative . . . the average white man will not associate with him on terms of equality.' (PAC, Sir Edward Kemp Papers, Vol. 110, file 3, Memo, 13 Apr. 1916.) In the end, a construction battalion was sent to France and individual Blacks served in battalions. There were also problems with American enlistments, largely because of diplomatic concerns, but the Governor General, the Duke of Connaught, was concerned that 'experience has so far shown that American citizens do not always make the best of soldiers.' (Borden Papers, Connaught to Bordon, 15 May 1916, f. 36377.)

sites, including armouries, harbours, hydro plants, locks and canals. In all, some 9,000 militia stood on guard in the first days of the war.[115] And the government took this chore seriously. Sir Joseph Pope, the Under Secretary of State for External Affairs, told Borden on 18 August 1914 of rumours that in the event of German success 'there would be a likelihood of inroads from the United States into Canada of bodies of armed men, drawn from certain German societies, united with members of the [anti-British Irish group] Clanna-Gael...'[116] Within a month, however, the Chief Commissioner of the Dominion Police was telling the Prime Minister that 'there is no evidence to be had of any present danger of raids.'[117]

Nonetheless Borden continued to fear that sabotage could be carried out by 'thugs, gunmen or other lawless individuals, instigated by German emissaries', and for several months he feared a major raid across the border.[118] Sabotage was always a possibility,[119] but there was never a real threat of raids or invasion.[120] As late as the summer of 1916, however, fears persisted, particularly in Saskatchewan where the Lieutenant-Governor warned of anti-British sentiment in the United States and of the warm response raiders would receive in Saskatchewan.[121] Borden took this seriously enough to order inquiries. General Gwatkin, the Chief of the General Staff, was scornful: any raiders, if there were any, 'would be back across the border before the local Militia had time to fall in on parade.'[122] Indeed Gwatkin had been skeptical for at least a year. In May 1915 he had pooh-poohed the requests for guards that flooded his office: 'Too often they are prompted by a desire to find employment for the unemployed; to put money in the pockets of tradesmen and contractors; to save Provincial Governments, Municipalities and private companies the cost of providing constables, caretakers and watchmen.'[123] And in February 1917, as the United States drew close to entering the war, Gwatkin referred mockingly to the German-American 'bugbear'. Two months later, finally, the CGS wrote his minister to say that 'it is incredible that anything in the nature of organized invasion could be sprung on us....'[124]

Chimerical as it was the fear existed, and the government felt obliged to keep enough troops in Canada to guard against invasion or insurrection. At their peak strength, almost 16,000 troops were on guard in Canada, and from October 1915 through to September 1916 there were never less than 50,000 CEF troops in training or serving in the Dominion.[125] But as casualties mounted in France and as reinforcements grew scarcer, the CEF men in Canada came to be seen as too valuable a resource to waste in guarding against raids that would never come. From the beginning of 1917, therefore, the question of calling out the militia to take over home-defence roles and thus, it was hoped, stimulating recruiting and releasing CEF men for overseas service, began to draw increased attention.

The CGS, General Gwatkin, informed Sir Edward Kemp in January 1917 that there were 62,000 men under arms in Canada, 50,000 of them CEF, the remainder militia on active service. The call for reinforcements, he said, might be such that in the coming months it might not be possible to maintain the stipulated figure of 50,000 men in Canada.[126] To meet this contingency, Gwatkin proposed four alternative courses:

(a) Conscription of 50,000 men of the first class for service overseas.
    . . .

(b) Enforce the Militia Act and call out for Home Defence 50,000 men of the first class, endeavouring to persuade them to volunteer for service Overseas and, in any event, retaining them continuously on active service in Canada. . . .

(c) Enforce the Militia Act, making it compulsory for certain classes . . . who are medically fit to train three or four nights a week in some Militia Unit. They will then be available for Home Defence in case of necessity, and a number of them will probably volunteer for overseas.

(d) Without resorting to compulsion, call out 40,000 Militia men (Volunteers) for Home Defence. . . . [127]

The Cabinet considered these proposals on 27 January and decided, as Borden noted in his diary, to raise an army for home defence, 'conscription to be used later if necessary'. On 8 February however, in the face of complaints from Kemp that this would stop overseas recruiting, the Cabinet 'Finally decide[d] to postpone for time and to utilize voluntary system at first.'[128] By early February, therefore, the Cabinet had decided to adopt Gwatkin's fourth alternative. Clearly the possibility of conscription for home defence was being held in reserve.

To head the recruiting for the home-defence army, Kemp, after great difficulty, secured Colonel S. C. Mewburn, a Hamilton lawyer, a Liberal, and a militia staff officer. Mewburn, a conscriptionist, was by no means convinced of the utility of the scheme, and certainly he had no expectation that men could be persuaded to volunteer for home defence. But Kemp pressed him to try, arguing that it scarcely seemed consistent to impose conscription for home defence without first trying the volunteer method. 'Moreover,' Kemp wrote, 'it has been represented to me that in certain parts of this country there are those who, while not willing to respond to the call for Overseas Service, would gladly do so for Home Defence.'[129] To Borden, in England for meetings of the Imperial War Cabinet, Kemp wired that 'It is intended to recruit for overseas as well as home defence upon a somewhat changed and new plan.'[130]

On 16 March 1917 Kemp announced plans for raising 50,000 men for the Canadian Defence Force. 'An appeal is now made to the manhood of Canada,' the Minister's press release said, for 'men to volunteer for home defence by joining the active militia. An opportunity is now afforded to those who have been prevented from undertaking Overseas service to join this movement.' Men enlisting for home or overseas service would train together, with pay and allowances slightly lower for home-defence men. The term of enlistment for both was to be the same—to six months after the war. Training was to take place on two evenings and one afternoon each week (at 50¢ per drill) with a May-to-September period of summer camp added. Men joining the CEF would wear a distinguishing badge to demonstrate that they were not CDF. The optimistic intent was that all 50,000 would be enrolled in April so they could attend the summer camp from May onward.[131]

To Borden, Kemp telegraphed that 'It is hoped that through this method of recruiting we may secure a fair number of recruits for overseas service. At any rate, it is about the only thing we can do now. Very strong pressure is being exerted in different quarters in the direction of conscription.'[132] Indeed many saw the CDF scheme as a last effort to avoid compulsion. Whether it was a fair trial was another question. Clearly there was no longer any threat of invasion from the south, particularly as the United States had broken off relations with Germany and was edging daily closer to a declaration of war, which came finally on 6 April. Why 50,000 troops were required for home defence in these circumstances was unclear. Secondly, why should men be expected to volunteer for home defence to soldier in a force that was clearly intended to serve as a pool of reinforcements for overseas service? Indeed, even if the pay was lower, the medical requirements for the CDF were explicitly stated to be the same as for the CEF. And why take men away from their employment to train over the summer if the purpose was really home defence? The motives for the CDF were confused at best, dishonest at worst.

Nonetheless by early April 1917, 49 city battalions of the CDF were authorized and Mewburn, now a Major-General, was in the process of forming his staff. A small newspaper publicity campaign was in train with the theme 'Release a Man to Fight in France by Enlisting in the Canadian Defence Force'.[133] In Quebec Colonel Armand Lavergne, a leading *nationaliste*, was placed in charge of CDF recruiting.

But nothing, not even Colonel Lavergne, could produce recruits for the CDF. The Toronto *Star* summed it up best when it noted that a soldier with CDF badges was simply advertising that while he was fit for overseas service he preferred to soldier as far away from the war as possible.[134] As a result Mewburn had no progress to report. In a memorandum on 25 April he had to say that 'practically no men are coming forward to enlist. . . . To date there are less than 200 recruits . . . after one month's recruiting efforts.'

Reports from all across the country, he maintained, indicated that no volunteers could be found for home service or for overseas. It was beyond doubt now: 'there is only one way to obtain this very necessary object, viz., by *Compulsory Selected Service for Home Defence*, and from this Home Defence Force, called out for actice service, I believe men will volunteer for Overseas Service.'[135] Officers across the country gave General Mewburn similar advice.[136] Yet another scheme had collapsed.

For Gwatkin, the Chief of the General Staff, this was a very difficult period indeed. His task was to supply the men that the Canadian Expeditionary Force needed, and every expedient seemed doomed to fail. The one certainty was that casualties at the front continued to rise. At the end of 1916 total casualties numbered 67,890, with 16,466 dead and a further 2,970 missing. There was every sign that 1917 would be worse. In the first three months of the year there were some 3,000 casualties, and in April, the month of the great Canadian victory at Vimy Ridge, and May, casualties would reach the horrific total of 23,939. Where could the men be found?

The CGS summed up the condition of the country's military strength in a long, despairing memorandum on 1 May. Canada had four divisions at the front, an effective fighting force of 100,000 all ranks. The annual wastage for this force would be about 75,000 men. To replace losses, Gwatkin said, there were 10,000 men available in England, but this pool was continuously drawn on and would be drained without a flow from Canada. Gwatkin estimated that 20,000-30,000 reinforcements would have to be sent from Canada by midsummer.*

*In fact in late March 1917 there were 125,465 CEF in France and 125,278 in the United Kingdom. Of the men in Britain, there were 40,000 unfit from wounds or other reasons, and the remainder were formed into 70 different battalions of widely varying strengths. There were also thousands of supernumerary officers and senior NCOs. (Borden Papers,

Where could the men be found? The CEF in Canada had been rapidly depleted since the beginning of the year, he said, there being only 18,496 left. Recruiting for the CEF had dropped to some 4,000 a month and the CDF was 'still born. The efforts to raise it have been rewarded by an enlistment of fewer than two hundred men'. But there was still some need for men to be kept in Canada, even though there was no longer a danger of raids. Public works had to be guarded 'against stealthy attempts at mischief', and this required 10,000 men. Thus, Gwatkin said, we are confronted with the following situation.

1. There is need, of the most urgent nature, for the prompt provision of some 20,000 or 30,000 recruits (mainly infantry recruits) for overseas.
2. It is necessary to provide a home service force of some strength.
3. Volunteering, either for overseas or for home service, has reached its limit.

To compel men to serve overseas is, probably, out of the question; but inasmuch as a Home Service Army of some size is needed, it should be raised forthwith by compulsion—in the frank hope that, once obliged to serve, a sufficient proportion of the recruits so obtained would volunteer for the C.E.F.[137]

Gwatkin had laid out the situation with care and frankness. Within a few weeks, much to the CGS's surprise, the Borden government would bite the bullet and announce conscription for overseas service. The CDF had achieved its purpose; from 24 May recruiting for it stopped and on 31 July it effectively vanished. Perhaps it really was, as the author of an anonymous pamphlet 'The Truth About Conscription' claimed, that the Canadian Defence Force had failed 'as it was intended to fail'.[138] Whatever the motives of the military and the government, the groundwork for compulsory service had been well laid. Only the politics remained to be worked out.

Strength of OMFC, 24 Mar. 1917, f. 43483. Also *ibid.*, Perley to Borden, 10 Nov. 1916, f. 39103.)

NOTES

1 See on this, Public Archives of Canada [PAC], Militia and Defence Records, GAQ file 4-124, 'The NPAM, 1914-21'.

2 PAC, W. G. Gwatkin Papers, file 2, Gwatkin to Col. Mason, 3 July 1915. Cf. PAC, Sir Robert Borden Papers, Gwatkin to L. Christie, 24 May 1915, f. 109601.

3 A. F. Duguid, *Official History of the Canadian Forces in the Great War 1914-1919*, Vol. I: *Appendices and Maps* (Ottawa, 1938), p. 58.

4 Militia and Defence Records, GAQ file 10-44, Maj. Scott to P.S., 7 Dec. 1926.

5 P. P. Hutchison, *Canada's Black Watch 1862-1962* (Montreal, 1962), p. 61.

6 *Ibid.*, p. 67.

7 G. R. Stevens, *A City Goes to War* (Brampton, 1964), p. 20.

8 Senate *Debates*, 14 Mar. 1916, p. 406.

9 *Census of Canada 1941* (Ottawa, 1943), II, 648-9, gives 1911 data.

10 Some Canadians viewed Canada as a principal in the war, not a colony. See Murray Donnelly, *Dafoe of the Free Press* (Toronto, 1948), pp. 76ff.

11 Militia and Defence Records, GAQ, file 10-44, Scott to P.S., 7 Dec. 1926.

12 D. P. Morton, 'French Canada and War: The Military Background to the Conscription Crisis of 1917', in J. L. Granatstein and R. D. Cuff, eds, *War and Society in North America* (Toronto, 1971), p. 93.

13 See Elizabeth Armstrong, *The Crisis of Quebec 1914-18* (New York, 1938), chapter IV. For Laurier's response, see O. D. Skelton, *Life and Letters of Sir Wilfrid Laurier* (Toronto, 1921), II, 432-4.

14 Morton, *op. cit.*, p. 96.

15 PAC, Sir George Perley Papers, Tel., Perley to Borden, n.d., f. 12.

16 PAC, Sir Lomer Gouin Papers, Wood to Gouin, 7 Sept. 1914, ff. 9907ff.

17 PAC, Sir Wilfrid Laurier Papers, Laurier to R. Lemieux, 14 Aug. 1914, ff. 190759ff.

18 Henri Bourassa, *The Duty of Canada at the Present Hour* (Montreal, 1914), p. 38.

19 Not everyone. See J. W. Dafoe, *Clifford Sifton in Relation to His Times* (Toronto, 1931), p. 388.

20 Skelton, *op. cit.*, 458.

21 'Our Volunteer Army' (Montreal, 1916).

22 *Ibid.*

23 Senate *Debates*, 14 Mar. 1916, p. 406. On the difficulty of using names as a guide, see W. H. Moore, *The Clash* (Toronto, 1918), pp. 271ff.

24 Not printed in *Sessional Papers*. Secured from House of Commons.

25 See Jacques Michel, *La Participation des canadiens français à la grande guerre* (Montréal, 1938); Robert Rumilly, *Histoire de la province de Québec* (Montréal, n.d.), tome XX, chapitre IV; tome XXI, chapitre III. Estimates of total French-Canadian numbers vary. Gwatkin put the total at 26,900 overseas. Militia and Defence Records, file HQ 54-21-12-26, Gwatkin to Pope, 3 Mar. 1919. A 1930 figure was 62,000. *Ibid.*, Col. Duguid to Maj. Culver, 28 Mar. 1930, file HQ 683-1-12.

26 N. W. Rowell, Ontario Liberal leader, gave figures in March 1916 showing that only 8.5 per cent of Ontario enlistments came from farm areas. Cited in W. R. Young,

'Conscription, Rural Depopulation and the Farmers of Ontario, 1917-1919', *Canadian Historical Review*, LIII (September, 1972), 299n.

27 'Our Volunteer Army'. This was the argument Laurier used. Skelton, *op. cit.*, 459-60. Militia and Defence Records, file HQ 54-21-12, Memo, n.d., supports this, showing 582,246 men of military age in Ontario and only 390,857 in Quebec.

28 Cited in Dafoe, *op. cit.*, p. 396. For another recruiting speech, see Skelton, *op. cit.*, 437-8. See also M. Hamelin, ed., *Les Mémoires du Sénateur Raoul Dandurand (1861-1942)* (Québec, 1967), pp. 189-90.

29 Duguid, *op. cit.*, pp. 344-5. For a history, see J. Chaballe, *Histoire du 22e Bataillon canadien-français*, tome I: *1914-1919* (Montréal, 1952).

30 D. P. Morton, 'The Short Unhappy Life of the 41st Battalion, CEF', *Queen's Quarterly*, LXXXI (Spring, 1974), 71.

31 See Rev. Williams' letter to Borden, 21 June 1917 in Borden Papers, ff. 33786ff. See also the anecdote in Hutchison, *op. cit.*, pp. 113-14 or Militia and Defence Records, file HQ 54-21-4-148, Col. Cross to Secretary, Militia Council, 22 June 1918, for examples of English-Canadian attitudes to francophone soldiers.

32 Morton, 'French Canada and War', 97ff. The brigade idea was not killed finally until June 1918. Borden Papers, Tel., Borden to Du Tremblay, n.d., f. 21326.

33 *Ibid.*, Meighen to Borden, 31 Oct. 1916, f. 33735.

34 Toronto *Globe*, 9 Aug. 1915. See other addresses reprinted in *Canadian Liberal Monthly*, Nov. 1914, Jan. 1915, Aug. 1915, etc.

35 E.g., Lemieux in Toronto *World*, 29 Nov. 1915; and in *Canadian Liberal Monthly*, May 1915.

36 A. H. U. Colquhoun, *Press, Politics and People* (Toronto, 1935), p. 225.

37 Lionel Groulx, *Mes Mémoires* (Montréal, 1970), I, 283.

38 Cited in J. C. Hopkins, *The Canadian Annual Review 1916* (Toronto, 1917), p. 342.

39 *Ibid.*, p. 343. For additional views of Bourassa, see Donnelly, *op. cit.*, p. 79; Armstrong, *op. cit.*, pp. 137ff.; Robert Rumilly, *Henri Bourassa* (Montréal, 1953), pp. 543ff.; Joseph Schull, *Laurier the First Canadian* (Toronto, 1965), 560; Skelton, *op. cit.*, 465ff.

40 E.g., E. Roux, *Henri Bourassa au service à l'Allemagne* (Montréal, 1917). See also L.-G. Desjardins, *England, Canada and the Great War* (Québec, 1918), pp. 251-320.

41 Translations in Militia and Defence Records, GAQ, file 4-49. Papineau's letter was dated 21 Mar. 1916 and published 28 July 1916. Bourassa's reply was in *Le Devoir* on 5 August 1916. Cf. Schull, *op. cit.*, pp. 576-7; Rumilly, *Bourassa*, pp. 559ff. In PAC, Talbot Papineau Papers, Vol. I, there is a letter, n.d., claiming to be Papineau's reply to Bourassa as well as a letter, 26 Oct. 1916, to 'My dear B.' complaining about political influence at front and saying 'The Canadian govt. deserves defeat and disgrace.'

42 PAC, Sir Charles Fitzpatrick Papers, Vol. 15, Bégin to Fitzpatrick, 31 juillet 1915.

43 See J. Bruchési, 'Service national et conscription, 1914-17', *Transactions of the Royal Society of Canada* (1950), 3-4; René Durocher, 'Henri Bourassa, les évêques et la guerre de 1914-18', Canadian Historical Association, *Historical Papers 1971*, 248ff.

44 Groulx, *op. cit.*, 285.

45 Borden Papers, Casgrain to Borden, 2 Sept. 1916, ff. 11643-4; cf. *ibid.*, White to Borden, 18 Apr. 1917, f. 33768. For a government view of the Quebec clergy, see PAC, J. S. Willison Papers, H. Clark to Willison, 1 Dec. 1916, ff. 2482ff.

46 Borden Papers, OC 310, Aitken to Borden, 1 Dec. 1916.

47 *Ibid.*, Borden to Perley, 16 Nov. 1916, f. 33745.

48 Militia and Defence Records, file HQ 1982-1-91, Adj.-Gen. to OCs, Military Districts, 24 Nov. 1916.

49 *Ibid.*, Mignault to Williams, 22 Dec. 1916.

50 *Ibid.*, Adj.-Gen. to Deputy Minister, 12 Jan. 1917.

51 Docs on *ibid.*, Feb.-Apr. 1917.

52 *Ibid.*, docs on MD 4, file 25-2-1.

53 Quebec Archives, F.-X. Lemieux Papers, file A-P-L-21-1, Lemieux to Borden, Jan. 1917.

54 Laurier Papers, Extracts from *Labour Gazette*, Feb. 1914, ff. 190597ff.

55 E.g., Public Archives of Ontario, Sir James Whitney Papers, Whitney to Beck, 6 Aug. 1914; University of Toronto Library, Sir Edmund Walker Papers, White to Walker, 15 Aug. 1914.

56 Willison Papers, Crothers to Willison, 8 Aug. 1914, f. 7279.

57 PAC, Arthur Meighen Papers, 'Memo Regarding Transfer of Canadian Workmen . . .', June 1919, ff. 18695ff.; R. C. Brown and G. R. Cook, *Canada 1896-1921* (Toronto, 1974), p. 240.

58 See Matt Bray, draft Ph.D. thesis, York University, chapter II, 10ff., 42; Walker Papers, E. B. Osler to Walker, 20 Oct. 1914.

59 Borden Papers, Address, 18 Dec. 1914, f. 34672.

60 Based on material in Department of National Defence, Directorate of History, file 190.013(D2), Capt. L. R. Cameron, 'Recruiting in Canada'; Toronto *Globe*, 6 July 1915.

61 Sessional Paper 124, 18 Mar. 1942, collects the enlistment data. (Not printed; secured from House of Commons.)

62 PAC, W. L. Grant Papers, Vol. 7, Macdonnell to Grant, 20 Feb. 1915.

63 Extracts in Willison Papers, att. to Rundle to Willison, 21 July 1915, ff. 26401ff.

64 Toronto *Globe*, 16 Oct. and 7 Nov. 1915.

65 Willison Papers, White to Willison, 26 Oct. 1915, ff. 35252ff.

66 Borden Papers, Memorandum, 1 Nov. 1915, f. 31606.

67 Perley Papers, Vol. 5, Bennett to Borden, 7 Dec. 1915.

68 Borden Diary, 30 Dec. 1915.

69 Cited in Henry Borden, ed., *Robert Laird Borden His Memoirs* (Toronto, 1938), I, 528. Rowell had urged this figure in the summer of 1915. See Margaret Prang, *N.W. Rowell Ontario Nationalist* (Toronto, 1975), p. 165.

70 Willison Papers, White to Willison, 25 Jan. 1916, ff. 35260-1; Skelton, *op. cit.*, 493; Young, *op. cit.*, 299ff.

71 Borden Papers, Borden to Hughes, 31 Jan. 1916, f. 108855.

72 Cameron, 'Recruiting in Canada'; Dafoe, *op. cit.*, p. 399; Public Archives of Nova Scotia, F. W. Borden Papers, S. Fisher to Borden, 7 Jan. 1916; Borden Diary, 5 Jan. 1916. Cf. O. D. Skelton's view 'This figure . . . has no magic weight. . . .' in 'Current Events', *Queen's Quarterly*, XXV (October, 1917), 225.

73 Sessional Paper 124, 18 Mar. 1942.

74 M. Bray, thesis draft, chapter III, 15.

75 'The Mulloy Memorandum', a Union Government election flyer.

76 *Christian Guardian*, 15 Nov. 1916, quoted in Michael Finnerty, 'Social Pressure and Enlistment in English Canada, 1914-17', York University undergraduate paper, 24; Toronto *Globe*, 15 Dec. 1915, 6 June 1916; Leslie Frost, *Fighting Men* (Toronto, 1967), p. 49; A. R. M. Lower, *My First Seventy-Five Years* (Toronto, 1967), pp. 89-90; Pierre van Paassen, *Days of Our Years* (New York, 1939), pp. 64-5.

77 Transcript in 'Canada and National Service', pamphlet (May, 1916).

78 Borden Papers, Borden to F. Churchill, 19 Apr. 1916, ff. 116071ff.; cf. Laurier Papers, Laurier to Sinclair, 4 Oct. 1916, ff. 193268-9. On American immigrant attitudes to conscription, see Borden Papers, Perry to Comptroller, RNWMP, 25 Oct. 1916, ff. 116686ff.

79 Cameron, *op. cit.*

80 Brown and Cook, *op. cit.*, p. 219.

81 'Canada and National Service'; Toronto *Globe*, 15 Apr. 1916.

82 PAC, J. M. Godfrey Papers, Vol. 2, 'The History of Bonne Entente', mss. copy.

83 *Ibid.*

84 *Ibid.*, and Laurier Papers, Hawkes to Laurier, 17 June 1916, ff. 192333ff. and Godfrey to Laurier, 20 June 1916, ff. 192363ff. See also John Witham, 'Bonne Entente-Was it Really?', York University undergraduate paper, 1968, *passim.*, and Hawkes' account, *The Birthright* (Toronto, 1919), pp. 240ff. and 375ff.

85 'History of Bonne Entente'.

86 *Ibid.*

87 Godfrey Papers, Vol. I, Godfrey to Mathers, 1 Aug. 1916 and Van Felson to Godfrey, 29 June 1916.

88 'The Bonne Entente: How it Began; What it has Done; and its Immediate Programme', pamphlet (1917). A list of participants is in 'History of Bonne Entente'.

89 'History of Bonne Entente'; Rumilly, *Histoire de la province de Québec*, XXI, 181ff.; Hamelin, *op. cit.*, chapitre XV.

90 M. Prang, 'Clerics, Politicians and the Bilingual Schools Issue in Ontario, 1910-1917', *Canadian Historical Review*, XLI (December, 1960), 305-6. For Newton Rowell's views on the schools' question, see his Papers in PAC, ff. 1656ff. See also Robert Choquette, *Language and Religion: A History of English-French Conflict in Ontario* (Ottawa, 1975), p. 201.

91 See Bray, draft thesis, chapter IV, *passim.*

92 Borden Papers, Borden to Tait, 11 Sept. 1916, cited in Cameron, *op. cit.*

93 Toronto *Globe*, 25 Sept. 1916.

94 Borden Papers, Tait to Borden, 3 Oct. 1916, ff. 34804ff.

95 *Ibid.*, Tait to Borden, 4 Oct. 1916, f. 116594.

96 Henry Borden, *op. cit.*, I, 609-11; Borden Papers, Tait to Borden, 12 Oct. 1916, ff. 34834ff. Cf. Laurier Papers, Godfrey to Laurier, 2 Feb. 1917, ff. 194716 ff.

97 *Canadian Annual Review 1916*, p. 326; Borden Papers, Tait to Borden, 12 Oct. 1916, f. 34614.

98 Laurier Papers, Laurier to Rundle, 6 Nov. 1916, ff. 193627ff. Cf. Borden Papers, Laurier-Borden correspondence, ff. 34616ff.

99 Montreal *Star*, 23 Oct. 1916; Laurier Papers, Laurier to E. M. Macdonald, 23 Oct. 1916, ff. 193177ff. and *ibid.*, Rundle to Laurier, 21 Oct. 1916, ff. 193621ff.

100 London, Beaverbrook Papers, Bennett to Aitken, 5 Dec. 1916, Bennett Scrapbook #6.

101 Borden Papers, Bennett to Borden, 17 Apr. 1918, unnumbered, Vol. 417, and Bennett in House of Commons *Debates*, 20 Sept. 1917, p. 6087. See also R. Blair, 'The National Service Board 1916-17', York University undergraduate paper, 1969, 20.

102 Card in Borden Papers, f. 34601. Sample M.P.'s letter in *ibid.*, ff. 34996ff.

103 Meighen Papers, encl. with Gosnell to Meighen, 16 Nov. 1921, ff. 11464ff.

104 E.g., Borden Papers, ff. 34606, 34635, 34650ff.

105 PAC, J. S. Woodsworth Papers, Vol. 2, Woodsworth to *Free Press*, 28 Dec. 1916. See also K. McNaught, *A Prophet in Politics* (Toronto, 1959), pp. 75ff.; Public Archives of Manitoba, J. S. Ewart Papers, letter, 'Food-Food-Food', n.d., f. 1118.

106 Bruchési, *op. cit.*, 7-8; Brown and Cook, *op. cit.*, p. 264; Borden Diary, 6-7 Dec. 1916. Earlier Bourassa had called Bruchési 'le Laurier de l'Eglise de Canada', no compliment. Durocher, *op. cit.*, 263.

107 Borden Papers, Borden to Watters *et al.*, 27 Dec. 1916, ff. 34643-4; Martin Robin, *Radical Politics and Canadian Labour* (Kingston, 1968), pp. 120ff. The TLC, unhappy, nonetheless urged cards be signed. Borden Papers, 'Statement', f. 34643.

108 Borden to C. H. Tupper, 2 Jan. 1916, quoted in Brown and Cook, *op. cit.*, p. 264.

109 *Canadian Annual Review 1916*, pp. 332-3; Prang, *Rowell*, p. 177. Borden's speeches are in Borden Papers, file OC 313 (5).

110 House of Commons *Debates*, 20 Sept. 1917, pp. 6088-9; PAC, Sir Edward Kemp Papers, Vol. 121, Gwatkin to Kemp, 15 June 1917.

111 Borden Papers, Bennett to Borden, 12 Feb. 1917, ff. 89089ff.

112 Toronto *Globe*, 11 Apr. 1917; G. W. L. Nicholson, *Canadian Expeditionary Force 1914-1919* (Ottawa, 1962), p. 220 gives results.

113 Kemp Papers, Vol. 118, file 12, Bennett to Kemp, 26 Apr. 1917.

114 D. P. Morton, *The Canadian General* (Toronto, 1974), p. 325; J. A. Boudreau, 'Western Canada's "Enemy Aliens" in World War I', *Alberta History*, XII (Winter, 1964),1.

115 Duguid, *op. cit.*, p. 15. Cf. Public Archives of Ontario, A. E. Belcher Papers, Lt-Col. C. F. Winter to Belcher, 13 Nov. 1914.

116 Cited in M. Boyko, 'The First World War and the Threat of Invasion', York University undergraduate paper, 1969, 7.

117 *Ibid.*, 14.

118 *Ibid.*, 17.

119 See Mackenzie Porter, 'The Men Who Tried to Capture Canada', *Maclean's*, 15 July 1950, 10ff.; *Canadian Annual Review 1914*, p. 315; *1915*, pp. 444, 455; *1916*, pp. 223, 226.

120 See C. T. Child, *The German-Americans in Politics, 1914-17* (Madison, 1939) and Carl Wittke, *German-Americans and the World War* (Columbus, 1936).

121 Borden Papers, Lake to Borden, 17 July 1916, file RLB 1281; Militia and Defence Records, file MD 1-C315 has correspondence from 1914-17 on this subject.

122 Borden Papers, Gwatkin to Insp.-Gen. Western Canada, 24 July 1916, f. 116334.

123 Gwatkin Papers, Gwatkin to Christie, 31 May 1915.

124 Kemp Papers, Vol. 71, Gwatkin to Kemp, 11 Feb. 1917 and Vol. 116, Gwatkin to Kemp, 8 Apr. 1917.

125 *Ibid.*, Vol. 71, 'Statement Showing Greatest Number Guards Employed', 10 Feb. 1917 and Vol. 115, file 7, 'CEF Strength in Canada'. On reinforcement problems, see Militia and Defence Records, file OSM 10-8-22, 'Report of the Overseas Deputy Minister . . . to Sub-Militia Council', 2 Nov. 1916.

126 50,000 had been stipulated since late November 1914.

127 Kemp Papers, Vol. 73, 'Suggestions for Calling Out Militia . . . , 15 Jan. 1917, Cameron, 'Recruiting in Canada'.

128 Borden Diary, 27 Jan. and 8 Feb. 1917.

129 Kemp Papers, Vol. 63, Kemp to Mewburn, 8 Mar. 1917. Cf. Morton, *op. cit.*, p. 324.

130 Kemp Papers, Vol. 73, Tel., 9 Mar. 1917.

131 *Canadian Annual Review 1917*, p. 309. See also Hugh Farmer, 'Sir Edward Kemp . . . and the Failure of Recruiting in the Canadian Defence Force 1917', York University undergraduate paper, 1968, *passim*.

132 Borden Papers, Borden to Kemp, 22 Mar. 1917, f. 43479.

133 Militia and Defence Records, file HQ 94-8, Vol. 5, McKim Ltd to Kemp, 29 Mar. 1917; Toronto *Globe*, 10 Apr. 1917.

134 Toronto *Star*, 21 Apr. 1917.

135 Kemp Papers, Vol. 119, file 17, Mewburn to Kemp, 25 Apr. 1917. To the end of June 1917, 1,858 men joined the CDF and 1,293 of them transferred to the CEF. Nicholson, *op. cit.*, p. 222.

136. Militia and Defence Records, MD4, file 25-2-1, Vol. I, Wilson to Secretary, Militia Council; Kemp Papers, Vol. 118, file 12, Mastin to Kemp, 7 May 1917 and atts. Cf. Rowell Papers, Rowell to Hearst, 14 Apr. 1917, f. 1529.

137 Militia and Defence Records, GAQ file 10-47c, Memo, 26 Apr. 1917. Cf. Skelton, 'Current Events', 225.

138 Copy in PAC, Brooke Claxton Papers, Vol. 137, conscription file.

Three

CONSCRIPTION 1917-1918

The groundwork for conscription had been laid through 1916 and into the first months of 1917. Pressure from the press, and the articulate public opinion created and moulded by it, demands from such groups as the National Service League, and the continuing high casualties at the front, coupled with declining enlistments at home all combined to make the issue of compulsory service a live one. The military chiefs, increasingly desperate to find the men they believed they needed, had turned to conscription, but few seemed to have much faith that Sir Robert Borden's government would act decisively to remedy their problems.

Indeed few in Canada had much faith left in Borden or his government. For French Canada he remained too imperialist; for English Canadians he was doing too little for the war; to the Opposition his government was weak and indecisive, strong only in protecting patronage. Almost no one believed that the Conservatives could survive an election in the conditions of 1917. But to Borden's surprise, and to the Liberals', conscription would provide the lever to move popular support behind the government. With it Borden created a Union Cabinet and destroyed the unity of the Liberal Party; with it he won his smashing victory in the election of 1917. Conscription proved to be the decisive weapon in the political wars, although something of a failure militarily. But to Quebec, conscription was the attempt to impose the Conquest yet again. As such it had to be resisted.

I

In a pamphlet published in the summer of 1917 denouncing conscription, Henri Bourassa rehearsed the story. First the Prime Minister in January 1916 had told Parliament that his government had no intention of imposing conscription, a statement that Bourassa considered particularly important because it was made after the decision to recruit 500,000 men had been taken and publicized. Then Albert Sévigny, named Minister of National Revenue on 8 January 1917, had informed the electors of his Dorchester constituency, where he was seeking re-election in a by-election, that there would be no conscription in this war. (Eleven months later Sévigny would have to be rescued from angry anti-conscriptionist mobs in his riding.)[1] Another minister, P.-E. Blondin, the Postmaster-General, had endorsed this pledge, Bourassa wrote, as had the 'paid organ' of the Conservatives, *L'Evénement*. The *nationaliste* leader continued by noting that the Speech from the Throne opening the 1917 session of Parliament had said nothing about conscription, adding that when Sir Robert Borden had left for England, the Imperial War Conference and War Cabinet, and the front on 12 February he had seemed convinced of the virtues of the voluntary system. On his return to Canada, however, the Prime Minister had come out for conscription. What, Bourassa wondered, had occurred to lead to 'such a sudden and complete somersault'?[2]

What had happened, in addition to Borden's visits to the trenches, was a great deal of polite pressure from the British. As early as December 1916 Prime Minister David Lloyd George was telling a colleague that 'We want more men from them. We can hardly ask them to make another great recruiting effort unless it is accompanied by an invitation to come over and discuss the situation with us.'[3] That invitation to the Conference and Cabinet was duly issued and Borden arrived in the midst of 'the gloom which pervaded London in the early spring of 1917'[4] to be subjected to strong moral suasion.

The British, for example, had been pressing the Dominion since November 1916 to agree to send the 5th Canadian Division, soon to be commanded by Sam Hughes' son, Garnet, from England to the front. The Canadians were cautious, fearing, as Sir George Perley telegraphed Borden, that 'sufficient reinforcements not in sight [to] keep five divisions full strength during balance year'.[5] A few days later nonetheless the British War Cabinet approved a recommendation 'That the Government of Canada be urged to agree to send the fifth Division to France as soon as it can be completed to establishment . . . and further to examine the possibility of raising a sixth Division.'[6] The War Cabinet's recommendation had been based on an Army Council manpower study that seemed to demonstrate that Canada had untapped reserves of men, having enlisted only 9.6 per cent of its male population. Additional data showed that while 37.5 per cent of British-born Canadians had already enlisted, the largest proportion of any group in the Empire, Canadians of British extraction but Canadian birth had enlisted in a slightly lower proportion than foreign-born Canadians (6.5 per cent to 6.1 per cent) while French Canadians (at 1.4 per cent enlisted) had the lowest rate in the white Empire.[7] Whatever the data demonstrated and whatever its reliability, the Canadian government was unmoved, agreeing, as the War Cabinet was subsequently informed, only to despatch the 5th Division if the British would agree to 'use in the front line not more than four Canadian Divisions at the same time, and this we clearly could not do.' The Chief of the Imperial General Staff was thereupon instructed to prepare an additional British division for despatch to France and to raise the matter at the Imperial Conference.[8]

Lloyd George helped prepare the ground for his military chief by telling the opening meeting of the Imperial War Cabinet on 20 March 1917 of British difficulties. He was proud of the Dominions' efforts, he said, paying particular tribute to the Canadians' great stand at Ypres against poison gas in 1915. But 'the first thing we must get is this: we must get more men.' In his reply Borden noted that in Canada there were 'certain elements to whom the purposes of the war do not appeal so strongly' and this led him to be cautious: 'I am not prepared to say at the moment how many men we can still send from Canada, but we shall do our utmost.'[9] And ten days later when the Chief of the Imperial General Staff finally raised the question of the 5th Division, Borden evaded answering directly, offering only a summary of the Canadian war effort to date. Sir George Perley, the Minister of Overseas Forces of Canada in the United Kingdom, had to step in to argue that the division could not be sent until the casualties in the other four Canadian divisions at the front were known. It was impossible to tell if there would be enough trained reinforcements to keep the Canadian forces up to full strength.[10]

All this must have been difficult for Borden. He had arrived in London almost unaware of the gravity of the war situation and his initiation had been 'sudden, violent and complete'. During the Conference he had seen the beginnings of the Russian collapse, the French army in agony and mutinous, and the entry of the United States into the war.[11] The Americans would be a fresh reservoir of manpower, but it was important for the postwar course of Empire that the United States should not be able to claim that it had won the war. 'What I saw and learned,' a shaken Borden wrote to Archbishop Bruchési of Montreal at the end of May, 'made me realize how much more critical is the situation of the Allies and how much more uncertain is the ultimate result of the great struggle. . . . ' Borden added that he had had 'the privilege of looking into the eyes of tens of thousands of men at the front who look to us for the effort which will make their sacrifice serve the great purpose for which it was undertaken.'[12] All this was undoubtedly true, as was Borden's conviction that Canada had to play a substantial role in the war in order to solidify its nationhood and its place in the Empire and the world.

Whatever the reason, when Borden returned to Canada in mid-May he had decided on conscription. Slow to move or to decide on his course, Borden normally worked his way through the facts of a situation, chewing over the details until he had mastered them. And then, once his mind was clear, he held to his direction with great tenacity and bulldog determination. So it would be with conscription. And after his process of decision-making, Borden could deny with a clear conscience that the British had forced any such step on Canada. This, a British Colonial Office official minuted on a despatch, 'is of course true but it is no doubt also true that it is the result of the impression made on his mind by discussions here.'[13] That seemed inescapably the proper conclusion.*

Borden met his Cabinet on 17 May for the first time since his return from England and told the assembled ministers that he had decided

---

*There is another and probably fanciful account of the decision for conscription in PAC, Mackenzie King Papers, Diary, 14 Feb. 1921: 'At the state dinner tonight Robert Rogers [Minister of Public Works until his resignation/expulsion from the Borden Cabinet in August 1917] told me in confidence that when he and Sir Robert Borden left England they had never thought of conscription, that they had promised Lloyd George another 100,000 men when he came to the boat to bid them farewell, that he and Rogers had given out an interview on landing in which he said they had promised the 100,000 and would get them anyway, the press taking it to mean conscription if need be. That that was the first that had been talked of conscription. . . . The day Borden spoke in the House on Conscription Rogers had been with him all the time advising against conscription. He said he had driven with Borden to his own house and B. had asked him what he better do, he told him by no means to speak of conscription, he had not taken up the matter in Council. No decision reached there. He was a weak man said Rogers. Then he got up in the House to speak and was carried on by the applause. He drifted into conscription. When he sat down he said to Rogers "well I have spilled the beans. I did not mean to, but I have done it." Rogers said "you have made a hell of a mess" and lectured him hard on it.' There are several flaws in this story, most notably that Borden did take conscription to the Cabinet on 17 May. Rogers in addition was bitter towards Borden and might easily have embellished the tale to make it more attractive to Mackenzie King.

Canada must have conscription. A small group of tired, overworked men, the Cabinet was not disposed to disagree; indeed, all the English-speaking ministers had been harassed by the demands of their constituents for a greater war effort and conscription seemed to offer surcease. 'All agreed that conscription necessary,' Borden jotted in his diary that night. All had agreed, but Patenaude and Blondin, the Secretary of State and the Postmaster-General, were worried. These two French-Canadian ministers were not powerful figures in the government or in their province, but they could readily discern what conscription would do to them and to the party. They said, Borden wrote, 'that they are prepared to stand by us but that it will kill them politically and the party for 25 years.'[14] The two were correct, even if they underestimated the duration of *bleu* death in French Canada. But for Borden, his mind made up that only conscription could maintain the Canadian Expeditionary Force and allow Canada to do its part towards winning the war, political considerations seemed irrelevant.

The next day, to great cheers from the Tory benches, and to stunned surprise from Sir Wilfrid Laurier, Borden announced his decision to proceed with conscription:

> We have four Canadian divisions at the front. For the immediate future there are sufficient reinforcements. But four divisions cannot be maintained without thorough provision for future requirements. ... Hitherto we have depended on voluntary enlistment. ... It is apparent to me that the voluntary system will not yield further substantial results. I hoped it would. ...
>
> All citizens are liable to military service for the defence of their country. ...
>
> I have had to take all these matters into consideration and I have given them my most earnest attention. The responsibility is a serious one, but I do not shrink from it. Therefore, it is my duty to announce to the House that early proposals will be made to provide by compulsory military enlistment on a selective basis, such reinforcements as may be necessary to maintain the Canadian army in the field. ... The number of men required will not be less than 50,000 and will probably be 100,000. ... [15]

When Borden spoke, he had no measure ready for the House of Commons and none would be introduced until 11 June 1917. Was a new bill even necessary? The Militia Act, as drawn in 1868 and amended most recently in 1904, provided for a *levée en masse* of 'All the male inhabitants of Canada, of the age of eighteen and upwards, and under sixty, not exempt or disqualified by law, and being British subjects....'[16] It was precisely because of this all-inclusiveness that Borden chose to proceed under a new measure, one that would provide selective service.[17]

The task of drafting the Military Service Act, 1917, as the conscription bill came to be called, was given to Arthur Meighen, the Solicitor-General. Easily the ablest member of the Borden administration, Meighen took every hard and dangerous job that the Prime Minister handed him and with brilliant oratory, enormous self-confidence, and a clear, lucid mind dealt with each problem with despatch. His biographer wrote that the conscription bill 'was Meighen's handiwork and his alone',[18] and certainly Meighen would bear the brunt of the blame for the rest of his long career. But in fact the Solicitor-General was assisted among others by Everett Bristol, a military aide to Sir Edward Kemp, the Militia Minister.

I was detailed [Bristol wrote in 1967] with the then Law Clerk of the Senate... to prepare a conscription Bill. We both felt that the United States' Act, which provided for national registration and therefore selection by lot from various Classes (in age groups, single and married), should be followed as being most democratic and having received a lot of favourable publicity....

We prepared a draft Bill accordingly, although adopting [different] classifications... We were then told that Mr. Meighen, as Solicitor-General and the 'work-horse' of the Cabinet, would have the conduct of the Bill through the House, and that we were to submit the draft to him. We had our first meeting with Mr. Meighen at his house. After reading our draft his keen mind, looking for shortcuts, jumped at the conclusion that national registration would take too long, and that what should be done was to provide that if and when a certain Class (as defined) should be called up... all members of that Class would thereupon be 'ipso facto' soldiers....

Very unfortunately, in my view, this was the form the Military Service Act in 1917 took....[19]

Indeed this short cut would be costly in the long run. Twenty-five years later, O. M. Biggar, one of the members of the Military Service Council set up to administer the 1917 Act and in 1941 the Chairman of the Canadian section of the Permanent Joint Board on Defence, singled out this same flaw: 'The Military Service Act proceeded on the assumption that everyone in the age groups 20-[24] was for the army.

The business of the administration was to exempt—entirely negative policy.'[20]

In any case, within a week Meighen had a draft bill ready for consideration. The bill was discussed clause by clause on 24 May, with Borden unhappy over what he felt was its verbosity and bad drafts-manship. By 30 May the revised bill was ready for printing.[21] As introduced in Parliament on 11 June, the bill provided that all male British subjects between the ages of 20 and 45 should be liable for military service. The manpower of the nation was divided into classes based on age and civil status, and these classes would be called for service as required by proclamation. Terms of exemption were vague and liberal, and men engaged in war industry, those who could not be spared from their work because of special qualifications, and conscientious objectors were among those declared exempt from service. Everyone and no one could be exempted, subject to the decision of exemption tribunals to be set up across the country.[22] With this bill, the government believed, Canada would place the required number of men in the field. With it the country would secure the necessary reinforcements for the Corps. And with it no one would be able to doubt that the senior Dominion had done its part in the war.

Had Canada done its share? This was one of the major arguments in the summer of 1917. To equal Australia's part in the war, critics charged, Canada should have had overseas by the beginning of 1917 fully 500,000 men; to equal New Zealand 450,000; to equal South Africa more than 400,000. But all Canada had in England and France was 284,000 officers and men. In addition the French and the British had respectively four and three times as many men in the armed forces in proportion to population as Canada. The Canadian effort was too weak and only conscription could make it respectable.[23] But as a Queen's University professor, O. D. Skelton, wrote at the time, 'as for Australia and New Zealand, it is only fair to remember that neither has been able to develop war manufacturing industries on a scale even faintly approaching the Canadian. . . . ' In addition, because of Canada's relative nearness to Britain, 'a farmer in Canada can be of very much greater service in the common cause than a farmer in Australia.' Skelton then looked at the United States, still in the process of mobilizing and organizing its armies. The Americans, he said, 'would have to enlist over 6,500,000 men . . . before they equalled Canada's present record.'[24] Skelton's words were rational ones, but conscription was not a subject on which rationality carried much weight.

There was more rationality—and calculation—in Borden's mind as he determined his government's course. Unless a further extension of the life of Parliament could be agreed upon between him and Laurier, a general election would have to be held no later than December 1917. But when on 17 July Borden brought a resolution to extend the Parliamentary term before the House of Commons, the Liberals voted against. Without near-unanimity on such a matter, Borden would not take a request to amend the British North America Act before the Imperial Parliament; a general election before the end of the year was now a certainty.

But Borden had already launched himself on another course. In response to a growing public clamour, begun and fostered mainly by the English-language Liberal press, the Prime Minister had approached the Leader of the Opposition on 25 May and offered a coalition, a Union Government, to the Liberal leader. The offer seemed sincere and genuine,* even generous in its terms; it would have seen equal numbers of Liberals and Conservatives serving under Borden in the Cabinet, and would have postponed the implementation of conscription until after a general election. For Borden, a coalition would help make conscription less a Tory policy and more a national policy. It would also ease many Conservative ministers' fears, for as Borden noted on 25 May, 'Our Ministers afraid of a general election. Think we would be beaten by French, foreigners, slackers.'[25]

Laurier thought the government could be beaten, too, as did many of his correspondents. John W. Dafoe of the *Manitoba Free Press*, a former supporter who was mightily disenchanted with both Borden and Laurier, still wrote to Sir Wilfrid in late April to say that the Conservatives' defeat 'when they appeal to the people appears inevitable, unless some new factor enters into the contest and gives them a good battle cry.'[26] Was conscription such a battle cry? It appealed to the urban English-speaking, to the press, to the military, and to the super-patriots, Laurier realized. But would it appeal to what Borden called the 'French, foreigners, slackers' and to those who were more concerned with Canada's fate than Europe's? Would conscription be enough to overcome the effects of six years of inefficient and often corrupt Borden government? Could it outweigh the repeated losses suffered by the Tories in provin-

---

*How sincere and genuine has been questioned, most notably by those who charged that the attempt to form a coalition was a screen behind which Borden thought he could solve the railway problems of the country. The manuscript sources are very scanty here and there seems little convincing evidence. A recent study, largely dismissive of this conspiracy thesis, is T. D. Regehr, *The Canadian Northern Railway* (Toronto, 1976), pp. 434-5.

cial elections and the patently obvious fears of the Borden government that had led to the delay of by-elections in 20 constituencies? Surely not.

As important as these political considerations to Laurier, conscription would shatter the country's already strained national unity. It would pit English against French in a contest that the majority would win. It would, for him, create a terrible choice between staying with his compatriots in Quebec and opposing compulsion or going into the government and trying to ameliorate its imposition of conscription. In essence, that was no choice at all, especially as Laurier feared that if he accepted Borden's offer Henri Bourassa would instantly—and permanently?— become the effective leader of French Canada. That would be a terrible end to Laurier's career and, he believed, a disaster for the country. So the coalition offer posed no serious choice for Laurier. The Prime Minister wrote on 6 June that Laurier 'told me he could not join coalition government as he is opposed to conscription. Fears Bourassa's influence &c. Says he will endeavour to have law observed.'[27] Thus Borden's honest and only attempt to minimize a racial split over conscription failed. The Prime Minister, however, with enormous patience and with a skill that few had believed he possessed, continued his efforts to entice Liberals into the Cabinet over the next several months.[28]

The long and heated debate on the Military Service Bill that occupied much of June and July confirmed the depth of division in the country. Ninety-nine M.P.s spoke during the debate, which lasted until 24 July. Given the Conservative majority, passage of the bill was inevitable, but Laurier's reluctance to countenance conscription began to split English-speaking Liberals away from the old chief. Laurier tried to counter this trend by calling for a referendum:

> What I propose is that we should have a referendum and a consultation of the people upon this question. . . . When the consultation has been made, when the verdict has been pronounced, I pledge my word, my reputation, that to the verdict, such as it is, every man will have to submit, and I claim to speak with knowledge at least so far as the Province from which I come is concerned. Is that an unfair appeal? Can anybody say that it is not in accordance with true democratic principles?[29]

But to the conscriptionists a referendum would entail delay, unacceptable delay, and the people might conceivably vote against conscription. Laurier's call for a referendum was defeated and the conscription bill passed in principle on a vote of 119 to 55. Twenty-five Liberals voted for the measure, as did every Conservative except for nine French-speaking M.P.s. Only five French-speaking Canadians voted for the bill: two ministers, one M.P. from Saskatchewan, one from New Brunswick, and the recent Deputy Speaker of the House of Commons. The racial split was complete, and when the bill was signed into law on 29 August 1917 the tension was almost palpable.

Laurier's last speech on the bill had expressed his fears movingly:

> ... I oppose this Bill because it has in it the seeds of discord and disunion; because it is an obstacle and a bar to that union of heart and soul without which it is impossible to hope that this Confederation will attain the aims and ends that were had in view when Confederation was effected. Sir, all my life I have fought coercion; all my life I have promoted union; and the inspiration that led me to that course shall be my guide at all times so long as there is a breath left in my body.[30]

The Liberal leader was a moderate on this issue, however, compared with opinion in Quebec, which was violently opposed to conscription. All the press, with the exception of two *bleu* sheets, vehemently opposed the Military Service Act. Public meetings in Montreal and Quebec City drew thousands night after night to hear orators such as Armand Lavergne denounce conscription. 'Je ne suis pas contre la conscription pour la défense du pays,' Lavergne, who had been in charge of recruiting for the Canadian Defence Force in his province, told a Quebec rally, 'mais je ne reconnais à aucun gouvernement le droit de nous imposer le service obligatoire pour prendre part aux guerres impériales. . . .'[31] And the night the bill became law there was a substantial riot in Montreal. French Canada seemed as one against conscription and the government.

But as a Canadian writing for a New York newspaper noted, 'it is perhaps not surprising that the rest of Canada* sees in the Quebec attitude nothing but disloyalty, and is more determined than ever to

---

*An anti-conscriptionist leaflet in PAC, Militia and Defence Records, file HQ 54-21-1-38, Vol. 2, expressed some contrary feelings:

> Citizens!
>
> The Borden Administration has no mandate from the people to pass a Conscription Bill . . .
>
> It is only the edge of the wedge to break up Canadian liberties and make this country cursed with militarism.
>
> Wives and Mothers! Men! Oppose this measure! . . .

make certain that Quebec shall not prevent the Dominion from doing its entire and splendid duty to the men at the front.'[32] The writer was Mackenzie King.

II

While the long debate in the House of Commons over conscription focused the country's attention in Ottawa, Sir Robert Borden continued his efforts to form a coalition. It could no longer be with Laurier, but it could include a substantial number of Liberals, either from the federal caucus or from the provincial parties, who favoured conscription and its immediate implementation. The Liberals were badly divided, but the residue of affection and regard for the leader who had made the party great was still substantial.

For example, a meeting in July of Ontario Liberal candidates who had already been nominated, a meeting expected to disavow the chief and to endorse conscription, did neither.[33] In part this was probably because rural Ontario, and rural Canada too, did not seem enthusiastic about conscription, a measure that would only speed the trend to rural depopulation that the war had accelerated. How could a farmer get his crops in if the city's high-paying jobs and the army's drill sergeants took away the son and hired hand alike?[34] Perhaps conscription would not win an election for Borden's administration. This seemed more likely after a western Liberal conference in Winnipeg in early August, called to endorse coalition and conscription, remained disconcertingly loyal to Laurier.[35] More ominously for loyalist Grits, a meeting of Ontario's Liberal newspaper editors on 26 July called with only one dissenting vote for a Union Government and compulsory service. This seemed a clear indication that if the candidates and the rank and file remained true to Laurier and the Liberal Party, the press was sliding very quickly towards coalition. A good indication, too, that the newspaper publishers, rich men all, would have nothing to contribute to party coffers and would turn the big guns of public opinion against those who opposed conscription.

Public opinion in favour of the Military Service Act and coalition was simultaneously being mobilized by the Win-the-War movement, based in Toronto. The successor to the National Service League and Bonne Entente, the Win-the-War and National Unity League, effectively led by J. M. Godfrey and his small crew of supporters, had begun organizing in February 1917 for a May meeting in Toronto. The purpose was to step up the pressure on the dilatory Borden and to force action on the question of military manpower.[36] But while the convention was meeting, Borden came out for conscription, and Godfrey and most of the English-speaking participants began to shift their support to the government and towards an antipathy to a French Canada that still objected to Canada's doing its duty to the fullest. So much for Bonne Entente, a phrase that would be forgotten until 1918. A second convention in August, now called simply a Win-the-War convention, came out strongly for coalition. Godfrey himself told the substantial audience that the 'old [political] machines must disappear.' It was now necessary 'to create a strong and vigorous and well-organized machine with a higher motive than power and patronage. The new machine,' he said lyrically, 'must throb with the impulse of national patriotism.' The one-time Liberal also declared that Sir Wilfrid Laurier had forfeited the right to national leadership. 'I earnestly believe that Sir Robert Borden will form the very best [coalition] government he can.' Hugh Guthrie, the Liberal Member of Parliament for Wellington South, Ontario, echoed this cry, telling the Win-the-War delegates that Borden was the only man who could form a government of national union. The villain of the piece was Quebec, no doubt of that. 'We must not forget that majorities rule,' Godfrey said, 'and if we win this election Quebec must accept the decision.'[37]

But if there was to be a coalition, some further solvent had to be applied to the still strong Liberal bonds, and Borden found it in the Military Voters Act and the War Time Elections Act. The first, introduced in mid-August, gave the vote to all soldiers regardless of their period of residence in Canada. A military voter would cast his ballot, not for a specific candidate as was the case in all general elections hitherto, but for either the government or for the Opposition. If the soldier could specify the constituency in which he had lived at the time of enlistment, or any constituency in which he had ever lived, his ballot would be counted there; if not, his vote would be assigned to a riding. There seemed to be ample potential for chicanery there.

There was just as much in the War Time Elections Bill, introduced on 6 September by Arthur Meighen. The Tories had been concerned at least since 1915 by their inability to draw support from naturalized Canadians,[38] and the too-clever Meighen had written to Borden in the fall of 1916 to suggest that the lifting of the vote from the disloyal and its award to the patriotic would be 'a splendid stroke'.[39] Similar advice came from Conservatives in the West,[40] and the results in the Alberta and Saskatchewan provincial elections in June 1917, where the Liberals swept back into power with near-solid 'foreign' votes, tended to confirm the worst Conservative fears.* The War Time Elections Bill was the answer. With one splendid stroke the mothers, wives, sisters, and daughters of soldiers were enfranchised, the first women to get the vote in federal elections, while naturalized immigrants from enemy countries who had arrived in Canada after 1902 lost the right to vote. Also disenfranchised were conscientious objectors, Doukhobors, and Mennonites.[41] With the solitary exception of Hugh Guthrie, all the Liberals argued strenuously in Parliament against this extraordinary gerrymander, but under closure the government forced its will on the country. As a Liberal would put it during the election, 'The Government chose the voters instead of the voters choosing the Government.'[42]

Laurier was now convinced that the government would stop at nothing to win: 'If you want any further evidence that the conscription act was passed for political purposes alone, you find it in the infamous act just passed for the disfranchisement of men who are by the laws of the land our fellow-citizens. . . . Do you see,' he asked a correspondent, ' . . . any evidence that the government intend to win the war, or to win the elections?'[43] O. D. Skelton, writing in the *Queen's Quarterly* just after the bill was passed, put the Act in perspective:

> The fact that a majority—a temporary majority—is honestly convinced that its policy is better than that of its opponents is no excuse for attempting to gerrymander the whole country, to manipulate the franchise to secure their own return. That would be a precedent for proscribing all of a contrary religious faith, or all who

*'The three main causes which led to the defeat of the Conservatives', Borden was told about the Saskatchewan election, were the disenfranchisement of soldiers, the influence of the Catholic Church in foreign settlements, and the introduction of conscription. The absence of the soldiers overseas upset 'the balance of power between British and foreign . . . and the German and Austrian had a voting strength double of what they would have had.' The foreign vote was said to number 31,000 out of a total poll of 108,000. 'In every single constituency in which the British predominated we had a majority or made a good showing and every Conservative who won did so in a preponderatingly [sic] English speaking constituency.' The French-speaking vote was solidly against Conservatives: 'Father Gravel was very active in Moose Jaw county and promised to deliver the vote of every French Canadian to the Liberals—which he very nearly kept.' Finally, 'the introduction of the Conscription bill was the most influential factor in the Conservative defeat. It was freely used among the foreign born.' What did this mean? Borden's unnamed correspondent was clear: 'There is in my opinion only one thing to do and that is to suspend the franchise right from all naturalized subjects whose country of origin is Germany Austria or Bulgaria. The right to vote in any election should only rest with British citizens by birth or citizens of 'Allies' origin. . . . ' (PAC, Borden Papers, Memorandum re Saskatchewan Provincial Elections 1917, n.d., ff.123132-4.)

differed on such a question as reciprocity or imperial relations. What guarantee is there against a similar high-handed proceeding when other issues arise on which the majority for the moment feel strongly? To find a sanction for the principle that the end justifies the means we must go to Germany. . . . [44]

The War Time Elections Act heralded the destruction of the Liberal base of support in the West and created a rush towards coalition. The Prairie Liberals, hitherto cautious, interested in securing a Prime Minister other than Borden, and in joining a coalition after rather than before an election, now changed their tune and ran towards Ottawa and Sir Robert. Two Liberals joined the Cabinet on 3 and 4 October and by 12 October the government had been completely revamped and a Union Cabinet was in place; over the next few days more new men were brought in. In all 13 Conservatives and 10 Liberals formed the government, only three Liberals coming from Laurier's federal caucus, the rest from the provincial parties in the West and Ontario.* How much strength Borden had added to his government was unclear. Newton Rowell, the leader of the Ontario Liberal Party, became the President of the Privy Council and the *de facto* senior Liberal. But Rowell was hated by the Liberals who had stayed loyal to the old leader and distrusted by many of the Conservatives. A. L. Sifton, Sir Clifford's brother and the former Premier of Alberta, joined the Cabinet as Minister of Customs but added little weight. J. A. Calder had come from the Saskatchewan government and Thomas Crerar from the United Grain Growers in Manitoba, and with Sifton they symbolized the West's rejection of Laurier. More directly they demonstrated that the provincial Liberal organizations on the Prairies had gone over to Borden.

As Minister of Militia Borden chose General Mewburn, the commander of the ill-fated Canadian Defence Force. His predecessor, A. E. Kemp, went to London as Minister of the Overseas Forces from Canada in the United Kingdom. Sir Thomas White remained as Minister of Finance, and Arthur Meighen became the Minister of the Interior, in his eyes and the country's the major portfolio of interest to western Canada. Only two French Canadians were included in the government: Albert Sévigny was Minister of Inland Revenue and P.-E. Blondin

---

*J. A. Calder, a Saskatchewan Liberal who joined the coalition, went to see Laurier before accepting Borden's offer. 'My dear Jim,' Laurier said, 'it is not for me to advise you as to what you should do, do what you think best and may God bless you.' (A. R. Turner, ed., 'Reminiscences of the Hon. J. A. Calder', *Saskatchewan History*, XXV (Spring, 1972), 73.)

remained as Postmaster-General. Both portfolios were minor, and Quebec had its least substantial representation ever in the Cabinet.

Whatever its weaknesses, however, the very existence of the Union Cabinet was a triumph of the first order for the Prime Minister. Borden had shown a political tenacity and skill that roused awe in observers and that has led to his high ranking among Canadian first ministers ever since. His performance in the face of quite extraordinary difficulties had been impressive, and J. D. Reid, his Minister of Railways, had not been far off the mark when he opined that he would back Borden against Job in a patience contest any day.[46] Patience was a virtue, no doubt of that, and the Union Cabinet was a creation of political legerdemain. Whether conscription had demanded such wizardry, however, was another question entirely.

Borden's difficulties were far from over when the coalition had been put together. A diary account by Main Johnson, Rowell's private secretary, highlighted the major trouble spots a few weeks after the new Cabinet had been formed:

> Gathering storm of hostility to the government—reflected over a widespread area, principally among Liberals but also among Conservatives (especially in Ontario). The worst disaffected areas were:—
>
> 1. British Columbia—no Liberal representative in Cabinet and general chaos there . . .
> 2. Ontario—
>   i) Strong Liberal opposition which had been growing steadily since the beginning of the war
>   ii) Conservative machine politicians disgruntled and hard to handle
>   iii) No Liberal member of the H. of C. in the Cabinet (except Guthrie) Guthrie considered unpopular to an intense degree, Mewburn not a member of the House & Rowell considered as a plotter against Laurier
>   iv) Organizational difficulties. . . .
> 3. Maritime Provinces—party spirit particularly strong and Union government evidently resented.
>
> Forces at first against the Union Government
> 1. French Canadians
> 2. all non-British Canadians
> 3. Roman Catholic Church
> 4. All those opposed to conscription

  i) men of 1st class
 ii) men of 2nd class
iii) families of these men
5. The farmers
6. At least part of labour
7. Strong Liberal partisans who rallied to Sir Wilfrid.[47]

That was an extraordinary list of problems, and still it omitted some potential difficulties; but in the weeks before the election on 17 December 1917 the government converted most of its liabilities into assets.

The farmers, probably the most important group initially hostile to conscription and thus to coalition, had to be pacified. One gesture to Manitoba farmers had been the bringing in to the Cabinet of T. A. Crerar, President of the United Grain Growers Ltd. Another, more important, was the pledge by General Mewburn, first delivered at Dundas, Ontario on 24 November and then confirmed in an order-in-council on 2 December that 'any farmers' sons who are honestly engaged in farm work and in the production of food stuffs—if they are not exempted by the Tribunals and are called up for military service—I will have them honourably discharged . . . provided they go back to the farm. . . .'[48] The Liberals tried to counter this promise—W. D. Euler in Kitchener, Ontario told his electors that 'After the election is over, if Borden should win, farmers will find conscription a terrible fact for them'[49]—but too few rural voters could be persuaded. Conscription would take the other fellow, not the farmers' sons.

The Conservatives were also worried about those women who, if they had relatives at the front, would be voting for the first time. In February 1917 a 'woman's parliament', organized by *Everywoman's World*, had found a six-to-one majority among its readers against conscription,[50] and there was some concern after conscription passed through Parliament that mothers might not be eager to force other women's sons into the charnel house of Flanders. There need have been no fear. The leaders of the major national women's organizations threw their support behind Union Government[51] and, although the data is necessarily unrecoverable, probably half a million women voted in the elections. One estimate had it that 70 per cent cast ballots for the Union Government.[52]

Organized labour was probably more intractable. Representatives from the Trades and Labour Congress had seen Borden on 21 May to demand that conscription not be imposed. But Borden, aware that only

2 per cent of the labour force was organized, could afford to ignore such protests. Labour leaders made fiery speeches, including one by TLC President Watters to a Hull audience that threatened that workers 'would lay down . . . tools and refuse to work' the day the conscription bill passed into law.[53] This did not occur, and the TLC, by helping to form the Canadian Labour Party and by supporting its electoral campaigns in a number of constituencies, simply divided the anti-conscription vote.

Other elements of opposition to the Union Government were less important. Many Catholics outside Quebec were upset that there were, counting Blondin and Sévigny, only three of their co-religionists in the Cabinet. But their options were limited—they did not want to appear to support the slackers, the foreigners, and the French Canadians any more than did their Protestant neighbours, and English-speaking Catholics largely appear to have supported the Union. Bishop Fallon, one of the leaders of the Ontario hierarchy and one who had bitterly opposed the attempts by Franco-Ontarians to secure school facilities in French in the Province, endorsed Union Government despite what he called the 'vile and indefensible anti-Catholic propaganda that certain supporters of Union Government are conducting in its name.'[54] If Catholics had nowhere to go but to the Union, the same was even more true for diehard Conservatives who had objected to submerging their party in the coalition. To co-operate with Grits was offensive to many, but what else could they do? The only options were to stay home or to vote for the Liberals and that was no choice at all.

Borden's government expected little support from French Canadians and it received little. But this was a positive element in the election campaign, one that permitted all the stops to be pulled and the flood-tide of Anglo-Saxon racism to be unleashed. Indeed this appeared to be a deliberate policy decision taken by the Prime Minister himself late in November when the government's strategists had a momentary panic. The initial requests for exemption from conscription were running over 90 per cent, and English-speaking men were proving as unenthusiastic about military service as the French. How could this be countered? On 25 November Borden jotted a note in his diary that his Finance Minister, Sir Thomas White, 'thinks we should make strong campaign against Quebec'. The next day he noted that 'White and Rowell agreed that we should attack in press and on public platform the attitude of Quebec,' and that same day Borden approvingly noted the anti-Quebec speech made by a politician with whom he shared a platform.[55] The word went out, and the press and politicians were quick to take advantage.

If Laurier wins, a Union Government pamphlet said, 'the French-Canadians who have shirked their duty in this war will be the dominating force in the government of the country. Are the English-speaking people prepared to stand for that?'[56] Another pamphlet, 'Plain Facts for English-speaking Electors', proposed to offer voters an understanding of the 'forces operating in the Province of Quebec against Union Government and against Canada's further participation in the war. The facts are plain and unmistakeable,' the pamphlet charged. 'Sir Wilfrid Laurier, who for years was afraid of the growing influence of Bourassa, finally capitulated to him, and an alliance has been formed between them. . . . ' Another government flier, 'English Canadians and the War', said bluntly that 'Laurier means to quit the war.'[57] Politicians made much the same argument. One Unionist Liberal in Winnipeg called Quebec 'the plague-spot of the whole Dominion', while the Tory Premier of Ontario, Sir William Hearst, promised to 'see that Sir Robert Borden and Mr. Rowell keep their promises to Ontario and that the people of Quebec are compelled to do their share before further sacrifices are demanded from Ontario.'[58] Again, the other fellow would be the conscript.

In Toronto, press and pulpit were mobilized with quite astonishing effectiveness by the Citizens' Union Committee. One Toronto Presbyterian minister told his Sunday congregation that 'Jesus Christ was a conscript for He said "No man is fit for my kingdom if he loves his life better than Me".'[59] Archdeacon H. J. Cody, one of the city's leading clerics, delivered on 26 November 1917 a sermon from notes:

Never did more turn on an election
> Defeat or Victory
> Honour or dishonour
> Union or disunion
. . . Exercise *vote at critical stage in war—need of men*, of union, of
> supplies—of determination [in] order to end war decisively. . . .
. . . *Real Issues*
Not past conduct of former government
Not grievances of self or soldiers
Not past party loyalty
Not Exemption tribunals
Not high cost of living
Not personality of individual candidates

but (i) how can our men at front be best backed up
(ii) Quebec über alles[60]

'Quebec über alles'—that summed up the thrust of Union Government propaganda. Main Johnson, a bit awed by the force of the campaign, noted that the electorate had been mobilized around the slogan 'Quebec shall not dominate the rest of Canada'. This, he wrote, 'was a watchword which, used as it was also in the official Unionist publicity, and by the government itself, had a great deal to do with the result. . . . ' He also noted that Rowell, attacked by critics as pious and prissy, had managed to adapt to 1917 electoral realities, adding 'truly it is strange how Mr. Rowell and his colleagues this time have adopted the very methods of campaigning, including the anti-Quebec cry, which formerly had been used against [English-speaking Liberals] with such telling effect, and which, on this occasion, had helped them so materially.'[61] Truly strange.

According to Meighen's biographer, the Union Government ministers 'knew that conscription would be unpopular, especially in Quebec, but, facing the facts as they had to do, they concluded that there was no honourable alternative.' That seemed fair. Less so is Professor Graham's next judgement: 'Nothing was further from their desires than that national unity should be destroyed, for nothing could be more disastrous to their own interest, let alone that of Canada.'[62] On the contrary. The Union Government campaign, founded on the Military Service Act and the War Time Elections Act, deliberately set out to create an English-Canadian nationalism, separate from and opposed to both French Canada and naturalized Canadians. No other conclusion can be drawn from this election campaign, one of the few in Canadian history deliberately conducted on racist grounds.

Against the unscrupulous tactics of the government Laurier and his party were helpless. The party's organizational base on the Prairies and in Ontario had gone over to the enemy, much of it was hostile in British Columbia and the Maritimes, and party finances, heavily dependent on corporate contributions from Toronto and Montreal, were weak. 'We are very much disorganized just now,' a weary Laurier wrote to one supporter at the end of October. 'Every riding must look after itself.'[63] Struggling to keep his men together, Laurier was willing to consider anyone a Liberal who was either against Union and against conscription, or against Union and for conscription, or an Independent Liberal. 'Anyone of these alternatives would be satisfactory to me,' he wrote to one M.P., 'not of course in the same degree, but I would be disposed to make allowances for the conscience of those who favour Conscription.'[64] The leader's imposed tolerance led to an extraordinary array of positions by party candidates. In western Ontario, for example, the position was this:

> *Kennedy* in North Essex is supporting the Conscription Act.
> *McCoig* in Kent will not repeal the Act.
> *McDougall* in West Lambton will enforce the Act.
> *Duncan Ross* no doubt the same.
> *London*, the same.
> *James Ross* in East Middlesex, *Tolmie* and *Charlton* in the Elgins and *Forrester* in South Perth, straight Laurier Candidates.
> *Hyslop* and *McMillan* in the Hurons, straight Laurier Candidates.[65]

The confusion this caused the public and party headquarters must have been substantial.

Laurier fought the election gamely, going through the motions in good spirits although he knew he had no chance. At Quebec City on 9 November he told his audience that 'I believe that our first and pressing duty is to share in the fight. I believe that it is our immediate duty to help our armies. . . . We must support them with men.' But not by conscription. 'We began with the voluntary system,' Laurier said, 'it is our duty to continue with it.' Lomer Gouin, Premier of Quebec, told the same meeting that 'There is no power here, there is no power in the world, that is able to impose Conscription on the Canadian people against their will.' And Rodolphe Lemieux, defending his leader, declared that 'Laurier is a Liberal, a Canadian patriot; above all, he is Laurier.'[66] That was enough for many Canadians. Hon. G. P. Graham, Laurier's Railways Minister and one of the senior Ontario figures, had wobbled badly when the Union Government was being formed, but now he returned firmly to the fold and told a Toronto crowd on 30 November that 'I voted for the draft of 100,000, and I am a follower of Sir Wilfrid Laurier in everything else. They tell you you can't be a follower of Laurier and disagree with him in one thing. I ask you how our friends can follow Sir Robert Borden and disagree with him in every issue but one.'[67] It was all magnificent and more than a little bit sad.

Overseas the government mobilized the military vote with some skill and great success. The British Commander-in-Chief, Sir Douglas Haig, was asked to give the Canadian Corps a rest behind the lines so 'they could be visited and their votes secured.'[68] General Arthur Currie, the first Canadian to command the Corps, received a wire from Ottawa: 'If Union Government wins election and Military Service Act is carried out survivors of First Division still at Front will be brought Canada on furlough.' Currie was asked to print that message in Corps Orders but the General, disturbed by this blatant political interference, refused.[69]

Currie was an interesting case. As a general, he wanted more men. And yet as a commander he was very careful and cautious in deploying his troops, preferring to use artillery and strategy rather than mass waves of infantry as other Empire commanders were wont to do. Currie cared for his men's lives. But the General could work himself into a rage over political interference and there was no shortage of that in the CEF. Officers were pressed forward for promotion by political influence, others were transferred to 'cushy' jobs in the rear. It was infuriating to Currie, and nothing galled him more than the case of the 5th Division.

Commanded by Major-General Garnet Hughes, Sam Hughes' son, the 5th remained in England with its 21,000 men, untouched and untouchable. It was just politics, Currie believed, damn politics. There were enough men there, he wrote a friend, 'to replace our casualties and many thousands more.'[70] This, the General Officer Commanding the Canadian Corps believed, would mean more to the CEF than conscription at home, for that politically dangerous course would take months to produce men. Thus when Sir George Perley, the High Commissioner, asked him to send a message to Canada supporting Union Government, Currie refused.[71] He would remain angry until February 1918 when the 5th was finally broken up for use as reinforcements.

Currie's silence on the election had no impact at all on the men of the CEF, however, as the troops at the front voted solidly Union. Writers at home could prate solemnly about the spirit in the trenches where men were 'void of fear' and happy to seek a chance of 'a fair death',[72] but the soldiers, dulled and tired by the constant fear of death, simply wanted succour. In some battalions no one could be found to act as the Liberal scrutineer; in another battalion Liberal voters were threatened with a ducking in a pond if they did not vote the right way. And in an Alberta regiment the orderly room sergeant sat beside the ballot box indicating where every soldier should put his mark 'and so assure a unanimous verdict for conscription.'[73] Major-General David Watson, commanding the 4th Division, wrote in his diary on 17 September that 'this Division has cast over 17,200 votes & I don't think that 5% will be for the opposition.'[74] He was very nearly right: 92 per cent of the military vote went to

Unionist candidates, enough under the peculiar terms of the Military Voters Act to swing 14 seats from the Liberals to the Unionists.*[75]

Not that the Liberals had many seats to lose. As early as the end of October Sir John Willison had written to Sir Clifford Sifton, 'Surely there can be no hope for Sir Wilfrid and his remnant.'[76] That seemed the right assessment, but there were a few nervous days as the Unionist backroom strategists attempted to determine who would receive which nomination where, even bringing in Sifton, probably the ablest election organizer/manipulator in Canadian political history, to sort out the Ontario situation.[77] Still, as one Ontario Tory wrote, 'Sir Wilfrid and Bourassa are too big a pill for Ontario to swallow today',†[78] exactly the kind of assessment that moved J. D. Reid, the Minister of Railways and Canals, to forecast that Union would win 76 of 82 seats as a minimum in Ontario.[79]

Reid had guessed a shade too high, the Unionists taking only 74 seats in Ontario. Laurier captured all of Quebec except for three seats, and both Sévigny and Blondin were defeated. Nationally the total was 153 for Borden and 82 for Laurier, although on the civilian vote the margin was surprisingly close, with Unionist candidates receiving 841,944 votes to the Liberals' 744,849. Significantly, Ontario had the highest percentage of its population enfranchised, 39.4 per cent, while Quebec had the lowest, 20.6 per cent. Saskatchewan, heavily ethnic,

---

*The best brief sample of Unionist manipulation of the overseas vote is found in this letter from a Unionist organizer of the soldiers' vote: 'Many [commanders] lined their men up and told them plainly what they wanted them to do as a matter of duty. . . . Also many of the Chaplains took up the stump and gave 10 minute addresses. . . . Great enthusiasm was worked up. . . . The special places I was asked to secure extra votes for, i.e., loose or non-resident votes were Ottawa 200, North Perth 200, Lennox 300, South Perth 200, South Grey 200, South Hamilton 200, Peel 200, Peterboro West 200. . . . I apportioned all the units in the whole four divisions among these constituencies. . . . It was only yesterday your cable was forwarded from London stating that your opponent had dropped out. Had we known earlier we could have utilized your vote to good advantage elsewhere.' (PAC, Borden Papers, Joseph Hayes to F. B. McCurdy, M.P., 18 Dec. 1917, ff. 41180a-b.)

†Although Bourassa and Laurier had agreed as early as 18 October to work together against conscription (Joseph Schull, *Laurier the First Canadian* (Toronto, 1966), p. 592) it was not until 15 December, two days before the election, that Bourassa advised his supporters to vote Liberal: 'Le mal à combattre, c'est la politique radicalement mauvaise du ministère. L'unique moyen de la combattre, c'est de voter contre les candidats ministeriels, ce qui implique la necessité de voter pour les candidats d'opposition.' (Robert Rumilly, *Henri Bourassa* (Montréal, 1953), p. 592.)

had the lowest percentage enfranchised, 22.9 per cent. The War Time Elections Act had effectively concentrated the vote, exactly as its drafters had hoped. And, as Professor John English has shown, 117 of the Unionist seats were rurally based, something that makes the government's pledges to the farmers about exemptions very understandable indeed.[80]

The Union victory did nothing to ease the bitterness felt by many in English Canada towards Quebec. Arthur Meighen's victory statement, for example, sounded militant still:

> Every appeal that could be addressed to the selfish, weak and the timid, every allurement that attended the prospect of immediate comfort, every temptation to seek immediate advantage rather than to use the ballot as the citizen of a nation, was brought into play. ... [The result of the election] was a call of duty to the absent; a call of honour from the State; and the conscience of the nation triumphed.[81]

The Minister of the Interior, never a man to forgive or forget, sounded no different in his private correspondence. 'The result is an indication that French-Canadian domination in political affairs in Canada is a back number,' Meighen wrote to a Kingston newspaper publisher. 'The time in my opinion has come to call a spade a spade, and if we have a disloyal element in our country it should be emphasized and ventilated.'[82] John W. Dafoe of the *Manitoba Free Press* was just as brutal in his correspondence with a Quebec friend. The crisis in Canada had become acute because Quebec had failed to do its duty in the war, Dafoe said, French Canadians 'being the only known race of white men to quit. ... You can do precisely as you please,' the Winnipeg editor wrote, 'and we shall do whatever may be necessary. When we demonstrate that a solid Quebec is without power, there may be a return to reason along the banks of the St. Lawrence.'[83]

The naked power of the majority had been brought into play and Quebec was severely shaken. One response was a motion introduced in the Quebec legislature by J.-N. Francoeur and debated on 17 January 1918: 'That this House is of the opinion that the province of Quebec would be disposed to accept the breaking of the Confederation Pact of 1867 if, in the other provinces, it is believed that she is an obstacle to the union, progress and development of Canada.' The discussion, held more in sorrow than in anger, saw many defend Confederation, most notably Premier Gouin, and the resolution was withdrawn without a vote.[84] But if Quebec had any goodwill left towards the rest of Canada, it must have been based on faith alone. That faith would be shaken in the next year.

III

The administration and operation of the Military Service Act were complicated. Two departments, Justice and Militia and Defence, had direct responsibilities, along with the courts, local tribunals, appeal and medical boards, and a host of paid and volunteer workers.

The basic directing body was the Military Service Council, appointed on 3 September 1917 to assist the Minister of Justice in securing the expeditious operation and full effect of the Military Service Act. The Deputy Minister of Justice, E. L. Newcombe, headed the Council, while the Militia Department was represented by a Military Sub-Committee under the Chief of the General Staff, General Gwatkin. The Sub-Committee's task was to assist the Military Service Council on all matters of military import and to assist the Minister of Militia in the administration of the Act from the point at which the Justice Department ceased control.[85]

A registrar for each province was appointed by the government and given responsibility for administering the Act. In provinces where there were two Military Districts a Deputy Registrar was also appointed. The next stage was the appointment of Boards of Selection, consisting of four men in Ontario and Quebec, and two men in each of the other provinces. The members of the Boards of Selection were chosen equally by the government and the Opposition.[86] The Boards in turn chose one member for each Local Tribunal for Exemption, of which some 1,253 were in place by mid-September. Another member for each Tribunal was chosen by the County Court Judge for the district, who could himself serve if he wished.[87] The intent clearly was to provide a fair and patronage-free process, something that was less successful perhaps than the framers of the procedure had intended. For example, the Minister of the Naval Service, J. D. Hazen, wrote to the New Brunswick Board of Selection member nominated by the government that he had been chosen because of his 'judgement, patriotism and good faith'. The Act had to be enforced fairly, Hazen said, adding prudently that 'while it is not desirable that any attempt should be made to gain political advantage out of it, at the same time our own friends should not be overlooked and undue consideration should not be given to those who are not in sympathy with the Government and opposed to the policy of selective conscription.'[88]

From the Local Tribunals appeals for exemption could be carried to one-man appeal courts, of which 195 were established throughout the land. And in a final resort, appeals could be taken before the Central Appeal Judge, Mr Justice Lyman Duff of the Supreme Court of Canada.

The Military Service Act declared all men between the ages of 20 and 45 liable for service, and these potential soldiers were grouped into six classes:

Class 1: Those who had attained the age of 20 years and were born not earlier than the year 1883, unmarried or widowers without child.

Class 2: Those who had attained the age of 20 years and were born not earlier than 1883, married or widowers with one or more children.

Class 3: Those who were born in the years 1876 to 1882 . . . unmarried or widowers without child.

Class 4: Those who were born in the years 1876 to 1882 . . . married or widowers with one or more children.

Class 5: Those who were born in the years 1872 to 1875 . . . unmarried or widowers without child.

Class 6: Those who were born in the years 1872 to 1875 . . . married or widowers with one or more children.

For the purpose of the Military Service Act, men married after 6 July 1917 were considered to be single.[89]

Essentially the individual had to make his own case for exemption. A man in a designated class had to secure a special form from the post office, complete it or have it completed on his behalf by his employer or a person with whom he was associated in business, or by a relative or dependant. All corroborative evidence had to be submitted in writing to the Local Tribunal, but personal attendance was not required. The Tribunal then reached its decision and notified the applicant. If the request for exemption was granted, the military authorities could appeal to the courts; if the request was refused, the man in question similarly had access to the appeal procedure.[90] Grounds for exemption were broad. A man could be excused military service if he had an essential occupation or if his work required special qualifications. He could be excused if serious hardship would result from his absence on military service or if he was a conscientious objector, a Mennonite, a Doukhobor, a clergyman, a member of the armed forces, or an honourably discharged veteran, or if he suffered from an obvious physical disability such as a missing limb.

Implementation of the Act began with a proclamation on 13 October as a consequence of a decision made by the first meeting of the Union Cabinet. All men of Class 1 were ordered to report 'for the defence and security of Canada, the preservation of our Empire and of human liberty'. These men had to present themselves before 10 November, and 200 medical boards were established to examine the potential soldiers. After the medical examination the men would either return home to await instructions or, voluntarily, report for service to a Depot Battalion (of which 12 were created across the country)[91] for the beginning of their military training.[92] The delicacy that had marked the entire discussion of conscription was to be preserved: by specific instruction of Militia Headquarters, men called under the Act were not to be known as 'conscripts' but as 'drafted men'.[93]

Once the men began to report, very slowly at first, it soon became evident that almost all were seeking exemption. The Montreal *Star* noted on 18 October that of the 896 men who had reported in Montreal so far, all but 59 had sought exemption, only 'a trifle over 7 per cent' being ready to serve. A report two days later in the Montreal *Gazette* showed 99 per cent seeking exemption in Hull, 98 in Saint John, 96 in Kingston, 90 in Toronto, 70 in Vancouver, and 86 per cent in Calgary. The figures demonstrated, said Montreal *La Presse*, that it was not just the French Canadians who opposed conscription. And Bourassa's *Le Devoir* could hardly hide its jubilation when it noted that 'Tout le monde demande d'être exempte du service militaire.... Certes, ce n'est pas très consolant pour les conscriptionistes....'[94]

By 2 November 157,603 men had reported and 144,628 had asked to be excused from military service. By 10 November, the cut-off date for reporting, 332,000 had been processed, and despite penalties for failing to register,[95] another 70,000 had failed to complete their forms. By the end of 1917 the final results were in hand: 404,395 had reported and 380,510 had sought exemption, leaving 24,000 who had been willing to serve in the army from the outset. In Ontario, 118,000 of 125,000 had sought exemption; in Quebec, 115,000 of 117,000. Nationally, 93.7 per cent of those called asked to be excused service.[96]

The Local Tribunals then took over, beginning the processing of exemption claims and operating with great speed. In Montreal, for example, after two days of sittings, the Tribunal had heard 2,595 cases and granted 2,021 exemptions.[97] Whole groups of men appeared to seek exemption: every student from Laval University and from the Manitoba Agricultural College, for example, appeared before the Tribunals with a letter signed by a university official and asking for exemption on the grounds of public interest.[98] Some tribunals granted exemptions in wholesale lots; others were tough. From St Catherines, Ontario, one army officer reported that his Tribunal 'is not likely to grant many exemptions, they are the hottest bunch I have seen, they will hardly excuse [low medical category] E-men, and I believe a dead man would even have to show good reason.'[99]

Many Prairie Tribunals must have acted in the same way. T. A. Crerar, the Minister of Agriculture in the Union Government, was flooded with protests from farmers complaining about the refusal of local Tribunals to exempt them. 'The action of a good many of the Tribunals is difficult to understand,' the Minister replied to one complainant with a frankness that marked him as a new politician. Some 'have not taken into consideration the fact that the removal of experienced farm help will materially affect our production of food stuffs at the present time.'[100] Newton Rowell felt similarly, and on 14 November he wrote to the Prime Minister to say that unless there was some reform in the process of granting exemptions 'the cause of Union Government [would] be imperilled.'[101] These and other complaints led to General Mewburn's pledge to farmers and to the order-in-council of 2 December granting a virtual blanket exemption to them.

Nonetheless, and despite all the complaints, the statistics up to the end of 1917 demonstrated that most exemptions had been granted. Of the 380,510 who had sought to be freed of service, 278,779 exemptions were granted by Local Tribunals and only 47,868 were disallowed. Another 53,788 cases remained to be heard, and 67,122 appeals had been lodged against Tribunal decisions, many by the military authorities.[102]

Significantly not a single man had yet been ordered to report for military training. In keeping with his pledge that conscription would not be enforced until after the general election on 17 December 1917, the Prime Minister had directed that conscripts not be called for training until 3 January 1918. And thanks to the exemption procedures, when the order to report for training was issued, there were only some 20,000 men ready. It was not, said Newcombe, the head of the Military Service Council, 'quite so many as the military authorities require'. Worse, the Deputy Minister said, only 1,500 would be from Quebec 'owing to the fact that there were very few reports for service there; that the claims for exemption have been generally allowed, and that very few of the appeals, which are very numerous, have been disposed of.'[103]

Another problem, particularly in Quebec where substantial numbers had failed to report, was that the military authorities received little cooperation from local police forces in their efforts to round up defaulters. The General Officer Commanding in Military District No. 5, based at Quebec City, had to report that both the municipal and provincial police refused to co-operate, and the General added that he was hesitant about employing military police on this duty.[104] The extent of the problem can be seen from the Montreal figures: 84 of 239 English-speaking conscripts ordered to present themselves on 3 January failed to do so; of 243 French-speaking, only 108 reported.[105]

The first concrete results of the Military Service Act, therefore, as presented to the War Committee of the Cabinet in a memorandum from the Military Service Council on 4 February were distinctly unimpressive:[106]

Men reported as having joined in advance of call	5,458
Men joined in pursuance of call	14,159
Men called but whose time for joining has not yet arrived	729
Men who appear to have disobeyed orders to report for duty	4,035
Men who still may appeal from the decisions refusing exemption	3,751
Men immediately available for a further call	5,108
	33,240
Claims for exemption still remaining undisposed of	52,185

The poor showing terribly depressed some members of the Cabinet. Sir George Foster, the Minister of Trade and Commerce, waxed gloomy and choleric in his diary:

19 January 1918: The M.S.A. is working fairly but slowly and I doubt if we get the 100,000 required out of this call. Quebec will make no show of active resistance but the pull will be a hard one to get a decent proportion from the number called. The passive resistence [sic] of Bourassa Priests Avocats Tribunals etc is a thick undergrowth from which to hunt out even a respectable proportion.

28 January 1918: The MS Act goes slowly and results are doubtful so far as our getting the 100,000 men.—Quebec does not show up well. We must jack up the machinery—the 100,000 must be got.

9 February 1918: Our M.S.A. is not panning out well. . . . So far 20,000 men is the max. we can see in sight.

12 February 1918: In Quebec little result, in Quebec district so far a dead failure. The tribunals follow the lead of public opinion and exemptions and appeals for exemptions are scuffled through. If counter appeals are made they involve delay. . . . The heart is sick

and that is the whole trouble. Quebec is badly led but alas does not resent the leading. Are there left a saving residue for the nation's salvation?[107]

But on 13 February when the government presented the public with the MSA results thus far, matters were made to look somewhat better. There were 30,248 draftees, the press statement said, and 16,448 volunteers up to the end of January, all forming a reinforcement pool of 46,696.[108] And although the release tried to explain the low numbers secured in French Canada, *La Presse* somehow managed to interpret the data to be able to assert that 'C'est Québec qui a le mieux répondu à l'appel au service militaire comparativement à l'évaluation de la population des districts.'[109] As later figures demonstrated, this was no more correct than the government public figures:[110]

Military Service Act—Statement as of 1 April 1918

Military District	Men Voluntarily Reporting	Reporting for Duty as Ordered	Apprehended After failing to report
M.D. 1 (London)	455	1,789	339
M.D. 2 (Toronto)	1,836	4,967	548
M.D. 3 (Kingston)	805	2,083	554
M.D. 4 (Montreal)	462	1,417	819
M.D. 5 (Quebec)	277	225	158
M.D. 6 (Halifax)	163	1,169	400
M.D. 7 (Saint John)	241	1,109	157
M.D. 10 (Winnipeg)	1,498	2,206	471
M.D. 11 (Victoria)	622	1,864	416
M.D. 12 (Regina)	278	1,896	437
M.D. 13 (Calgary)	138	1,300	196
	6,775	20,025	4,495
Grand Total	31,295		

In addition, on 1 April there were 107,559 exemption claims granted or pending across the country; of these 47,313 were in Quebec.[111]

Meanwhile the German army had launched a massive attack on 21 March against the Allied trenches. On the first day gains of three miles were made, and the breakthrough deepened as March wore on. Although the Canadian Corps fortunately held a quiet sector, it seemed clear that the Western front had been breached and that the war could be lost. To Sir Clifford Sifton in England the crisis of the war was at hand, and he wired Borden his views:

Every available first line fighting man should be got over here at earliest possible moment. If necessary all other traffic except food convoy should be suspended. In meantime I urge that drastic steps be taken to clean up first draft and that second class should be called forthwith. Suggest second class should be asked to waive formalities and join up at once so as to get into immediate training. Make no mistake situation desperately serious. . . . [112]

Telegrams from the British government carried the same sombre message, including one from Lloyd George that was promptly made public. In return, Borden promised to do everything he could to get reinforcements across the Atlantic as quickly as possible.[113]

What Borden could do to step up the pace was, however, limited by public opinion in French Canada. The government had been pressing the appeal courts in Quebec to work faster,[114] and increased efforts had been launched to arrest defaulters. The pressures exploded into several days of rioting in Quebec City over the Easter weekend of 28 March to 1 April. At least four civilians were killed by troops, five soldiers and a substantial number of *Québécois* were wounded, and the jails were full. The government intervened with crushing military and legal force, calling in infantry reinforcements (unfortunately choosing a Toronto unit, which some in Quebec saw as deliberate provocation), and passing an order-in-council under the War Measures Act that suspended *habeas corpus* for those arrested during the riots, summarily drafted any man who participated in the riot, and gave summary court-martial powers to the military *in any area in Canada* designated by the Governor-in-Council.[115]

The rioting in the old city had seemingly confirmed that Quebec would not accept the Military Service Act and that public opinion there supported those who refused to serve. How could the situation be turned around? One Cabinet Minister, Newton Rowell, the President of the Privy Council, considered these questions in the course of a long conversation with his private secretary on 7 April 1918:

Mr. Rowell . . . was in bed [Main Johnson recorded in his diary] . . . said it was about Quebec he wanted to speak. He felt that a crisis was coming rapidly, and that drastic action would have to be taken. More men had to be obtained for the army—this was clear from the German offensive—but to take more men, especially of other classes, while Quebec was still supplying so few, even under the Military Service Act, was becoming an impossible proposition. Opinion in Ontario and the other provinces was growing restless. . . .

Mr. Rowell admitted that the M.S.A. was being carried out constitutionally, in the province of Quebec as elsewhere, but the methods of appeal were so long drawn out, that, where, as in Quebec, public opinion was hostile, actual results under the act could be postponed to an unreasonable time.

Mr. Rowell felt that

1) either more men must be obtained from Quebec at once, or
2) the government should take the people of the rest of the country into their confidence and say that, owing to certain specified causes, men could not be obtained under the present methods in Quebec.[116]

Neither course would be easy to follow and Rowell knew this. The government was caught and, as a British observer later noted, 'Freely denounced as an engine of oppression, the Military Service law, in point of fact, contained so many safeguards against oppression that it had been made to no small degree inoperative.'[117] Borden was now ready to remedy the Act's deficiencies.

Cold and determined, the Prime Minister told the Cabinet on 12 April that alterations to the Military Service Act were necessary, thanks to the situation at the front where the Germans continued to make headway. That day an order-in-council was prepared in draft, cancelling all exemptions heretofore granted, prohibiting future exemptions for men in Class 1, and calling up all men between 20 and 24 years of age.[118] The Cabinet thrashed through the question during the next three days, with Rowell in particular being full of doubts about cancelling all exemptions. What would such a step do to war production?[119] Again the Ontario minister rehearsed his fears with his secretary:

The advantage of [the plan suggested in the order-in-council] would be that it would not be necessary to call out the married men yet. To call out Class 2 at this time, when, owing to exemptions and appeals, the showing from Class 1 in the Province of Quebec was so disappointing would probably arouse great unrest . . . in addition to creating inevitable social and economic derangement.

The disadvantages, on the other hand, were that, if all physically fit men in Class I were taken it would mean principally that thousands of men exempted on national grounds, especially in farming, would be taken, and the agricultural situation would be interfered with.*

*The government was still operating in the dark about the numbers and availability of

There was also this difficulty. In calling out all men of Class 1, irrespective of occupation, you would get a considerable number in Quebec from perhaps the ages of 20-24 but, above that, you would get very few men from the province owing to the early marrying-age prevailing there. The disparity between Quebec and the other provinces, therefore, would likely continue. . . .

On the general question of cancelling all Class 1 exemptions Mr. Rowell pointed out the particular difficulty which would arise in quite a large number of cases, especially in the West, where unmarried men were the owners and operators of farms. It would surely be a bad thing to take them away. 'Couldn't a special exemption be made to fit this case?' I asked. But Mr. Rowell said it would mean continuing some sort of machinery to hear appeals and it was felt that this would be a fatal obstacle. . . . [120]

Rowell had foreseen some of the difficulties that the proposed order-in-council could produce, and alterations were made before the order was presented in the House of Commons on 19 April. The age limits of those whose exemptions were to be lifted were fixed at 20 to 22 years, and men of 19 years were ordered to report. The only ground for exemption remaining was the 'death, disablement or service of other members of the same family while on active service. . . .'[121]

Why an order-in-council and not an amendment to the Military Service Act that could have been processed through Parliament in the normal fashion? The answer was the scope of the emergency, the need for immediate action, the same reasoning that justified breaking the pledges made to the farmers in November and December 1917. Or so Borden told the Commons. But as Rowell noted, a bill could have been rushed through Parliament with the aid of closure in scarcely more time than that required by Borden's extraordinary procedure of amend-

---

men. The National Service Board's registration of early 1917 could not readily be used, and from early 1918 planning for a new registration was under way in the Canada Registration Board. The count would take place on one day, 22 June 1918, and all men and women over 16 years would be obliged to register. Despite some minor opposition in Quebec, the process worked well, and 5,044,034 people registered, of whom 2,471,280 were males. None of the data was ready for use until November 1918, by which time the war was drawing to its close. Government planning for the classification of industry and the control of labour therefore went unused. (PAC, Borden Papers, Rowell to Borden, 29 Jan. 1918, ff. 52172-4; *ibid.*, Robertson to Borden, 18 May 1918, ff. 52241ff.; PAC, Militia and Defence Records, file HQ 54-21-146, Robertson to Mewburn, 7 Oct. 1918; *Canadian Annual Review 1918*, pp. 490ff.)

ing an Act of Parliament with an order-in-council.[122] Closure, however, would have been no more palatable to the Opposition, to Quebec, and to the farmers.

The sweeping alterations to the procedures of the Military Service Act met with fierce opposition, particularly from the farmers who thought that the order-in-council was deliberately aimed at them. The Prime Minister had tried to counter the complaints in advance by preaching stoicism, urging Canadians to accept increased hardship and decreased production. 'It is impossible to avoid this in war,' he told Parliament.[123] The opposition mounted nonetheless, leading Borden to comment with a touch of sarcasm in his usually anodyne *Memoirs* that 'This was not unnatural, as by Order-in-Council in the previous autumn we had provided that farmers' sons should be exempt under certain conditions. It was indeed inevitable that the farming population would greatly prefer to have their sons at home and engaged in producing large crops which could be sold at unusually high prices rather than that they should be placed on active service. . . .'[124]

One immediate result of the lifting of exemptions was the huge delegation of farmers, largely from Ontario, that descended on Parliament Hill on 14 May, a delegation that received extremely short shrift from Borden and his government. To the end of April, the farmers claimed, there had been 41,852 agriculturalists exempted from service; if they were now to be called up the results would be serious and each township in Ontario, for example, would see 4,400 acres go out of production.[125] Henry Wise Wood, the head of the United Farmers of Alberta and the leading agricultural figure in the country, also complained bitterly to his friend T. A. Crerar, the Minister of Agriculture, that the end of exemptions would be a 'serious blow to production. Many cases leaving family helpless and farm unworked.'[126] Worse still was the way the press reacted to the farmers' complaints. The *Round Table*, a British imperialist organ, sneered that farmers' minds do 'not easily grasp abstract facts', while the journalist H. F. Gadsby mercilessly parodied the farmer delegation in *Saturday Night*:

> . . . the Sons of the Soil met together in a painted chamber to chide King Borden for that he did not let them stay at home to charge ninety cents a pound for turkey at Christmas. . . .
>
> And King Borden and three of his council sat on the high seats at the far end of the chamber, and the Sons of the Soil saw that King Borden's back was up also, which was another omen.

And there were scribes present with long pencils and a nose for news.

And one scribe said to another: 'An odor prevaileth.'

And the other answered: 'Why not? They are five thousand strong.' . . .

And another said: 'It is the livery stable'. . . . But it was not the livery stable.

And another scribe said: 'It is the esprit de corps.' And it was a true word.[127]

The farmers would not forget their treatment in Ottawa or the way they had been portrayed in the press, and the political implications of conscription would have a major effect on farm politics well into the 1920s.

But in fact the new regulations could not be enforced with the rigidity set out in the order-in-council. The process was speeded up, but exemptions were lifted only after investigation, and the Tribunals continued their work. Rowell wrote to the Prime Minister on 8 May to reiterate his support for selective conscription as soundest in principle, arguing that the government had abandoned it only for certain exempted men and only because of the 'present emergency'.[128] The same day the Minister of Justice reported that there were 150,000 exemption cases presently before the Central Appeal Judge, with hundreds of new cases being added each day.[129]

Although hardship cases were officially recognized by an order-in-council of 25 May,[130] farmers continued to be pulled off the land and directed to the army. On 2 May General Mewburn had told Parliament that farmers could be given leaves of absence, subject to the judgement of the District Officers Commanding, but as the Minister of Agriculture learned shortly afterwards, such leave was only for two weeks 'for seeding purposes' and could not extend beyond 1 June.[131] For Crerar, desperately trying to ensure that the maximum amount of food could be produced, and trying with equal desperation to balance his obligations to his Cabinet colleagues while simultaneously maintaining his position as one of the leaders of rural Canada, this was a difficult time. To one correspondent, a farm-journal editor, he wrote that 'I have no hesitation in telling you *privately* that I think the whole thing has been poorly handled. The Militia Department have acted in a stupid manner and a good many of the judges in the country . . . are acting in an equally stupid way.' The Union minister added that the situation gave

the United Farmers of Ontario, the powerful and growing farm organization, 'a magnificent opportunity.... It does appear to me that there
has not been a time in years when there has been such a ferment....
Wisely directed, it could be productive of much good. One result that
will come out of this whole thing is to create a strong feeling of
antagonism throughout Canada against things military.'[132] That was
true enough.

The Minister also noted, with a good deal of puzzlement, that the
ending of exemptions had not created an uproar in Quebec. The
French Canadians 'are, apparently, accepting it in good spirit, and I
have no doubt a good many of them are quietly enjoying the situation
in Ontario.'[133] Sir George Foster noted the same effect: 'Quebec has
apparently had a change of heart or it is becoming clear to the powers
that be that accommodation to the general wish is expedient.'[134] Whatever the reason, the change was marked. The Church began to throw
its weight behind the upholding of law and order, and soon the universities began encouraging students to enlist. The Quebec riots and
the uncompromising government response presumably had frightened
everyone, and when, for example, an officer from Montreal headquarters toured Vaudreuil County he received only co-operation from
clergy and political leaders, all of whom claimed to be encouraging the
citizenry to obey the law. The officer, a Captain Duchastel, concluded
that if tact were exercised there would be no problems there in
future.[135] Matters were helped along, too, by the announcement of a
general amnesty for all defaulters under the Military Service Act, providing they reported before 24 August, and of a six-week leave granted
farmer conscripts in August.[136]

Overseas, however, the attitude was a little cooler to the conscripts
and particularly to French Canadians. The otherwise sensible General
Currie, in command of the Corps, wrote to the commander of Canadian troops in Britain to urge that French-speaking reinforcements be
split up among different units. He had found a 'unanimous opinion'
among his commanders 'that they should be spread about.... There
was a decided objection ... to having as many as a French Canadian
company together.' His own opinion was the same, Currie added:
'They should not be kept separate. They are Canadians the same as
everybody else, and the sooner it is so regarded the better it will be for
the national life of our country.'[137] The General's views would not have
been pleasing to Quebec had they been known, unlike those of the
Minister of Militia, General Mewburn, who wrote to urge that French
Canadians be well treated in the army. 'I honestly think it would be a

good policy to have your officers go out of their way to treat them decently,' he told Sir Edward Kemp. 'It will make all the difference in the world. . . .'[138] The sentiments were splendid; how sad that Mewburn felt any need even to express them.

Different sentiments about conscription and conscripts were being expressed in Canada by the courts. In a series of cases in the summer of 1918 the legality of the government's cancellation of exemptions by order-in-council was severely challenged, and Sir George Foster moaned in his diary that 'The court decisions are not agreeable helpmeets to recruiting.'[139] On 28 June the Alberta Supreme Court had ruled that a conscript named Lewis, represented by R. B. Bennett, was being illegally held by the army, ordered his release, and ruled in addition that the order-in-council of 20 April was invalid. The government immediately appealed the decision to the Supreme Court, and Cabinet passed a new order-in-council declaring that the government would continue to act as before 'notwithstanding the said judgement and notwithstanding any judgment or any Order that may be made by any Court . . .', a simply astonishing course of conduct. Matters deteriorated to such an extent that when the Alberta courts sought to force an army officer to appear, the Militia Department ordered the officer in question to remain in barracks. The court issued an order for his arrest, and the military authorities responded by posting guards with machine guns around the camp and by saying publicly that any attempt to arrest the officer would be resisted with force. The extraordinary affair was not resolved until 20 July when the Supreme Court of Canada saved the federal government by finding in a 4-2 decision that the order-in-council was valid.[140]

The government had escaped from this challenge. But despite the Military Service Act, its exemptions and cancelled exemptions, the exhortations of politicians, clergy, and the press, it is inescapable that the war effort remained unsystematized, indeed disorganized. Newton Rowell said this bluntly in a letter he wrote to Borden, in which he called on Canada to increase its war effort:

To do so, however, we must have definite objectives, and plan, organize and increasingly work to secure these objectives, and to subordinate less important interests to this supreme task. . . . One of the first problems we must face is in what particular channels shall we direct the national effort, and what emphasis shall we place upon the various branches of the war activities.

Shall we take men from agriculture for the army, or is the food situation so urgent that we should call the remainder of the men from other occupations? . . .

Rowell's concerns were proper ones;[141] that he could raise them in June 1918 after four years of war is a measure of just how makeshift Canadian war organization had been.

There were signs by September 1918 that this situation was beginning to be remedied. General Mewburn was now able to provide fairly detailed estimates of his manpower requirements for the next year and to propose policy actions to meet those needs. Not that the policies were particularly palatable. According to the Minister of Militia, to meet his requirements for the year ending August 1919 he would need 120,000 reinforcements; he had only 45,000. In his view, he told Borden, 'The time has arrived when a proclamation calling out the remaining classes under the Military Service Act should issue.'[142] That the Union Government would have taken this step had the war continued seems certain; fortunately within a few weeks of Mewburn' s letter the imminent collapse of the German army seemed apparent and the necessity for calling out married men disappeared. The Military Service Act in effect became a dead letter with the armistice of 11 November.

What had the Military Service Act produced? The most complete, if still not entirely accurate and reliable, figures are contained in the official history of the Canadian Expeditionary Force:[143]

Status of Men	Dept. of Justice figures	Dept. of Militia & Defence figures
Class 1 Registration	401,882	
Granted Exemption	221,949	
Liable for Military Service	179,933	
Unapprehended Defaulters	24,139	
Available 11 Nov. 1918 but not called	26,225	
Reported for Military Service	129,569	
Permitted to enlist in U.K. Forces	8,445	
Taken on strength CEF	121,124	124,588
Performed no military service, struck off strength	16,108	16,300
Available for service with CEF	105,016	108,288
Discharged prior to 11 Nov. 1918 for misc. reasons	8,637	8,637

On Strength CEF 11 Nov. 1918 (includes 16,296 on unexpired harvest leave etc.)	96,379	99,651
Proceeded overseas		47,509
Taken on Strength CEF units in France		24,132

Another estimate, that of Charles Stacey, had 7,100 men on compassionate leave and 15,333 on agricultural leave at war's end.[144]

Additional detail in government reports fleshes out the picture. The cost of operating and enforcing the Military Service Act was $3,661,417.20, H. A. C. Machin, the Director of the Military Service Branch, indicated in his final report dated 1 March 1919. Much of the cost resulted from efforts to apprehend defaulters, not a few of whom had been created by the 20 April order-in-council. According to Machin, 65,610 men of the 20-22 age group had been called as a result of the order, of whom 11,961 had been found to be unfit, 12,000 had defaulted, 8,200 had been sent home, and still others were on temporary leave. The net increase in strength from the order was 25,449.

Machin also provided final data on exemptions. Of the 401,882 men who registered, 379,629 sought exemption. The Tribunals heard 395,162 cases and found 112,625 men unfit, granted exemptions to 222,364, ordered 59,991 to report for service, and had 3,182 cases yet to be determined at the end of the war. Appeal tribunals heard 120,448 cases, granted exemptions to 65,224 men, declared 8,443 men unfit, and ordered 36,781 men to report for service. By 11 November 1918, 9,990 cases remained unresolved. The Central Appeal Judge, Mr Justice Duff, heard 42,300 cases, found 369 unfit, declared 17,140 exempt, and ordered 20,240 to report for military service.

Of the men made available for military service by the Military Service Act, Quebec provided 55,814 and Ontario 55,145, with Saskatchewan producing the next largest total, 14,863. Quebec also had the largest number of defaulters, 18,827.[145] Later data demonstrated that 64,745 conscripts were English-speaking and Canadian-born, while only 27,557 were French Canadian.[146] Most conscripts were farmers, as a chart showing the occupations of conscripts and volunteers demonstrated:[147]

	Professional	Clerical	Manual	Farmers	Students
Conscripted	10,039	8,610	46,573	55,421	1,053
Volunteered	63,110	50,391	289,355	70,155	13,584
	73,149	59,001	335,928	125,576	15,087

Was conscription a military success? Borden had indicated in May 1917 that conscription was to produce 100,000 men. According to the military's figures, the Military Service Act had put 99,651 men on strength of the Canadian Expeditionary Force by 11 November 1918. In that single sense it had done the job, although at least 22,000 of those men were on leave, some for long periods. But only 24,132 conscripts got to France, a very small number indeed when we recollect that it had been 18 months from Borden's decision for conscription through to the armistice. Had the war continued into 1919, many thousands more would have reached the trenches, to be sure, but the war did not go on. On the basis of the results, on the basis of the reinforcements produced for the CEF, conscription at best can be considered only a partial military success. 'The results of this measure,' Canada's leading military historian wrote, 'fell somewhat short of the expectations.'[148]

And if, as was the case, conscription had been designed to compel the French Canadians to fight, this too was a failure. No more than 23 per cent of the conscripts were *Canadiens*, a number substantially below the French-speaking proportion of the population in 1917. Almost a quarter-century after 1917, Mr. Justice Lyman Duff recollected the results of the Military Service Act in a conversation with Grant Dexter, the *Winnipeg Free Press* journalist:

After the last war, he could not bear the thought of having the conscription records placed anywhere where the public could reach them. The papers of the local tribunals and appeal bodies in Quebec were full of hatred and bitterness and would have been a living menace to national unity. He had, therefore, . . . burned them and he was glad to say no real record of conscription existed. Nobody, he thought, except himself was aware of the fact that practically no French-Canadians were rounded up. The Quebec tribunals . . . gave exemptions automatically to French-Canadians and it was meaningless for the national appeal court to reverse their decisions. But they applied conscription against the English-speaking minority in Quebec with a rigor unparalleled.

It has been claimed that the war fostered a spirit of nationalism in the men who served in the Canadian Corps and for many, if not all, English Canadians. Perhaps. But for Quebec the Great War produced only bitterness and division. 'It is one of the great tragedies of Canadian history,' Professor Charles Stacey wrote in 1967, 'that this tremendous experience, the most powerful nation-building force ever brought to bear upon English-speaking Canada, was actually divisive in its effects upon the relations between English and French.'[150] A tragedy indeed, and a pointless one.

NOTES

1 Robert Rumilly, *Maurice Duplessis et son temps* (Montréal, 1973), I, 35.

2 Henri Bourassa, 'Conscription' (Montréal, 1917), p. 37.

3 David Lloyd George, *War Memoirs* (London, 1938), I, 1026.

4 Stephen Roskill, *Hankey Man of Secrets* (London, 1970), I, 368.

5 Public Archives of Canada [PAC], Sir Robert Borden Papers, Tel., 18 Jan. 1917, ff. 39123-4.

6 Public Record Office [PRO] (London), Cabinet Records, Cab 32/1, Min. 5 to Meeting 41, War Cabinet, 23 Jan. 1917.

7 Appendix 1 to *ibid.*

8 *Ibid.*, Cab 23/2, Min. 5 and 6 to Meeting 97, War Cabinet, 15 Mar. 1917.

9 *Ibid.*, Cab 23/43, Procès-verbale of 1st Meeting, Imperial War Cabinet, 20 Mar. 1917.

10 *Ibid.*, Cab 23/40, Imperial War Cabinet Minutes, No. 6, 30 Mar. 1917.

11 George Cook, 'Sir Robert Borden, Lloyd George and British Military Policy, 1917-1918', *Historical Journal*, XIV (1971), 374.

12 Borden to Bruchési, 31 May 1917, quoted in G.W.L. Nicholson, *Canadian Expeditionary Force 1914-1919* (Ottawa, 1962), pp. 342-3.

13 PRO, Colonial Office Records, CO 42/1000, Min. to Devonshire to Colonial Office, 15 June 1917. Cf. PAC, Devonshire Diary, 17 May 1917.

14 Borden Diary, 17 May 1917. Patenaude would resign because of conscription, effective 12 June 1917.

15 Quoted in Henry Borden, ed., *Robert Laird Borden His Memoirs* (Toronto, 1938), II, 698-9.

16 Quoted in PAC, Arthur Meighen Papers, 'Memorandum re Conscription', ff. 037320ff. and following; *Revised Statutes of Canada 1906*, c. 41; PAC, Loring Christie Papers, memo, ff. 1260ff.

17 Public Archives of Nova Scotia, E. N. Rhodes Papers, Rhodes to J. L. Ralston, 30 Oct. 1917.

18 Roger Graham, *Arthur Meighen* (Toronto, 1960), I, 121.

19 Queen's University, C. G. Power Papers, Bristol to Power, 17 Mar. 1967.

20 Queen's University, Grant Dexter Papers, Memorandum, 11 Dec. 1941.

21 Borden Diary, 24, 30 May 1917.

22 See C. P. Stacey, *Historical Documents of Canada*, Vol. V: *The Arts of War and Peace, 1914-1945* (Toronto, 1972), pp. 572ff.; Toronto *Globe*, 10 July 1917. American exemptions from conscription were substantially less liberal. See F. H. Epp, 'Canada and the American Draft-Dodger in World War I', a paper presented at Canadian Historical Association, 1972.

23 See in particular A. M. Willms, 'Conscription 1917: A Brief for the Defence', *Canadian Historical Review*, XXXVII (December, 1956), 343.

24 O. D. Skelton, 'Current Events', *Queen's Quarterly*, XXV (October, 1917), 225.

25 Borden Diary, 25 May 1917.

26 Dafoe to Laurier, 26 April 1917 in Willms, *op. cit.*, 340. Cf. Dafoe in *Manitoba Free Press*, 28 June 1917, quoted in Ramsay Cook, 'Dafoe, Laurier and the Formation of Union Government', *Canadian Historical Review*, XLII (Spring, 1961), 199.

27 Borden Diary, 24, 25, 29 May and 4, 6 June 1917; Henry Borden, *op. cit.*, II, 720 ff. Prof. John English in his 'Sir Robert Borden, the Conservative Party and Political Change, 1901-1920' (Ph.D. thesis, Harvard University, 1973), 251 suggests that 'Probably neither was serious in this political flirtation.'

28 On the coalition efforts, see English, *op. cit.*, chapters 7 and 8, and the most recent detailed account, Margaret Prang, *N.W. Rowell, Ontario Nationalist* (Toronto, 1975), chapter 12.

29 Quoted in 'Conscription and Coalition', *Round Table*, VII (September, 1917), 784.

30 House of Commons *Debates*, 24 July 1917, pp. 3723-7.

31 Robert Rumilly, *Histoire de la province de Québec* (Montréal, n.d.), XXII, 86.

32 Typed copy of article for New York *Outlook*, 25 July 1917, in PAC, Mackenzie King Papers, ff. C39236-8. For English-Canadian popular opinion on conscription, see J. Castell Hopkins, *The Canadian Annual Review 1917* (Toronto, 1918), pp. 339-40, 347.

33 *Ibid.*, pp. 566-7.

34 See W. R. Young, 'Conscription, Rural Depopulation and the Farmers of Ontario, 1917-19', *Canadian Historical Review*, LIII (September, 1972), 303-4.

35 *Canadian Annual Review 1917*, pp. 569ff.; Cook, *op. cit.*, 199ff.

36 PAC, A. K. Cameron Papers, Cameron to Laurier, 5 May 1917, indicates the anti-government tone. For a speech at the May conference by the Auxiliary Bishop of Montreal, Mgr Georges Gauthier, see *L'Action française*, I (octobre, 1917), 315ff.

37 Toronto *Globe*, 3 Aug. 1917; *Canadian Annual Review 1917*, pp. 567-9; Prang, *op. cit.*, pp. 201-2.

38 Borden Papers, Blount to Borden, 21 Aug. 1915, f. 31946.

39 Quoted in Graham, *op. cit.*, 165.

40 Borden Papers, J. G. Harvey to Borden, 5 June 1917, f. 123088.

41 F. H. Epp, *Mennonites in Canada, 1786-1920* (Toronto, 1974), pp. 372-3. For the travails of another group, see M. J. Penton, *Jehovah's Witnesses in Canada* (Toronto, 1976), chapter II.

42 W. R. Motherwell in Regina, 11 Dec. 1917, cited in J. C. Hopkins, *The Book of the Union Government* (Toronto, 1918), p. 63. Church groups, strongly for conscription, were troubled by the WTEA. See Patricia Oxley, 'Toronto Clergy, Conscription and Union Government', York University undergraduate paper, 1968, 28-9; J. M. Bliss, 'The Methodist Church and World War I', *Canadian Historical Review*, XLIX (September, 1968), 222 suggests that Methodists were less critical.

43 O. D. Skelton, *Life and Letters of Sir Wilfrid Laurier* (Toronto, 1921), II, 521.

44 *Queen's Quarterly*, XXV (October, 1917), 231. See also Mackenzie King's diary entry of a discussion with Robert Rogers about the WTEA. King Diary, 14 Feb. 1921. For an authoritative academic account see Norman Ward, *The Canadian House of Commons: Representation* (Toronto, 1963), p. 226.

45 For Rowell's account of his decision to enter the Cabinet, see PAC, Newton Rowell Papers, ff. 3353a ff.

46 Quoted in Arthur Ford, 'Some Notes on the Formation of Union Government in 1917', *Canadian Historical Review*, XIX (December, 1938), 359.

47 Toronto Public Library, Main Johnson Papers, Diary, Notes on General Election Campaign, 1-19 Nov. 1917.

48 Cited in a pamphlet in King Papers, f. C3622. A useful study of western agriculture in this period is John Thompson, ' "Permanently Wasteful but Immediately Profitable": Prairie Agriculture and the Great War', a paper presented to the Canadian Historical Association, 1976. See also F. J. K. Griezic, 'The Hon. Thomas Alexander Crerar, Marquette Riding and the Union Government Election of 1917', *Transactions of the Historical and Scientific Society of Manitoba*, Ser. III, no. 28 (1972), 108-9; Young, *op. cit.*, 306-7.

49 John Witham, 'Opposition to Conscription in Ontario', M.A. thesis, University of Ottawa, 1970, 119.

50 Borden Papers, M. Simonski to Borden, 24 Mar. 1917, f. 35092. Cf. F. M. Beynon, 'Conscription', in Ramsay Cook and Wendy Mitchinson, eds., *The Proper Sphere* (Toronto, 1976), pp. 252 ff.

51 *Canadian Annual Review 1917*, pp. 630-1. See also Catherine Cleverden, *The Woman Suffrage Movement in Canada 1900-20* (Toronto, 1974), pp. 124ff.

52 *Round Table*, VIII (March, 1918), 359-60.

53 Martin Robin, 'Registration, Conscription and Independent Labour Politics 1916-17', *Canadian Historical Review*, XLVII (June, 1966), 109; Toronto *Telegram*, 15 June 1917.

54 Toronto *Globe*, 7 Dec. 1917.

55 Borden Diary, 25, 26, 29 Nov. 1917.

56 Cited in Hopkins, *Union Government*, p. 74.

57 Pamphlets in Pamphlet Collection, PAC, and in Rhodes Papers.

58 Hopkins, *Union Government*, pp. 67, 74.

59 Toronto *Globe*, 8 Dec. 1917.

60 Public Archives of Ontario, H. J. Cody Papers, Sermon File. Reported in Toronto *Globe*, 27 Nov. 1917.

61 Johnson Diary, 17 Dec. 1917.

62 Graham, *op. cit.*, 194-5.

63 PAC, Sir Wilfrid Laurier Papers, Laurier to W. Charlton, 29 Oct. 1917, f. 197743. For a mythic U.K. view of Liberal finances, see Roskill, *Hankey*, I, 464.

64 Laurier Papers, Laurier to W. German, 1 Nov. 1917, f. 197623.

65 PAC, G. S. Gibbons Papers, Vol. 1, Gibbons to Goddard, 8 Nov. 1917.

66 Hopkins, *Union Government*, pp. 61, 88, 89.

67 Toronto *Globe*, 1 Dec. 1917.

68 Robert Blake, *The Private Papers of Douglas Haig 1914-19* (London, 1955), p. 266.

69 PAC, Sir Arthur Currie Papers, Vol. 2, Tel., 3 Dec. 1917.

70. A. M. J. Hyatt, 'The Military Career of Sir Arthur Currie', Ph.D. thesis, Duke University, 1965, 170; A. M. J. Hyatt, 'Sir Arthur Currie and Conscription', *Canadian Historical Review*, L (September, 1969), 292-3. For detail on the 5th Division, see Nichol-

son, *op. cit.*, pp. 218, 231. The Division was not broken up for reinforcements until February 1918.

71 Hyatt, 'Military Career', 167.

72 Andrew Macphail, 'In This Our Necessity', *University Magazine*, XVI (December, 1917), 476.

73 K. Weatherbe, *From the Rideau to the Rhine and Back* (Toronto, 1928), p. 292; Kim Beattie, *The 48th Highlanders of Canada 1891-1928* (Toronto, 1932), p. 282; G. R. Stevens, *A City Goes to War* (Brampton, 1964), p. 108.

74 PAC, General David Watson Diary, 17 Dec. 1917.

75 The best account, and one minimizing the fraud, is D. P. Morton, 'Polling The Soldier Vote', *Journal of Canadian Studies*, X (November, 1975), 39ff. Cf. W. T. R. Preston, *My Generation of Politics and Politicians* (Toronto, 1927), chapter 46. The total military vote cast and counted was 234,371, of which Unionists got 215,849.

76 PAC, Sir Clifford Sifton Papers, Vol. 206, Willison to Sifton, 29 Oct. 1917.

77 Johnson Diary, Notes. On Unionist organizational chaos, see English, *op. cit.*, 331ff.

78 Meighen Papers, W. M. Dickson to Meighen, 3 Dec. 1917, ff. 718-20.

79 Borden Papers, Vol. 417, Reid to Borden, 13 Dec. 1917.

80 English, *op. cit.*, 384-5. Cf. J. A. Boudreau, 'The Enemy Alien Problem in Canada, 1914-24', Ph.D. thesis, UCLA, 1965, 150ff.

81 Hopkins, *Union Government*, p. 115.

82 Meighen Papers, Meighen to W. R. Givens, 9 Jan. 1918.

83 PAC, J. W. Dafoe Papers, Dafoe to T. Côté, 1 Jan. 1918. For an attempt by Rowell and J. S. Atkinson of the Toronto *Star* to undo the harm they and others had done in the campaign, see Johnson Diary, 18 Dec. 1917.

84 Mason Wade, *The French Canadians* (Toronto, 1956), pp. 754ff.

85 PAC, Militia and Defence Records, file HQ 1064-30-6, Memo, 'Military Service Council and Sub-Committee', n.d.

86 Borden Papers, Borden to S. N. Parent, 10 Sept. 1917, f. 4015; Hazen to Borden, 31 Aug. 1917, f. 4007; *Canadian Annual Review 1917*, p. 347.

87 Rhodes Papers, F. McCurdy to Rhodes, 29 Aug. 1917.

88 University of New Brunswick, J. D. Hazen Papers, Hazen to M. G. Teed, 11 Sept. 1917.

89 Militia and Defence Records, file HQ 1064-30-2, Secretary, Militia Council to Principal Black, 26 Sept. 1917; Memo on Directorate of History, Department of National Defence, file 949.033 (D1).

90 Raymond Ranger, *Report on the Operations of National Registration and Military Mobilization in Canada During World War II* (Ottawa, 1949, mimeo), pp. 76-7. (Copy in Directorate of History, Department of National Defence.)

91 Militia and Defence Records, file HQ 1064-30-2, Adj.-Gen. to Officers Commanding Military Districts, 9 Aug. 1917.

92 *Ibid.*, file MD 7-45-4-1, Memo, 'Organization and Administration under the Military Service Act', n.d.

93 *Ibid.*, file HQ 1064-30-6, Adj.-Gen. to General Officers Commanding, 24 Sept. 1917.

94 Montreal *La Presse*, 20 octobre 1917; *Le Devoir*, 23 octobre 1917.

95 Militia and Defence Records, file HQ 1064-30-6, Adj. -Gen. to GOC MD No. 4, 12 Nov. 1917 and docs on file.

96 *Report of the Director of the Military Service Branch to the Minister of Justice, March 1, 1919*, (Sessional Paper 246, tabled in the House of Commons, 6 May 1919), pp. 94, 96; *Canadian Annual Review 1917*, p. 351.

97 Montreal *Star*, 15 Nov. 1917.

98 Queen's University, T. A. Crerar Papers, Reynolds to Crerar, 21 Nov. 1917; *La Presse*, 14 novembre 1917.

99 Militia and Defence Records, file MD 2-34-3-105, Vol. 2, Capt. Gibson to Capt. Van Norman, n.d.

100 Crerar Papers, Reynolds to Crerar, 21 Nov. 1917, and atts; reply, 26 Nov. 1917.

101 Rowell Papers, Rowell to Borden, 14 Nov. 1917.

102 *Canadian Annual Review 1917*, p. 351.

103 Borden Papers, Newcombe to Borden, 19 Dec. 1917, f. 53483.

104 Militia and Defence Records, file MD 5-M-123-4, GOC MD No. 5 to Secretary, Militia Council, 21 Dec. 1917.

105 Montreal *Star*, 4 Jan. 1918.

106 PAC, Sir George Foster Papers, Vol. 43, 'Memo Prepared for War Committee. . .'.

107 *Ibid.*, Diary.

108 Borden Papers, 'For the Press', ff. 5350ff.

109 *La Presse*, 14 février 1918.

110 Borden Papers, f. 53556.

111 *Ibid.*, Statement by Provinces, f. 53561.

112 *Ibid.*, Tel., 26 Mar. 1918, f.53539.

113 Christie Papers, Tel., Long to Governor General, 30 Mar. 1918 and reply 2 Apr. 1918, ff. 23214ff. But cf. Cabinet Records, Cab 23/5, Minute 5 to Meeting 378 of War Cabinet, 30 Mar. 1918.

114 Borden Papers, Borden to Kemp, 14 Mar. 1918, ff. 51163-4.

115 Henry Borden, *Borden Memoirs*, II, 787ff.; Jean Provencher, *Québec sous la loi des mesures de guerre* (Trois Rivières, 1971), *passim*; N. Ward, *A Party Politician: The Memoirs of Chubby Power* (Toronto, 1966), pp. 83 ff.; Elizabeth Armstrong, *The Crisis of Quebec* (New York, 1937) chapter IX.

116 Johnson Diary, 7 Apr. 1918.

117 Sir Charles Lucas, *The Empire at War* (London, 1923), II, 57.

118 Borden Diary, 12 Apr. 1918; draft order in Borden Papers, ff. 53570-2.

119 Borden Diary, 14 Apr. 1918.

120 Johnson Diary, 14 Apr. 1918.

121 The order is printed in Stacey, *Historical Documents*, V, 581-3. Exemption for those with relatives at the front had been urged by soldiers. Borden Papers, ff. 126769ff.

122 Borden Diary, 19 Apr. 1918; Foster Diary, 19 Apr. 1918; Johnson Diary, 14 Apr. 1918; Prang, *op. cit.*, pp. 244-6; Lucas, *op. cit.*, 58.

123 House of Commons *Debates*, 19 April 1918, p. 933.

124 Henry Borden, *Borden Memoirs*, II, 801. For an indication of the extent of rural resentment see Crerar Papers, war files.

125 L. A. Wood, *History of Farmers' Movements in Canada* (Toronto, 1975), pp. 279-81.

126 Crerar Papers, Tel., Wood to Crerar, 21 May 1918.

127 *Round Table*, VIII (September, 1918), 839ff.; 'The Sons of the Soil', *Saturday Night* (1 June 1918), 4.

128 Borden Papers, ff. 53524ff.

129 *Ibid.*, Doherty to Borden, 8 May 1918, ff. 44336ff.

130 *Canadian Annual Review 1918*, p. 462; Borden Diary, 19 May 1918; Borden Papers, Crerar to Borden, 18 May 1918, ff. 53600ff.

131 House of Commons *Debates*, 2 May 1918, p. 1366; Crerar Papers, Deputy Minister of Agriculture to Crerar, 3 May 1918. For earlier agricultural leave policy, see Militia and Defence Records, file MD2-34-3-105-20, Asst Adj.-Gen. to OC Toronto Artillery Brigade, 26 Feb. 1918; for detail on the impact of the 20 Apr. order on this, see *ibid.*, Asst Adj. -Gen. to J. Fraser, n.d.

132 Crerar Papers, Crerar to H. B. Cowan, 29 May 1918 and Crerar to J. Kennedy, 30 May 1918.

133 *Ibid.*, Crerar to Cowan, 29 May 1918.

134 Foster Diary, 17 May 1918.

135 Militia and Defence Records, file MD 4-60-1-29, Duchastel to District Intelligence Officer, 15 July 1918.

136 PAC, Sir Charles Fitzpatrick Papers, Vol. 17, Doherty to Fitzpatrick, 2 Aug. 1918; *La Presse*, 9 aôut 1918. 5,477 defaulters took advantage of the amnesty.

137 PAC, Gen. R. E. W. Turner Papers, Currie to Turner, 14 Mar. 1918, f. 5756.

138 *Ibid.*, Kemp to Turner, 17 June 1918, f. 7051. Cf. Militia and Defence Records, file OSM-10-8-33, Adj.-Gen. Canadians to Deputy Minister OMFC, 22 Jan. 1918.

139 Foster Diary, 9 July 1918.

140 *Canadian Annual Review 1918*, pp. 468ff. Cf. R. B. Bennett's extraordinary correspondence with Borden on this subject. Borden Papers, ff. 53611ff.

141 *Ibid.*, Rowell to Borden, 8 June 1918, ff. 53626ff.

142 *Ibid.*, Mewburn to Borden, 19 Sept. 1918, ff. 53534ff.

143 Nicholson, *op. cit.*, pp. 551-3.

144 C. P. Stacey, *The Military Problems of Canada* (Toronto, 1940), pp. 79-80.

145 *Report of Director of Military Service Branch, passim.*

146 Militia and Defence Records, file GAQ 10-473, Asst Director Records to DOC, MD 12, 9 Mar. 1928.

147 *Ibid.*, file HQ 54-21-12-26, Col. Armstrong to DAG Organization, 14 Jan. 1919, and atts.

148 Stacey, *Military Problems*, pp. 79-80.

149 Dexter Papers, Memo, 22 Dec. 1941.

150 C. P. Stacey, 'Nationality: The Experience of Canada', *Canadian Historical Association Report 1967*, 12.

Four

CONSCRIPTION AND POLITICS
1919-1939

'It is not the Canada I expected it to be,' General Sir Arthur Currie wrote on his return to Canada in 1919. 'I came back from the war feeling that all the suffering and sacrifice must have meant something. But I found, as others have done, that there was little change.... Men were fighting for the dollar in the same persistent way. There seemed to be little difference in the viewpoint towards life, little indication of any growth in national spirit and very little appreciation of the world situation and its attendant problems....'[1] The General Officer Commanding the Canadian Corps was undoubtedly correct. There was no change in the basic attitudes of businessmen, politicians, or the public at large. Only the troopers who had returned from France and Flanders were different. With many this change was readily apparent in missing limbs, blinded eyes, or seared lungs. With others it was less noticeable until the returned men began to talk. The bitterness was deep and genuine, a detestation of all politicians, a passionate loathing for all who had not shared the hell at the front, a hatred of all things military. As late as 1935 one returned man wrote: 'The majority of those of us who fought—a not inconsiderable body—sum up their experiences in two words, "Never again".'[2]

Such attitudes were important and long-lived, and they played a crucial part in shaping the course of the simmering controversy over conscription between the two wars. This is not to suggest that conscription was a vital issue from 1919 to 1939. It had its proponents among the officers of the tiny Permanent Force, in the militia, and in Parliament, but conscription was not a key issue, except for its use as a propaganda device in some general elections in Quebec and for the way it helped to blight the career of Arthur Meighen. What is interesting, however, is the way the conscription question lingered on, the way its proponents felt compelled to justify and explain their roles, and the way both of the major parties used the remembrance of things past for their partisan ends. Equally significant, by the time of the Second World War both Liberal and Conservative Parties had rejected compulsory service as an acceptable means of raising men. After the experience of 1917, conscription had become a curse word.

I

The idea of peacetime universal military training was raised even before the Great War had ended. To many in Canada the lesson of 1914 seemed clear: Canada had been unprepared then and could not afford to be so again. How best be prepared, then? The answer—train every fit man in peacetime so that he will be ready when war comes again. The most serious proponent of this scheme was Colonel William Hamilton Merritt, the president of the virtually defunct Canadian Defence League. In his book *Canada and National Service*, published in the summer of 1917, Merritt discoursed on the national spirit, on various military systems, especially that of the Swiss, and on the estimated costs to Canada of universal military training. Nothing, the Colonel claimed, 'but a changed Militia Law—back somewhere to what it was a hundred years ago—will give us the stability of purpose, upbuilding of character and physique, and safety to Dominion and Empire which comes from a virile system of national organization, based on *Universal Military Training and Service*.'[3] Stability of purpose, mental and physical character, safety of the realm—in sum these were what all proponents of peacetime military service trumpeted as the benefits of their scheme.

Certainly this was the message of H. M. Mowat, the Liberal Unionist Member of Parliament for Toronto-Parkdale and a brigade major at Camp Borden for part of the war. Major Mowat spoke learnedly in an October 1918 article about the demands that modern war posed for nations. 'It would be inhuman to send insufficiently trained men to the front line with war conducted as scientifically as in 1917-18,' he wrote, apparently unconcerned with the inhumanity of scientific war itself. 'No country could get a numerous force under the voluntary system, and such countries will, in the future, be at a great disadvantage. The volunteer system is obsolete.' According to Mowat, the war had demonstrated this to be a truism. Canadians had enjoyed the 'swagger' of the peacetime militia in the past, but 'when after the war [had started], and peril was imminent, we were let in for the odious task of cajoling or threatening men into joining the overseas forces, when we attempted to pose as persons of superior loyalty and patriotism . . . it was then that many military officers concluded once and for all that the voluntary system was a mistake. . . . ' Another concern for the Parkdale M.P. was the physical condition of Canada's young manhood. 'It appears that the young men of the First Class, recently called [under the Military Service Act], were deficient to the extent of 65%—that is to say, more than one half were unfit for the rigors of modern service. Conditions in factories, child labour, watching games from bleachers instead of playing, frequenting pool rooms and moving picture shows, may account for this loss of manhood. . . . ' The solution, Mowat maintained, was for all men to be trained for six weeks a year until they reached the age of 25. Then they would go into the reserve list. 'Let people look upon defence as an essential part of their life duty,' the Major maintained, 'as great as paying their taxes, extinguishing fires, and obeying their laws.'[4]

Such arguments were accepted as revealed truth by some officers of the General Staff at militia headquarters in Ottawa. To them the war had demonstrated clearly that Canada needed universal military training, and no sooner had the war ended than the planners, apparently blind to the political realities, were preparing their proposals. On 20 November 1918 the Chief of the General Staff, General Sir W. G. Gwatkin, advised the Deputy Minister of Militia 'that a scheme for universal training should be submitted to Parliament at the approaching Session.' A committee preparing the reorganization of the militia and chaired by General Sir William Otter was also conscriptionist to a man, and the Minister of Militia, General Mewburn, was said to agree. But General Otter was more of a realist, and when he was pressed by some eager Hamilton militia officers on conscription, he warned them that 'There is throughout Canada a feeling that there shouldn't be any militia at all.'[5] Some of the same thoughts must have been going through General Currie's mind. When he heard that militia headquarters were pressing universal military training, he was shrewd enough to suggest that the matter should first be raised from within some such body as the Great War Veterans Association, one of the predecessors of the Canadian Legion. 'They ought to realize,' Currie said, 'that much of the dissatisfaction amongst the returned soldiers is primarily due to the unsatisfactory way in which the manhood of our country served during the war. . . . '[6]

The organized veterans were concerned with conditions of service, but not quite in the way their former commander had foreseen. Returned soldiers bitterly resented the privileges that staff officers had received during the war:

> Oh, the generals have a bloody good time
> Fifty miles behind the line.
> Hincky, dincky, parley voo.

'We have learned who our enemies are,' one soldier wrote in *Generals Die in Bed*, probably the best Canadian novel about the war, 'the lice, some of our officers, and Death.' And with the peace the officers seemed to get the good jobs and the best deal from the government. No wonder then that the returned men sought service gratuities for themselves now that peace had returned. Conscription scarcely interested them. Occasionally, as at the British Columbia Great War Veterans' Association convention in 1921, some zealot would introduce a motion calling vaguely for peacetime compulsory service; on occasion the motion would carry.[7] Others would demand resolutions calling for the conscription of wealth as well as manpower in the event of war.[8] But the predominant talk was of pensions, pensions, pensions, and the organized veterans soon became a pressure group like the others, fruitlessly demanding their due. Certainly they were not a great machine pressing for conscription.

As a result, universal military training along the lines suggested by Colonel Merritt, Major Mowat, and General Gwatkin was quickly seen to be an impossibility. But perhaps a modified scheme, calling for one or two days' service each month and a full month's training in each of four years, might be possible. This at any rate was the proposal of Brigadier A. G. L. McNaughton in a memorandum he prepared for the Otter committee in 1919.[9] This idea, like the others, proved simply unacceptable in the light of public opinion. Sentiment, Currie was reluctantly forced to concede, was 'overwhelmingly against any form of universal training', and the best plan was 'not to attempt to force the issue and proceed meanwhile with other things.'[10]

Anti-military feeling in general, and not just that against univeral military training, was also growing. The Minister of Militia introduced a bill on 24 June 1919 to amend the Militia Act by increasing the establishment of the permanent force from 5,000 to 10,000 men. His reasoning was simple: 'I do not feel pessimistic about the future but I think that without any doubt I would be negligent in my duty ... if I did not propose that we should have some force that would be available for the preservation of law and order in the country.'[11] His reference was clearly to the great general strike in Winnipeg, and the Minister referred at one point to a letter he had received from that city 'urging that the Government should have a permanent force that can deal with the situation there.'

The Opposition response was not enthusiastic. Pius Michaud, a Liberal from New Brunswick, said simply that 'I do not see that the country should be asked to pay for a larger force than that which we had before the war.'[12] Andrew McMaster, another Liberal from Brome, Quebec, was more explicit and more eloquent. The requested increase, he said, 'is due not to apprehension of outside danger but to the fear of domestic trouble. . . . I say to this House that force is no remedy; that it is not necessary that the Canadian people should be overawed by an increase of 100 per cent in our military establishment.' Surely the government could trust the people of Canada? 'Trust the people; the heart of the Canadian people is as sound as our No. 1 Hard Manitoba wheat.'[13] To the Minister's defence—in a manner of speaking—came the Radical M.P. for Springfield, Manitoba, R. L. Richardson. Richardson had talked with senior officers in Winnipeg during the late disturbances, he said, and he had been informed that demobilized men did not want to join the militia to keep order. The returned men 'did not manifest any willingness to organize again,—they had been demobilized, were sick of the job, and did not wish to participate in military service again immediately.' The only source of recruits had been businessmen, Richardson said. The defence of their businesses had produced a patriotic fervour that apparently the war had not, although Richardson did not draw that conclusion. The M.P. did note, however, that there were dangers loose in Canada:

Hon. Members should bear in mind the heterogeneous nature of the population in this far western country. . . . Hundreds of thousands of these people do not understand our constitution, many thousands of them are not even familiar with our language; and until they are assimilated with our own people it would be wise to have a very considerable permanent force.[14]

W. F. Cockshutt, the wealthy plow manufacturer who represented the Unionist interest in Brantford, Ontario, gave the hard-pressed General Mewburn still more assistance of a kind when he said that a force of 25,000 would not have been too much. 'Ten thousand men is the very minimum for a permanent force in this country.' Causes of unrest in Canada would not be increased 'by having a kind of respectable police force. Even Toronto "the good" has never been able to abolish its police force, and I do not believe it will in our time.'[15] Despite the assistance of its supporters, the bill passed the House of Commons. The Opposition criticisms might have had an impact, however, for although the permanent force establishment was fixed at 10,000, the government forbade the enlistment of more than 5,000 men. And because proper accommodations were never provided, the force was kept below even that number.[16]

Many of the same participants were involved in another debate some nine months later. The subject was a motion by Parkdale's Mowat calling for universal military training for men between the ages of 18 and 25. Mowat raised many of the arguments he had used in 1918. The most contentious new part of his long speech was perhaps his disquisition on the militia. 'We all know that the militia until now has been looked upon by large portions of the community as a class or caste,' he claimed with some truth, 'and the militia themselves get to feel that they are such. . . . If we could have a force which would get the rich man's son and the poor man's son living together for some weeks, we would produce a good feeling between the classes. . . . ' To finance his scheme, which would see a man do four weeks' training each summer for seven years, would be simple, Mowat maintained. The permanent force of 3,700 was maintained for $1,300 each a year. 'For that amount we could train thirteen citizen soldiers; for I think $100 a year would cover the cost of maintaining a man in camp or barracks for one month each year.' Who would train the conscripts was never mentioned, for Mowat did not seem to realize that regulars would have to be maintained on strength—and certainly in larger numbers than 3,700—to train the men.[17] None of Mowat's critics realized the flaw in the argument, although many spoke with eloquence and passion. J. A. Maharg, an Independent from Saskatchewan, said that Canadians 'have had sufficient fighting and military display, at least for a time. We are a war-weary people; we are heartily sick and tired of strife; and almost on the heels of peace . . . we are now talking of taking up the matter of compulsory training.'[18] Dr. Henri Béland, the Liberal M.P. who had been a prisoner of war, was equally critical, tearing apart Mowat's fiscal arguments and noting that 'throughout the length and breadth of Canada the rural constituents are to a man opposed to this proposal of universal military training.'[19] The debate was adjourned without a vote, and the subject was not raised again.

Defence matters came before the House one more time in 1920 when the Militia Department estimates were discussed in Parliament. Mackenzie King, the Liberal leader, took after the new minister, Hugh Guthrie, with a will and in a fashion that was uncommonly direct for that cautious gentleman:

> Before the war . . . it was certainly said in official quarters that a menace was threatening the world, and that it was necessary to meet that menace by increasing our military expenditures, and it was largely in anticipation of a great international disturbance that this country voted for military and naval purposes the sums of money which were appropriated at that time. But conditions are wholly different today. There is no world menace. Where does the minister expect invasion to come from? The minister says that this expenditure is needed for the defence of Canada—defence against whom? There is no answer; there is no answer to be made.[20]

There was no answer. Moreover, there were very few men willing to join the militia. The Militia Department's *Report* for 1919-20 said that 'The recruiting of the rank and file has . . . been slow, as the majority of men with overseas service are not prepared at once to assume further obligations and make the necessary sacrifice of time for training, while men who have not served in the war are at present slow in coming forward.'[21] The military simply was not popular, and Mackenzie King could get good mileage during the election of 1921 by claiming that the government was wasting large sums for ammunition.[22]

King should not then have been surprised when members of his own party, led by Chubby Power, the wartime major who had won Quebec South for the party in 1917 and 1921, began to press for reductions in the defence budget almost from the beginning days of the first postwar Liberal administration. 'Not only Quebec but all Canada was war weary,' Power recalled. 'The ex-soldiers themselves were violently anti-brass-hat . . . [and] many thousands of voters regarded the Liberals as an anti-militaristic party. I felt that to continue to support defence expenditure on the same level . . . and for such outmoded and futile purposes as the thoroughly discredited militia training camps, which had largely been a pretext for an orgy of petty graft and alcoholic festivity, was not keeping faith with Liberal thinking. . . .'[23] A blunt-speaking, forthright, and able man, Power and his fellow Quebec M.P.s won their point and the defence appropriations were reduced by $700,000. It would be a long time before expenditures rose much, and until 1935 Canada existed for all practical purposes with only the barest rudiments of a military force.*[24] That, after all, was more than enough.

*Small as it was, the army was still an English-Canadian preserve, almost as much as it had been before 1914. French was used only in King's Regulations, pay and dress regulations,

II

Mackenzie King was too shrewd a politician, even in his first years as party leader and before he became Prime Minister in late 1921, to get out of step with the rank and file. If he attacked military expenditures in peacetime Canada it was because his instincts advised him that this fitted the popular mood. Only rarely would King fly in the face of prevailing winds, and when he did it invariably redounded to his advantage. Conscription, for example, had required some courage to oppose in 1917, yet oppose it King did. He had toyed with the idea of supporting the Union Government and he had tried to persuade Laurier to accept conscription, but in the end he had stuck with his chief; two years later he was party leader, helped into power by the votes of the Quebec delegates. Certainly King himself believed 'that it was my stand in the Federal elections of 1917 which won me the leadership.'[25] To a lady friend he added that the convention victory became possible 'when I went to certain defeat at the time my mother was dying, and left her side to fight for the principles which I felt were just as sacred in the preservation of liberty as any the men were fighting for at the front.'[26] His own view of the principles that had shaped his decisions did not blind him to the possibility that others might have seen things differently. 'I am, of course, in entire accord with you as to the attitude that should be taken by all Liberals toward those of the Party who gave

---

and Cadet regulations. Orders, decorations, and regimental names were not ordinarily translated. The militia in Quebec had only 14 French-language units in 1930 with a strength of 2,292 officers and men out of a total militia of some 30,000 officers and men. In the permanent force, the breakdown of officers by rank and language was as follows:

	1930		1935	
	Fr.	Eng.	Fr.	Eng.
Maj.-Gen.	—	3	—	7
Col	5	36	2	19
Lt Col	8	55	7	53
Maj.	7	82	9	84
Capt.	13	71	7	69
Lt	7	45	15	129
2Lt	—	—	5	14
	40	292	45	375

(Royal Commission on Bilingualism and Biculturalism, 'Armed Forces Historical Study' (n.d., mimeo), part II, pp. 35, 41, 63.)

their support to the Union Government at the last election,' he wrote to Professor George Wrong of the University of Toronto. 'I have on two or three occasions publicly expressed my own belief that only the most patriotic and honourable of motives actuated practically all of those who . . . found it necessary to break with old associations and friends during that trying period.'[27] On the other hand, King did not want to take any action that might weaken Liberalism's hold on a solid Quebec, and this moderated attempts to welcome back too overtly the fallen men of 1917.

King's opponents were not always charitable in their criticism of King's own part in the war, and the new leader felt justified in taking the extraordinary step of making a very personal speech in Parliament in April 1920 explaining his wartime actions. His work for the Rockefeller interests in Colorado, he maintained, was a service to the war effort for it had ensured harmony between labour and management. And as for his failure to serve at the front, the explanation was simple enough. He was 40 when the war broke out, unfitted by his training for rough work and saddled with onerous family obligations.[28] One who commented on King's defence was J. M. Macdonnell, an officer of the National Trust Company, a wartime artilleryman, and a Conservative. 'I am slow to criticize a man for not having been in France,' Macdonnell wrote, 'and your answer on that score seemed to be perfectly adequate.' What dissatisfied Macdonnell, however, was that in his speech King had not explained his support for Laurier and his rejection of conscription in the 1917 election. King's reply rehearsed his position on conscription in detail, stressing the disunity in the country and the mess that had been made of voluntary enlistment procedures. He concluded with his by now slightly pious appeal for broadmindedness: 'It is . . . I believe, due to those who were prepared publicly to advocate their views, to recognize that all alike were equally sincere in the opinions held.' The Toronto Conservative was still not satisfied, claiming that there were 'insuperable' objections to King's record, but he added, 'you are not called upon to worry unduly about what I think.'[29] King knew what Tories thought of him, but he could be assured that there were more voters than Conservatives in Canada.

This simple arithmetical fact was worrying the Conservatives. The Union Government was desperately weak by 1920, and some would say it had always been so. No government can be effective in Canada without support from both English Canadians and French Canadians, and the Unionists had no strength whatsoever in Quebec. Prime Minister Borden tried to remedy this, talking to notables in the province about his and their shared concerns for the tariff during a highly political boat trip down the St Lawrence in the summer of 1919. The politicians were friendly, but if Borden underestimated the political complications that conscription had created in 1917-18 they could not.[30] Borden got nowhere in trying to strike a *rapprochement*, and within a few months he was tired and worn out, made old by the strain of the war years. The uneasy Union coalition continued to exist in an organizational limbo, uncertain of leadership, unsure of its future policies, and gradually many of the Liberal Unionists returned to the party of Laurier. The lack of direction was partially corrected when Borden chose Arthur Meighen as his successor in July 1920. The Governor General, the Duke of Devonshire, wrote of the new Prime Minister that he is 'distinctly clever, keen, and a good parliamentarian and has, moreover, the advantage of being young and active.' All this was true, but so was Henri Bourassa's description of Meighen as a 'révolutionnaire à froid'. Devonshire was not the shrewdest of observers, but he was certainly correct when he noted that Meighen's 'great difficulty will be in the Province of Quebec.'[31]

Arthur Meighen's trials with French Canada have been illuminated by Professor Roger Graham and there is little point in attempting to duplicate his efforts. All that needs to be said is that Meighen was unable to attract French Canadians of genuine stature to his side (his three French-Canadian ministers in 1921—Normand, Monty, and Belley —were certainly not strong men), and lacking an effective lieutenant he was never able to overcome the bad press he had received in Quebec during the Great War. To be sure, the Liberals did their best to ensure that Meighen's 'bloody hands' were not forgotten, but much of the resentment would have existed in any case. Meighen himself spoke openly about the issue. 'I never try to ride two horses,' he said in Quebec. 'I favoured conscription. I introduced the Military Service Act. I spoke for it time and time again in the House of Commons, and in every province in the Dominion. I did because I thought it was right.'[32] This was magnificent, but it was not Canadian politics, and as one French-Canadian nationalist writer noted, Meighen 'reste attaché aux principales erreurs qui ont causé sa perte.'[33]

Nor was the new Prime Minister helped much by his English-Canadian supporters. The Toronto *Telegram* was still fighting the war each day, and one Conservative was moved to write that the *Telegram* thinks 'that it is helping to weaken the Liberal Party by picturing it as one which is dominated by French Canadian slackers . . . '; the editors seem to 'overlook the fact that anything it may gain in that direction is only going to make more difficult the swinging of the French Canadian block into line on the [tariff] issue.'[34] Nothing, however, could keep the Orange fire out of Black Jack Robinson's newspaper.[35] Nor, it seemed, could anything weaken the distrust that many Ontario Conservatives had for the Liberals who had joined them in 1917 and who remained with them still.[36]

More to the point were the defections from the Unionist Government and the Liberal Party, particularly among farmers. From Ontario to the West, farmers were turning their backs on the two old parties, and one of the major causes of the desertions was reaction to the Military Service Act. Indeed even before the war was over the backlash had begun. The United Farmers of Ontario captured their first seat in a provincial by-election in Manitoulin in October 1918 despite the efforts of the Premier, Sir William Hearst, to pin the blame for conscription on Ottawa alone. Everything 'pertaining to Military Affairs belongs to the Federal Government,' Hearst argued futilely, 'and the Ontario government has nothing to do with it.' That was correct, but the farmers could not forget that Hearst had been a tireless campaigner for Union Government and for conscription. The next year the UFO captured the government, the first victory won by the resurgent farmers. In the West, the situation was even more bleak for the old parties. The party machines had been weakened first by the reciprocity election of 1911 that had undercut the Tories and then by 1917 when the Liberal provincial organizations had essentially changed allegiances. There was continued resentment about the broken promises over conscription exemptions. Other farm voters remained furious about the gerrymandering of the vote in the 1917 election, while still others claimed that aliens were the only Canadians who had prospered during the war, thanks to their having escaped conscription. Contradictory as these complaints were, they all supplemented the historic farmers' grievances over the tariff and together they provided enough motive force to create, with almost bewildering speed, a new and powerful political organization.[37] The Progressive Party was a reality and all Ontario and the Prairies could fall to it.

For the leaders of the old parties, the losses and potential losses to Progressivism were explained most easily by referring to conscription, and both did so. King was the readiest to place blame there. 'The Farmer movement,' he wrote in late September 1921, 'as the present [election] campaign is clearly indicating, is mainly the result of Unionist Government and conscription . . . the people of Canada were really against conscription, and . . . it would never have carried but for the change of the Franchise Act and the unholy alliance between some of the leading Liberals and some of the leading Conservatives for the sake of power rather than for the sake of principle.' The truth of the matter, King maintained, was that 'the whole Unionist Government is thoroughly discredited.'[38] But to many farmers the Liberals were equally tarnished. Jimmy Gardiner, the Saskatchewan Liberal, told an interviewer in 1931 of the difficulties he had faced in campaigning for King in 1921. One old German farmer said, 'I voted Liberal in 1911 and the Liberal M.P. changed to Union Government in 1917. How do I know that if I vote Liberal this time the M.P. will stay Liberal?' The farmer couldn't know, and he voted Progressive.[39] Only in Quebec were the Liberals truly safe from the contagion of Progressive ideas because, as Progressive leader T. A. Crerar said, there was no use in his going to that province. He, too, was thoroughly tarred with the Unionist brush, and he simply did not believe that a radical farm party could operate effectively in what he saw as a clerically dominated province,[40] particularly one that seemed unwilling to forgive and forget the war.

Still, the extent to which memories of conscription affected the election results in 1921, an election in which most discussion concerned the tariff, is almost impossible to determine, even in Quebec. Who can know why people vote?* Who can know the factors that determine where the 'x' on the ballot is placed? But many Quebeckers and many politicians blamed the Conservative *débâcle* in Quebec on conscription. One resident of Quebec City, for example, wrote to Meighen that 'The conscription bogy [sic] again did service. The election was principally run on LAURIER'S grave: and induced fear in an immaginary [sic] war was due if you were elected, and all the young men would be conscripted.'[41] Even Sir Robert Borden could believe that in Quebec the people voted against Meighen because of resentment against conscription and because of a desire for revenge.[42] There is no question that the Liberals frequently referred to conscription and its baneful effects in their speeches,[43] but so too did the Conservatives; in the Conservatives' own propaganda there was more than a little gleeful wallowing in the mud thrown by their opponents—the Liberal victory in the Yamaska, Quebec by-election in early June 1921, for example, was attributed to

*This question puzzled the Governor General, Lord Byng, who wrote most confidentially to Sir John Willison: 'The point that I do not understand is whether Quebec will follow King when he offers them a policy which differs in no way from Meighen's except the possible flogging of an extremely dead horse, viz. conscription.' PAC, J. S. Willison Papers, Byng to Willison, 9 Sept. 1921, f. 3752.

conscription by Meighen's *National Liberal and Conservative Bulletin* and trumpeted as 'a notification to the rest of Canada that Quebec remains isolated in order to dictate.'[44] The Liberals used other techniques in Quebec to place the blame for 1917. Ernest Lapointe, for one, claimed in Parliament that the Conservative government's French-Canadian ministers had told Quebec that the Liberals were responsible for conscription. 'That was the campaign in the Province of Quebec in the last election . . . ,' Lapointe maintained.[45]

But was the fact that Meighen's candidates were all defeated and his party received only 18.4 per cent of the popular vote in Quebec attributable only to conscription? If so, how can the Conservative losses in English-speaking Quebec be explained? Certainly the Montreal business newspapers' attacks on Meighen's railway policy of nationalization hurt, but how much? And how can one explain Saskatchewan voters giving Meighen's party only 16.7 per cent of the ballots, a percentage markedly less than the Tories received in Quebec? Conscription was important, but a fairer view may be that of Sir John Willison, the former publisher of Toronto *News* and the friend of the rich and powerful, who wrote that it was his 'own deep conviction that the so-called Coalition from 1917 to December 6, 1921 was engaged chiefly in committing suicide.'[46]

Whatever the causes, Mackenzie King was now in power. The new Prime Minister was delighted that conscription was no longer hurting his party, but many Canadians were still bitter about the manpower question. Senator Gideon Robertson, late of the Unionist coalition, could write to remind King during the Chanak crisis of 1922, when Lloyd George's government called on Canada to pledge military aid in a potential war with Turkey, that 'Canada's large french [sic] population [had been] notoriously anti British in so far as helping in the late war was concerned. . . . ' Mackenzie King may have been correct in characterizing these words as 'propaganda of a most diabolical character', but according to Tory sources Liberals were not above playing the same game. Tom Blacklock, the reporter, wrote to Sir John Willison in 1924 about P. J. A. Cardin, King's new Minister of Marine and Fisheries, 'the most vicious of racial agitators in Quebec'. In a recent by-election, Blacklock claimed, Cardin had raised 'the race cry of "bloody ballots" and "bloody hands". He even resurrected the expulsion of the Acadians and wept of the wrongs inflicted on Evangeline by the cruel English. With Lapointe and Cardin in charge,' the reporter concluded, 'we can look for a "bloody shirt" revival in Quebec.'[48]

The bloody shirt was always useful, and its use continued to affect

Quebec politicians. E. L. Patenaude, Meighen's choice as his lieutenant, was reluctant to commit himself to the Conservative leader, one reason being his belief that Meighen was never going to do well in Quebec. A memorandum of a confidential interview with Patenaude in 1924 in the papers of Sir Robert Borden made this very clear: 'While he appreciates the very cordial reception given to Mr. Meighen in the City of Quebec, he does not think that any material change has taken place such as would lead to different results at an early election.' Then Patenaude hit at a crucial point: 'He considers that Mr. Meighen has not acted wisely in referring so frequently to compulsory military service, and he believes that Mr. Meighen's speeches in that Province should omit any reference thereto and should relate to future progress and development.'[49] Meighen, too, was keeping the issue alive.

Certainly conscription was still talked about in the 1925 election, and particularly in Quebec. Candidates in Sherbrooke, for example, traded charges and counter-charges about who had been most against conscription in 1917.[50] Conservatives wrote long memoranda on conscription, claiming that 'Sir Robert Borden did not introduce conscription into Canada. He merely lightened the burden of it and made it more bearable. It fell to him to enforce it and he but did his duty.' The same memorandum also looked at the 23 Liberals who had voted for conscription in 1917. Six had died, nine had become Conservatives or had received rewards from the Borden or Meighen governments, while the remaining eight stayed as Liberals. Three of the latter were made senators, two became judges, one became a minister of the crown, and two had stayed as Members of Parliament. In the 1925 government, the memorandum noted, Mr King was surrounded by eight conscriptionists. The point was simple. Liberals in Quebec were attacking Patenaude, an anti-conscriptionist who had left the government in 1917 because of its policies, for consorting with the conscriptionist Tories. The 'spectacle of a government so strongly conscriptionist in personnel as the King Government, a Government whose hand has so richly rewarded those who "ratted" from Laurier and the Liberal party in 1917, attempting to defeat upon the issue of conscription *Patenaude*, who then was anti-conscriptionism personified, is surely one for which a fitting stage would be a madhouse with audience and actors alike bereft of sense.'[51] There was some substantial justice in this complaint, but the Conservatives were still hurting. C. C. Ballantyne, one of Borden's Unionist ministers, wrote to his former chief to indicate that he had decided not to run in Montreal in the 1925 election. The reason was that 'G.H.Q. on St. James St. did not want any men that had been closely associated with Mr. Meighen or in his government to be candidates.... Another reason for taking this attitude was that it might hurt Mr. Patenaude's prospects.'⁵² Despite his vigorous campaign, however, Patenaude's prospects were not promising. Meighen stayed out of the province and Patenaude, stating that 'I am free of Mr. Meighen, even as I am free of Mr. King,' cut virtually all ties, but to no avail. The *Canadien* was very suspicious, Frank Carrel of the *Quebec Chronicle-Telegraph* noted, and the feeling persisted that 'Patenaude is playing a double game, or, in other words, Meighen is trying to steal the Province through subterranean methods.' And Meighen still frightened Quebec. The Liberals had only to refer to Meighen's 'ready, aye, ready' approach to British requests for aid against the Turks in 1922 and they could 'paint the picture of another war with Meighen in power, conscription and the taking out of the homes of our finest young men for the armies, etc.'⁵³

Was King responsible for the 'vilification' of Meighen?, Professor Neatby has asked. The biographer of Mackenzie King concludes that he was not, although he admits that King apparently made no effort to moderate the attacks. 'Part of the price which any English Canadian leader must pay for French Canadian support,' Neatby notes, 'is that the Quebec wing of the party must be allowed autonomy in its own affairs.... The Liberal abuse of Meighen was no more misleading or hypocritical than Patenaude's fictional repudiation of his leadership.'⁵⁴ This, too, is true. Still, the most important factor that militated against the Conservatives in Quebec and elsewhere was not conscription but the personality and record of Arthur Meighen. Borden summed up his successor's strong and weak points in a confidential letter to Lord Beaverbrook:

If the Conservatives do not win in the present contest, the result will, in no small measure, be due to Mr. Meighen's unwisdom in the use of his remarkable intellectual gifts, (especially his great debating power) and his lack of capacity for political organization. When Parliament was dissolved the country was in a mood to overthrow the King government.... But to a certain extent [Meighen] has played Mr. King's game by engaging in a wordy duel with him; and he devoted his entire energies to a speech-making campaign, in which his speeches are not always helpful ... he sometimes does more harm than good by violent attack and bitter sarcasm, which arouse the anger of the Liberals disappointed with their party and its leadership, and ready to assist in driving it from power.⁵⁵

Borden apparently believed that Meighen's speeches improved during the course of the campaign,[56] and certainly the Conservatives made a remarkable comeback after their dismal record in 1921. Still it was not enough to tumble King. In Quebec, Meighen and Patenaude received 34 per cent of the vote and gained 123,000 votes. Four English-speaking Conservatives were elected, but once again no French-Canadian Conservative survived.

The Quebec results were disappointing to Conservatives, but more heartening were the conversations Meighen was having with French-Canadian leaders. After being defeated as a Conservative in Montmagny, the old *nationaliste* Armand Lavergne wrote to Bourassa that 'après les conversations nombreuses que j'avais eues avec Meighen, je croyais et je crois encore, que c'est auprès de lui que nous pouvions trouver chez les anglais les plus grandes raisons d'espérer; car je vous dis franchement, même au risque de passer pour un naif, j'ai constaté chez lui, et vous serez à même de constater avant peu, un véritable sens national, pour ne pas dire vraiment nationaliste.'[57]

Praise from Lavergne was praise indeed, and on 16 November 1925 Meighen did his considered best to make that praise widespread throughout the province of Quebec. The occasion was his famous Hamilton, Ontario speech in which he tried to influence the forthcoming Bagot, Quebec by-election by pledging that should 'the spectre of 1914 . . . again appear I believe it would be best, not only that Parliament should be called, but that the decision of the Government, which, of course, would have to be given promptly, should be submitted to the judgement of the people at a general election before troops should leave our shores.'[58] The Hamilton speech represented the Conservative leader's response to the problem posed for him by conscription 1917.

Meighen had been considering this speech for some months—according to Borden since 'last winter',[59] and as he told a reporter in a confidential interview in October 1927, 'I arrived at the policy only after prolonged thought. The last war convinced me that it would be impossible for this country to ever engage in a war in Europe on a great scale without an election, and, if we tried to do so, we would in all human probability have caused a revolution. Certainly, without the mandate that we got in 1917, it is extremely doubtful whether we could have put conscription in force without trouble. The Borden Government alone could not have done it.' 'That much being fairly clear,' Meighen continued, 'having convinced myself, and I think rightly, that we couldn't get through the next war . . . without a similar experience . . . I concluded that it would be wiser to get the necessary mandate at the beginning, when the country would in all probability be more unanimous than later on . . . it wouldn't mean delay of an hour.' There had been a political aspect to the speech, Meighen admitted frankly, both in its intended long-term effect on the Tory position in Quebec and its short-term application to the Bagot by-election. 'The Conservative Party had been crucified in Quebec on the cross of suspicion,' Meighen said. 'We were the jingo Party, the Imperialist Party, the War and Conscription Party. I said to myself, why, if I believed, in addition, that it would allay suspicion in Quebec, and thus make for a better feeling and greater harmony—I asked myself why the Conservative Party, which believed that it could do good service for Canada in office, couldn't adopt such a policy as part of its programme?' According to Meighen, the result of any such wartime election as he proposed was inevitable. 'No Government, asking for such a mandate, would ever dare put up candidates against an Opposition who were also for war. The result would be union—Coalition. That would be the logical, the inevitable outcome. . . . That would be the one thing to save the country from strife.'[60]

Both Meighen's speech and his explanation for it were extraordinary. In the first place he drew upon himself the most bitter attacks from among the members of his party and its press. Very few of these attacks were answered, because, as Meighen said to the reporter, he was 'persuaded . . . against my own judgement to let my position go without defence rather than rock the boat when we were so near the harbour of office.'[61] Then the by-election was lost, and English Canadians could say, as many did, that 'Meighen & King are bidding against each other for the disloyal vote, and Meighen is becoming an active party to propaganda and policy that, if there is trouble between the Empire and another country, Canada leaves the Empire. . . . '[62] This talk did Meighen no good. But more serious was Meighen's misjudgement of Quebec. Could he believe that an 'inevitable' wartime coalition would ever appeal to that province, haunted as it was with memories of Union Government and conscription? And what *Québécois* could believe that a national election would have any other result than to reaffirm Canadian support for Empire? The only policy that could have appealed to Quebec was that suggested by Sir John Willison—a pledge 'that we would never apply conscription for a war outside Canada.' Such a promise, of course, was impossible for Meighen to offer, for it involved an implicit admission that the policy of 1917 had been an error, and Meighen was no man to admit to error.[63] Armand Lavergne could see in Meighen 'un véritable sens national' and Patenaude could align himself openly with his leader at last, but few others in Quebec apparently believed they could trust the man.[64] The best judgement, perhaps, was Borden's. 'If I had been in Mr. Meighen's place I should not have selected the occasion nor used the phraseology which he chose; further, I should have got much more closely in touch with leading men of the party and with the Conservative press. . . .'[65]

Whatever the effect of Meighen's speech, the election of 1926 appears to have been fought on other grounds, notably the King-Byng constitutional crisis and the perennial issue of the tariff. For the Conservatives the results brought few gains and many losses. In Quebec, where conscription was scarcely mentioned, itself an indication of non-response to the Hamilton speech, the Tories won only the four seats they had held since 1925 and a bare 6,000 votes more than they had received in that election. In Ontario, however, 60,000 votes and 15 seats were lost. If it was remembered at all after the King-Byng affair, Meighen's ploy at Hamilton would seem to have been remembered unfavourably, particularly in Ontario.[66] After the election Meighen resigned as leader. Quebec had its revenge at last.

As the post-war era gradually became the prewar one, and as the Great Depression began to bring the country to a halt, conscription once again became an issue very briefly during the 1930 election. R. B. Bennett, Meighen's successor at the head of the Conservative Party, was occasionally attacked as the father of the national registration of 1916, 'le premier pas vers la conscription',[67] and the Montreal newspaper La Presse did what it could to mount a scare campaign by giving banner headlines to a London report that British sources expected Bennett would be amenable to conscription to support British moves in Egypt.[68] But not even the 'Menace de Conscription' could stir an electorate that was more concerned with joblessness and finding enough money to buy food. As Chubby Power noted in his memoirs, instructions went out to Liberal speakers to 'Forget all about conscription. Nobody is interested in it, and if you mention it on the hustings, it will be looked upon as evidence that you are ignorant of the matters of real importance. . . .'[69] Conservatives, too, it should be noted, once again tried to drag Mackenzie King's war record out of mothballs, presumably with a similar lack of success.[70] The results, of course, produced a Conservative victory and 24 seats in Quebec, the best Tory effort since 1911. Conscription was disappearing as an issue, and if the motto of Quebec was still Je me souviens, the Québécois did not seem to remember quite so sharply as they had in 1921 and 1925.

III

Memories of past wrongs were soon to be replaced with fear of the future. The world situation worsened with great rapidity during the 1930s, with Japan, Italy, and Germany pressing their ends with increasing aggressiveness. People were frightened of another war, and many turned to disarmament as the best hope for peace. Almost half a million Canadians between 1930 and 1932 expressed their support for a petition organized by the Women's International League for Peace and Freedom:

> The nations have renounced war. Let us also renounce the instruments of war. The undersigned men and women ... STAND FOR WORLD DISARMAMENT. They are convinced: that competition in armaments is leading all countries to ruin without bringing them security; that this policy renders further wars inevitable; that wars in future will be wars of indiscriminate destruction of human life. ... [71]

The signers of the petition were correct in their views, but certainly the Canadian armed forces had no part in the world arms race. The effects of the Depression had led to cuts in defence expenditures, and the military were forced to seek 'civilian'-oriented roles to remain alive. The Chief of the General Staff, General A. G. L. McNaughton, eagerly seized on the administration of relief camps for single, unemployed men as such a function in 1932. The official rationale for this plan was that problems of declining morale and health made transient men easy prey to Communism. To prevent this fate, the unemployed men's independence and initiative had to be restored by useful work and discipline. There may have been something to this argument, but whether regular army officers would or could understand the problems of the dislocated was uncertain. What is significant, however, is that almost no one appears to have demanded either compulsion or universal military training to force the unemployed into the army or the relief camps. As one student of the relief-camp scheme has commented, many of the unemployed would not have been medically fit for military service in any case.[72]

The Liberal government returned to power in 1935 was no more disposed to large expenditures on the military forces than the Conservatives, and one of its first acts was to end the army's role in the relief camps. Mackenzie King's personal predilections were still explicitly anti-military, and his political career had been based in part on a distrust of Empire and alliances—he was less than enthusiastic about the League of Nations, that great-power-dominated body that could drag the world to war through collective security.[73] But what seems to have annoyed the Prime Minister most on his return to power was the discovery that the military staff were planning for Canadian participation in a European war. The armed forces were tiny, ill-equipped, underpaid and understrength, but the tenor of staff discussions, nonetheless, was based on the assumption that a Canadian expeditionary force would fight at Britain's side in any future war. According to a paper, 'Notes on the Defence of Canada', prepared for King in February 1936, this had been the policy since 1932 (at which time the previous priority of planning for both offense and defence against the Americans had been dropped), and the policy had been reaffirmed in 1935.[74] The army was organized so that an overseas expeditionary force could be mounted, the air force had army co-operation as its main task, and only the navy, the weakest of the services, seemed to be geared to home defence. The unnamed author of the 'Notes' was appalled that this should be the basis of planning, and recommended that all consideration of an expeditionary force should be stopped until such time as the requirements for the forces to defend Canada were studied.[75] An additional memorandum bitterly attacked the defence planners: 'On general grounds there must surely be a striking lack of proportion, an immense incongruity, in a conception which accepts major overseas operations as the ordinary permanent basis of design and strength for Canada's army organization. . . . For Canada especially the incongruity seems underlined by the circumstances that, even if the extraordinary should happen and a force be sent overseas, it could not at the outset affect the issue materially.'[76] This was unquestionably true. Of equal import to Mackenzie King was the simple fact that a large expeditionary force implied heavy fighting and large casualties. Such an eventuality would lead inevitably to a demand for conscription, and this was a course that the Prime Minister could not accept with equanimity.

The Liberal government was soon persuaded that its major defence efforts should be directed to improving the air and sea defences of the nation, that air force and navy budgets should be increased, and that the militia services should be allowed to slip further into disrepair.[77] As King told his party caucus on 20 January 1937, in a speech that was designed to soothe Quebec members troubled by any increase in the defence budget, Canada was 'not concerned with aggression. We are concerned with the defence of Canada. . . . The possibility of conflict with the United States is eliminated from our mind. There is nothing here for an expeditionary force—only for the defence of Canada against those who might wantonly assail us or violate our neutrality. The defence of our shores and the preservation of our neutrality—these are the two cardinal principles of our policy.' The Prime Minister concluded by urging the caucus to 'be united on a sane policy of defence— let us explain that policy to our people and let us above all strive at all times to keep Canada united.'[78]

Many members of the Co-operative Commonwealth Federation shared the fears of French Canadians that increased expenditures on defence heralded involvement in future wars.* J. King Gordon of the Fellowship for a Christian Social Order wrote in 1936 that 'it goes without saying that churches must take the negative stand of separating themselves from the war aims of the governments in their respective countries....' But Gordon was realistic enough to add that 'Such a negative stand...while it may do something to save the soul of the church, will do little to prevent war.'[79] That seemed all too true, and it was this type of reasoning that led T. C. Douglas, the CCF Member of Parliament for Weyburn, Saskatchewan, to urge in January 1937 that any future war should be fought with all the resources of the state. Douglas gave notice of motion in the House of Commons 'That in the opinion of this House, legislation should be immediately brought down by the Government of the Day providing that, in the event of another war involving Canada's active participation, every agency, financial, industrial, transportation or natural resources, shall automatically be conscripted for the duration of such a war....' This was, commented Loring Christie of the Department of External Affairs, 'about the "largest order" on the Order Paper'. Such steps were impossible, he maintained. 'Canada's necessities and impulses are not those of a Great Power. She is distant from the battle fronts that all these projects assume as their justification. She therefore is in a position to take a cooler view of the "totalitarian" idea and wait to measure the risks.'[80] O. D. Skelton, the Under Secretary of State for External Affairs, added a brief personal note for the Prime Minister: 'The assumption of war

---

*M. J. Coldwell, the chief assistant of J. S. Woodsworth and his eventual successor: 'I favour neither [voluntary enlistment nor conscription]. The use of force is unnecessary and wrong' (1934); 'The C.C.F., whether in or out of office, will oppose the sending of one Canadian youth for sacrifice to the god of war on a foreign field...' (1935). In 1938 the Saskatchewan provincial CCF convention passed the following resolution: 'In the event of war to bring about the socialization of all munitions and armament plants to eliminate profits, and the conscription of wealth before men.' That was Coldwell's position too in 1939. Cited in A. J. Groome, 'M. J. Coldwell and C.C.F. Foreign Policy, 1932—1950', M. A. thesis, University of Saskatchewan, 1967, 14, 19, 59.

being imminent which underlies the proposal is not warranted by the existing facts. . . . ' Such a policy was wholly uncalled for in Canada under an administration that has made 'no commitments for participation in wars abroad and is equally opposed to conscription of men and regimentation of national life.'[81]

Skelton's note notwithstanding, war was moving perceptibly closer. The German Chancellor, Herr Hitler, had begun the rearmament of Germany, even striking an arrangement with Britain that permitted him to build submarines, a forbidden weapon under the terms of the Versailles Treaty that had ended the Great War. Hitler had moved his troops back into the demilitarized zone along the Rhine, and soon a succession of 'peaceful' aggressions would expand the Reich to the east. Mussolini, the Italian Duce, had had success in Ethiopia, capturing that formerly independent African country and adding it to his domain; his territorial ambitions were not yet satisfied. And the Japanese were actively engaged in war in China, consolidating their power on the mainland and controlling huge territories.

War was moving closer, and the 'Empire right or wrong' element had begun to gather its forces in Canada. Gordon Conant, the Attorney-General of Ontario, for example, told a banquet in his home town of Oshawa in April 1938 that 'When England is at war, Canada is at war . . . if England is forced into another war it is the British Empire upon which she must depend.'[82] In a by-election in Lotbinière a few months earlier, on the other hand, the candidates all spoke of the possibility of war and conscription. The victor, the Liberal J.-N. Francoeur, maintained 'that we were in favour of defending our country, that we believed that the first line of defence was now in Canada, but that we did not want to contribute one cent for arming or equipping an expeditionary force, in short, that we do not intend to take part in foreign wars.'[83] Chubby Power, who also spoke in the campaign, put it more succinctly: 'With regard to war, I went overseas in one war. I returned. I'll never go back, and I'll never send anybody else.'[84]

Power's position was not the government's; it could not be in a country with a large Anglo-Saxon majority, one where people still looked to England as a mother country. For the Prime Minister, pressed towards neutrality by French Canada and towards involvement by the majority race, the dilemma was a sharp one. Since the passage of the Statute of Westminster in 1931 neutrality might now be a legal possibility—there was some doubt on this—but political realities made neutrality almost impossible. The best King could do, temporizing as always, was to promise that Parliament would decide the nation's course. Very few had any doubt that when Britain went to war, if Britain went to war, Parliament would decide that Canada should follow.[85]

And what of conscription when the inevitable took place? Quebec attitudes were unaltered;*[86] so unfortunately were Ontario's. On 23 March 1939, just after Hitler had swallowed the remains of Czechoslovakia, the Ontario legislature adopted a resolution calling on Ottawa 'to immediately pass Legislation providing that in the event of a War emergency the wealth and manpower of Canada shall be mobilized... for the duration of the War, in defence of our free institutions.'[87] Other pressures too were forcing the Prime Minister to take a public position. Colonel Wilfrid Bovey of Montreal, probably responding to recent *nationaliste* moves in the Quebec legislature, passed on advice that the fear of conscription was affecting all classes in Quebec. A majority in the province would be prepared to fight for Canada, Bovey told one of King's aides, 'but only on a voluntary basis.'[88] More to the point, perhaps, in forcing King's hand on the manpower question was the statement by Conservative leader R. J. Manion, which was quoted in the press on 28 March. 'I do not believe Canadian youth should be conscripted to fight outside the borders of Canada,' the recently elected Conservative chief said. 'Canada can play her full part in the empire and in support of our democratic institutions by full cooperation with Great Britain through volunteer units, through supplying munitions, foods and other necessities to our allies, and by fully protecting Canada's own territories.'[89] This was probably enough for the Prime Minister. Two days later he told the House of Commons that he would not countenance compulsion. 'Let me say that so long as this government may be in power, no such measure will be enacted.'[90] The Liberals and Conservatives both were now committed flatly against conscription for overseas service.

But in fact there remained substantial pro-conscription sentiment within the ranks of the Conservative Party, even if it did not surface in

---

*In the midst of the Czech crisis of September 1938 the Acting British High Commissioner in Ottawa reported that French-Canadian opinion seemed to be moving in the proper direction, and if war became necessary Mackenzie King would have his party prepared to back him—and war—unanimously. 'Provided', he added, 'it is made absolutely clear by the Canadian Government at the outset that there can be no question of coercion of individuals by imposition of conscription French Canadians... will not oppose a policy of active support of the United Kingdom... and further that French Canada will take their [sic] share in the burdens which this may involve.' (Public Record Office, London, Dominions Office Records, DO 114/94, Tel., 26 Sept. 1938.)

public. Certainly all those who had been in the Union Government seemed to believe that conscription was still a great and good thing, and former senior army officers still believed in compulsion. Dr Manion had alienated the true blue Tories with his pledge against conscription. But an election was close after all, and Manion had been chosen leader because some people thought he might appeal to French Canadians—his wife was a *Canadienne*—in a way that no Tory chief had been able to do for years. Better then to remain silent, to talk of party solidarity in public, to confine the grumbling to intimates, to plan for the future.

Mackenzie King faced difficulties too. His blanket pledge was sincere when offered, but few could have foreseen the scope of the war that would burst upon Canada a bare six months in the future. In his speech in the House on 30 March the Prime Minister had said that 'The idea that every twenty years this country should automatically and as a matter of course take part in a war overseas for democracy or self-determination of other small nations, that a country which has all it can do to run itself should feel called upon to save, periodically, a continent that cannot run itself, and to these ends risk the lives of its people, risk bankruptcy and political disunion, seems to many a nightmare and sheer madness.'[91] The nightmare was about to begin.

NOTES

1 H. M. Urquhart, *Arthur Currie* (Toronto, 1950), p. 284.

2 A. R. M. Lower, 'Foreign Policy and Canadian Nationalism', *Dalhousie Review*, XV (April, 1935), 33. Cf. Douglas Durkin, *The Magpie* (Toronto, 1974).

3 W. H. Merritt, *Canada and National Service* (Toronto, 1917), p. ix.

4 'A Citizen Army', *Queen's Quarterly*, XXVI (October, 1918), 181-90. See also Brig.-Gen. Critchley, 'Conscription After the War', *Maclean's*, (October, 1918), 13-14.

5 Public Archives of Canada [PAC], Militia and Defence Records, HQC 2862; D. P. Morton, *The Canadian General: Sir William Otter* (Toronto, 1974), p. 360; John Swettenham, *McNaughton*, Vol. I: *1887-1939* (Toronto, 1968), pp. 182-3.
1968), pp. 182-3.

6 A. M. J. Hyatt, 'The Military Career of Sir Arthur Currie', Unpublished Ph.D. thesis, Duke University, 1965, 261. Cf. Hyatt's contradictory introduction to 'Sir Arthur Currie and Conscription', *Canadian Historical Review*, L (September, 1968), 285.

7 Charles Y. Harrison, *Generals Die in Bed* (1930; reprinted, Hamilton, 1975), pp. 138 and introduction; J. C. Hopkins, *The Canadian Annual Review 1921* (Toronto, 1922), p. 346.

8 *Ibid.*, 1926-7, p. 639.

9 Swettenham, *McNaughton*, 182-3.

10 Hyatt, 'Military Career', 261.

11 House of Commons *Debates*, 24 June 1919, p. 3969.

12 *Ibid.*

13 *Ibid.*

14 *Ibid.*, p. 3972.

15 *Ibid.*, p. 3973.

16 Hyatt, *op. cit.*, 261-2.

17 House of Commons *Debates*, 31 Mar. 1920, pp. 923-5.

18 *Ibid.*, p. 942.

19 *Ibid.*, p. 947. On the other hand, cadet training continued, and although efforts, particularly on the Prairies, were made to ban it, none succeeded. See Donald Page, 'The Development of a Western Canadian Peace Movement', in S. Trofimenkoff, ed., *The Twenties in Western Canada* (Ottawa, 1972), pp. 93ff. See also R. Allen, *The Social Passion* (Toronto, 1970), chapters 20-1.

20 House of Commons *Debates*, 16 June 1920, p. 3646.

21 *Report of the Department of Militia and Defence for . . . 1920* (Ottawa, 1921), p. 13.

22 For details, see *The Canadian Annual Review 1921*, pp. 495-7.

23 Queen's University, C. G. Power Papers, Vol. 9, Power to N. Ward, 9 July 1959. See also N. Ward, ed., *A Party Politician: The Memoirs of Chubby Power* (Toronto, 1966), p. 104.

24 See C. P. Stacey, *Official History of the Canadian Army in the Second World War*, Vol. I: *Six Years of War* (Ottawa, 1955), 3-6.

25 PAC, W. L. M. King Papers, King to V. Markham, 10 Dec. 1919, f. 41657.

26 *Ibid.*, King to Elizabeth Norton, 23 Dec. 1919, ff. 42383-4.

27 *Ibid.*, 19 Dec. 1919, ff. 45098-9. But conscription still blighted Liberal careers. See Margaret Prang, *N. W. Rowell, Ontario Nationalist* (Toronto, 1975), pp. 431-2.

28 House of Commons *Debates*, 20 Apr. 1920, pp. 1405-16.

29 King Papers, correspondence on ff. 47451-6.

30 Craig Brown and Ramsay Cook, *Canada 1896-1921* (Toronto, 1974), pp. 328-9.

31 New College, Oxford, Lord Milner Papers, Vol. 170, Devonshire to Milner, 9 July 1920. (I am indebted to Prof. Charles Humphries for drawing this letter to my attention.) Cf. Robert Rumilly, *Histoire de la province de Québec* (Montréal, 1952), XXV, 16 and the Robert Borden Diaries, 28 June-9 July 1920.

32 Quoted in R. M. Dawson, *William Lyon Mackenzie King*, Vol. I: *1874-1923* (Toronto, 1958), 351.

33 L. Richer, *Silhouettes du monde politique* (Montréal, 1940), p. 47.

34 PAC, Arthur Meighen Papers, G. M. Murray to J. Bain, 16 Sept. 1921, ff. 12101-2. The effects of such press campaigns, however, were such that King felt obliged to keep French-Canadian leaders out of Ontario during the campaign of 1921. King Papers, King to L. Gouin, 4 Nov. 1921, ff. 52460-1, and Dawson, *op. cit.*, 354.

35 See, for example, Wilfred Eggleston, *While I Still Remember* (Toronto, 1968), p. 81.

36 PAC, J. S. Willison Papers, Willison to Hale, 10 Nov. 1921, ff. 12980-2 and Willison to J. Harold, 13 Oct. 1921, f. 14596; Peter Oliver, *Public and Private Persons: the Ontario Political Culture 1914-1934* (Toronto, 1975), p. 30.

37 A very able description is D. E. Smith, *Prairie Liberalism* (Toronto, 1975), chapters III and V.

38 King Papers, King to V. Markham, 29 Sept. 1921, ff. 55332-3.

39 PAC, Escott Reid Papers, J. G. Gardiner interview, 9 Aug. 1931.

40 *Ibid.*, T. A. Crerar interview, 20 July 1931. Cf. the Liberal's pamphlet, *Liberaux et fermiers* (octobre, 1921) which indicates the Liberals were taking no chances, however. For discussion of Crerar, see F. J. K. Griezic, 'The Hon. T. A. Crerar: The Political Career of a Western Liberal Progressive in the 1920's', in Trofimenkoff, *Western Canada,* pp. 107ff.

41 Meighen Papers, T. Delany to Meighen, 23 Dec. 1921, f. 11342. Cf. Rumilly, *op. cit.,* chapitre IX.

42 PAC, Robert Borden Papers, Borden to Perley, 24 Dec. 1921, f. 156805.

43 *The Canadian Annual Review 1921*, pp. 487ff. refers.

44 Vol. I, no. 4, 4 June 1921. Copy in PAC, Sir George Foster Papers, v. 67, folder 163. Cf. issues of 17 Sept. and 1 Oct. 1921.

45 Quoted in E. M. Macdonald, *Recollections Political and Personal* (Toronto, n.d.), p. 404.

46 Willison Papers, Willison to Beatty, 9 Dec. 1921, f. 1235.

47 King Papers, Robertson to King, 28 Sept. 1922 and reply 30 Sept. 1922, ff. 67926-9.

48 Willison Papers, 3 Feb. 1924, f. 1935. Rumilly, *op. cit.,* XXVII, 175, maintains that the Conservatives began the conscription mudslinging.

49 Borden Papers, 'Memorandum . . . 27th October 1924', ff. 155796. Cf. Rumilly, *op. cit.,* 51-4.

50 'Sachez donc la verité', flyer in Meighen Papers, f. 57371.

51 Borden Papers, Memorandum re Conscription, n.d., ff. 157242-6. *Ibid.*, S. White to Borden, 21 Oct. 1925, f. 157170 indicates this memo was sent to friendly press sources. See also *ibid.*, ff. 157205ff.

52 *Ibid.*, 20 Oct. 1925, f. 146162.

53 Willison Papers, Carrel to Willison, 22 Oct. 1925, f. 4917. Cf. Roger Graham, *Arthur Meighen,* Vol. II: *And Fortune Fled* (Toronto, 1963), 340ff.; Rumilly, *op. cit.,* XXVIII, 79ff.

54 H. B. Neatby, *William Lyon Mackenzie King,* Vol. II: *1924-32* (Toronto, 1963), 74.

55 Borden Papers, 29 Sept. 1925, f. 146272.

56 *Ibid.*, 2 Nov. 1925, f. 146275.

57 PAC, Henri Bourassa Papers, Mf. M-722, 5 Nov. 1925.

58 Arthur Meighen, *Unrevised and Unrepented* (Toronto, 1949), p. 193.

59 Borden Papers, Borden to Christie, 23 Nov. 1925, f. 148201. Cf. Rumilly, *op. cit.,* XXVIII, 99, which indicates that the speech was suggested by two Quebec senators.

60 Queen's University, Grant Dexter Papers, Memorandum of a conversation . . . 27 Oct. 1927. Cf. Borden Papers, L. C. Christie to Philip Kerr, 14 Dec. 1925, ff. 148210-12 and Borden to Beaverbrook, 6 Jan. 1926. ff. 146282-3.

61 Dexter Papers, Memorandum, 27 Oct. 1927.

62 Willison Papers, Blacklock to Willison, 27 Nov. 1925, f. 1973. There is substantial correspondence in the Meighen and Borden Papers on this point.

63 Graham, *op. cit.,* 363-4.

64 Cf. the Liberal reaction in 'Mr. Meighen in Quebec', 11 Dec. 1925, a press release. Copy in Meighen Papers, ff. 37384p-s.

65 Borden Papers, Borden to Beaverbrook, 6 Jan. 1926, f. 146282.

66 Cf. Willison Papers, Blacklock to Willison, 22 Sept. 1926, ff. 1984-5.

67 Rumilly, *op. cit.*, XXXI, 229-30, 237; see also M. La Terreur, *Les Tribulations des conservateurs au Québec* (Québec, 1973), p. 20.

68 *La Presse*, 25 juillet 1930. See also PAC, R. B. Bennett Papers, Dandurand to Bennett, 2 Aug. 1930, ff. 38066-8; La Terreur, *op. cit.*, p. 21.

69 Ward, *op. cit.*, p. 116.

70 See the reference to Dr. R. J. Manion's speech in *The Canadian Annual Review 1929-30*, p. 86.

71 Page, *op. cit.*, p. 106n.

72 G. M. Lefresne, 'The Royal Twenty Centers', (Unpublished B. A. thesis, R.M.C., 1962), 9-10; Public Record Office, London, Cabinet Records, Cab 63/81, 'Impressions of Canadian Defence Policy—December, 1934', by Sir Maurice Hankey.

73 Some colleagues professed to believe otherwise. PAC, Brooke Claxton Papers, Paul Martin to Claxton, 20 Feb. 1936.

74 In May 1935, Gen. McNaughton officially reported that 'the direct defence of the national territory...had not been given a high degree of priority.' Power Papers, 'The Requirements of Canadian Defence', 28 May 1935.

75 King Papers, 20 Feb. 1936, ff. C112277-85. To determine the extent to which these views affected policy see the report 'The Defence of Canada', prepared by the C.G.S. and submitted on 10 Jan. 1938. Copy in Power Papers. Cf. a series of memos during 1937-9 in PAC, Department of External Affairs Records, v.8 (e.g., 17 Nov. 1938 and 10 Feb. 1939).

76 King Papers, 20 Feb. 1936, ff. C112275-6.

77 Stacey, *op. cit.*, 13.

78 *Ibid.*, 14. In many respects this involved countering British attempts to link Canada into the Imperial Defence net, a problem that became acute at the 1937 Imperial Conference. See 'Review of Imperial Defence...', 22 Feb. 1937, a U.K. paper; and Canadian comments on it. 'Preliminary Notes Respecting Canadian Position,' King Papers, ff. C126675ff. and C124163ff. For U.K. comment on Canadian 1937 defence estimates, see King Papers, Massey to SSEA, 29 Jan. 1937, ff. 204805-10. L. B. Pearson, *Mike: The Memoirs of the Rt. Hon. L. B. Pearson*, Vol. I: *1897-1948* (Toronto, 1972), 125 indicates that he disagreed with this view by 1937, but that the public accepted it until 1938-9.

79 Cited in D. Rothwell, 'United Church Pacifism, October 1939', [United Church] *Bulletin*, no. 22 (1973), 45.

80 King Papers, Memo, n.d., ff. C111882-90. Cf. Doris Shackleton, *Tommy Douglas* (Toronto, 1975), pp. 102ff.

81 King Papers, 27 Jan. 1937, ff. C111880-1. Such attitudes in Canada infuriated the British. The Chief of the Naval Staff, for example, said that 'he considers the Canadian attitude to defence matters can only be described as "pitiful"...' Cabinet Records, Cab 21/671, Secretary to C.N.S. to Gen. Ismay, 23 Mar. 1939.

82 Oshawa *Times*, 13 Apr. 1938, clipping in Gordon Conant Papers, Oshawa.

83 House of Commons *Debates*, 31 Jan., 1938, p. 19.

84 Ward, *Power Memoirs*, pp. 122-3.

85 J. L. Granatstein, *Canada's War: The Politics of the Mackenzie King Government, 1939-1945* (Toronto, 1975), pp. 2ff. For a U.K. view of neutrality, see PRO, Dominions Office Records, DO 114/94, Tel., 26 Sept. 1938, pp. 62-4.

86 'I hope you have noted that, with the exception of Lapointe, every French-Canadian who has spoken in parliament . . . has not only spoken against conscription but against Canada sending a man overseas. They represent 95% of the population. Make no mistake about it. . . .' Claxton Papers, v. 137, Claxton to K. Lindsay, 19 May 1939. See also Jacques Michel, *La Participation des canadiens français à la grande guerre* (Montréal, 1938); Rumilly, *op. cit.*, XXXVIII, 124; *Action Nationale*, XIII (avril, 1939), 289-90.

87 King Papers, Notes and Memoranda, file 1589, ff. 121514-5.

88 On 23 March René Chaloult introduced a neutralist motion. Rumilly, *op. cit.*, 191-2. Chaloult's *Mémoirs politiques* (Montréal, 1969), make no reference. King Papers, Memo, 28 Mar. 1939, f. C111895.

89 Toronto *Star*, 28 Mar. 1939; J. L. Granatstein, *The Politics of Survival* (Toronto, 1967), pp. 23-4; La Terreur, *op. cit.*, pp. 87-8. Manion's statement sounded very much like O. D. Skelton's memo on 24 Aug. 1939 proposing a 'Canadian War Policy', King Papers, v. 228.

90 House of Commons *Debates*, 30 Mar. 1939, p. 2425. For CCF comment see Walter Young, *The Anatomy of a Party: The National CCF 1932-61* (Toronto, 1970), pp. 223ff.

91 House of Commons *Debates*, 30 Mar. 1939, p. 2425. For a comment on the lack of enthusiasm for war in Canada see Skelton's memo of 10 Sept. 1939 in External Affairs Records, v. 13, folder 74, v. 6. See also H. B. Neatby, *William Lyon Mackenzie King*, Vol. III: *The Prism of Unity* (Toronto, 1976), chapters 15 and 16 for a good account of King's attitudes and role.

Five

TOWARDS THE PLEBISCITE AND BILL 80

The Second World War began on the morning of 1 September 1939 when Germany invaded Poland. That day Prime Minister Mackenzie King called Parliament to meet on 7 September, and the government also announced that a state of 'apprehended war' existed and had existed since 25 August when the permanent forces had been placed on alert and the RCMP had undertaken security actions.

For Mackenzie King and his government the war was something that had been feared, not in any way an event that Canada could welcome. The memories of the casualties of the Great War and of the social and political strains it had produced were all too clear. For the Prime Minister in particular the recollections of the effects conscription had had on the country, on French Canada, and on the Liberal Party constituted a guide to action. In March 1939 King had pledged there would be no conscription in any future war. Now, with Parliament assembled, King repeated his promise on 8 September:

> I wish now to repeat the undertaking I gave in Parliament on behalf of the government on March 30 last. The present government believes that conscription of men for overseas service will not be a necessary or an effective step. No such measure will be introduced by the present administration. We have full faith in the readiness of Canadian men and women to put forward every effort in their power to defend free institutions, and in particular to resist aggression on the part of a tyrannical regime which aims at the domination of the world by force.[1]

Two days later, after brief flurries of neutralist and anti-war sentiment from a few Quebec members, Canada was at war.

The national war effort as envisaged by Mackenzie King's government entailed co-operation with Britain and its allies. Military participation would be subordinated to economic assistance, in particular agricultural and industrial aid. In fact, until the late spring of 1940 and until a series of disasters had overtaken Britain and France, very few orders of any kind were placed in Canada. British firms sought for themselves such contracts as were issued, there was still unemployment in the United Kingdom, and patents and blueprints were only rarely passed along to Canadian firms. And Britain was unwilling to pay the prices Canadians asked for wheat, cheese, bacon, and other farm products. The result was that for the first nine months of war British orders in Canada were merely a trickle. Orders placed by the Department of National Defence were no greater, for the government had determined that the war would be fought essentially on a pay-as-you-go basis.[2]

Similar approaches prevailed on manpower questions. An order-in-council on 1 September 1939 authorized the recruiting of men for the newly created Canadian Active Service Force (CASF). In effect this permitted certain designated units of the Non-Permanent Active Militia (NPAM), the part-time soldiers who trained on Saturdays and in the summers, to recruit up to full strength and to place themselves on active service, along with the units of the permanent militia, the professional soldiers. The NPAM units would now become the active battalions of their particular regiments and would ordinarily be moved to training camps to join with the other battalions and units of the CASF. The remainder of the regiment would organize a second battalion at home, retaining its NPAM status until such time as the Department of National Defence would order it activated for CASF service. This was the procedure followed throughout the war years. In November 1940 the militia designation was dropped, however, with the CASF now being called the Canadian Army Active Force (CA(AF)) and the NPAM now being known as the Canada Army (Reserve) (CA(R)).

In September 1939 there was no shortage of volunteers, in part at least because the country was still wracked by unemployment—there were at least half a million men without work, many of them having been jobless for years. Yet recruiting officers had some problems. Their instructions obliged them to discourage enlistment in the ranks by university graduates, professional men, and youths under 18, all of whom might be utilized to better purpose later. Further, married men with more than two children received the warning that dependants' allowances could not cover families of more than three dependants. Finally, aliens were barred from enlisting. Despite these limitations on recruiting, on 24 September, a week after the government had announced its intention to despatch an expeditionary force of one division overseas, all recruiting was suspended except for men selecting the infantry. The tap would not be opened until February 1940 for tradesmen and until 18 March 1940 for all comers.[3] By that time some 80,000 men had enlisted in the army, and as the war in Europe had stagnated, degenerating to a battle of leaflets and loudspeakers across the Rhine, that seemed more than enough.

The phoney war in Europe was not paralleled on the Canadian political front. Just a few weeks after war was declared, the Premier of Quebec, Maurice Duplessis, sought and received a sudden dissolution of the legislature and announced that an election would take place on 25 October 1939. In the normal course of events the federal government would have been delighted to see Duplessis toppled—his support was essentially Conservative-*nationaliste* at base and he had crusaded against Ottawa without cessation since coming to power in 1936. But in the context of the war, Duplessis's dissolution seemed to pose a particularly serious problem. Perhaps too quickly, and perhaps as much for political reasons as for national ones, the federal government and the English-language press perceived Duplessis's dissolution as an attempt to win the election by crusading against Canada's—and French Canada's—participation in the war. In his initial comments, however, the Premier had staked his ground around provincial autonomy and he had talked of the way Ottawa was using 'le prétexte de la guerre déclarée par le gouvernement féderale' to foster 'une campagne d'assimilation et de centralisation'.[4] This was far different than a crusade for Quebec to opt out of the war.

Significantly, however, it was the Quebec ministers in the King government who insisted on action. Chubby Power, King's Postmaster General, argued that Duplessis's action challenged the position of the federal ministers from Quebec and, by weakening them, brought conscription nearer. There was some logic behind this contention. Ernest Lapointe, the Minister of Justice, P. J. A. Cardin, the Minister of Public Works, and Power had all pledged themselves to stand against the imposition of conscription in this war; if Duplessis could win his implicit anti-war campaign, their prestige in the nation would suffer, and with it their ability to impose their will on the conscription question on their colleagues. For this reason, Power and his colleagues persuaded the Prime Minister that the Ottawa Liberals had to intervene actively against Duplessis's Union Nationale in the election campaign. Most important, the federal ministers felt so strongly that their prestige was at stake that they announced they would resign if Quebec repudiated them. This, they maintained, would inevitably bring conscription. In essence then, the people of Quebec were being asked to defeat Duplessis or to see conscription imposed, an unfair choice at best.

Lapointe, Cardin, and Power campaigned actively throughout the province, appearing often with Adelard Godbout, the Quebec Liberal leader. Repeated pledges against conscription were offered, and Godbout himself delivered an unequivocal pledge that if the King government ever resorted to conscription he would leave the Liberal Party and fight it. The war had recreated the conscription bogey and, as the Liberals were demonstrating, it had potency still.

Against this unexpected campaign from Ottawa Duplessis could do nothing. His splendid tactic of dissolving quickly and seeking a snap mandate had turned to ashes, and although he campaigned vigorously his language began to moderate as he sought to hold his supporters. It was all in vain. The Union Nationale's huge pre-election majority—Duplessis had 77 of 90 seats in 1936—was swept away; Godbout took 53 per cent of the popular vote and 69 seats. It was a triumph for Lapointe, Cardin, and Power, a triumph for those in English Canada who wanted to believe that Quebec was heart and soul in the war. The Toronto *Globe and Mail*, for example, proclaimed on 26 October that 'Quebec has answered' and confirmed 'the confidence of the rest of the country in the soundness of the French-Canadian people.'

This was simply not so, of course. The election results had demonstrated not support for the war but a deep and abiding fear of conscription. Professor F. R. Scott was one of the very few who perceived this. In an article in the *Canadian Forum* for December 1939 Scott argued that Quebec had voted against compulsory service, not for the war. 'That is why Mr. Lapointe's intervention was so supremely important. Once he had announced . . . that in the event of a Duplessis victory he would resign with all his French colleagues in the Federal Cabinet, it became clear that a vote for Mr. Duplessis would be more likely to bring on conscription than retard it.' That was all too true, and the failure of English Canadians to draw the correct lessons from the October election would have fateful effects.

I

Despite the success with which the Liberals had employed the fear of conscription in the Quebec election, there was very little overt sign of support for compulsory service anywhere in the country. Mitchell Hepburn, the Premier of Ontario, could write to a friend that 'I agree with you thoroughly that conscription should be put in force at once',[5] but a private letter was different from a public statement. However there was some pro-conscription sentiment, and most of it was to be found within the ranks of the Conservative Party.

The leader of the party, Dr Robert Manion, had announced his position in March 1939 when he came out against conscription for overseas service in any new war. But Manion was considered to be slightly suspect by many in his party, too radical on economic questions and too soft on imperial ones. Conscription was an imperial issue, one that cut close to the bone and, as in the Great War, brought unhappy racial and economic instincts to the fore. For example, the York East Conservative association in Toronto put itself firmly on the line at the beginning of October 1939, voting for compulsion 'as the only fair means of selecting men and preserving a proper balance of British stock in Canada'.[6] Other Conservatives wanted conscription for more direct economic reasons. Harry Price, a Toronto businessman and one of Manion's key advisers, wrote him on 9 September to urge compulsion:

I very strongly believe that public opinion in Canada is rapidly becoming crystallized to the view of mobilization of manpower for every purpose. Particularly is this important in connection with two of our basic industries, namely gold-mining and farming.

It is of the utmost importance that our gold mines continue to operate on a wage scale that will allow of a reasonable return to the investors, which would not be possible unless mine labour was mobilized.[7]

Another Tory, Brigadier J. A. Clark of Vancouver, also urged his leader towards conscription. As he wrote to former Prime Minister R. B. Bennett,

From the outset ... a resistance is built up in Quebec with the full approval of the Government and I regret to say our own Party, against performance of duty. I can understand men like Lapointe taking this stand but I cannot understand my own Party falling in line. It may be that the Party could not declare for conscription at the particular moment but it did not need to declare against it. I may add that I have been severely rebuked by the Party leader for these thoughts.[8]

Indeed Manion had vigorously assailed Clark and others who thought like him. 'Apparently you do not see the need of trying to keep Canada from splitting down the middle,' he wrote. 'I cannot see for the life of me what good it would do to the Empire for Canada to get into a sort of semi-Civil War of its own.' Manion was certainly correct on this score, but in his party there were large numbers of conscriptionists biding their time. Some, like Clark, sought a way to make French Canadians fight; others, like those Tories in York East, feared that the war would see 'loyal' Britishers enlisting and being killed while the 'disloyal' French and immigrant classes stayed home to breed in safety; and finally men like Price, worried over the intrusions of organized labour into the mining areas of northern Ontario, and fearful that their exorbitant profits would fall if decent wages were paid, wanted compulsion to keep labour's demands in check and to keep a plentiful supply of workers underground. To his great credit Manion saw that these forces within his party were dangerous and had to be resisted. It was his misfortune that he had to grapple with them during an election campaign.

Like the Quebec election in October of the previous year, the federal general election of 26 March 1940 was quickly called when Mackenzie King, a fine judge of the opportune, saw his chance. This came when Premier Hepburn, joined by the bulk of the Ontario legislature's Liberal caucus and by the entire Conservative Opposition, whooped through a resolution on 18 January denouncing Ottawa's lacklustre war effort. After a momentary panic at the effects this might have, Mackenzie King quickly saw that Hepburn's impulsive act gave him the chance to go to the people before the expected campaigning in Europe began in the spring. A snap election would also catch Manion's Tories in a disorganized state, and it would provide a chance to strike Hepburn Liberalism, long a divisive force in the Ontario Liberal Party, a fatal blow. The result was that the Speech from the Throne, intended to open the 1940 session of Parliament, instead announced its dissolution.

Exactly as King had foreseen, the Conservatives were caught with their plans unmade. Desperately trying to recover, the caucus unwisely found itself supporting a call for a national government of the 'best brains'. This would not have been a bad idea had the Union Government of 1917 not created resentment and alienation in Quebec and among labour, immigrants, farmers, and independents. A national government made up of unspecified 'brains' could not be a winning hand in the Canada of 1940. As for Manion himself, he was against conscription and for national government, and he quickly found himself squeezed between the millstones of his party's past and present. Significantly, as Manion later noted, 'before every meeting ... the first demand by our candidates was that I make it very clear I was opposed to conscription for overseas service.' So he did, again and again, but to no avail. The Conservatives won only 40 seats in the election, and all across the country the party's surveys afterwards pointed to a fear of conscription, a fear that the Tories would implement it, as the key reason.[9]

The Conservatives were not alone in suffering for their conscriptionist beliefs in the 1940 election. Social Credit, transformed under the hand of W. D. Herridge, R. B. Bennett's Minister to the United States, into the New Democracy Party, flatly endorsed compulsory service in its election platform. The Herridge-ites paid for their folly, dropping seven seats. The policy of conscription, a student of the New Democracy wrote, 'had alienated many ... former supporters and had attracted no new ones'.[10]

Curiously, if the Conservatives and Social Credit were punished by voters who feared their bellicosity, the CCF seems to have been punished because it was seen as too pacifist, too lukewarm about the war. CCF policy had been tortuously reached, a product of deep divisions between men like party leader J. S. Woodsworth, who believed that no war was just, and pragmatists like M. J. Coldwell, Woodsworth's deputy, who recognized that such a stand would destroy the party. The compromise—that Canada should send economic aid but not men to Britain—seemed to satisfy no one, and the CCF took a beating at the polls.

Only Mackenzie King and the Liberals seemed to hold the requisite middle ground. Most impressive of all was that the Liberals fought the election exactly as planned. In a memorandum prepared on 1 February 1940, probably by Norman Lambert, President of the National Liberal Federation, the strategy was defined: 'we shall blow both hot and cold on the subject of preparedness for war, showing that the government in its wisdom and foresight did actually make great strides in the matter of preparedness while, at the same time, the Government had to fight against a Canadian public opinion which was definitely antagonistic to anything approaching military preparedness measures.' Only in Ontario, the author of the assessment went on shrewdly, 'only in the Province of Ontario does Canada's wartime effort completely overshadow all considerations of the normal functions of Government. ... '[11] That was a very accurate assessment of the national mood, and in playing to it the Liberals allowed their opposition to destroy itself with programs that offered either too little or the prospect of too much.

The results of the voting on 26 March exceeded everyone's expectations. The Liberal government was returned with 181 seats and a majority over the combined opposition parties of 117. Manion's Tories were devastated yet again, and Manion lost his own seat. The CCF took only eight ridings, Social Credit ten. It was the largest majority in history, a sure indication that King's 'limited liability' war effort was gauged correctly.

II

The complacent attitude that had characterized Canadian response to the war began to change quickly with the collapse of the Anglo-French front in May 1940. The myth that had been the Maginot Line was exploded; along with it went the Allied hope that Germany could be brought to its knees by economic means. In the changed atmosphere that was created by the defeats in Belgium, by Dunkirk, and by the surrender of France, the Canadian war effort was dramatically altered.

By the time the British Expeditionary Force had escaped from the continent, Canada had prepared to send to England all the aid it was possible to give. Four destroyers and two RCAF squadrons were under orders, and military units were preparing to occupy Newfoundland, Bermuda, and Jamaica, while troops of the 2nd Division were under orders for Ireland. Units for a 3rd and a 4th Canadian division were being mobilized, as were nine additional infantry battalions, five motorcycle regiments, forestry corps troops, coast-defence units, and a Veterans Home Guard for home service made up of older men.

But there was at first no move to emulate the efforts at total war under way in Britain. There a national government under Winston Churchill had taken power, and as one of its first acts had passed the Emergency Powers (Defence) Act, 1940 on 22 May. This sweeping bill gave the Minister of Labour power to order any person to perform such services as directed. The United Kingdom, of course, already had conscription in force, and had had since before the outbreak of hostilities.

For Mackenzie King, fresh from his smashing victory of 26 March, national government was unthinkable. In his view his government, representative of all provinces, all races, and all classes was already a national government, and King believed that little could be gained by taking in the dispirited Tories or CCF. Much could be lost, however, most notably the support of Quebec, which would be certain to see any attempts at a coalition as presaging conscription. Nonetheless King did secretly attempt to bring some individuals into the government in an effort to broaden its base; but whether businessman, banker, or labour leader, whether Liberal or Tory, all declined, terribly disillusioning the Prime Minister. His only success came on 28 June when Angus L. Macdonald, Liberal Premier of Nova Scotia, agreed to join the government.[12]

Despite the government's efforts to reassure Canadians that everything possible was being done to help Britain, conscription was on everyone's mind in the late spring and summer of 1940. In the House of Commons Opposition speakers began to press for a national registration, while organizations such as the Canadian Legion openly advocated conscription.[13] For a time the government simply stonewalled, turning aside queries with polite parliamentary evasions. But in the Cabinet, King was worried. When he learned of the Emergency Powers Act at Westminster, he wrote in his diary, 'I saw clearly that instant demand would be made for so-called national service in Canada . . . , I told my colleagues we might easily see the party divided into conscriptionists or non-conscriptionists. . . . That I certainly would resign before I would accept any move in the direction of conscription. . . .'[14] Some two weeks later Arthur Slaght, M.P., raised the necessity for a national registration in the Liberal caucus. In his diary the Prime Minister noted that the Minister of Justice, Ernest Lapointe 'answered as to the devilment it would make of the situation in the province of Quebec.'[15]

But as the situation in France grew more perilous, King slowly began to alter his position. On 16 June, the day France capitulated, he wrote:

My heart aches for the people in the British Isles. However, I see wherein now that there is a real possibility of invasion of our shores, an effort will be made to seize this country as a prize of war. We have, therefore, changed now to the stage where defence of this land becomes our most important duty.[16]

The next day the Conservative Party's house leader, R. B. Hanson (selected by caucus to replace Dr Manion, sent packing by his followers) came to see the Prime Minister. Hanson urged that Parliament pass legislation similar to the British Emergency Powers Act, that a state of emergency be declared, and that a national government be created. King gave the Leader of the Opposition scant ground to expect anything, but at the Cabinet War Committee that night King was surprised to find that his most senior colleagues agreed 'that we should have a measure that would enable us to call out every man in Canada for military training for the defence of Canada.' This accorded with King's perceptions, and this suggestion had the support of Lapointe and of C. G. Power, another key Quebec minister and the acting Minister of National Defence since Norman Rogers' death on 10 June.* '[I]t was a relief to my mind, in that it amounts to what is right in the mobilization of all resources', he noted.[17]

The Prime Minister himself subsequently drafted the bill that would become known as the National Resources Mobilization Act (NRMA). In a speech to the Commons introducing the bill on 18 June, Mackenzie King noted that this legislation 'will relate solely and exclusively to the defence of Canada on our own soil and in our own territorial waters.' Later in his remarks he returned to this theme, dealing with conscription explicitly:

> Recruitment for service overseas will be continued on a voluntary basis. No difficulty has been experienced and no difficulty is anticipated in raising by the voluntary method the men required for service outside Canada. The bill to be introduced today in no way affects the raising of men to serve in the armed forces overseas. Once again I wish to repeat my undertaking, frequently given, that no measure for the conscription of men for overseas service will be introduced by the present administration.

King added that a national registration would be held in the near future. 'Let me emphasize the fact that this registration will have nothing to do with the recruitment of men for overseas service,' the Prime Minister reiterated, sounding much as Sir Robert Borden had in late 1916.[18]

The key provisions of the NRMA gave the government great powers, almost unlimited in their ability to determine the role of every individual:

> 2. Subject to the provisions of section three hereof, the Governor in Council may do and authorize such acts and things, and make from time to time such orders and regulations, requiring persons to place themselves, their services and their property at the disposal of His

---

*Rogers was killed in an air crash on 10 June. His death forced King to turn to Col. Layton Ralston, the Minister of Finance from the outbreak of the war, to become Rogers' replacement, which he did on 5 July. Earlier, on 23 May, Power had been named Minister of National Defence (Air) and Associate Minister of National Defence. On 12 July 1940 Angus L. Macdonald became Minister of National Defence for Naval Services, thus completing the structure under which the Department of National Defence would fight the war.

Majesty in the right of Canada, as may be deemed necessary or expedient for securing the public safety, the defence of Canada, the maintenance of public order, or the efficient prosecution of the war, or for maintaining supplies or services essential to the life of the community.

3. The powers conferred . . . may not be exercised for the purpose of requiring persons to serve in the military [,] naval or air forces outside Canada and the territorial waters thereof.[19]

Further details of the government's intentions were given to Parliament by Power:

Every able-bodied man in Canada will be given the opportunity of training in the use of arms, so as to come to the defence of the homeland if necessary. The procedure will be that the men will in due course be called up for a period so as to be prepared for the active defence of this dominion. The training . . . will be entrusted to units of the non-permanent active militia which will be recruited voluntarily or filled under the powers of the new legislation according as the facilities for training and accommodation permit.

The length of the period of training will be determined by regulation. Whether this will be for a continuous period of three months or for a lesser depends on: (a) the advice of the technical officers of the department; (b) the requirements of industrial and productive manpower as shown by a survey to be immediately undertaken.[20]

In fact the period of service for men conscripted under authority of the NRMA was initially fixed at 30 days. Only the unmarried would be called at first. After some debate the bill was moved speedily through the three readings in the House of Commons and in the Senate and became law on 21 June. On 12 July a bill to create the Department of National War Services, necessary to administer the call-up, was introduced.

The initial response to the passage of the NRMA was generally favourable throughout the country. Even Quebec did not seem unduly alarmed at this first break in the solid front of pledges against conscription. The dangers to North America seemed clear enough—France and Western Europe were gone and Britain was on the brink of defeat; Canadian markets and trade were in serious jeopardy, to say the least, and if the Royal Navy and the French Navy fell into Hitler's hands, the actual physical safety of Canada could be endangered. Nonetheless there was some opposition. In the Quebec legislature on 19 June, René

Chaloult, a *nationaliste* Liberal, put a motion objecting to the NRMA on the grounds that it would eventually be used to force overseas conscription. There was substantial prescience in that motion, but the Liberal majority handily turned down Chaloult's intervention.[21] In addition *Le Devoir*, joined by some other newspapers, fulminated against the NRMA, but when the Church hierarchy supported the government, alarm did not spread.[22] Opinion was similarly steadied by Ernest Lapointe's firm pledge that overseas service 'demeura voluntaire, tel que je vous l'ai toujours dit.' He said he and his colleagues from Quebec 'n'accepterons jamais une telle mesure'.[23]

Meanwhile planning for the NRMA conscripts' training was under way at Army Headquarters. The new Chief of the General Staff, Major-General H. D. G. Crerar, had returned from London early in July to take on the job of mobilization. The task was a difficult one, in large part because of the new public pressure for a greater war effort. As Crerar wrote to General A. G. L. McNaughton, commanding the Canadian troops in Britain, the 'pressure of public opinion' to 'get on with the war' had developed to such an extent that National Defence was going in all directions at the maximum possible speed.[24] One sign of this was the NRMA. Crerar believed that the government's program of compulsory military training 'was a very superficial scheme', but he felt it was already too late to change its basis. In his opinion all that could be done in such a short period of training and with such a shortage of modern weapons was to make the men 'military-minded'.[25]

Before any of the 30-day soldiers could appear, the national registration had to be held. This was a task that fell to the Department of National War Services under J. G. Gardiner, also King's Minister of Agriculture. The registration was under the control of a Chief Registration Officer, appointed on 9 July, and the regulations called for a registrar to be appointed in each federal election district with two deputy registrars in each polling division. In effect the same organization as that used in the 26 March general election was employed again, the sitting Member of Parliament even nominating the Registrar and Assistant Registrars for his constituency, and the Chief Electoral Officer changing titles to become the Chief Registration Officer. The Governor-in-Council in two Privy Council Orders (P.C. 3086 of 9 July and P.C. 3156 of 12 July) called on all Canadian men and women over 16 to register during the period 19-21 August. Provision was also made for registration of those turning 16 at future dates.

Earlier Gardiner had announced that only men wed on or before 15 July 1940 would be considered married men under the terms of the

NRMA, and there were an unusual number of July weddings as a result. Nonetheless there was still a substantial number of single men and childless widowers between 19 and 45:[26]

PEI	6,664
NS	40,110
NB	29,200
PQ	234,241
Ont	251,570
Man	53,558
Sask	70,023
Alta	61,766
BC	55,326
	802,458

These 800,000 men (a figure that did not include those already enlisted in the three services) formed the basic manpower pool out of which Canada's armed forces would be found.

The registration was conducted in a general atmosphere of calm and resignation. The solitary major incident that marred the process was a statement by Mayor Camillien Houde of Montreal on 2 August. The ebullient, corpulent Houde declared himself against the national registration, calling it 'unequivocally a measure of conscription'.[27] The federal government over-reacted, slapped censorship restrictions on the Mayor's statement, and promptly seized Houde and shipped him off to internment. Surprisingly there was no great outburst in Quebec at these draconian measures. Le Devoir observed that he had acted like a fool and deserved what he received; and La Presse remarked on the Mayor's defiance of authority, noting that this shocked law-abiding Canadiens.[28] The absence of response probably did indicate that Québécois were willing to do everything possible to defend Canada; it did little to show any regard for civil liberties in Quebec—or Canada.

Preparations for the call-up continued. Recruiting for the Non-Permanent Active Militia, the peacetime militia organization of the country, had come to an end on 15 August 1940. Thereafter entry to NPAM units was to be open only to men who had undergone their 30 days' training, and every 30-day soldier was automatically deemed to be a member of the NPAM unit nearest his home. At the end of July there were only 47,343 men still serving in the NPAM, but by the end of August, even before any conscripts had reported for training, there were 107,219 all ranks.[29] Clearly a substantial part of the increase must have occurred when young men joined the NPAM to avoid any stigma

arising from their being made to undergo compulsory service. Colonel
J. L. Ralston, named Minister of National Defence on 5 July, had tried to
deal with the supposed 'shame' of being conscripted when he told Parliament,

> I should like to stress again that all these members of the non-
> permanent active militia, whether they have been enlisted or called
> for training, are to be regarded on exactly the same basis. Training is
> being given so that they may be ready and able to defend their
> country. The call for training is a summons to the highest service
> which any citizen can render. They are all Canadian soldiers...
> there will be no distinction between them.[30]

But the distinctions would be there and over the course of the war they
would grow and solidify, eventually coming close to destroying the
Liberal government.

To select the men for training the government created 13 administrative divisions across the country. Each divisional registrar was responsible to the Minister of National War Services in Ottawa for selecting the
trainees from the men registered in his district. The original plan was
to train 240,000 men annually, 30,000 in each of eight 30-day training
periods. The registrars were instructed to begin with single men in the
21-24 age group and to requisition enough men to meet their quotas
after medical rejections. Unfortunately medical examinations were left
to any practitioner to do. Busy doctors, not always interested in the $1
fee for each recruit, sometimes used their own judgement. If they
thought a borderline case would benefit from healthy outdoor living,
he was passed. After reporting at training centres, however, the conscripts were examined yet again by army doctors and thousands more
were rejected. In the three classes that reported for 30-day training, the
statistics were as follows:[31]

	Men Reported	Rejected	Trained
1st	27,559	2,092	25,507
2nd	30,904	2,604	28,300
3rd	30,623	2,552	28,071
	89,086	7,248	81,878

Provision was also made for exemptions from service and for defer-
ments. As had been the case throughout the long series of Militia Acts
since Confederation and before, judges, clergymen, RCMP, provincial
policemen, municipal police, firemen, and prison and mental asylum
workers were automatically exempted from call-up. In addition neither

Doukhobors, Mennonites, nor conscientious objectors were liable for service.[32] Each man was told at the time he received his order to report for medical examination that an application could be made to have his military training postponed. Such applications, made in writing within 8 days (later 14 days) to the division registrar, were heard by a National War Service Board, one or more of which were established under a judge in each of the 13 areas. Except for farmers, who could be given postponements until further notice, no postponement order could be issued for more than six months. Extensions could be granted, but a Board had the right to cancel postponement orders at any time.[33]

The NRMA soldiers were to be trained in 39 militia training centres scattered across the country and located close to the NPAM regiments for which they were to provide reserves. Camps varied in size and, according to population density, had one to four training companies. By deliberate policy, decentralization was encouraged—local pride and local business both would benefit from having the men trained close to home. Administrative and training staffs came from the nearby NPAM units.[34]

All across Canada men reported for the first 30-day training period on 9 October 1940. The atmosphere in the camps was generally good, and morale was high. The training focused on competition between individuals in events such as athletics and rifle marksmanship, and proficiency was rewarded with suitable ceremony. In fact the army saw its task being not so much to train soldiers—everyone knew that 30 days was too little time for this—as to 'sell' the military way of life.[35] Books were provided, movies screened, and the instructors demonstrated a camaraderie that was not usually found among drill sergeants as a class. The 'compulsory training recruits', as they were known, seemed to agree that 'the time had been well spent, from the standpoint of health, education and downright fun', or so said the Toronto *Globe and Mail*.[36] The second batch of trainees reported on 22 November and the third on 10 January 1941. The same atmosphere prevailed throughout, and the Toronto area registrar actually issued a statement to the press just prior to the third group's service date that 'Trainees reporting Friday are urged to bring along any basketball or badminton equipment they have available'.*[37]

---

*On the other hand at least one observer was impressed with the military value of the training, feeling it produced better results than the three-month CASF course in some units, and certainly better results than the NPAM annual training periods of past years. (PAC, W. L. M. King Papers, Extracts from Report of Maj.-Gen. J. W. H. T. Pope, encl. with Ralston to King, 3 Nov. 1940, ff. 249027.)

The 30-day scheme was clearly a stop-gap, and even the defence made of it in the House of Commons by the Minister of National Defence was curiously circular and definitely lukewarm. The recruits, Ralston told Parliament, 'have had the benefit of what is probably the most effective and efficient course of basic training that has ever been furnished to the men of this country in thirty days time.' As the only 30-day courses in basic training in the country's history were those run for the NRMA men, the Minister was certainly correct.[38] Worse, no one had any idea how—or if—the men called up for training were to be incorporated eventually into the armed forces. A survey of the conscripts showed that some 20,000, or roughly one-quarter of the men trained, were considering military service,[39] itself an indication that the war was still not taken very seriously by Canadians, even after the disasters of the summer of 1940. Incredibly there was no system for taking enlistments in the 30-day camps, nor was there any attempt to preserve lists of those who had expressed interest. And although there was a *pro forma* attachment of the men to NPAM units, there was no system for ensuring that the men reported for the weekly training sessions.

The slapdash inefficiency that marked the 30-day scheme cannot easily be justified, although it can be explained. In the first place there was little or no equipment. 'Thirty days' training was all I wanted, initially', General Crerar, the Chief of the General Staff, later recalled, 'because all we could train with were U.S. rifles of last war vintage— and no ammunition.'[40] What the scheme was intended to do, and what it did do to some extent, as General E. L. M. Burns later wrote, was to persuade 'the public that determined action was being taken to defend Canada, and . . . that young men were obliged to serve in the armed forces.'[41]

Crerar indicated his agreement with this concept in a memorandum he sent his minister on 3 September 1940, a full month before the first group of conscripts reported. 'We should assert the principle and put it into practice that men may be compelled to serve for the defence of Canada in this hemisphere. . . . Once this principle is established, a detailed plan of organization for the Canadian Army can be built up, but if home defence and training for it are left mainly on the voluntary, part time militia basis, no sound system of defence can be organized.'*

---

*In private Gen. Crerar was more outspoken. 'He was particularly angry about the national training scheme,' Grant Dexter wrote privately after an interview, 'which as a military policy was very costly and completely useless. Of what possible utility could it be to train men

But Crerar argued, carrying the concept further, 'Individual training requires 4 months, collective training a further 6 months continuously, thus the programme contemplated under the National Resources Mobilization scheme ... will be inadequate. We don't need the number of men [for] which those schemes cater, but we require a longer and more thorough training for a smaller number of men.'[42] These arguments apparently proving unavailing, Crerar wrote his minister again three weeks later. 'The power of the modern army,' the CGS said, trying a new tack,

> resides in its arms and equipment—not in the number of men in its ranks. Our first objective in military organization must then be *to produce the arms and equipment we need* for our Army. In the unhappy event of the defeat of the United Kingdom, production of arms on this continent would be absolutely vital; we cannot defend Canada by masses of half-trained men with a variety of rifles in their hands. Therefore at this stage nothing in the way of military training should be allowed to interfere with production.[43]

What the General Staff wanted, as a minimum, was a four-month training scheme for conscripts, a reduction in the total number to be called, and the transfer of the trainees to the home-defence formations of the active army.[44]

Others were arguing similarly. J. G. Gardiner, the minister responsible for producing the conscripts through his National War Services Department, told the Prime Minister that industry was more important than half-trained non-soldiers.[45] In the Senate the former Prime Minister, Arthur Meighen, was raising similar queries, although in a more vitriolic fashion. What was the point in defending Canada, he asked, when the only defence lay in a strong Britain? The NRMA scheme, he said later, was a 'colossal waste' that would produce nothing except 'half-trained ... hot-house soldiers'.[46]

All these criticisms had their effect, and the government moved slowly to deal with them. On 1 October 1940 the Cabinet War Committee began its consideration of the army program for 1941, a plan prepared by General Crerar and calling for a corps of three divisions and a tank brigade overseas by spring 1941, and for the next few months there was sharp debate around the Council table. One point occasioned little debate, however. On 3 October the Committee agreed

---

for 30 days? None. We now had in Canada a direct conflict in policy—compulsion at home, voluntary enlistment for overseas. These were mutually destructive.' (Queen's University, Grant Dexter Papers, Memorandum, 13 Sept. 1940.)

that the 30-day scheme was causing too much dislocation to industry and it determined that postponements henceforth could be given to key workers in war industry. On 31 October and again on 4 December tentative approval seems to have been given to a four-month compulsory scheme, but the argument about the form of this training continued.* Not until 28 January 1941 was the army program agreed to, accompanied by Mackenzie King's warning that the country should not undertake too much. The total cost of the 1941 military program was fixed at a maximum of $1.3 billion, and it included a four-month compulsory training plan, subject to Ernest Lapointe's carefully stated proviso that such a plan could not be construed as a prelude to conscription for overseas service. A proclamation to this effect was published on 20 February and henceforth men at age 21 were liable to four months' training.[47] Only three classes of 30-day men had been called in all.

The new scheme would have major implications. Under its terms both the four-month conscripts and active-force recruits would train together. The trainees, Colonel Ralston told Parliament on 11 March 1941, would be known as 'A' recruits – those who had volunteered for overseas service – and 'R' recruits – those conscripted under the NRMA. 'A' and 'R' recruits would work together in the same platoons through basic and advanced training and would receive the same pay and allowances. Upon completing this training 'A' recruits would become eligible for further specialist training until posting to an 'active' unit in Canada or overseas; 'R' recruits, on the other hand, would be posted back to their nearest reserve unit. A total of 10,000 men each month would enter the training stream, roughly divided into equal numbers of volunteers and conscripts.[48] The first 4,668 'R' recruits reported for their training on 24 March 1941.

The problem was that 'A' recruits were starting to dwindle in number. Although almost 200,000 men had enlisted for service anywhere to that point, nearly 7,000 fewer men had enlisted in the first three months of 1941 than were needed to complete reinforcement pools. Whether men were still there or not, simply biding their time as civilians before enlistment, was a bit unclear; Ottawa really did not

---

*'Apart from the Army Programme for overseas,' Gen. Crerar wrote to McNaughton, 'the other principal issue which required, firstly, to be sold to the Minister and then to the Cabinet, was the changeover from one month to four months compulsory training. That took quite as much work and argument ... no doubt because there were more local angles to it.' (PAC, A. G. L. McNaughton Papers, CC7/Crerar/6, Crerar to McNaughton, 4 Mar. 1941.)

know, and there had as yet not been a sustained national recruiting drive to try to determine this, nor would there be one before May 1941. This fact notwithstanding, the shortage worried the defence planners, who hit upon the obvious solution of retaining the NRMA conscripts in service not for four months but for the duration of the war, thus releasing overseas volunteers from home-defence units and freeing them for service with the growing Canadian army overseas. On 26 April, just a month after the extension of the NRMA scheme to four months, this alteration was announced by the Minister of National Defence, the Cabinet War Committee having approved it on 23 April.[49] 'R' soldiers then in training would be retained in the service as 'members (home defence)' of the Canadian Army for coast defence or internal security duties.*

The government presented this change to the nation as a natural development in government policy, not at all as a response to emergency conditions. It was also implied that the policy might apply only to the 9,830 men expected to complete their four months' training in July and August 1941.[50] This last was left vague, deliberately so because the numbers of 21-year-olds were dwindling fast and because the success of organized national recruiting remained to be discovered.

Reaction to the extension of service for the NRMA conscripts was generally favourable in the press, English-language newspapers seeing this as a long overdue step. The response of the NRMA men affected was also much as expected. Many applied instantly for a postponement, others transferred to the active force, while the remainder reluctantly persuaded themselves that service in the home-defence army might not be too bad.[51]

The response from the Opposition in Parliament was less enthusiastic. Although the Conservative Party itself was still nominally committed to a policy of opposition to conscription for overseas service, this line was becoming increasingly difficult to maintain. In the party caucus the rural members, remembering the attitudes of their constitutents after 1917, remained in general steadfastly opposed to compulsory service, while the metropolitan representatives, more exposed to the

---

*'The decision to retain the "trainees" in the Service for an indefinite period after they have finished their 4 months in the Training Centres has been well received...' General Crerar wrote. 'All these rather represent several bites at the cherry – the cherry being conscription for service anywhere. On the other hand, this progressive process is educating the public... and I believe that... the final stage will be taken with a minimum of fuss by all concerned.' (Directorate of History, National Defence Headquarters, H. D. G. Crerar Papers, file 958.009 (D12), Crerar to McNaughton, 19 May 1941.)

pressures of the press and an articulate public opinion, were more vociferous in supporting the measure. One of the most vehement city members was Herbert Bruce, the Member for Toronto-Parkdale and a former lieutenant-governor of Ontario. In a speech in the House on 12 May, Bruce, stating he spoke only for himself, called upon the government 'to take immediate steps to meet the present urgent situation and make available by a national selective process the men necessary to bring our armed forces up to the strength that represents the fighting might of Canada. We should have the compulsory selective service which was visualized by the sweeping powers of the National Resources Mobilization Act . . . without the hamstringing clause that prevents men who train under that act from being used wherever the need is urgent.' That was about as far as any Conservative dared to go in May 1941, and for his pains Bruce took a good deal of criticism from his colleagues.[52] All the Tories could do given the split in the caucus was, as R. B. Hanson said, 'to manoeuvre the position so the Liberals will have to adopt conscription.' The time as yet was not opportune for a more forthright policy, Hanson said. 'My own view is in favour of conscription but I cannot carry the rank and file of the Party in the House with me and it is useless to take this step without that unanimity. . . .'[53]

While the Conservatives agonized over conscription, the first national recruiting campaign was beginning. On 11 May Colonel Ralston opened the drive with a nation-wide radio address, and on 15 May Ernest Lapointe spoke to Quebec. The radio, the press, the billboards were all employed in a professionally conceived and co-ordinated advertising campaign that stressed the theme of service in 'Canada's Mechanized Army'. Local citizens' committees were created in the cities to work with recruiting officers, and, in conjunction with the Victory Loan drive, a 'Victory Torch was dedicated and carried across Canada.'[54]

Despite the drum-beating, the campaign began with near-glacial slowness. Recruiting was very slow indeed, Ralston admitted to the press, adding that there was less glamour in this war than in the Great War and that a passerby could stroll the streets of Ottawa without realizing there was a war on.[55] The recruiting problem was compounded because Canadian troops thus far had not been involved in any fighting. The solitary experience of war for the army had been the rather inglorious (but fortunate) effort of the 1st Division in embarking for France in June 1940, unloading its equipment, and then heading back to England just ahead of the blitzkrieg. This was not the stuff of which recruiting campaigns were made, and potential volunteers asked why they should give up their jobs in industry or agriculture, also vital to the war, when the army was not fighting. In addition the RCAF had a long waiting list of volunteers, thousands of young men having learned a lesson from their fathers' experiences in the infantry in the 1914-18 war.

All this concerned the Cabinet War Committee as the first discouraging reports of the recruiting campaign trickled in. Already there had been some minor conscriptionist rumblings from Ralston, including his statement on 23 April that although conscription did seem impossible from the point of view of national unity, 'it might be the proper policy to meet the whole situation'.[56]   Again on 9 May the question came up in Committee, when Mackenzie King insisted that his colleagues not countenance conscription. 'All were agreed to that,' the Prime Minister wrote in his diary, 'Ralston merely asking that conscription . . . not be barred wholly should situations later arise. Lapointe stated he, of course, would not stay in the government. Gardiner also stated he would have to leave if there were conscription. . . .'[57]

Perhaps the recruiting drive could be made to work, however, if the army overseas could get into action. On 20 May Ralston told his colleagues in the Cabinet War Committee that the lack of fighting 'accounted for the degree of apathy evidenced by the public as regards the war efforts and prevented enthusiasm being aroused . . .'[58] King was appalled to hear his ministers seemingly advocating fighting for the sake of fighting, deaths for the sake of recruiting publicity purposes,[59] but the result was a Cabinet War Committee decision to telegraph Churchill reaffirming the government's willingness to have Canadian troops serve in any theatre.[60]

In addition the recruiting drive was increased in tempo. The Prime Minister himself launched a speaking tour of the West on 24 June, and for the next three weeks he travelled by rail throughout the Prairies and British Columbia urging men to come forward. In some cities, Calgary in particular, there was an organized effort to press for conscription now, and there was a concerted attempt in the Opposition press to paint the recruiting drive as a total failure, the only remedy being compulsion.[61]

The doomsayers notwithstanding, the campaign did meet its objectives. The projected quota was 32,434 men; enlistments were 34,625. Over 48,000 men had come forward during the two-month-long drive, but 14,000 had been rejected for medical or other reasons. During the same period the RCAF had signed up over 12,000, while the Navy had enlisted about 3,500.[62] At the same time a Directorate of Army Recruiting was established to capitalize on such continuing enthusiasm as might remain from the drive.[63]

There was one additional result that sprang from the slow start of the recruiting drive. The training camps needed their quotas of men, and when the flow of recruits slowed, additional numbers had to be summoned under the terms of the NRMA. These men and their fellows soon found themselves the subject of appeals to 'convert' from 'R' status to 'A'. Previously the expectation had been that simply mixing the volunteers and the conscripts could acclimatize the 'R' men and lead them to volunteer. But with the seeming shortage of recruits and with the four-month training scheme drawing to its end, the Adjutant-General telegraphed the District Officers Commanding on 5 July to point out the 'Great opportunity to obtain 'R' recruits for active service at this time when those completing four months will otherwise be going to coast defence or other home service units.'[64] From this point on pressures of various kinds began to be exerted on the NRMA men.

The actions taken depended on the local commanders, but it seems clear that in the training camps some commanders harangued men unmercifully en masse or singly. Others promised passes for entire training platoons if every 'R' man converted to active duty. The pressures were very great indeed, and many men succumbed. Those who did not bore a grudge of monumental proportions, and when crisis arose in the fall of 1944 these men had no inclination whatsoever to assist.

Ralph Allen, war correspondent and later editor of *Maclean's*, wrote about this kind of pressure in two novels, *Homemade Banners* and *The High White Forest*. Both employ many of the same characters and scenes, and although the setting is imaginary, the ring of verisimilitude is clear:

> . . . it was a hard, mean game all of them were playing. At Camp Salute . . . there was at first no hostility between the R-men and the A-men, or even anything that could be called coolness. Since most R, or reserve, men went A, or active, within a week or two anyway there was, in most cases, no occasion for it.
>
> But later the climate of their ninety man hut came to be as carefully and expertly managed as though it were controlled by a thermostat. The visible differences between the R-men and the A-men began to achieve some importance. . . . An active soldier wore the cap badge of the corps to which he would soon be posted . . . A

reserve soldier wore a non-committal maple leaf. An active soldier had badges saying Canada on his shoulders and the ribbon of the Canadian Volunteer Service Medal on his chest. A reserve soldier had nothing on his shoulders and nothing on his chest. . . .

Almost every day two or three of the R-men were fallen out of the squad and told to report to the company commander's office. Sometimes they returned looking virtuous and a little sheepish, avoiding the anxious glances of the other R-men. Sometimes they were sullen and defiant. . . .

'. . . If good old Number Nine platoon can show a one-hundred-percent-active roster by Thursday night [the company commander said in a speech to the platoon] the whole platoon will go out on seventy-two-hour passes on Friday morning and I am confident. It just means all pulleen together and talkeen it over among yourselves. I know that some of you, perhaps for what seem to you good personal reasons, haven't been as fast as the rest to decide about goeen active, but I know that no man in Number Nine would want to deprive his whole platoon of the last leave they'll be getteen for a long time. . . . So talk it over among yourselves and pull together among youselves, this is your own decision and it's none of the business of your officers and NCOs. And after all that's the British way, the way that means so much to all of us.'

As Allen describes it, that speech set an entire platoon to beating up and verbally abusing the hold-out 'R' men. In the end, the platoon took its leave together, all having caved in.[65]

Nor did the pressures end when NRMA soldiers were posted to coast-defence formations or to other home-defence formations. Small numbers of the conscripts would be drafted into units where they suffered both as outsiders and as conscripts. Often coming directly into a regimental formation, the NRMA troops found themselves treated as pariahs who neither shared the regiment's spirit nor its desire to proceed overseas eventually as a unit. In the Canadian Scottish regiment, for example, the regimental historian noted, 'generally the H[ome]. D[efence]. men were received with reservations on the one hand and yet as potential G[eneral]. S[ervice]. men on the other. The volunteers could not and did not appreciate the arguments advanced by the H.D. men as to why they did not choose to fight overseas. . . . [their] reasons were brushed aside by the volunteers with contempt and some talked openly of cowardice'.[66]

The NRMA soldiers' lot was not a happy one. And yet despite the pressures exerted by their volunteer comrades in arms and their officers, most of the NRMA men resisted. In the first three groups of four-month trainees, 64, 63, and 57 per cent respectively completed their training as 'R' recruits. In addition a further 19, 14 and 18 per cent of these classes were lost to the RCAF and the RCN. Army headquarters thereafter estimated that 60 per cent of the 'R' recruits would continue indefinitely as members (Home Defence) of the army, 20 per cent would volunteer for overseas service and 20 per cent would transfer to the air force or navy.[67]

This percentage of men going active was not going to be sufficient, for the army brass had expansive plans. By the fall of 1941 Canada had completed the program approved in January and had an overseas army of three infantry divisions, an army tank brigade, and various supporting units. The military wanted more—a total force of five divisions organized into two corps. General Crerar, firing the first shots in the military's offensive, wrote to Colonel Ralston on 29 September:

> It is important that plans for the expansion of the Canadian Army should be such as can be implemented with our present system of voluntary enlistment for overseas service. On the other hand, within whatever restrictions may be imposed upon army expansion by the availability of manpower and other limiting factors, it is essential, from the military point of view that Canada provide the maximum force overseas that it is possible to organize and maintain. It is certain that the land forces of the British Empire can never reach such numbers that we will become overinsured in that respect. And it is eminently desirable that we should now tentatively explore the various alternatives for providing a larger and more offensively effective Army overseas. . . .[68]

Crerar's successor as Chief of the General Staff, General Kenneth Stuart, put the final details on the plan, the army program for 1942-3, and it was brought to the Cabinet War Committee on 2 December 1941.

The next day discussion on the army proposals began in earnest. The Prime Minister, bereft of his French-Canadian lieutenant after Ernest Lapointe's death on 26 November, saw himself as the main bulwark against conscription, and he was as a result understandably leery of proposals for a larger army. Such schemes required reinforcements in huge numbers, and there were too few men left in the country to satisfy the ever-expanding demands of the three services and war industry. The whole army scheme, King wrote after a morning spent reading the proposals, 'is based on the assumption that recruiting as of a certain period can be maintained up till March 1943, this notwithstanding that it is known that there has been already increasing difficulty in keeping recruiting up to earlier standards and that it is bound to become more difficult as time goes on.'[*][69] This was true enough. The army's manpower needs for the four months after the recruiting campaign ended in July had been some 37,000; but only 24,000 men had enlisted.[70]

As a result, before the War Committee met, King took the highly unusual step for him of setting down his thoughts on the army demands in a memorandum.

> If the military authorities can give reasonable assurance that, by any plans that can be devised, or arrangements made short of conscription for overseas service, and the Minister of Finance is prepared, along with other commitments, to assure the War Committee that in his opinion it would be possible to have the armed forces overseas so increased without creating in itself a situation which will make impossible the raising, by taxation, war loans or other means, the revenues necessary for the purpose, I shall be prepared . . . to support the programme . . .
>
> In other words, it would be impossible for me . . . to sanction in advance any programme which would be in the nature of committing the country by the government itself to a policy of conscription for overseas service.[71]

The Prime Minister's memorandum provoked the Minister of National Defence to say to the War Committee that he could not be certain if conscription would become necessary, but if it was the government should support it. Later in the discussions, the Chief of the General Staff was summoned to the Council Chamber. 'Was this the last demand the army would make?' King asked. It was. 'He did not think there would have to be a further demand on Canada so far as the army was concerned.' Could the program's targets be met without resort to compulsory service? Stuart replied that 'the programme had been worked out so as to fit into the government's policy of voluntary enlistment for overseas. That is what the staff had aimed at, had worked for, and what he believed could be accomplished in that way.'

---

*In the fall of 1941 the Black Watch in Montreal ran an elaborate recruiting campaign at the expense of regimental funds, and found only 50 recruits. 'It was beginning to appear that the youth of the country would not continue to volunteer in large numbers without a more direct indication from the Government at Ottawa of the needs of the armed forces, and an assurance that all who were fit would be obliged to serve', or so said the regimental historian. P. P. Hutchison, *Canada's Black Watch 1862-1962* (Montreal, 1962), p. 209.

Were there enough reinforcements to meet the needs of the army once it became involved in battle? Yes, Stuart replied, enough to cover the 'foreseeable circumstances'.[72] In spite of himself, King was impressed by Stuart's straightforward responses, and from this moment King's eventual support for the army program was guaranteed. His other colleagues were less satisfied. T. A. Crerar, the Minister of Mines and Resources, continued to tell the War Committee that too much emphasis was being placed on the military and too little on production, a view that C. D. Howe, the Minister of Munitions and Supply, certainly shared.

But with King's still tentative support now assured, the military would get the big army it wanted. And when the Cabinet as a whole approved the proposal on 6 January 1942, the generals were exultant. General Stuart told Grant Dexter of the *Winnipeg Free Press* on 12 January 'with the greatest satisfaction' that this was 'absolutely all' the army wanted. 'This is the kind of army a soldier dreams of commanding, hard hitting, beautifully balanced, incredibly powerful. It was, for example, an army which could beat Rommel in Libya.' Dexter added that he expected King to tell the Canadian people that this was all the army that the generals wanted. The problem, the reporter added with his usual perspicacity, 'will be one of reinforcements—not new units'.[74]

Dexter was correct, but the problems with reinforcements would take some time to arise. What was certain, however, was that a crucial decision had been taken and Canada was now committed to maintaining a large army, possibly one larger than the country could support. Given the enormous scope of the industrial and agricultural effort, an army of five divisions plus the thousands of ancillary troops, as well as a very large air force and a substantial navy would be exceedingly difficult to maintain. In retrospect, it is clear that the conscription crisis of 1944 became almost a certainty with this decision.

By the time the army program was finally approved, however, the complexion of the war had altered irrevocably. With Japan's entry into the war on 7 December 1941, the struggle had truly become a global conflict, and there would be new political and military pressures with which the King government would have to contend.

III

The surprise Japanese assault on Pearl Harbour, the Philippines, Hong Kong, and other British and American possessions in the East finally brought the United States into the war. American participation meant eventual victory for the Allied cause and that thought heartened everyone. But Japan's entry to the war simultaneously heightened the demands for an increased war effort and altered its focus in Canada. The new situation almost forced Canada to do more in this world war. But at the same time the Japanese threat to the West Coast increased the demand for troops for home defence. Those NRMA men, hitherto scorned by the super-patriots, could now be seen as a wise precaution and the zealous conscriptionists as those who were willing to sacrifice Canada to save Britain. The entire problem had increased in complexity.

The Cabinet was forced to grapple with this new situation, but so too was the Conservative Party. Once again the Tories began to gird themselves for a frontal assault on the King government and its policies of military service and one-party government. At the head of the attack would be Arthur Meighen, the Prime Minister's most feared and most detested opponent, and the one man who symbolized the mentality of English Canada at War. Or so, at least, French Canada perceived it.

Isolated in the Senate at the beginning of the war, Meighen had quietly fumed as events unfolded. He had been enraged when King insisted on a separate Canadian declaration of war, furious at the Ogdensburg agreement, outraged by the half-measures taken under the NRMA. But he had kept silent in public, saying nothing and loyally following the lead of R. B. Hanson, the cautious Tory leader in the Commons.

This did not mean that Meighen was inactive. He kept up a vast correspondence with like-minded men across the nation and with his old cronies who increasingly were coming to the conviction that conscription was necessary because this appeared the only way Quebec could be made to do its share. In a sense Meighen seemed to be forced back to this position—his and his government's during the Great War. He had consciously tried to widen his outlook in the interwar years, and in March 1939 he had even written a French-speaking militia officer that 'Personally I have never felt that one could naturally expect as generous a recruitment among our French-Canadian population as would take place among our English-speaking population.' The reasons, Meighen acknowledged, were the closer links of Anglo-Saxons to the Mother Country. 'I think now, as I have always thought, that there should be a measure of tolerance based upon this consideration among all our English-speaking citizens'.[75]

But this tolerance in Meighen and others like him was worn away by two years of defeats in Europe, and by mid-1941 if not sooner Meighen was again wholeheartedly in favour of compulsory service. His own calculations suggested to him that French Canadians were not volunteering in anything like comparable numbers to their English-speaking fellow countrymen:[76]

Quebec population (1939 est.)	3,210,000	(Quebec's is 85.5% of Ontario's)
Ontario population (1939 est.)	3,752,000	

As of 31 October 1941

Ontario voluntary enlistments	147,114	
Quebec share (85.5%)	125,783	
Quebec actual	61,247	(48.7% share)
Ontario overseas troops	89,618	
Quebec share (85.5%)	76,624	
Quebec actual	34,293	(44% share)

To Meighen these figures were near-conclusive proof that conscription had to come.

The former Prime Minister's figures were, in fact, fairly close to the best official estimates. A calculation made in June 1941 put French-Canadian enlistments at 60 per cent of English-speaking enlistments in per capita terms.[77] But there were reasons for this, best canvassed in letters by Ernest Lapointe to Colonel Ralston and in subsequent studies undertaken in the Colonel's department.

To Lapointe, one of the difficulties was a lack of able officers in the Quebec military district. 'In Quebec,' he wrote, 'we have been cursed for years with military chiefs who know nothing about the rank and file of the people, had no contact with them and have bungled the situation in the most deplorable way.'[78] Another was the anti-*Québécois* attitude that in his view permeated the General Staff. In a letter to Ralston in August 1941 he conveyed information he had learned: 'I hate the sight of French-Canadians,' one general was said to have remarked. 'None of them should go over the rank of Lt. -Col.' Lapointe said that this seemed unbelievable to him, 'but knowing the mentality of many Tories in Canada I am compelled to think that this is genuine.'[74] In this particular instance the facts may have been false, but the attitude that Lapointe feared was certainly present at headquarters and in the ranks. Intelligence reports on attitudes in home-based units showed widespread prejudice directed at French Canadians—and also at Jews and other minorities.[80]

How this problem could be met tended to bedevil the military. It was easy enough to suggest translating training manuals into French page by page, or putting able journalists into the army's public relations posts. It was simple to advocate working with the hierarchy and the Primate or to suggest a French-Canadian brigade.[81] But in the military's view such suggestions overlooked key factors. General Crerar, for example, wrote to Ralston about one such difficulty:

> ... I am fully seized with the importance of increasing to a proportionate basis French-Canadian representation on Staff and in Command. It is a problem which cannot be quickly solved, however, because the civil educational system of Quebec does not tend to produce in equivalent numbers to English-speaking Canada, the 'officer-type' so essential to the purpose. As a result not only is the supply of prospective officers restricted, but difficulties in language make higher military qualifications a more lengthy process.[82]

Nor did it seem a solution to have a unilingually French-officer training camp. The Director of Military Training, sounding very much like General Currie in 1918, told his superiors that the officers had to fight together eventually so they had better learn to co-operate early on.[83] Unfortunately, to French Canadians, co-operation seemed to be a one-way street, requiring the virtual abandonment of their language.

Worse yet, even the Minister of National Defence sometimes seemed to be less than sympathetic to the problems faced by French Canadians. His department tended to view the *Québécois* as technically backward, and thus unsuited for the more demanding jobs in the RCAF, RCN, or the technical corps of the army. This posed a problem, forcing the French Canadians into the front-line units, a fact raised with the Minister by the Master General of the Ordnance, Victor Sifton, late of the Sifton newspaper chain. 'When Victor pointed [this] out,' Grant Dexter of the *Winnipeg Free Press* wrote in a private memorandum after a conversation with Sifton, 'Ralston protested. The army would not have masses of Quebeckers under any conditions: they would not be able to do anything with them. There is only limited room in our army for these men. They can't speak English. We have no French Canadian officers to handle them. Their fighting ability is questionable etc. etc.'[84] This is hearsay and has to be treated with caution. But if Ralston ever did express such views, even in heat, his staff officers must have believed that their attitudes were sanctioned.

Arthur Meighen may or may not have been aware of the attitude of the military. If he was, this probably affected his determination to act, and by the late fall of 1941 the opportunity seemed at hand. The Conservatives had scheduled a party meeting at Ottawa to select the date and place for a national-leadership convention designed to find a permanent successor to the ill-fated Manion and the temporary leadership of Hanson. For a variety of reasons, but largely out of a belief that conscription was an idea whose time had come, a small group of Conservatives, aided greatly by a substantial publicity drive launched by the Toronto *Globe and Mail*, determined to use the meeting to select a leader then and there. The ideal man was Arthur Meighen.[85]

The former leader was probably a party to the attempt to push the Conservatives along faster than the conference planners had intended; it was certain, however, that he did not want the leadership himself. Nonetheless when the gathering turned to him, when appeals were made, 'I became convinced,' Meighen wrote, 'and certainly my wife became convinced, that I would lose what respect and regard the people felt for me if in the full light of day...I refused to try to do the one thing I can do, if, indeed, there is anything I can do, entirely well...'[86] His decision reached, Meighen came out full blast on 13 November with a statement demanding an end to one-party government and for conscription.[87]

Meighen's return let loose the pro-conscriptionists. All the restraint that had marked the press and people of English Canada fell away, and over the course of the next three months the language and passion escalated. In December the Manitoba legislature unanimously passed a resolution calling for conscription; in January the Liberal Premier of New Brunswick, J. B. McNair, endorsed compulsion. And in Toronto 200 prominent citizens met at a carefully orchestrated meeting on 10 January 1942 to demand 'Total War Now'. The 'Toronto 200', as they became known, particularly in Quebec, placed full-page advertisements in every daily and weekly newspaper in Ontario and deliberately attempted to shape a public opinion favourable to conscription, to a coalition government—and to Arthur Meighen.[88]

That there was a sense of unease in the nation was certain, and the press and publicity campaign fed it and fed on it. But whether this unease was widespread and shared by all Canadians was less clear; indeed, opinion polls taken by the Canadian Institute of Public Opinion in late 1941 suggest otherwise. When asked shortly before Pearl Harbor if they were satisfied with Canada's war effort 61 per cent indicated they were and only 35 per cent indicated dissatisfaction;

54 per cent of Conservatives, surprisingly, were satisfied—and this was at least two weeks after Meighen's return to the leadership. Respondents also approved of Mackenzie King's leadership, two-thirds of those questioned so indicating. On manpower questions the response was interesting indeed. When asked in mid-December if they would vote for overseas conscription if they had the opportunity, 60 per cent indicated they would while 30 per cent said they would not. But when asked at the same time if Canada's army was large enough, 37 per cent said it was, while only 47 per cent said more men were needed.[89] There was a public opinion in the country to suit every politician's needs.

Nonetheless Meighen's acceptance of the Conservative leadership, coming less than a month before the growing debate in the Cabinet War Committee over the army program for 1942-3 and before Pearl Harbor, put together all the factors necessary to make the first half of 1942 a harrowing time for Mackenzie King. The Prime Minister had repeated his pledges over and over again that his administration would never bring in conscription. Now, however, the Opposition, headed by the one politician whom King feared mightily and detested bitterly, was in full flight, demanding the policy of 1917 again. The Liberal government and, King fervently believed, the country as well faced its greatest crisis thus far in the war.

IV

In such a situation King's every instinct was to seek a way to delay, to allow time for matters to become clearer. The long discussions in the Cabinet about conscription on 9 and 10 December had demonstrated that virtually all the ministers except Ralston, Ilsley, the Finance minister, and Macdonald were, if not completely opposed to conscription, at least prepared to recognize that its introduction would cause enormous difficulties.[90] Delay, here too, would be useful, and fortunately a method to achieve delay was at hand. As early as mid-November[91] King had begun toying with the idea of a plebiscite on the conscription question. If the country were against conscription then a plebiscite, giving every citizen a chance to vote on the question, would make this evident; if, on the other hand, the country wanted compulsory overseas service, then its verdict would provide a way for the government to back off from its pledges that overseas service would never be imposed. Clearly a plebiscite had some real advantages, and for Mackenzie King, pre-eminently a pragmatist, they were obvious. The Prime Minister was not opposed to conscription on ideological grounds. He did not think it unfair or the wrong way to man an army. His objections to it, based on the experience of 1917, were wholly political, and if a way could be found to impose it without dire effects on the body politic, he would do so. But conscription would divide the Cabinet, the caucus, the party, and the country; if it would cause a repetition of the national disaster of 1917, then he would fight it to the end.

Complicating matters was the building panic in British Columbia at the prospect of a Japanese invasion. Few in the military took such a threat very seriously, but the public clamour could not be ignored. One sign of Ottawa's yielding to it was the increasing restrictions placed upon Japanese Canadians and their ultimate dispersion across the country; another was the despatch of more troops to the Pacific coast. An intangible factor, but one that greatly concerned Mackenzie King, was the impact of the Japanese threat on conscriptionist sentiment. Now that there was a threat to Canada, would conscriptionists realize the worth of the government's policy? This was yet another aspect of the considerations that ran through the Prime Minister's mind as he contemplated his course.

Finally on 18 December, after the long discussions about the army program had shortened tempers, King took his courage in his hands and, as Angus L. Macdonald noted, told his ministers that 'this government must be kept in power for the good of the country. Conscription is likely to divide the Government. Therefore let us take a plebiscite and be guided by it.'[92] There were other advantages, too. A plebiscite, introduced with care as to timing, could hit at the Tories and their effort to make conscription the centrepiece of their attack. How, after all, could they object to bringing the question to the people? And the plebiscite could be used directly against Arthur Meighen, who would be leaving his sinecure in the Senate and seeking a seat in the House of Commons in a by-election.

But before these great, good things could come about the entire Cabinet and influential leaders in Quebec would have to be brought to see the wisdom of going to the people. In Cabinet the major obstacle was P. J. A. Cardin, the senior Quebec minister since Lapointe's death. Cardin was a man better known for his devotion to patronage than for his statesmanship, but he now saw himself as the protector of his people, and he remained unmoving for almost a month. Québécois, he believed, could only see a plebiscite on conscription as a sign that the King government was considering a switch in its policy—why else ask the people to release the government from its pledges? But as time passed and as the full dimensions of the growing campaign in English Canada for conscription became evident, Cardin began to waver. There were suggestions that Cardinal Villeneuve had come to accept the idea of a vote, and the Quebec minister was becoming convinced that without a plebiscite or some such action, the result might well be a Meighen-controlled national government. That would be a disaster. In the circumstances Cardin persuaded himself that a plebiscite would be the lesser of two evils, and if Quebec could see the alternatives clearly it might even vote to free the government from its pledges. The Cabinet was now solidly behind King.[93]

The Prime Minister, however, still had his own doubts. As late as 8 January 1942, two days after the army program for 1942-3 had been accepted, King was still torn between simply putting the question of conscription to Parliament or taking a plebiscite. But in the end King decided on the plebiscite because it would allow the government to impose conscription (or not) at its discretion. That, he believed, was the best course, because the views of the majority of the Cabinet would determine policy 'and probably government would find ways and means of holding together to prevent division in country which would destroy war effort. . . . '[94] The decision, as with many of the Prime Minister's, remained tentative right to the last moment, but finally King determined to announce his move in the Speech from the Throne opening the 1942 session of Parliament on 22 January. The final wording of the announcement was thrashed out in three meetings on 19, 20, and 21 January. 'My ministers,' it read, 'accordingly will seek, from the people, by means of a plebiscite, release from any obligations arising out of any past committments restricting methods of raising men for military service.'[95] The date for the plebiscite would eventually be fixed for 27 April.

The reasons for King's decision to hold the plebiscite were not totally complicated. In a long conversation in May with Georges Pelletier of Montreal's *Le Devoir*, no friend to the government, its leader, or its policies, the Prime Minister explained his reasoning:

Il continue en disant qu'en janvier 1942, la situation était en train de devenir la même [as in 1940]. Il était attaqué d'un côté par les conservateurs dans le pays et dans la presse tory de Toronto et d'ailleurs, qui reclamaient tous ensemble la conscription, bien qu'en février et mars 1940, ils n'en voulussent point. D'un autre côté, à la Chambre, M. King se trouvait à avoir affaire à Hanson et à son petit groupe de Tories qui, dit-il, menaçaient de répéter les tactiques de 1940, en même temps que Hepburn et les *Deux Cents* de Toronto insistaient pour avoir un effort de guerre total. De plus, la candidature Meighen était affichée depuis plusieurs semaines; Meighen devait remplacer Hanson comme chef du party tory, et il paraissait impossible d'admettre qu'il fut bon pour le Canada de laisser entrer Meighen à la Chambre. 'J'ai travaillé toute ma vie, dit M. King, pour faire l'accord entre les deux races. On m'a accusé de faire des concessions à Québec, mais, en fait, pour avoir l'accord entre les deux grandes races du pays il faut pratiquer une politique de concessions. Or Meighen, qui est l'âme damnée d'un groupe de Toronto, fanatique et d'esprit très étroit et très égoiste, aurait extrêmement compliqué la situation, à une periode dangereuse, s'il fût entré aux Communes. Je ne pouvais tout de même pas décider de faire des élections générales comme en 1940, pour écraser les adversaires de tous les camps. J'avais déjà fait entendre à Calgary et à Victoria qu'il ne pouvait pas être question de conscription sans un appel au peuple. Or, s'il n'y avait pas d'élection, le seul moyen d'en appeler au peuple c'était un plébiscite. Cela s'imposait, parce que si je n'avais pas annoncé de plébiscite, il y aurait en toutes les chances du monde que Meighen revînt aux Communes et nous aurions alors perdu le temps de la Chambre dans les querelles interminables et des debats extrêmement acerbes et inutiles pour autant; car Meighen est d'une force considérable dans l'invective. . . . En décidant la plébiscite et en l'annoncent avant l'élection de Meighen, j'ai cru que c'était une excellente façon de lui barrer la route. . . .'

The other major factor that concerned King, he told Pelletier, was the force of the pro-conscription argument:

'. . . devant l'insistance de tout un groupe qui réclamait la conscription, j'ai cru et je crois encore que la plébiscite était le meilleur moyen de remettre les choses dans l'état où elles devaient être. En effet, s'il n'y avait pas eu le plébiscite, la campagne en faveur de la conscription de la part des conservateurs et des feuilles tory aurait été en s'accroissant, et elle fût devenue un danger pour le Canada. Je me suis dit que si nous allions devant le peuple avec un plébiscite, nous obtendrions l'avis de la masse des électeurs, la libération de nos promesses de 1939 et qu'ensuite il serait assez facile de démontrer au peuple qu'il n'y avait pas besoin de conscription, pendant plusieurs mois en tout cas, peut-être pas de tout.'[96]

The Prime Minister's reasoning was not unpersuasive with Pelletier; there was to be more difficulty with Quebec.

The French-Canadian members of the Liberal caucus were unhappy with the plebiscite. The press, the Church, notables at all levels—all shared the deep unease at the government's course. The Lieutenant-Governor, Sir Eugene Fiset, for example, told the American Minister in Canada that the average *Québécois* asked himself 'Is it not strange that within a very few weeks of the death of Mr. Lapointe, Mr. King should be asking a release from his solemn pledges?...He is asking for a release from his promise at a time when voluntary enlistments are good and getting better. Ergo, he must be made to feel that the Province is disappointed in his volte-face.'[97] That attitude, however shortsighted it may have been in the face of the Japanese and German successes of early 1942, and however much it may have underestimated the fervour of English Canada, was nonetheless widespread. Even the Liberal Premier of Quebec, Adelard Godbout, could tell a Montreal audience that if he believed conscription was the only way to win the war he would accept it, but 'le service obligatoire pour outre-mer dans le moment, serait un crime...' and in a petulant outburst, directed at some *nationaliste* hecklers, Godbout could even suggest that Mackenzie King agreed with this view.[98] This proved embarrassing to both men.

The plebiscite, however, did have one anticipated effect. Arthur Meighen, running in a by-election in Toronto's York South constituency against a CCF candidate (the Liberals wisely having chosen to honour the longstanding arrangement that party leaders should not be opposed in by-elections), promptly reacted as expected. The plebiscite, he said, left him 'shamed and humiliated by our Government's despicable evasion....It is a base and cowardly insult ...'[99] But the voters in the riding, already being subjected to an intensive CCF door-to-door campaign that stressed social-welfare issues and Meighen's reactionary views on the subject, seemed to respond differently. The plebiscite, they might have said, would give everyone a chance to vote on conscription, so why keep pushing the issue in this by-election? The result of the vote in York South on 9 February, therefore, was a victory for the CCF candidate with a majority of some 4,500 votes out of 28,000 cast. It was also a triumph for Mackenzie King, freed at last of the hated Meighen; whatever the results of the national vote in April, the plebiscite idea had done yeoman service already.[100] If there was any threat to the King government now, it had to come from within the Cabinet or caucus.

The two ministers most upset by the course of events were J. Layton Ralston and Angus Macdonald, both Ministers of National Defence, both Nova Scotians. Neither man could really grasp the reasons for Quebec's hesitancy about accepting conscription for a war that was so evidently a just war, and while both accepted the plebiscite, they wanted to know what would happen once the vote was held. About all they could get from Mackenzie King was a promise that a decision would then be made 'considering everything', the whole country, not Quebec alone. This was not particularly satisfying to either man, and Macdonald came away from an interview with the Prime Minister shrewdly convinced that King's response to the results, whatever they were, would likely be that 'Conscription might give you a few more men here and there, but it would create a terrible situation in the country and consequently will not be worthwhile.'[101]

Macdonald and Ralston did not believe that conscription would create 'a terrible situation', but King, looking at the campaign under way in Quebec against the plebiscite and for a 'non' vote, did. The campaign was brilliantly organized, uniting a sweeping cross-section of French Canada in an umbrella organization called La Ligue pour la défense du Canada. The LPDC sprang from the group of *nationalistes* clustered around the journal *L'Action Nationale* and its editor André Laurendeau. Before the organization was through it encompassed such groups as the Société Saint-Jean-Baptiste, the Montreal Catholic Labour Council, the Voyageurs de Commerce, and farm and youth groups. The chief publicity organ was and remained *Le Devoir*, but a wide variety of handbills, local newspapers, and radio programs was also employed in this massive attempt to organize French Canada.[102]

The essential argument of the LPDC was simple and compelling. Quebec should vote 'non' in the plebiscite because no one asked to be released from a pledge unless he intended breaking that pledge. Furthermore, of all the promises made by the King government, the most important one, the one that King was most obliged to honour, was his pledge not to conscript men for overseas service. In addition, LPDC speakers argued, the pledge against conscription was a pledge made to Quebec alone as part of the bargain under which Canada went to war in 1939. Now all Canada was being asked to release the government from its pledge made to French Canadians. Where was the justice in this?[103]

There was no justice in it, and the LPDC, harassed by Ottawa through its control of the Canadian Broadcasting Corporation and through the Liberal Party's hold on the key newspapers in the province, found receptive ears despite the opposition. In Montreal a poll-by-poll organization was created to spread the message, and in the legislature at Quebec and the Parliament at Ottawa sympathizers moved motions and made speeches denouncing Ottawa's plebiscite and calling on

Quebec to resist. Even Ernest Lapointe, in his grave since November, was summoned forth in LPDC publicity: 'Jamais, Jamais. . . a dit M. Lapointe'; 'L'Honorable Ernest Lapointe a dit: La Conscription Jamais Votons NON'.[104] The result of this campaign was a virtually solid Quebec. In mid-March, according to opinion polls, 79 per cent of Quebec residents opposed conscription, a figure that would have been substantially higher had French-Canadian respondents been separated out; at the end of April, just before the ballot, the figure was higher still, a stunning 81 per cent.*[105]

The solidity of Quebec opinion on this issue was frightening to the government, particularly as its own efforts to mobilize a 'oui' campaign

---

*Opinion polls demonstrated that 54 per cent thought the government wrong to call the plebiscite, 31 per cent that it was correct; 45 per cent thought the plebiscite was designed to free the government from its pledges, 42 per cent thought it a vote for or against conscription. This confusion about the government's aims tended to shape the attitude of respondents. When asked on 20 April, just a few days before the plebiscite, how they would vote, for conscription or against it, only 55 per cent indicated they would vote in favour. But when asked on 1 April how they would vote on the plebiscite, a vote many interpreted as a vote to free the government from its pledges, 62 per cent said they would vote 'yes' and 27 per cent said they would vote 'no'. The results of the questioning on 1 April were correlated by income, by rural or urban living place, and by province:

Overall		By Income Bracket		
		Upper	Middle	Lower
Vote to free	62%	72%	70%	54%
Vote against	27	20	21	34
Undecided	11	8	9	12

By Living Location				
	Farm		Small Town	City
Vote to free	57%		59%	68%
Vote against	29		30	23
Undecided	14		11	9

By Province		For	Against
N.S./P.E.I.		80%	20%
N.B.		65	35
Que.		26	74
Ont.		88	12
Man.		90	10
Sask.		82	18
Alta.		81	19
B.C.		91	9

The undecided were eliminated in the provincial calculations. (Polls in *Public Opinion Quarterly*, VI (Summer, 1942) 312-13, and (Fall, 1942), 488-9.)

in the province had floundered. Part of the problem was simple incompetence at the helm, the Prime Minister having assigned the job of securing a favourable vote to lesser lights in the ministry; part of it, too, was the unwillingness or lack of enthusiasm of Quebec political leaders to go out on a limb and support the campaign in the face of the opposition in the province. About all that could be done was to urge the *Québécois* to put their trust in Mackenzie King: 'AYEZ DONC CONFIANCE EN M. MACKENZIE KING ET VOTEZ OUI le 27 Avril 1942'. 'N'oublions pas,' voters were told, 'que le Gouvernement en général et que tout particulièrement notre premier ministre, dont le sain canadienisme est bien connu, n'ont aucun intérêt à demander au Canada des sacrifices qui ne seraient pas nécessaires.' A different tack was taken by Chubby Power in a pamphlet prepared in French and English for his Quebec South constituents. The government had to be released from its pledges, the Air Minister said, because the situation was 'so serious'. Canada had to 'be ready to do anything and everything to meet whatever comes, and to do it quickly. . . . We have to save our homes and our religion and our right to think and speak and act and live instead of being slaves to Hitler.' Power's approach was more aggressive and forthright than that of the official 'Yes' campaign, but it would be no more successful.[106]

If Quebec did not accept the government's propaganda, one man who appeared to was the Prime Minister. Just before the plebiscite Mackenzie King met with Bruce Hutchison and Grant Dexter, the two star reporters of the Sifton chain and two newsmen with whom King could relax. The Prime Minister repeatedly made cracks at Ralston during the long interview, Dexter's memorandum recorded, and also at the advice proffered by the General Staff. 'I have talked to him again and again,' King said. 'I have asked him not once but many times why he does not tell the generals what we, the cabinet, think instead of continually telling us what the generals thinks [sic]. Generals,' King added, 'are almost invariably wrong.' As for the plebiscite, the prospects were good. 'The people who had opposed the plebiscite so bitterly around Meighen were now . . . supporting it and urging an affirmative vote.' What else, after all, could the Conservatives do? Then in a curious comment, one that revealed the full pragmatic approach of King to the question of conscription, he told the reporters that getting conscription with a united country would be the biggest triumph of the war.*[107]

---

*Earlier King had been drafting a speech with his assistant, J. W. Pickersgill. The latter had

The plebiscite results, however, demonstrated that the two nations of Canada each had their own—and separate—unity. French Canada voted solidly 'non', with Quebec registering 72.9 per cent against the government's request for release from its pledges and with six heavily French-speaking constituencies outside the province doing the same. French Canadians, whether they lived in Prescott or Russell, Ontario, in Provencher, Manitoba, or in the ridings of Gloucester, Restigouche-Madawaska, and Kent in New Brunswick, opposed conscription for overseas. So, too, did many non-Anglo-Saxons. Vegreville, Alberta and Rosthern, Saskatchewan, both heavily ethnic in composition and including large numbers of voters of German and Ukrainian origin, voted no. On the other hand the majorities throughout the rest of the country were huge in support of the government's request for release from its past promises. In Prince Edward Island 82.4 per cent voted 'yes', in Ontario 82.3, in Alberta 70.4, and in New Brunswick, the smallest 'yes' percentage, 69.1.[108] The overall results showed that 2,945,514 Canadians had voted 'yes' and 1,643,006 had marked their ballots 'no'. Curiously, the military voters in Canada had replied 'yes' to the tune of 84 per cent while of those overseas only 72 per cent had done so. Some have speculated that the all-volunteer army in Britain preferred to remain that way. There was no doubt, however, that the results were a smashing triumph for the Ligue pour la défense du Canada in Quebec, and a clear demonstration of the differences in attitude and emotive feeling towards the war, England, and the duty of a citizen that co-existed uneasily in Canada.

Shaken by the outcome, the Prime Minister was pensive as he contemplated the results of the vote: 'I felt very strongly that to keep Canada united we would have to do all in our power [to keep] from reaching the point where necessity for conscription overseas would arise,' he wrote in his diary. The plebiscite confirmed him in this belief, but the Prime Minister added that if conscription ever did become necessary it could be implemented 'with the will of the majority, expressed in advance, and if proceedings are taken in the right way, will be gradually acquiesced in by those in the minority.'[109]

---

suggested some phrasing that King felt would create a wrong impression. 'They would be taken as meaning that there would never be conscription for overseas service, and make it impossible, even if given freedom from past commitments, to so much as consider the compulsory selective service for overseas however necessary it might be and remain true to the will of the people.' (King Diary, 26 Jan. 1942.)

V

The problem now was to rein in the majority. Mackenzie King knew that he would have to take some action to satisfy those English-Canadian voters who had assumed almost as a matter of course that the plebiscite would settle the conscription question once and for all.* But national unity, as King perceived it, certainly did not permit the introduction of conscription for overseas service at this point, nor was there any demonstrable need for it, the great bulk of the army overseas remaining unblooded. What was to be done?

King had pondered this question while he waited for the results of the plebiscite to come in, and as he wrote in his diary:

> We will repeal the clause in the National Resources Mobilization Act, which limits the government's power to the confines of Canada. I will announce that we intend to extend the application of the provisions of the N.R.M.A. to cover the coasts of Canada, possibly going the length of using Canadians anywhere in the northern half of this hemisphere. I doubt if we shall ever have to go beyond that . . . If there is any pressure on the part of our men to enforce conscription, just for the sake of conscription, I will fight that position to the end. Quebec and the country will see that I have kept my promise about not being a member of the government which sends men overseas under conscription. The only exception I will make in that will be that our own men need additional numbers which could not be obtained voluntarily, but I do not think this will be the case. . . . [110]

In this remarkable diary entry, King laid out the essentials of the policy he would hold to for the next two-and-a-half years. He would amend the NRMA's limiting clause; he would oppose conscription for its sake alone; he would abide by his promise against conscription unless and until there were insufficient reinforcements to maintain the army overseas. Everything he said that 27 April 1942 he implemented.

There would be difficulties along the way in the Cabinet and country about the amendment of the NRMA and about the course that would

---

*Opinion sampling, however, showed that most Canadians realized after the vote that it had been intended only to free the hands of the government, not to force conscription immediately—37 per cent believed it meant immediate implementation of overseas conscription, 58 per cent that it was to free the government's hands. In Quebec the proportions were 21 and 72 per cent; in English Canada 42 and 54 per cent. (*Public Opinion Quarterly,* VI (Fall, 1942), 488-9.)

follow upon that. When the Cabinet War Committee met the day after the plebiscite vote, all those difficulties became clear. Ralston and Macdonald instantly began to press for the total elimination of geographic restrictions on the use of conscripts, and not, as King had hoped, just to authorize the use of NRMA men anywhere in North America. Furious that the Prime Minister was ignoring the expressed will of the people, Macdonald even hinted broadly at resignation if he did not win his point. The debate swirled around the table, and Louis St Laurent, the Minister of Justice and Lapointe's successor in the riding of Quebec East, argued that if section 3 were eliminated, overseas conscription would have to be enforced at once. This was not so, Macdonald countered. The people had given the government release from its pledges, but there was nothing in the vote that demanded that conscription come immediately.[111] This was an approach that squared with King's own, but in the rush of angry words it slipped away.

The response from the War Committee disheartened the Prime Minister, who now came to realize—as he should have much earlier—that the plebiscite had heated up the debate. The signs were everywhere. The Ontario ministers met privately and decided to press the issue, an occurrence that provoked a fierce exchange between King and C. D. Howe, the Minister of Munitions and Supply.[112] T. A. Crerar, an opponent of conscription since his experiences in the Union Government of the Great War, now wrote to suggest that section 3 should be deleted from the NRMA and a declaration made that conscription would come if it became necessary to maintain an effective war effort.[113]

Under this pressure King agreed to do what he had told his diary on 27 April he would. The NRMA would be amended to delete section 3, but the government's policy would be to extend conscription 'for the present' only to the Western hemisphere. In addition King would offer a pledge that 'would bring us back to Parliament before we actually enforce conscription. In that event I can always have my colleagues understand that they will have to find another leader if there is an attempt to bring conscription into force where that is not necessary.'[114] But there was no willingness on the part of Ralston and Macdonald to accept this new position. 'What benefits would occur by going back to Parliament?' they asked. There might be an urgent need for men, and going back to Parliament would only delay matters. The proper course, the two Defence Ministers argued insistently, was for the Cabinet to pass an order-in-council when conscription became necessary. After further discussion, and without agreeing on anything beyond the fact that there would be no commitment 'for or against going to Parliament first or later', the Prime Minister informed the War Committee on 8 May that he would give Parliament notice of his intention to amend the NRMA.[115]

For P. J. A. Cardin this meant that his life in the government was at an end. The Works Minister felt that his prestige in Cabinet had been weakened by the negative vote in Quebec; now if he was unable to block the government from clearing the ground for conscription, his prestige in Quebec among his own people would be gone completely. Cardin told Mackenzie King that he did not want to suffer the fate that had befallen the few French Canadians in the Borden government — 'he did not want to be like Blondin or other men who had to walk across the city of Montreal accompanied by a policeman.'[116] So Cardin resigned from the government, leaving Quebec represented by no one of genuine public regard. St Laurent would soon come to fill the position of lieutenant to the Prime Minister, but in the spring of 1942 he had yet to speak in the House, he was still too new, too untried to be *le chef*. The other Quebec ministers, with the exception of Power who was an Irish Catholic, were not men of great ability or prestige among the people.

In fact, Quebec's influence to some extent rested more on the Ligue pour la défense du Canada than on any individual in the Cabinet. After its incredible success in mobilizing the people for the plebiscite vote, the LPDC continued its efforts, now attacking the government's decision to proceed with the amendment of the NRMA. King had introduced the bill, Bill 80, into the House on 11 May. Within a few weeks hundreds of municipal councils throughout the province of Quebec were passing resolutions, obligingly supplied them by the Ligue, against Bill 80.[117] Quebec was still on fire, and the plebiscite had settled nothing.

Many English-Canadian journals, however, seemed to believe that it had. *Saturday Night*, for example, agreed that French Canadians had had the right to vote 'no', but argued that Quebec did not have the right to prevent the rest of the country from putting its desires into effect.[118] And the *Financial Post* was convinced that the vote 'indicates decisively that the vast majority of Canadians are willing to undertake any task, to accept any sacrifice needed to win the war.' French Canadians, on the other hand, although they were in the war 'at heart', have permitted 'the conscription issue of the last war [to] overcloud their good judgment ... [This] will not help to gain for Quebec the goodwill and understanding of English-speaking Canadians.'[119]

Very little goodwill would be evident in the debate in Parliament over Bill 80, a debate that dragged on into July. Each party faced its own peculiar problems with this question, not least the Tories. Immediately after the plebiscite R. B. Hanson, still the Leader of the Opposition, believed that the government should be left to squirm on the hook. 'Our members take the position that King must assume the onus and burden of introducing conscription,' he wrote to one of the party's most vociferous conscriptionists. 'Our members are averse to assuming the whole responsibility. They say that we, a small minority, have shown our position repeatedly and that the onus is on the government and that King should be made to assume it.'[120] Clearly Hanson remembered the weight conscription had placed on Conservatism's back after 1917; this time it was the Liberals' turn to carry the burden. But to his great surprise Hanson found his caucus on 12 May far more militant than previously and, as he wrote to Meighen, 'it has been decided that we shall press for immediate institution in full of a programme of compulsory selective service over the whole field of war.'[121] No one could have been more delighted than Meighen, still the nominal (if slightly irregular) leader of the party. Conservative policy, he replied, should take 'a direct, definite and unchanging line—that is, press for compulsory selective service now and all the time . . .'[122]

But the Conservatives still had their problems. How could they draft an amendment to Bill 80 that would not, as Hanson saw it, 'challenge directly the principle of the Bill and leave the impression in the country that we were opposing it but would urge the Government to take immediate steps to put into effect those principles which we, as a Party, advocate?'[123] No one could find a way, and after much wrangling the caucus decided to vote for the Bill. This pleased no one very much— King had manoeuvered the Tories first into supporting his plebiscite and now into supporting Bill 80. Hanson, for one, expected there might be 60 Liberal 'bolters' on the Bill: 'If we were to vote against the Government might possibly be defeated. . . .' But to do this would be to force an election, a delay for conscription, and the possibility of another shattering defeat for the Conservative Party. The only option was to vote for the Bill.[124]

The CCF moved through a similar tortured process to a decision. The socialists were no less distrustful of Mackenzie King, but they too could be swayed. At a special caucus on 12 May the Members decided to move an amendment to Bill 80 demanding the conscription of wealth and industry, not of men alone. This had been the CCF position at least since the York South by-election, but the party's past positions had been less clear. Entering the war divided, the CCF had called only for economic aid to Britain. This had been followed by support for conscription of wealth not men, and finally to support for the conscription of all the human and material resources of the state. This position seemed set, but the caucus decided that if its amendment to Bill 80 lost, as everyone knew it would, then the CCF members would vote against Bill 80. There was substantial opportunism here, many seeing a vote against the Bill as a sure way to crack Quebec's solid opposition to socialism.[125] But soon some members began to waver, particularly after the government budget, introduced in May, imposed stiff new taxes. From the party point of view the budget was a good one, almost conscription of wealth, but as David Lewis, the head of the party organization, argued in a memorandum that was designed to check potential bolters, it was not good enough. There were no initiatives towards social security, no moves to maximize production through the conscription of industry, and no limitation on profits. In addition, Lewis argued, Bill 80 was the climax to government rule by order-in-council, and the government still sought control over life, not property. The 'vested interests', he concluded, 'must not be placed above human life and rights.'[126] The CCF M.P.s would do their duty.

Whether Liberal Members of Parliament would do theirs was less certain. At a caucus on 12 May the Prime Minister found his Quebec M.P.s 'deeply concerned' and discouraged by the situation they seemed to be facing,[127] and there were clear indications—the same ones Hanson had seen when he forecast Liberal bolters—that it would be difficult indeed to keep the party together on the Bill 80 vote. Another indication of trouble was the 61-7 vote in the Quebec legislature on 20 May in favour of a motion demanding that Ottawa retain the voluntary system. This result, one newsman told the American Minister, meant that Premier Godbout 'had lost all control of the situation'.[128] Mackenzie King's hold on his ministers was no less feeble. Even Chubby Power, the Associate Minister of National Defence and one of the very few English-speaking ministers with a genuine understanding of Quebec, even Power was standing with Ralston and Macdonald in opposing a second debate on conscription should such a thing become necessary. 'In fact,' King wrote, Power 'thought he would have to consider carefully his own position, if the Quebec members went against it, and resign, being without any support in the Province and his own constituency having voted against him in the plebiscite.'[129]

For the Prime Minister the task was extremely difficult and delicate. If he promised to come back to Parliament for a second debate, his

English-speaking ministers and members would be in revolt; if he did not, his francophone supporters might bolt. As a result King hedged and trimmed, choosing his words carefully and cautiously, seeking desperately for a way out of the dilemma the plebiscite had put him in. In caucus on 27 May he suggested that 'if conscription is necessary, Parliament must decide the matter' because he would not. This upset Angus Macdonald who felt King had violated the understanding of 8 May in the War Committee that no commitment either for or against going to Parliament would be offered. Not so, King replied to the Navy Minister's hot complaint. 'I had not gone further in caucus than make clear that responsibility to Parliament would have to be my guide.... I had made no commitment on the part of the government.'[130] Similarly when the Prime Minister made his famous speech on the second reading of Bill 80 on 10 June he left many members and observers confused. He had said that his policy was 'not necessarily conscription, but conscription if necessary'.[131] That statement was actually very precise in meaning but it nonetheless baffled many. So too did King's words on whether or not he would return to Parliament to debate conscription a second time. King had decided to omit any reference to this from his speech, but at least two observers, Grant Dexter of the *Winnipeg Free Press* and Pierrepont Moffat, the American Minister, were convinced that he had promised not to come back to Parliament.[132] Mackenzie King carried the art of oblique references to its very pinnacle.

But to the Cabinet on 12 June the Prime Minister was more precise. He told his ministers that he believed it essential 'when the time came, if it did come, to put conscription into force, Parliament's approval should be given.' 'How could a long debate be avoided?' Ralston asked. He could tell the House, King replied, that it had 'a day or two—at the most—to express its approval or disapproval of the Government's action. If they approved, well and good. If they did not, then the Ministry would resign....' Ralston objected to the delay this course entailed, and Macdonald supported his colleague. King then suggested that he could see the Governor General and ask him to name one of the ministry as Prime Minister if such an eventuality arose.

I said to them I would like you to consider the position exactly as I see it now. We are sitting here. The House is in session, will be in session again this afternoon in an hour or two. Does anyone suppose that if this action had to be taken today, with the knowledge of what is owing to Members in the House of Commons, that I could sign an Order to put conscription into force and go an hour later and tell the

House that this had been done, and ask for confidence in my action? . . . I said I would never do that.

There was complete silence in the Cabinet. . . . I could see that all my colleagues excepting Ralston and Macdonald were solidly with me.

It had taken more than a month but Mackenzie King had finally made his position clear to his colleagues. 'If it is agreed that Parliament will approve the Government's action before any action is taken,' he told his ministers, 'I will, d.v., stay and do my best . . . I shall never be at the head of a Government that will enforce conscription without having Parliament share that responsibility to the full with me.'[133]

Now that he at last understood precisely what King intended, Ralston began to consider leaving the Cabinet. An honourable, upright man, a courageous soldier himself during the Great War, Ralston felt a deep devotion to his 'boys' overseas. He wanted them to have the best in food, medical care, weapons, and reinforcements because he knew that if there were shortages or delays men would suffer and die. Every casualty weighed on his mind; needless losses would torment him forever, and this he could not tolerate. In his view, the course King was proposing now could lead to precisely the situation he feared. And for what? To Ralston the answer was clear: to appease Quebec, to pander to French Canada when soldiers might be dying overseas for want of reserves. As the representative in the government of the army, of the soldiers overseas, he could not accept such a situation.

When Ralston came to see him on 12 June to say that he thought he should resign, King, not at all surprised, nonetheless tried to persuade him to reconsider. The differences between them were not that great, he said, and, as he privately noted, such relatively minor procedural points as going to Parliament before or after an order-in-council 'would never stand in the light of day'.[134] The two met again on 15 June and made no further progress. The Prime Minister, however, had decided to accept Ralston's resignation rather than to yield,[135] but Ralston continued to agonize over where his duty lay.

Meanwhile the debate in the House of Commons continued. The splits in the Liberal Cabinet and caucus could not be concealed, with ministers and members carefully carving out their own position. Under tremendous pressure from the LPDC and from their constituents, Quebec M.P.s hedged in many cases or spoke out flatly against the government's policy. English-Canadian Liberals often sounded as hot for conscription as the Tories; so too did some CCFers.

In the Cabinet on 7 July King at last told his ministers that he would close the debate on second reading that day. If he could not get the support of a majority of his party he would see the Governor General and ask him for dissolution or to name a new first minister. 'On the question of going back to Parliament,' Macdonald wrote in his diary, King 'announced that what he had in mind to say was that the Government should come to a decision and then report to Parliament. If Parliament were not in session it should be called immediately. Upon meeting Parliament he would ask for a vote of confidence.' King added that he would tell Parliament that this was his own opinion as one member of the government. Ralston, for one, indicated he could not accept such a course, and Macdonald and J. L. Ilsley, the Minister of Finance, also raised objections.[136] The Prime Minister, however, supported by the great majority in the Cabinet, won his point.

Before King spoke in the Commons to end the debate that night Ralston came to hand in his resignation. The letter sat in King's folder on his desk while he told the members that his position was set, that there would not be a second full debate on conscription but only on whether the government's decision merited the confidence of the House.

In the vote that followed the government won a substantial majority, 158-54. Only a handful of French Canadians outside the ministry voted for Bill 80, while 48 opposed it, supported by six CCF M.P.s. This was a climatic moment for French Canada, as André Laurendeau observed:

> In our eyes, then, the discussion of Bill 80 was the last phase of the conscription debate. Once the amendment was voted, the system was watertight, even if the government chose not to proceed to the brute exercise of its powers. From then on, the question was closed.[137]

For French Canada the conscription crisis of 1942 was the crucial point of the war. Pledges directed to French Canada had been freely offered by the government; those pledges had now been violated despite the expressed will of all *Québécois* in and out of Parliament. How could Ottawa ever be trusted completely again?

The Prime Minister was virtually unaware of this feeling. With the vote in the House, the Bill 80 matter was finished. His short-term task was to resolve the question of Colonel Ralston's resignation, while his long-term task was to prevent the necessity for compulsion if at all possible. The first task was soon solved. Under strong pressure from his friends, Ralston wavered badly. His health was starting to break down under the strain, and Macdonald and Power, his closest colleagues, had eventually determined that they could not resign on the question of courses to be followed in the event of actions that might never occur.[138] At last, on 13 July Ralston wrote to the Prime Minister and set out the terms on which he would stay in the government. Essentially he reserved for himself the right to take any stand he chose on the manpower question.[139] This was extraordinary in every respect, but King agreed, sending his thanks to Ralston for 'consenting not to press your resignation for the present. I sincerely hope the occasion may not arise when you will feel it necessary to give the matter a further thought.'[140] No truer words were ever said by Mackenzie King.

For him the crisis was over, successfully handled. Cabinet now had the right to bring in conscription if it became necessary, but only in dire circumstances. The procedure to be followed had been laid down. Except for Cardin, the ministry had stayed together. And although Quebec was unhappy, the wounds would heal when the province saw that King kept his word and did not impose conscription for overseas service. Certainly this was his intent, and Mackenzie King was almost certain that conscription would never become necessary.

NOTES

1 House of Commons *Debates*, 8 Sept. 1939, p. 36.

2 See J. L. Granatstein, *Canada's War: The Politics of the Mackenzie King Government 1939-1945* (Toronto, 1975), chapters 1-2.

3 Public Archives of Canada [PAC], Department of National Defence Records, file HQC 6974, Vol. 4, Whitelaw to DOCs, 10 Jan. 1940. Aliens could be enlisted providing they had an RCMP certificate of good character. Later Americans were permitted to enlist without taking the oath of allegiance.

4 On the Quebec election, see Robert Rumilly, *Maurice Duplessis et son temps*, Tome I: *1890-1944* (Montréal, 1973), 529-33; Conrad Black, *Duplessis* (Toronto, 1976), pp. 204ff.

5 Public Archives of Ontario, Mitchell Hepburn Papers, Supplementary Files (Private) 1939 (H2), Hepburn to T. Wayling, 15 Sept. 1939.

6 Toronto *Star*, 2 Oct. 1939.

7 PAC, Manion Papers, Vol. 10, Price to Manion, 9 Sept. 1939.

8 PAC, Bennett Papers, Series H, Vol. 3, Clark to Bennett, 25 Sept. 1939. Bennett's own view was much less bellicose. See *ibid.*, Bennett file (Family) (W. D. Herridge), Bennett to Herridge, 15 Sept. 1939.

9 J. L. Granatstein, *The Politics of Survival* (Toronto, 1967), pp. 48-52.

10 M. E. Hallett, 'W. D. Herridge and the New Democracy Movement', M. A. thesis, Queen's University, 1964, 152.

11 Queen's University, C. G. Power Papers, 'Memorandum re 1940 Election Campaign,'

1 Feb. 1940.

12 On these efforts, see Granatstein, *Canada's War*, p. 105.

13 House of Commons *Debates*, 23 May 1940, p. 138; Montreal *Gazette*, 10 June 1940.

14 PAC, W. L. M. King Papers, Diary, 22 May 1940.

15. *Ibid.*, 5 June 1940.

16. *Ibid.*, 16 June 1940.

17 J. W. Pickersgill, *The Mackenzie King Record*, Vol. I: *1939-1944* (Toronto, 1960), 95.

18 House of Commons *Debates*, 18 June 1940, p. 854.

19 *Statutes of Canada* (1940), chapter XIII, pp. 43-4.

20 House of Commons *Debates*, 18 June 1940, pp. 961-2.

21 See André Laurendeau's account, 'The Conscription Crisis, 1942', in Philip Stratford, ed., *André Laurendeau, Witness for Quebec* (Toronto, 1973), pp. 42ff. René Chaloult's *Mémoires politiques* (Montréal, 1969) make no mention of this motion.

22 See Elizabeth Armstrong, 'French Canadian Opinion on the War', *Contemporary Affairs* (Toronto, 1942), pp. 15ff.

23 *Texte complet des discours sur le mobilisation générale ... 23 juin 1940* (Ottawa, 1940), p. 7.

24 PAC, A.G.L. McNaughton Papers, Vol. 227, CC7/Crerar/6, Crerar to McNaughton, 8 Aug. 1940.

25 *Ibid.*

26 Raymond Ranger, *Report on the Operations of National Registration and Military Mobilization in Canada during World War II* (Ottawa, mimeo, 1949), pp. 9ff., 48. Copy in Directorate of History, National Defence Headquarters.

27 Quoted in House of Commons *Debates*, 3 Aug. 1940, p. 2402 by Mr Hanson.

28 Armstrong, *op. cit.*, pp. 19-20.

29 House of Commons *Debates*, 29 July 1940, pp. 2098-9.

30 *Ibid.*, p. 2097.

31 W. R. Feasby, *Official History of the Canadian Medical Services, 1939-1945*, Vol. I: *Organization and Campaigns* (Ottawa, 1956), 419ff.

32 Ranger, *op. cit.*, p. 55.

33 *Ibid.*, pp. 77ff.

34 Documents on Department of National Defence Records, file HQS 8624, Vol. 1.

35 A report from a Quebec military district noted that the scheme helped end legends 'after 20 years of pacifist debauchery'. PAC, Ernest Lapointe Papers, Vol. 16, 'Survey of Conditions Prevailing in M.D. 5, 9-22 Feb. 41'.

36 Toronto *Globe and Mail*, 8 Nov. 1940, cited in Cam Macpherson, 'The Birth of a Minority: The Army System and the Zombie Myths', York University undergraduate paper. This fine paper is relied on heavily for discussion of the NRMA.

37 *Globe and Mail*, 7 Jan. 1941 in *ibid.*

38 House of Commons *Debates*, 17 Mar. 1941, p. 1581.

39 *Ibid.*

40 Directorate of History, National Defence Headquarters, H.D.G. Crerar Papers, 958C.009 (D129), Crerar to Gen. Montague, 11 Dec. 1944.

41 E.L.M. Burns, *Manpower in the Canadian Army* (Toronto, 1956), p. 117.

42 PAC, J.L. Ralston Papers, Vol. 38, 'The Canadian Army', 3 Sept. 1940.

43 PAC, C.D. Howe Papers, file S-14ND(1), Vol. 48, Crerar to Ralston, 24 Sept. 1940.

44 Ralston Papers, 'The Canadian Army'.

45 Saskatchewan Provincial Archives, J.G. Gardiner Papers, Gardiner to King, 7 Nov. 1940 and atts.

46 Quoted in Macpherson, *op. cit.*

47 King Diary, 13 Nov. 1940, 4 Dec. 1940, 27-8 Jan. 1941; PAC, Privy Council Records, Cabinet War Committee Minutes, 1, 3 Oct. 1940, 4, 18 Dec. 1940, 28 Jan. 1941; Directorate of History, Records, file 112.1013 (D2), 'The Nature of the Canadian Army Effort in Mid-Summer 1941. . . . ', 18 May 1941.

48 House of Commons *Debates*, 11 Mar. 1941, pp. 1428-30.

49 Cabinet War Committee Minutes, 26 Apr. 1941.

50 Ottawa *Journal*, 28 Apr. 1941.

51 Toronto *Telegram*, 28 Apr. 1941.

52 House of Commons *Debates*, 12 May 1941, p. 2729; Queen's University, H. A. Bruce Papers, Bruce to C. G. McCullagh, 15 May 1941.

53 PAC, R. B. Hanson Papers, file 0-160, Hanson to H. C. Farthing, 27 May 1941.

54 Montreal *Gazette*, 26 May and 2 July 1941.

55 Ottawa *Journal*, 18 June 1941.

56 Cabinet War Committee Minutes, 23 Apr. 1941.

57 King Diary, 9 May 1941.

58 Cabinet War Committee Minutes, 20 May 1941.

59 King Diary, 20 May 1941.

60 Cabinet War Committee Minutes, 20, 21 May 1941. In fact, the telegram was not sent.

61 Granatstein, *op. cit.*, pp. 203-4. Cf. PAC, Arthur Meighen Papers, Vol. 220, G. A. Drew to key Western Tories, 24 June 1941.

62 Material on Directorate of History file 112.3S2009 (D262). See also DND Press Release No. 759, 16 July 1941.

63 Public Archives Record Centre, Department of National Defence Records, War Diary, Directorate of Army Recruiting.

64 Department of National Defence Records, file HQS 20-6, Vol. 13, Tel., 5 July 1941.

65 Ralph Allen, *The High White Forest* (New York, 1966), pp. 234ff.

66 R. H. Roy, *Ready for the Fray* (Vancouver, 1958), pp. 147-8.

67 Department of National Defence Records, file HQS 20-1, Vol. 2, Adj.-Gen. to Minister, 27 Nov. 1941.

68. *Ibid.*, Vol. I, Crerar to Minister, 29 Sept. 1941.

69 King Diary, 2 Dec. 1941.

70 House of Commons *Debates*, 5 Nov. 1941, p. 4115.

71 King Papers, 'Personal View With respect to 1942-3 Proposed Programme of the Army', 3 Dec. 1941, ff. C244478ff.

72 King Diary, 3 Dec. 1941; Cabinet War Committee Minutes, 3 Dec. 1941.

73 Queen's University, T. A. Crerar Papers, Crerar to King, 17 Dec. 1941; Cabinet War

Committee Minutes, 2, 3 Dec. 1941.

74 Queen's University, Grant Dexter Papers, Memorandum, 12 Jan. 1942.

75 Meighen Papers, Vol. 139, Meighen to Capt. Laclaire, 28 Mar. 1939.

76 *Ibid.*, Box 4, memo, n.d.

77 Directorate of History, file 112.3S2099 (D36), 'The Recruiting Problem in the Province of Quebec', 9 June 1941.

78 Lapointe Papers, Vol. 18, Lapointe to Ralston, 27 May 1941.

79 Ralston Papers, Vol. 45, file 499-75, Lapointe to Ralston, 7 Aug. 1941. See also docs on *ibid.*, Vol. 46, file 492-43 and material on Department of National Defence Records, file HQS 8841.

80 *Ibid.*, Col. Gibson to Crerar, 27 Mar. 1942 and att.

81 As suggested in 'The Recruiting Problem . . . '.

82 Directorate of History, file 112.3S2009 (D36), Crerar to Minister, July 1941. Cf. *ibid.*, Lawson to Crerar, 25 June 1941.

83 *Ibid.*, Lawson to Crerar, 8 July 1941.

84 Dexter Papers, Memorandum, 9 Dec. 1941. Cf. J.-Y. Gravel, 'Le Québec militaire, 1939-45', in Gravel, éd., *Le Québec et la guerre* (Montréal, 1974), pp. 84ff.

85 See Granatstein, *Politics of Survival*, pp. 80ff.

86 Meighen Papers, Meighen to Hugh Clark, 14 Nov. 1941.

87 *Globe and Mail*, 13 Nov. 1941.

88 See Granatstein, *Politics of Survival*, pp. 104-5; *The Round Table* (March, 1942), 303-4.

89 Polls reported in *Public Opinion Quarterly*, VI (Spring, 1942), 158ff.

90 King Diary, 9, 10 Dec. 1941.

91 *Ibid.*, 14 Nov. 1941; Pickersgill, *op. cit.*, 280.

92 Public Archives of Nova Scotia, Angus L. Macdonald Papers, Diary, 18 Dec. 1941.

93 King Diary, 15 Jan. 1942; T. A. Crerar Papers, 'Memo dictated by Minister . . . ' 16 Jan. 1942.

94 King Papers, 8 Jan. 1942, ff. C244522-4.

95 The wording was accepted on 20 Jan. *Ibid.*, Memo by Heeney, f. C257021. House of Commons *Debates*, 22 Jan. 1942, p. 2.

96 Fondation Lionel-Groulx, Fonds Georges Pelletier, 'Entrevue Georges Pelletier—King 1942', 26 mai 1942, pp. 9-11.

97 Harvard University, Pierrepont Moffat Papers, Memorandum of Conversation . . . , 19 Feb. 1942.

98 Robert Rumilly, *Histoire de la province de Québec* (41 vols; Montréal, 1969), XXXIX, 184; Ottawa *Citizen*, 10 Jan. 1942.

99 Meighen Papers, Meighen to John Bracken, 23 Jan. 1942.

100 On York South, see Granatstein, *Politics of Survival*, pp. 97ff.

101 Macdonald Diary, 31 Jan. 1942, 'Conversation Ralston and I had with P.M. . . . '.

102 See Rumilly, *op. cit.*, 187ff.; Stratford, ed., 'Conscription Crisis', p. 62ff.

103 See Granatstein, *Canada's War*, pp. 222ff. for detail.

104 In *ibid.*, p. 224.

105 *Public Opinion Quarterly*, VI (Fall, 1942), 488-9.

106 PAC, L.-P. Picard Papers, leaflets; Power Papers, Vol. 78, conscription file, leaflet, 18 Apr. 1942.

107 Dexter Papers, Memorandum, 28 Feb. 1942.

108 See F. A. Angers, 'Un Vote de Race', *L'Action Nationale*, XIX (mai, 1942), 299ff.

109 Pickersgill, *op. cit.*, 364.

110 King Diary, 27 Apr. 1942.

111 Macdonald Diary, 28 Apr. 1942.

112 King Diary, 1 May 1942.

113 T. A. Crerar Papers, Crerar to King, 1 May 1942.

114 Pickersgill, *op. cit.*, 366.

115 King Diary, 8 May 1942.

116 *Ibid.*, 9 May 1942.

117 Fondation Lionel-Groulx, Fonds LPDC, Circular File, letter of 26 mai 1942; *ibid.*, unnumbered file, 'Trois cents conseils municipaux. . .'.

118 *Saturday Night*, 2 May 1942.

119 *The Financial Post*, 2 May 1942.

120 Hanson Papers, file P-450-C, Hanson to J. A. Clark, 6 May 1942.

121 *Ibid.*, file S-175-M, Hanson to Meighen, 12 May 1942.

122 Bruce Papers, Meighen to Bruce, 19 May 1942.

123 Hanson Papers, file S-175-M, Hanson to Meighen, 14 May 1942.

124 *Ibid.*, file S-175-J, Hanson to Sen. Jones, 16 June 1942.

125 M. S. Horn, 'The League for Social Reconstruction: Socialism and Nationalism in Canada 1931-1945', Ph.D. thesis, University of Toronto, 1969, 477.

126 PAC, M. J. Coldwell Papers, Memo on Bill 80, 30 June 1942.

127 King Diary, 12 May 1942.

128 Rumilly, *op. cit.*, 260-4; Moffat Papers, Memo of Conversation with F. C. Mears, 21 May 1942.

129 Pickersgill, *op. cit.*, 377.

130 Macdonald Diary, 28 May 1942 and att. letter; *ibid.*, 4 June 1942.

131 House of Commons *Debates*, 10 June 1942, p. 3236.

132 Dexter Papers, Memorandum, 16 June 1942; Moffat Papers, Memorandum, 11 June 1942.

133 Pickersgill, *op. cit.*, 383-4; Macdonald Diary, 12 June 1942.

134 Pickersgill, *op. cit.*, 384-6.

135 King Diary, 15 June 1942.

136 Macdonald Diary, 7 July 1942; Pickersgill, *op. cit.*, 392ff.; Ralston Papers, Vol. 85, Diary Notes, 7 July 1942.

137 Stratford, ed., 'Conscription Crisis', p. 99.

138 Macdonald Diary, 8-9 July 1942; Power Papers, Memorandum for the record, entry of 12 July 1942.

139 Ralston Papers, Vol. 85, Ralston to King, 13 July 1942.

140 *Ibid.*, King to Ralston, 15 July 1942.

Six

THE CRISIS OF 1944

For more than two years after the resolution of the conscription crisis of 1942, manpower problems seemed to disappear largely from the public ken. Attention focused on the great battles overseas—on Alamein, Stalingrad, the Coral Sea, on Torch and Husky. Particular notice was taken of the Canadian forces, naturally enough. Although the first battles at Hong Kong and Dieppe were slaughters, by July 1943, with Canadians taking part in the landing in Sicily, the bad times seemed to be forgotten. Canadian troops were now in the fighting, and the public desire for action was largely satisfied.

But if manpower problems were obscured until the fall of 1944, it was not because matters of great import were not occurring. Over the course of the years from 1942 to 1944, the nation developed and implemented a massive selective-service program that controlled the lives of virtually every man and woman in the land. Conscription for overseas service would not come until the end of 1944; conscription of the human resources of Canada in almost every respect had been implemented long before then.

I

While the Cabinet was dealing with the political problems that the plebiscite and Bill 80 had created it was simultaneously tackling other matters of substantial concern to the employment of the nation's manpower. Out of these discussions would come the National Selective Service system, an attempt to satisfy the demands for manpower made by the military and war industry.

As early as June 1940 the Cabinet had created the National Labour

Supply Council to advise on all matters pertaining to the supply of industrial manpower. One of this Council's offshoots was the Interdepartmental Committee on Labour Co-ordination, a body that was to bring together representatives of all the government agencies in any way concerned with manpower. As part of its task, the Interdepartmental Committee established the Labour Supply Investigation Committee, which in October 1941 produced a long and detailed report on the manpower resources of Canada.

The Investigation Committee's report showed that the absolute limit of the man- and woman-power resources of the Dominion was 7,863,000, a highly exaggerated total that included every person of appropriate age. The total potentially available for military service from this pool was 2,124,000 but of this number only a small portion could be spared from civilian work. At least two-thirds of the executive and administrative classes, for example, had to be kept out of the military, and up to 80 per cent of skilled workers; only one-sixth of the farmers could be spared for the armed forces, and students and skilled artisans had to be permitted to continue their studies and work in the interests of the nation's future. In addition, at least one-third of those remaining could be expected to be medically unfit. After various additional deductions were made to the potential military pool remaining, only 609,000 at most were available for military service, and these 'only if the most drastic measures [were] adopted'.[1]

The problem of finding the men for the armed forces was compounded by their unequal distribution across the country. If existing recruiting methods were continued, the manpower reserve in the Maritimes (49,340), the Prairies (117,000), and British Columbia (40,340) would be barely adequate. Ontario with 195,790 men still available and Quebec with 206,530 were held to have sufficient resources. From these remaining men, a maximum of 437,000 men would have to be found for the army, 132,000 for the air force, and 40,000 for the navy, all without disrupting too severely the normal functioning of the country or drawing too heavily on one part of the country while leaving other areas relatively untapped.

The report recommended in brief that the competition for manpower between the military and industry be stopped. Priorities had to be established, and if workers could not be induced to move to areas where they were needed, then the jobs should be moved to them. The report also urged a greater utilization of woman workers in key industries, and it offered some sound opinions about the flaws of the hitherto existing system:

While an individual responsible for the success of a given enterprise may be the best judge of the best uses to which labour may be put in the operations of that enterprise, he is not necessarily the best judge of whether labour should be available for this enterprise. Each man worth his salt will do everything he can to make his particular enterprise a success; but the success of this enterprise may be at the expense of another serving even more valuable national purposes.

. . . Thus there is competition between the armed forces and industry, and among industrial concerns generally. The Committee doubts that this situation results in the most effective use of the nation's manpower.[2]

The Labour Supply Investigation Committee's report came to the Cabinet War Committee early in December 1941, where it provided fuel for both the conscriptionist and anti-conscriptionist ministers in the debates about the 1942-3 military program. On 10 December, in part at least in an effort to cool matters, the War Committee agreed to set up a special Cabinet Manpower Committee with Joseph Thorson, the Minister of National War Services, as Chairman and Louis St Laurent and Colin Gibson, the Ministers of Justice and National Revenue, as members. The secretary of the committee was Alex Skelton, the son of Dr Oscar Skelton, the long-time Under Secretary of State for External Affairs, who had died in January 1941. The younger Skelton was a powerful bureaucrat in his own right, and as secretary he was in a position of some substantial power. This fact was quickly recognized and, as Grant Dexter of the *Winnipeg Free Press*, a friend of Skelton's, noted, he was courted by both sides. Colonel Ralston was in to see him as soon as he was named, and Skelton talked with Mackenzie King within a few days. 'There is no lack of efforts to influence him,' Dexter said, adding that Skelton knew what he wanted to do:

The grand strategy of the war, he says, should require us to close down on army recruiting and take perhaps half of those in uniform at home and train them for war industry. This kind of report, of course, would be impossible. He knows that.

He thinks he will proceed by requiring all essential services— army, air, navy, munitions, base metals, lumber, agriculture to estimate their requirements. Where they are expanding, he will want the desired rate of expansion. With agriculture he would want some idea of how many men could be given up. He will then make his survey which will disclose that there are far too few men to meet requirements—after making every allowance for transfer of women and those in unessential occupations, etc. He will point this out, give the figures and tell the government that co-ordinated control and priorities are required.[3]

Events proceeded much as Skelton envisaged. At the Cabinet Manpower Committee's first meeting on 16 December Thorson suggested that selective-service machinery, backed by sanctions if necessary, should be readied, although the goal should be to retain the maximum degree of voluntarism. The next meeting a week later got down to business, to the gathering of information, and to staking of positions. The representative of the Department of Munitions and Supply, for example, complained about the army's raiding industry 'indiscriminately' for trained personnel. By 8 January it was clear that a form of national selective service would be recommended, with the power to assign manpower from industry to the armed forces or from non-essential to war industry.[4]

At the end of January the first reports of the Cabinet Manpower Committee were before the War Committee. By 4 February, at which time the Cabinet War Committee discussed the question in some detail, three immediate steps were proposed: refusal to permit men eligible for military service to enter certain non-essential industries; the freezing of agricultural labour and the institution of government subsidies to control prices; and the placing under government control of a limited number of the technical and skilled personnel required for industry.[5] No immediate conclusions were reached and the question of selective service did not come back to the War Committee for serious discussion until 26 February.

By this date the Manpower Committee was proposing a 'freeze' on the transfer of skilled and other workers out of war industry. This suggestion, in part a reflection of the concern expressed by the Department of Munitions and Supply, was sharply resisted in the Cabinet War Committee by Colonel Ralston. The Defence Minister argued that such a scheme would enhance service on the home front at the expense of overseas service and thus discourage recruiting for the armed forces.[6] Ralston's arguments essentially persuaded his colleagues, and the result, apparently on 6 March, was the adoption of the Manpower Committee's report, including the administration of a national selective-service system by the Department of Labour, but with the proviso that the needs of the armed forces were paramount and that every effort should be made to encourage enlistment.

The new system was announced by the Prime Minister in the House of Commons on 24 March. In his long address and in some 13 orders-in-council tabled the same day, the outline of National Selective Service was made clear. The NSS would be under the Department of Labour, and its director would be Elliot Little, an industrialist who had been serving in the Wartime Bureau of Technical Personnel since 1941. Selective Service would be run by Little, assisted by the NSS Advisory Board, which would consist of representatives of government departments and agencies, labour, and management.

The NSS was to make extensive use of the Employment Service, and every area served by the Unemployment Insurance Commission would have an NSS officer attached. Utilization of industrial manpower would be handled by the Employment Offices, while the procurement of men for compulsory military service would remain with the Department of National War Services. Appeals against orders affecting civilian labour would henceforth be heard by the National War Service Boards, thus far concerned only with appeals against service under the NRMA. In addition, the maintenance of the records of the national registration were transferred from the Department of National War Services to the Department of Labour.

Liability for service in the military under the NRMA was substantially broadened. All single men and childless widowers born between 1912 and 1921 were henceforth liable for call-up, and the severe restrictions that had prohibited aliens from service were relaxed. The question of aliens had troubled the government for some time, and by including them—or most of them—in the manpower pool, at least 25,000 men were made available for service. There were also felt to be positive benefits to be gained by encouraging their assimilation into Canadian society.[7] Nonetheless, Canadians of Chinese and Japanese origin were still to be excluded as were German and Italian enemy alien nationals. Canadian citizens of enemy national origin including the Japanese Canadians would eventually be permitted to enlist.[8]

One class was excluded from the broadened call-up provisions. Farmers and farm labourers were now declared to be 'frozen' to the land and henceforth were forbidden to seek employment elsewhere without written permission from an NSS office. As the Prime Minister put it, demonstrating that one lesson had been learned from 1917,

> The policy of stabilizing employment in agriculture represents what, in effect, is a block allocation to agriculture of the persons best suited to food production. It constitutes a form of large scale selection for national service which should go far to ensure the supply of man-power essential to the food production aspect of the national war effort.

Mackenzie King also laid down the procedures that would be followed to force fit men of military age out of non-essential occupations and into the armed forces or war industry. After 23 March 1942, he told Parliament, no physically fit man between the ages of 17 and 45 could be employed as a bookkeeper, a cashier, a stenographer or typist, as a messenger, a sales clerk, a taxi driver, in advertising or real estate. Nor could a fit man work in entertainment-related industries, or in the manufacture of biscuits, bread, beer, tobacco, leather goods, textiles, jewellery, china, soap, sporting goods, toys, and a host of other areas. The government had opted to restrict employment, rather than to allocate it, by deliberate choice, Mackenzie King said:

> By applying the negative compulsion of restriction, where possible, in preference to the positive compulsion of allocation, the waste of man-power in unessential activities is prevented. At the same time, men and women are maintained in or directed into the form of service they prefer. It is obvious that the greater the measure of willingness that can be preserved, the more effective the service will be.
>
> ...It is essential that at a time of war, the service of men and women should not be consumed in unnecessary tasks. It is imperative that the services of all should be directed into war-time tasks. In those aspects of our war effort in which voluntary methods are working satisfactorily, voluntary selection...has been and will be continued. The more expensive and complicated methods of compulsion have been employed only where it is felt that compulsory selection is necessary in order to increase efficiency in the prosecution of the war. Compulsion, however, will be applied without fear or favour wherever in the opinion of the government its use will aid in the achievement of a maximum war effort.[9]

The NSS announced by the Prime Minister set in train a vast body of regulations and an increasing regimentation of all aspects of life. And as time passed the NSS system began to extend to other areas. In May all unemployed males were required to register; in September all women between the ages of 20 and 24 were registered by the Women's Division of the NSS. And in June the government passed an order-in-council providing, with a few exceptions, that no man or woman could take employment anywhere without a permit from an NSS officer.[10] For the first time the impact of war was directly, inescapably felt by the Canadian people at home. The state had intervened massively and its efforts to create an economy geared for total war had begun to alter society. The implications of this new role were important and far-reaching, but few complained. The war excused much and justified everything.

The sweeping new measures did not solve the manpower question, far from it, and in July 1942, at the same time that the Bill 80 debate was reaching its apogee in the House of Commons, the Cabinet again was fighting about numbers. As early as 8 July the National Selective Service system had produced estimates that 638,000 men were potentially available for military service, a small increase over that reported in October 1941 by the Labour Supply Investigation Committee. This new figure became the basis on which subsequent discussion—and argument—was based. At a special Cabinet War Committee meeting on 17 July the whole question of manpower resources was canvassed. Colonel Ralston told his colleagues that the army would need to enlist 184,980 men by 31 March 1943 to meet its needs. There were needed, he said, 83,980 men for service in Canada, 93,300 more for overseas, and an additional 26,000 to maintain the training centres. The remaining 31,000 were 'wastage'—men who would be released from service and who could return to civilian employment. For the air force Chubby Power reported that 37,950 men would be needed to retain 26,500 aircrew and that his total requirements would be 53,193, a figure that included 10,000 women. The navy, on the other hand had smaller demands, only 1,500 a month to 31 March 1943 for a total of 13,755 plus 300 women. Munitions and Supply, C.D. Howe insisted, required a further 100,000 workers to reach the 910,000 workers necessary to run the war plants. Already, Howe added, there were 175,000 women working at essential war industries.

Thorson, the Minister of National War Services, expatiated on the problems his department faced in securing enough men to meet the army's needs. The age of the men eligible for call-up under the NRMA had been extended yet again, and now men of 20 and men from 30 to 40 were being drafted. But the wastage in this higher age group was substantial, Thorson said. Of 93,000 men between 35 and 40 years of age, no more than 10,000 could be expected to be fit for service, and thousands were applying for deferment. The manpower pool, he prophesied gloomily, might well be exhausted by September 1942, after which the only remaining men would be those under 20 and those men married before 15 July 1940. Humphrey Mitchell, the Minister of Labour since joining the government in December 1941, argued that more men could be found if non-essential industry was curtailed, a view that matched that expressed by Colonel Ralston at the outset of the discussions. The only decision reached was that the Cabinet Manpower Committee should study the situation and quickly bring forth new recommendations.[11]

This it did on 22 July, recommending among other things that the Unemployment Insurance Commission become an integral part of the Department of Labour and that new measures for controlling employment be taken. The Cabinet War Committee accepted these recommendations, and on 31 July they came before the full Cabinet. On the recommendation of the Prime Minister, it was agreed that the Unemployment Insurance Commission should come under the Department of Labour and be strengthened in personnel so that it might handle National Selective Service. During the two or three months required to reorganize, the National War Service Boards would continue to function, but thereafter their functions of selection and deferment would be transferred to the Employment Service under the Director of the NSS, Mr Little. The Boards would then function only as appellate tribunals responsible to the Justice Department.

Essentially what had occurred was the gutting of the Department of National War Services, a fact that infuriated its minister, Thorson. The Department of Labour, Thorson told Grant Dexter, had no organization capable of handling the job, and the result of the transfer of power would be chaos. T. A. Crerar, Thorson's fellow Manitoban in the Cabinet, did not share the dark view of Mitchell that obsessed Thorson. But Crerar essentially seemed to agree that power was being shifted away from Thorson because of the incapacity in his department.[12] In a private letter Crerar expressed his view that 'in our war effort we have extended ourselves about as far as it is safe to go, largely because of the exhaustion of our able-bodied manpower.'[13]

The results of the shuffling of responsibilities came into effect on 1 September 1942. From that date the NSS organization had virtually complete responsibility for the manpower problem, including the allocation of men to the armed forces and industry. Additional regulations at the same time forbade employers to discharge workers and workers to quit their jobs without seven days' written notice. Workers could not seek new employment and employers could not engage new workers without an NSS permit, and the permit might be worded so that the opportunities were limited to a single community or industry. Advertising for employees was forbidden to anyone except the NSS, and its officers were given the power to summon anyone who was unemployed or under-employed and compel him to accept a designated job.[14] These powers were substantial, almost sweeping, and they concentrated in one agency control over the lives of Canadians to an unheard-of degree. But the manpower problem remained fundamentally unsolved.

At the Cabinet War Committee on 17 September the same gloomy forecasts were presented yet again. Colonel Ralston, Power, and Macdonald reported on the difficulties they faced in finding the requisite numbers of men. Ralston, in particular, emphasized the dangers in the army-reinforcement system and warned that he might be forced to denude units in Canada of volunteer personnel if all or part of the Canadian army overseas became involved in battle. No allowance, he said, had been made for casualties to occur before 1 April 1943, but the 'wastage' up to that date was nonetheless expected to be 41,802 men. Elliot Little, the Director of the NSS, reported that his calculations now showed a potential of 427,000 fit males who might be secured for the armed forces. This was a drop of some 200,000 in about six months. Little added that these men could be secured only by drastic measures and the closing down of non-essential industries. The War Committee, facing difficult decisions ahead, asked Little to confer with Donald Gordon, head of the Wartime Prices and Trade Board, and to report on the measures that might be taken to close down non-war industries.

One week later Little and Gordon submitted separate—different— reports. Little argued that the armed forces and war industry would require almost 50,000 men and women each month until 1 April 1943. The only way to get these people would be by curtailing non-essential industry and by utilizing women workers in greater numbers. The NSS Director believed that 11 per cent of the labour force employed in non-essential industry—or 27 per cent of its male labour force—would have to be redirected to more essential work.[15]

Donald Gordon based his report on the implications he saw in Little's. The only way 50,000 men could be found each month would be by a direct draft, a course of action that would have severe dislocating effects on industry and commerce. To implement Little's proposals, the WPTB chairman said, would require the withdrawal of virtually every able-bodied man from the age of 16 to 44 from all industries and services that could be regarded as non-essential. The result would be a spartan Canada with widespread rationing of consumer goods, the disappearance of whole categories of goods from the marketplace or a decline in quality, a curtailing of exports such as newsprint, furs, and rye whisky, and a substantial concentration of industry along with a simplification and standardization of products. Gordon warned that such a plan would require a huge bureaucracy, and he added that the

Canadian people would have to be made to understand that their lives would have to alter substantially.[16]

All the sugar coating was off the bitter pill. The Cabinet had been appalled by Little's proposals—Ilsley said no democracy could live with such a system while King was convinced it would produce only chaos—and there was little disposition to go ahead. The Prime Minister was convinced that a gradual process had to be adopted and that matters could not be pressed in one fell swoop.[17] In his diary that night King noted that 'we have reached the point where it is going to be most difficult to get the numbers at which we have been aiming. I feel very strongly that we have gone much too far particularly in relating to the army. It makes a desperate effort for everything else.'[18]

This was the problem. Those decisions in January 1942 that had given the generals the army they wanted were putting a great and lasting strain on the country's limited manpower reserves. There were three infantry and two armoured divisions overseas, plus two tank brigades and all the ancillary troops required to maintain and support such a force. There were thousands and thousands more troops at home maintaining the supply lines to Britain, and in Canada, in addition, there were three further divisions in various states of readiness, providing a measure of protection against the possibility of Japanese or German assault. Thousands more men and women served on coast-defence duties or in internal-security roles. The army was too large.

Clearly the Prime Minister was not alone in this view, for the Cabinet on 25 and 29 September refused to go the full distance of accepting Little's proposals if they meant the fulfilment of Donald Gordon's predictions. Drastic action that would dislocate the economy was forbidden, but the Cabinet did reaffirm that National Selective Service should be empowered to make available the numbers of men required for the military and industry. How this was to be done without drastic action was unclear.[19]

These Cabinet decisions made Elliot Little's position almost impossible. His problem was compounded by his inability to persuade the Minister of Labour, Humphrey Mitchell, to give him the support he needed. What the Director wanted was to be a deputy minister in what amounted to another department with the right to an establishment of his own and under his own control, not one for which approval had to be sought elsewhere. Little also wanted the right to review all the plans for concentration of industry that emerged from the Wartime Prices and Trade Board, and he sought the right to take men away from industry, regardless of such plans, if the manpower needs required it.

Compounding matters was Little's dislike for Humphrey Mitchell. But at root was the unwillingness of Cabinet to face up to this situation. In a long memorandum based on conversations with key civil servants, Grant Dexter summed up the difficulty:

> I am surprised to discover that Little well knows that the manpower demands are ridiculous; cannot be met. He put in his memo to Cabinet . . . that the demand could be met if certain things were done —[the forcing out of] sub-marginal farmers, the wheat industry, concentration of industry and so on. He refused . . . advice to say that theoretically it could be done but that practically it was impossible because he believed that his 'ifs' would make that plain to cabinet and that cabinet would say no. He was dumfounded [sic] when cabinet said that the expansion programme must stand approved and that he should go ahead—but without wrecking the economy. He has been back twice since then and got the same impossible advice on both occasions—which he finds completely baffling.

It was baffling, but Dexter thought he had found the answer. The Cabinet could not deal with the matter, Dexter suggested, because Mackenzie King feared another conscription drive. Dexter explained:

> The army is wrecking the economy. Eight divisions cannot be sustained. But to restrict the army would expose King to [another] conscription cry. Ralston would resign and claim that army was limited to save gov't from applying overseas conscription. He had no intentions of exposing himself to this attack and his reason is that by so doing he would imperil national unity.
>
> . . . Under these circumstances King intends to pursue the line that everybody can extend the war effort as far as they like until the country rises up and co-ordinates things by demanding a roof on the army.[20]

Dexter's sources of gossip were occasionally inaccurate in detail, but he was clearly correct in his appraisal of Little's position. On 16 November the Director of National Selective Service confronted the Prime Minister and Humphrey Mitchell with the choice between meeting his demands for changes in the operation and status of the National Selective Service or of accepting his resignation. Two days later, after King's attempts to reconcile the two men had failed, Little resigned. For the Prime Minister this was a difficult time. He had no admiration for the way Mitchell ran the affairs of his department and he would come close to sacking him in the near future; but instinctively he backed the minister against the civil servant, and he soon persuaded himself that Little had deliberately acted so as to hurt the government.[21] There were some grounds for this belief, for Little carried his case to the public in a letter printed in *The Financial Post* of 28 November. The government was guilty of unnecessary and lengthy delays in implementing regulations for the curtailment of unessential industry, he charged, and he could not get the support and authority he needed to do his job effectively. 'If the government is really serious about implementing its professed desire to tackle the manpower problem,' Little argued, 'the very minimum powers that are needed by anyone selected to carry out that responsibility are at least commensurate to those of a deputy.' There was a note of pique there, showing through the outrage.

Little's successor was Arthur MacNamara, the Chief of the Unemployment Insurance Commission and the Associate Deputy Minister of Labour. As its gift to the new director, the government made substantial alterations to the NSS in December 1942 and January 1943. The administration of manpower functions under the NRMA was officially transferred to the Department of Labour and the existing National War Services Regulations were replaced. The new National Selective Service Mobilization Regulations dealt with the call-up of men for military service while the National Selective Service Civilian Regulations consolidated all orders-in-council relating to civilian employment and the war effort. And the Department of Labour received authority to circulate 'interpretive' letters to ensure uniformity across the country.[22] Finally at the end of 1942 MacNamara became Deputy Minister of Labour. Much that Little had sought was eventually given his successor.

There was one additional and important change before the end of 1942. On 10 December the Cabinet War Committee agreed to accept an army request made on 18 November that married men born between 1917 and 1923 henceforth be eligible for call-up under the NRMA. The Prime Minister was upset by this decision:

> I spent the afternoon in Council from 3:30 until nearly 7:30. Agreement was finally reached on having young married men up to 25 called up for military service. It was felt that this would have the additional advantage of bringing pressure on single men who have not yet responded to the colours. I would say that over half of Council was strongly opposed to the idea, but felt, with the United States and Great Britain having called out married men, and the war situation demanding this step and, in particular, bringing the reinforcements up, this action was necessary in Canada.[23]

There may not have been the co-ordination that critics of government policy like Little sought, but the war's demands were affecting almost everyone now.

By the beginning of 1943, then, Canada was almost fully mobilized. Certainly the Canadian statistics compared favourably with those in Britain and the United States, and those two countries, of course, were principal powers with world responsibilities of a kind that Canada did not have. The statistics, with figures in thousands, were as follows:[24]

	Canada 31 Jan. 1943		USA 1 Jan. 1943		UK Mid-1942	
War Employment Industry	1,036	9.0%	8,700	6.4%	5,110	10.9%
Essential Non-Agricultural Ind.	1,089	9.5	7,700	5.7	4,566	9.7
Less Essential Non-Agricultural Ind.	1,317	11.4	26,600	19.7	7,000	14.9
Agriculture	1,020	8.9	8,900	6.6	1,107	2.4
TOTAL INDUSTRY	4,462	38.8	51,900	38.4	17,783	37.9
Armed Forces (Projected to Mar. 1944)	778	6.8	10,800	8.0	4,500	9.6
Total Ind. and Forces	5,240	45.6%	62,700	46.4%	22,283	47.5%
Population	11,500		135,000		47,000	

II

While the pressures on the civilian population increased, the NRMA troops continued their duties in Canada. The home-defence conscripts were popularly known by the unfortunate name of 'Zombies,' a term derived from Hollywood horror movies where it generally applied to soulless victims of voodoo rites. The term, one that probably did much to increase bitterness among NRMA troops, had apparently first come into use during the plebiscite campaign in the winter of 1942; soon its use was widespread throughout the country.[25]

The bitterness of the NRMA troops was increased as well by the way the government progressively expanded their field of service. As early as February 1942 there was not a single battalion in Canada without its quota of conscripts, and as newspapers unfriendly to the government pointed out, these troops could not even be sent to the United States in an emergency. It was September 1942 before action was taken. An order-in-council on 4 September authorized the inclusion of NRMA men in three anti-aircraft batteries being despatched to Alaska. An order on 14 September authorized the use of conscripts in infanty battalions in Newfoundland and Labrador. On 18 June 1943 the government approved the employment of NRMA conscripts in the four-battalion brigade Canada provided for the American-commanded force that was to attack Kiska in the Aleutian Islands. Finally on 11 August 1943 blanket authority was provided for NRMA soldiers to serve with any unit in Newfoundland, Bermuda, the Bahamas, Jamaica, British Guiana, Alaska, and the United States. Thus everything in the northern part of the Western hemisphere was covered—by the time there was no longer any real possibility of attack.

The efforts to persuade NRMA troops to convert to active service continued, indeed increased in intensity, as the pressures on manpower grew. But as the volunteers for General Service were gradually combed out for service overseas as reinforcements, the efforts at persuasion shifted entirely to the training system. There every method was employed, ranging from lectures, posters, and fair treatment to the 'transfer of 'R' personnel to less pleasant duties', as a frank official at Defence headquarters put it.[26] The General Service troops were encouraged to exert pressure on their fellow NRMA trainees, something that worked better with English-speaking units than with French Canadians.[27]

But once training ended and the soldier was posted to a unit in Canada or North America, pressure from fellow soldiers virtually ended. From the spring of 1942, most battalions in Canada had a majority of NRMA troops in the ranks; in the Canadian Scottish Regiment, for example, by January 1943 there was scarcely a soldier who was not NRMA. Even the non-commissioned officers were Zombies, only the officers being volunteers. What made it worse for the military brass was that the NRMA units did their duties well and efficiently and with high morale. The NRMA troops did even boring duties willingly, and those who decided to go active seemed to do so on their own initiative.[28] There were few enough of these: in all of 1942 only 18,274 men went active; in 1943 only 6,560.[29]

Thus the scarcity of reinforcements for the army overseas continued, and Colonel Ralston and his staff redoubled their efforts to win the army a larger share of available and untapped manpower. In the first four months of 1943, a memorandum prepared for Ralston showed, the army had fallen 20,074 men short of its needs in NRMA men. Voluntary enlistments on the other hand, including conversions by NRMA men, were running about 8 per cent ahead of expectations, but the net result was still a shortage of 17,500.[30] The problem, in the army's view, was that military service was by no means the top national priority. According to a Labour Department survey in January 1943 there were 277,000 single men and 369,000 married men aged 18 to 40 working in war industry of high priority and a further 115,000 single and 160,000 married men in low-priority employment. The requirements of industry, therefore, were the heart of the problem.[31]

So strongly did Colonel Ralston feel on this score that he wrote his colleague the Minister of Labour on 4 June in strong terms:

> There seems to be an ineradicable impression that [men who were being moved out of non-essential areas] must be transferred to some other industry. But it seems essential that the Army be recognized for what it is, namely an integral part of the national economy—the front-line for the factories, farms, railroads, mines, etc. The system has been designed to transfer workers to the jobs where their efforts will count most, and the Army is the primary occupation for the young and strong who are released. The older men and women and the less physically fit should be the ones primarily to man the other components of the economy.
>
> The Army's needs can only be met if National Selective Service makes it clear that young men, physically fit, should go to the Army *as soon as* their jobs can be taken by older men or by women or by unfit men.[32]

Everyone could agree with Ralston's general comments on the desirability of fit men going into the armed services while the young, the old, the unfit, and the women manned the industrial plant. But the practice was different than the wish. Donald Gordon of the WPTB put his finger on the problem:

> Six months ago we assumed that a curtailment program would, *in itself*, produce manpower. No doubt this assumption is true in the sense that a curtailment program will release men and women from civilian employment. However, the value and usefulness of the people thus deprived of their livelihood is quite a different matter.
>
> . . . In a word, the types of labour releasable by a curtailment policy which seeks to *produce manpower* are likely to be, in a large measure, useless to and remote from war industries, or unfit for the armed services. Certainly every acceptable person obtained will be at

the expense of throwing numbers of men and women out of employment.[33]

There were, therefore, relatively few potential soldiers still to be squeezed from the labour force, and every one of those could be secured only at the cost of social dislocation. The men remaining were among those who were reaching their majority, among those who could be brought to the requisite physical standards, among the older and the married, and, of course, among General Service volunteers on duty in Canada. The NRMA soldiers, as well, formed a potential body of reinforcements for the overseas army.[34]

The military employed a variety of expedients in their efforts to get the men their organization tables showed they needed. For example, as approximately 80 per cent of volunteers for military service offered their services only upon receipt of their notices to report for medical examination or for military training under the NRMA,[35] the pace of securing men from the designated classes was stepped up.[36] So, too, was the hunt for defaulters. And as the Japanese threat to the Pacific coast, as well as the Nazi threat to the East coast, had clearly diminished, two of the three divisions on home-defence duties could be disbanded. On 30 August 1943 the Chief of the General Staff recommended this action, and the Cabinet soon accepted it. This had the net result of freeing several thousand General Service men for overseas postings; it also permitted the use of the divisions' NRMA men as replacements for volunteers in other units across the country.[37]

In addition, an effort was made to reduce competition between the air force and the army for high-calibre men. By 1942 the RCAF was having increasing difficulty finding candidates of sufficient mental and physical standards for aircrew training; the army actively sought the same men as candidates for officer training. This led in January 1943 to a suggestion by Chubby Power, the Minister of National Defence for Air, that the RCAF could trade 'washed out' aircrew candidates for potential aircrew then in khaki. In the resulting meetings on this proposal, meetings that had the appearance of being between two separate powers rather than between the armed forces of the same nation, a tentative agreement was reached: the army would make available monthly 1,000 potential aircrew and 500 low-category men for ground-crew duties in exchange for the RCAF's failed aircrew who were still fit for overseas service. Because of each service's suspicion that the other was getting a better deal, the arrangements fell through. Not until August 1943, and not until the Prime Minister intervened, did a solution result. The RCAF and the army would launch a recruiting campaign in concert and help meet each other's needs.[38]

Throughout this same summer further changes took place in the operation of National Selective Service. The Minister of National Defence, for one, was upset at what he saw as the inefficiencies in the operation of the NSS. Thousands of men simply failed to respond to orders to report, the NSS seemed to lack the ability to follow up such failures, and there was no adequate enforcement machinery.[39] Ralston took these complaints to the Cabinet War Committee on 24 June, and there his strictures on the administration of the NSS were echoed by C. D. Howe, the Minister of Munitions and Supply—and Ralston's major competitor for men. As a result, the War Committee authorized the Prime Minister to discuss the separation of the posts of Director of National Selective Service from that of Deputy Minister of Labour.[40] The Minister of Labour resisted these attempts strenuously,[41] and Arthur MacNamara, the Director of NSS and the Deputy Minister of Labour, fired off his own salvo, urging that the NRMA men be disbanded from their unproductive labours and returned to industry.[42] That suggestion, needless to say, met no favour within the General Staff, the argument being that there remained some necessity for home defence and that the NRMA constituted a source of potential reinforcements for the army overseas, if and when needed.[43]

But in the War Committee on 21 July the ministers decided to have the military staff prepare a study, a re-examination, of the army's manpower requirements within Canada. There was also support for the formation of an army works battalion, notwithstanding Ralston's comment that he would agree to such a body providing its manpower was not drawn from the army.[44] The result in the end, in a defeat for Ralston, was the creation of two port companies for use as longshoremen, and military personnel were employed on this duty.[45]

But if Ralston lost this battle, he won the war against Humphrey Mitchell. An order-in-council on 10 August drastically re-organized the NSS system. An Administration Board was created under the chairmanship of the Director of NSS, with associate directors placed at the head of nine divisions:

Mobilization
Labour Priorities
Essential Civilian Services
Agriculture, Forestry, Fisheries
War and Heavy Industry

Coal Mining and Transportation
Employment of Women
Employment Service
Industrial Mobilization Survey

Further decentralization was achieved by appointing directors for each of the country's five employment regions and by naming Regional Selective Service Advisory Boards.[46] Shortly thereafter the 'new' NSS issued a Compulsory Employment Transfer Order, a clear attempt to get tough with industry and labour. Henceforth single and married men between 16 and 40 years of age in a lengthy list of jobs were required to register with their Employment Office and hold themselves ready for transfer to higher priority work.[47]

The acrimony between Ralston and Mitchell continued into 1944. On 6 March the Minister of National Defence wrote to insist that his requirements of 5,000 fit men each month be met. Mitchell was willing to try, but he did not know where he could find the men. During the last six months, he said, the three services 'have obtained 65,021 men. During this period to obtain the foregoing result National Selective Service had sent orders-medical [the order to report for medical examination] to 184,971 men. During this period the Army obtained 34,040 men. To obtain 5,667 men for the Army,' he complained, 'we had to call 184,971 men.'[48] The requirements for 1944-5 totalled 98,000 men for the three services, a demand of over 8,000 men each month. Ralston was not mollified by this account of Mitchell's problems. His reply was sharp:

> You say that 'No stone has been left unturned to meet the demand'. I of course, have to accept that, but I can suggest that there are some stones that, while they may have been turned, have, perhaps not been turned all the way over, under which there will be found quite a number of prospective recruits.

There were too many defaulters, Ralston argued, perhaps as many as 125,000; postponements of military service could be reduced, particularly as war production had started to decrease somewhat and employment taper off.

> There are still those in the designated classes who have not yet been called at all [Ralston went on]. Apparently the bulk of these are married men in the Province of Quebec. My information is that the Registrars in Montreal and Quebec have refrained from calling these men because the boards automatically grant them postponements on

compassionate grounds, for the reason that there are still some single men not called.[49]

In his reply, Mitchell denied most of Ralston's allegations. In Quebec, he argued, the responsibility lay on poor management in the early days of the war. Although the population was almost as large as Ontario's, there were only two Mobilization boards there, compared with four in the latter province. And part of the blame, Mitchell said, had to rest with the shortage of army doctors to cope with the 700 men that NSS was calling-up each day in the Montreal area. There was no meeting of minds. But Mitchell did assure his colleague that 'not only is the Labour Department doing its best but . . . everything within the bounds of possibility is being done.'*[50]

What more could be done was strictly limited, primarily because the country had effectively reached the bottom of the manpower barrel. As Arthur MacNamara, the Deputy Minister of Labour, pointed out to the Secretary to the Cabinet, as of 1 December 1943, 5,057,000 men and women over 14 years of age were either in the armed forces or at work, and this out of a total population of 8,820,000 over 14. From the beginning of the war the labour force had increased by 1,317,000 or 35 per cent. In 1939, he added, there had been virtually no employment whatsoever in war industry; on 1 December 1943 there were 1,104,000 people working in munitions factories, including 240,000 women. And in 1939 again, there had been only 10,000 men in the armed forces; today there were 734,000 men and 35,000 women. Where had the additional workers and soldiers come from? Part of the growth was natural increase, but civilian industry employed 140,000 less than in 1939, there were 159,000 fewer students, 628,000 fewer unemployed men or housewives, and 331,000 fewer men on farms.[51] The country had gone almost as far as it could. Significantly, perhaps, the public was beginning to realize this. A poll conducted by the Wartime Infor-

---

*How 'the bounds of possibility' were defined was a matter of calculation. At the end of January 1944 Mitchell informed the Cabinet War Committee that he believed efforts should be made to compel Sons of Freedom Doukhobors to enlist. The sect's members, living in British Columbia, were as liable for service as anyone, Mitchell argued, although they regularly ignored call-up notices and 'staged nude parades if any pressure is brought to bear' on them. This could be ended, the Labour Minister believed, if a battalion of infantry was moved into the Doukhobor area 'for a show of strength'. The War Committee, however, refused to act as requested. Too many RCMP would be required to maintain order, and the military effectiveness of the Doukhobors was considered doubtful in any case. (PAC, Privy Council Office Records, Box 6, file M-5-6, Mitchell to Heeney, 31 Jan. 1944 and reply 7 Feb. 1944. Cf. Toronto *Globe and Mail*, 19 Apr. 1976.)

mation Board for the government in the summer of 1944 showed that most people now believed that the best use for manpower was on the farms, 45 per cent indicating this. Only 11 per cent believed that war industry was most important, while 28 per cent still said that the military should have first call on men.[52] Those results indicated with some clarity that Canadians were concerned about the impact of the war on their lives and were beginning to be concerned about food shortages and rationing. And there was a suggestion here too that the public believed the military took too many men.

No one would maintain that the armed forces were unpopular, but there were suggestions that the best use was not always made of men. Some of the difficulty sprang from the actions of the navy and the air force in continuing to recruit men apparently in numbers above the agreed totals. To Ralston, harassed and tired from his five years of Cabinet service and from fighting for more men against the Labour Department and Howe's Munitions and Supply Department, it would be insupportable if his colleagues in National Defence, Chubby Power and Angus Macdonald, also began 'chiselling' him.[53] His complaints had the desired effect. At a Cabinet War Manpower Committee meeting on 21 June Power agreed to cease recruiting for three months and to cut the RCAF home establishment by 10 per cent; Macdonald also agreed to cut his service's intake substantially.[54] Still there was relatively little co-ordination among the three services, and in October 1944, for example, the RCAF was releasing some 4,200 surplus men at a time when the army's need for infantry reinforcements was beginning to become clear to the government.[55]

The army was also doing its utmost to build its General Service rolls by encouraging NRMA men to volunteer. Following a conference of the District and General Officers Commanding in mid-April, the Adjutant-General approved a 'gloves off' recruiting campaign that would include particular efforts aimed at persuading the NRMA to go active.[56] Preparations began at once, and within a few days the NRMA troops were being paraded to hear speeches from their officers. 'No man should wear "that khaki uniform" unless he is willing to wear it anywhere,' General George Pearkes, commanding in British Columbia, was reported to have said. 'Many young soldiers are quite satisfied to say they are doing their duty by defending this coast. That is not 100 per cent service. The appeal has gone out to every soldier to volunteer heart and soul to support his comrades who are now ready to launch the invasion.'[57]

But such speeches could not persuade NRMA soldiers to enlist. One senior officer, Brigadier W. H. S. Macklin, one of Pearkes' brigade commanders, reported on 2 May 1944 of his unavailing efforts to persuade his men to volunteer during April. Macklin could even promise that units would stay together if sufficient numbers came forward, but this too had little impact:

25. As arranged, I spoke during the early afternoon to the officers of all three battalions. . . .

26. After discussion with the Officer Commanding Régiment de Hull I decided that it would be sounder for him to speak to his own NCOs and men in their own language.

27. The response of all officers and of active NCOs and the very few active men in the brigade was immediate, and enthusiastic to a degree. Their spirits rose, and I have never seen any announcement greeted with greater eagerness.

28. On the other hand the response of the NRMA men, and of a large proportion of the NRMA NCOs was very disappointing. There was no great rush to enlist, and although officers at once began to interview their companies and platoons, by evening less than 100 had enlisted from each of the two English-speaking battalions. . . .

29. In Le Régiment de Hull matters were even worse. This unit had, to begin with, no more than a mere handful of active personnel, probably not more than a dozen. . . . Warrant Officers and NCOs gave little or no support to their Commanding Officer. . . .

30. . . . Lieut.-Col. Schimnowski, senior R.C. Chaplain, . . . stayed two days . . . and he personally interviewed large numbers of R.C. personnel of all units . . . He informed me that the resistance of the NRMA soldiers to enlistment was amazingly strong, and that he had reduced more than one man to tears without succeeding in persuading the men to enlist. . . .

36. Major Paul Triquet, V.C., arrived and spoke to the men of Le Régiment de Hull. All other French-speaking soldiers . . . were paraded as well. Triquet's speech was excellent, but the results were again disappointing. Only about two dozen men answered the appeal on the spot. . . .

37. By this time it was clear that there were a number of NRMA NCOs who would not enlist. . . . I . . . reduced several sergeants and corporals in various units to the ranks as unsuitable, and a considerable number reverted at their own request.

By 1 May Macklin's efforts at a gloves-off campaign had produced only 769 conversions.

In his report Macklin ventured some opinions about his NRMA men. The NRMA soldier, in his view, was a sullen man, one who slouched, had no pride in himself or his unit, and hated the army. 'These men take pride in only one thing: they have beaten "the army"; they have beaten "the government".' The volunteer, by contrast, was proud of his position, anxious to work, self-confident. And Macklin added, 'It was not too much to say that the volunteer soldier in many cases literally despises the NRMA soldier.'

To Macklin the reasons for the strong feelings of the Zombies were many. But prime among them was the failure of the nation to inculcate patriotism into all its citizens:

> 60. As regards the English-speaking NRMA soldiers who refuse to volunteer they vary all the way from a large number who have no patriotism or national feeling whatever, to a few intelligent men who, I believe, honestly think that by holding out they will some day force the Government to adopt conscription which they feel is the only fair system.
>
> 61. The great majority are of non-British origin—German, Italian, and Slavic nationalities of origin probably predominating. Moreover most of them come from farms. They are of deplorably low education, know almost nothing of Canadian or British History and in fact are typical European peasants, with a passionate attachment for the land. A good many of them speak their native tongues much more fluently than they speak English and amongst them the ancient racial grudges and prejudices of Europe still persist. Here again the process of converting these men into free citizens of a free country willing to volunteer and die for their country will be a matter of education, and I think it will be slow. At present there is negligible national pride or patriotism among them. . . . They do not know what they are fighting for and they love nothing but themselves and their land. . . .[58]

Macklin was an intelligent, able, and experienced officer, but he was perpetuating myths. In his eyes and those of the volunteers, the Zombie slouched and had no respect for himself, his unit, or his country. But such men do not withstand moral and physical pressure of the kind the NRMA were subjected to for long periods. Certainly the kind of appeals employed—speeches, interviews with officers and padres, appeals to patriotism—could not crack them, probably because the NRMA men had their own conception of duty and patriotism, a conception vastly different—and no less correct—than Macklin's.

Nor was Macklin correct in general in lumping the NRMA soldiers together as being of non-British origin. A study prepared later in 1944 found that of the approximately 60,000 NRMA men, 17,000 spoke English as their native tongue, 12,000 spoke French, 14,000 English and French, and 15,000 some other language. There was a smaller proportion of English-speaking NRMA than one might have expected, a larger proportion of French-speaking, and a roughly equivalent number of those of non-British origin. In no case was the discrepancy enormous, and the figures suggested that the NRMA soldiers were roughly representative of the nation at large.[59]

Finally, the army promoted an advertising campaign in mid-1944 to appeal to the NRMA soldiers and their relatives and friends. The appeal centred on the 'G.S.' badge that the volunteer wore on his sleeve: 'Canada's badge of honour—wear it on your arm'. In one advertisement, seen in virtually all the national media, the 'V' for victory symbol was intertwined with the 'G.S.' badge: 'These two go together...the fight is OVERSEAS in the face of the enemy...and you must be an OVERSEAS soldier to get into it...you can't share the victory unless you are ready and willing to take your place with boys who are earning it.' Another advertisement showed a member of the Canadian Women's Army Corps saying, 'Gee, there's something about a G.S. man', while a third had children seeing the badge and saying, 'Gee, he's a G.S. soldier'.[60] There was a cheap psychology in such efforts that today seems mawkish in the extreme; to the NRMA men of 1944 it must have been offensive.

The failure of the campaigns to persuade the NRMA men to convert to overseas service was probably fore-ordained, given the methods and tactics employed. The tragedy was that by late 1944, for the first time in the war, there were extremely heavy casualties and a developing shortage of infantry. Only the NRMA men would seem to be available for use, but so hardened were the men by that date that no efforts could persuade them to volunteer. The ensuing crisis came near to destroying the government, disrupting the war effort with victory only months away, and dividing the nation.

III

The conscription crisis of 1944 sprang from military causes, but it was a political crisis at root. At stake was the continuance of the Liberal government of Mackenzie King; at stake, too, was the maintenance of the

Prime Minister's promise to Quebec that conscription would only be implemented 'if necessary', and hingeing on that was the continuance of Liberal ascendancy in the province. For the Opposition, the crisis seemed to provide the opportunity to hit the government at its most vulnerable point, perhaps to implement the policy that Arthur Meighen had tried and failed to carry out in 1941-2.

One problem facing the Conservatives was that the party was very different indeed than it had been in November 1941. The new leader, selected at a national convention in Winnipeg in December 1942, was John Bracken, long-time Liberal-Progressive Premier of Manitoba. Bracken was a conservative-progressive; he had never been a Tory; and he shared only a very few of the attributes that tended to distinguish English-speaking Conservatives from the great majority of their fellow Canadians. But he could become incensed at Mackenzie King's policy on manpower, and in late 1941 he had encouraged his Manitoba legislature to pass a resolution in favour of conscription. As leader of the newly christened (at his request) Progressive Conservative Party, his course was, and had to be, cautious, but occasionally he would let go: the war policy of the government, he said on 2 July 1943, 'having been in too many of its aspects prompted by political cowardice, could not fail to result in the chaotic and . . . disgracefully wasteful conditions which now prevail. . . .'[61] That was strong language that drew the huzzahs of Arthur Meighen,[62] but it was rather different than a demand to send the NRMA men overseas immediately. No Conservative asked for that for almost a year.

The first open and direct Progressive Conservative demand for immediate conscription for overseas service came on 19 June 1944 at a nomination meeting in Guelph, Ontario. The speaker was C. P. McTague, the party's national chairman and a former chairman of the government's National War Labour Board. With John Bracken sitting on the platform with him, McTague made a strong demand for action:

> Now as to where this party stands on this matter, let me state in simple unequivocal terms. To our army overseas and their relatives here we say you should have reinforcements now, and they are all available now, from the trained troops not now and never required for home defence, so-called. . . . National honour demands that without an hour's delay the necessary order in council should be passed making these reinforcements available.

> The government's persistence in leaving these trained soldiers of the home army in Canada, can only be construed as deference to the

will of the minority in the Province of Quebec as voiced in the plebiscite. . . .[63]

The magic words had been said; with them went the bare chances the Conservatives had been working on to develop their fortunes in Quebec.

Behind McTague's remarks was the Saskatchewan election held a few days earlier on 15 June. There the CCF had swept the boards, taking 47 of 55 seats and winning a clear majority of the popular vote.* Saskatchewan seemed a defeat for John Bracken's Progressive-Conservatism, for Saskatchewan was his backyard and he and his party had devoted much time and money to bolstering the organization in the prairie province. The party's failure in the election—of 40 candidates, none had won, all had run third, and all had lost their deposits— seemed to require resort to more traditional weapons. As a result, at a secret meeting in Toronto just after the debacle, Bracken, Gordon Graydon, his House leader, and one or two other Conservatives apparently decided that conscription was now the best card for the Tories to play. It would clearly differentiate the party from the government and, equally important, from the CCF as well. 'The Tories,' Grant Dexter wrote privately after talking to some who had attended the meeting, 'seem to have been perfectly cold-blooded about it . . . On careful assay they figured conscription is good for one hundred seats right now.'[64] What better weapon could there be than the manpower question? And what better time for it than two weeks after the Normandy invasion, the long awaited D-Day? Canadian troops involved in the fighting in Sicily since July 1943 were now fighting in France, and within a few weeks the entire army would be in action. Surely conscription would be necessary now.

This was not the advice the government was receiving from its military advisers. In the third week of June, shortly after the Tory

---

*The CCF was not above some politicking with manpower. T. C. Douglas, the man who led the party to victory in Saskatchewan, spoke in a by-election campaign in Humboldt, Saskatchewan on 2 August 1943: 'Your vote . . . will inform the Government what you think of their handling of the manpower situation. Despite a solemn promise made last year that no more men would be taken off the farm, the Government has continued to take thousands of men from Prairie farms. The same policy has not been followed elsewhere . . . 36% postponements [in Saskatchewan, while] in the Military district of Quebec 80% of those seeking postponements were successful.' Your vote, Douglas concluded, reaching back to an unfortunate Great War phrase, will tell the government you want equality of sacrifice. (Saskatchewan Provincial Archives, J. G. Gardiner Papers, 'Speech by T. C. Douglas', CKCK, 2 Aug. 1943.)

switch to open conscriptionist activity, Ralston could assure a journalist friend that the army had on hand enough reinforcements to take care of eventualities well into 1945.[65] And Lieutenant-General Kenneth Stuart, the Chief of Staff at Canadian Military Headquarters, London since December 1943, had visited the Canadian fronts in July. The next month he flew to Ottawa and on 3 August he appeared before the Cabinet War Committee to report on what he had learned. His words seemed unequivocal, at least as they were expressed in the minutes:

> General Stuart reported that although the Army had been fighting for some twelve months in Italy and two months in France, the reinforcement situation was very satisfactory. At present there were reinforcement personnel available for three months at the intensive battle casualty rate.[66]

The General's statement to the War Committee seemed the triumphant vindication of Mackenzie King's policies. There could be no doubt that the war would be won, that Canada had done its part and that conscription had not proven necessary. He had kept the nation together and prevented a repetition of 1917.

But in Stuart's words was the seed of the crisis. He had referred to the 'battle casualty rate' on which the planners based their reinforcement calculations. As early as the summer of 1942 the Canadian army had determined to follow reinforcement calculations similar to those employed by the British army, a fateful move. The British had estimated that 48 per cent of the total casualties of a field force would fall among general duty infantrymen; the actual figures were closer to 77 per cent. The Imperial General Staff had also operated on the assumption that 50 per cent of the wounded would be recoverable for active duty, while experience would demonstrate that these men, while able to continue in the army, would not be capable of shouldering a rifle in an infantry battalion. No reinforcement pool, British or Canadian, could cope with this discrepancy unless the most vigorous measures were taken to remuster large numbers of soldiers from other duties to infantry. For the Canadian army the only possible answer would seem to be to despatch as many men as possible from the home war establishment—from the General Service men and the NRMA men in Canada.[67]

Ralston had not been fully aware of the reinforcement difficulties facing the army overseas until he flew to Italy in late September 1944. As he had told a friend, George Currie, head of a large firm of chartered accountants based in Montreal and his executive assistant and deputy minister from 1940 to 30 September 1944,

towards the end of August he began to feel uneasy as to the reinforcement situation due to cables from the other side asking for specific
authority to do certain things which he felt were obviously for the
purpose of increasing reinforcements for the infantry. This included
remustering, continuation of trades pay [extra pay received by specialist soldiers], compulsory transfer of tradesmen to the infantry, etc.
They were all said to be for the purpose of remedying a purely temporary situation. All of them together, however, caused him to become quite nervous about the situation in spite of reassuring cables
sent by General Stuart. By about the first week in September, he decided that it was necessary for him to go over himself and obtain information on the spot.*[68]

Ralston would see the difficulties for himself.

His conversations with officers and men in Italy and later in North
West Europe persuaded him that there was a severe shortage of reinforcements already and one that would build into a crisis in the months
ahead. At headquarters in London, at his order, forecasts and projec-
tions were made and calculations derived. General Guy Simonds, the
acting army commander in North West Europe, had told the Minister
that the object should be to have sufficient reinforcements available so
that casualties could be replaced promptly and units not allowed to be
run down so far that only large numbers of 'green' reinforcements
could bring them back to strength. This did not seem to be the case.†
Ralston later told the House of Commons of the difficulty:

> I found that on account of the heavy infantry casualties, the infantry
> reinforcement pool which had been established in France on D-Day
> had been completely exhausted, and that at one time there had been
> aggregate shortages in the units themselves of over 3000. This had
> been gradually overcome in aggregate numbers, but not in individ-
> ual units, by vigorous efforts to retrain men from other units as

*Stuart has often been painted the villain in this piece and in events that followed. Chubby
Power, an anti-conscriptionist, discounted the criticism: 'I think of all the brass Stuart best
understood the Quebec position. He had been born in Three Rivers and he knew the
Quebec people. He understood King's aversion to conscription, and I think all along he had
been playing the game honestly and fairly . . . I believed then in his integrity and have not
changed my mind since.' (Queen's University, Power Papers, Power to Bruce Hutchison, 15
May 1952.)

†Simonds does not seem to have been convinced of the dire nature of the crisis. Early in
October, for example, he had told CCF leader M. J. Coldwell, in Europe on a visit to the
front, that the reinforcement situation was satisfactory. (PAC, M. J. Coldwell Papers, Vol.
17, Coldwell to E. B. Jolliffe, 12 Oct. 1944.)

infantry. No pool had been built up. The week I was there, there would be sufficient infantry . . . to bring the units up to strength. To do so would leave only about ten percent of what should have been on hand to provide the pool for which the acting army commander had asked.[69]

The statistics prepared for Colonel Ralston put numbers onto his fears. There was an overall surplus of 13,000 men but a deficiency of some 2,000 infantry. There had been 34,000 casualties up to the end of September, and estimates were for a further 29,000 by the end of the year. This pessimistic total of 63,000 was 23,000 more than the original estimates before D-Day. If the estimates were correct, then the army would have eaten into its capital by 23,000 and reduced its reinforcement pool by that much. This deficit in the pool would have to be restored to a level sufficient to provide men to cover the wastage that could be expected from two months of intense fighting. This would require the provision of 15,000 general-duty infantrymen before 31 December 1944. For the first six months of 1945, in addition, a further 25,875 men would be required.[70]

This was the gloomy news that Ralston and Stuart brought back to Canada on 18 October 1944.* It was amplified in a memorandum that General Stuart brought with him:

. . . Until about two months ago, I was satisfied with the general reinforcement position both in respect to First Canadian Army and 1 Cdn Corps in Italy.

There were three main reasons for my optimism; the general strategic situation, our overall reinforcement holdings and my expectation, based on 21 Army Group forecast of activity, that casualties for balance of 1944 would be intense and normal in alternative months.

In early August every indication pointed to an early collapse of Germany. I felt very strongly . . . that the German Army was in the process of being decisively defeated and would probably collapse before December 1944. Today, largely because of the successful German

---

*Certainly Ralston was gloomy on his return. Chubby Power talked with him on 19 October: 'I found him in a very bad state of health with a heavy cold and feeling greatly depressed.' But the Prime Minister was not buoyant either when Power saw him on 26 October: ' . . . he seemed to be much depressed . . . I felt he was not reasoning very well. He kept repeating his argument. . . .' The general degree of tiredness that affected all the ministers after five years of war cannot be underestimated as a factor in the events that followed. (Power Papers, Notes of Discussions on the Conscription Crisis, 19, 26 Oct. 1944.)

strategy of denying the Channel Ports to us, a German collapse cannot be regarded as imminent . . . Intelligent planning demands, therefore, that we must prepare for the prolongation of the war against Germany into 1945.

There would be a shortage of infantry reinforcements, Stuart said, of about 2,000 men. But, he added, 'nothing is certain' and the situation could be worse.

I say this because of what has actually happened in the last two months. Our casualties in infantry have been greater than was anticipated for two main reasons. The first was that we anticipated infantry casualties at 55% of total casualties; they proved to be 75% of casualties. The second was that forecasts must also be based on an anticipated scale of activity. We used 21 Army Group scale of activity with intense and normal casualties alternating monthly. Actually since 'D' day our casualties in 21 Army Group have been at an intense rate continuously.

The implications of this state of affairs were clear to Stuart:

. . . The only solution that I can see is to find an additional 15,000 infantry to add to our reinforcement pool on or before 31 Dec 44, and to ask that replacements sent monthly from Canada in 1945 shall be increased to 5300, of which 4300 should be infantry.
. . . I recommend, therefore, if the numbers required cannot be found from General Service personnel in Canada, that the terms of service of N.R.M.A. personnel be extended to include service overseas in any theatre.*[71]

For Prime Minister Mackenzie King the information brought back

*What this crisis meant was neatly stated by General E. L. M. Burns in his *Manpower in the Canadian Army* (Toronto, 1956), pp. 5-6: ' . . . there were 465,750 men and women in our Army. Of these 59,699 were NRMA and 16,178 were nurses . . . leaving 389,873 soldiers and officers available for "general service". Of that number, some 254,242 were in North-West Europe, Italy and the United Kingdom. There were some 158,000 in the field formations; that is divisions and troops of the 1st Canadian Army and the 1st and 2nd Canadian Corps, about 90,000 more in the base and lines of communications units in Italy and North-West Europe, and in the United Kingdom in reinforcement holding units and various other establishment.

. . . The establishment strength of the Canadian divisions was about 85,000 and that of the infantry battalions for which, as it was thought, reinforcements could not be provided, was about 37,817.

Those figures mean that with some 390,000 "general service" (GS) men on its strength, the Army could not find the bodies to reinforce the 38,000 infantry.'

from overseas by Ralston and Stuart came as a shock. He had truly believed that he had brought Canada through the war without a divisive and destructive battle over conscription, and now, with the war all but won, it seemed to be his task to deal with this most difficult of problems yet again. His first thoughts, expressed in his diary, were that 'more harm than good would be done with any attempt to force conscription at this time.' Certainly he could not head a government that would attempt any such course. 'It would be a criminal thing, and would destroy the entire War record.'[72] The Prime Minister and the Minister of National Defence met on 18 October for their first conversation since Ralston's return, and instantly the lines were drawn. The NRMA men in Canada had to be sent overseas, Ralston said. He had seen wounded leave the hospitals to return to the front, and the lack of reinforcements was hurting the men at the front. 'He did not wish to be emotional,' King recorded Ralston as remarking, 'but this had affected his feelings as to the necessity of easing the situation.' Clearly Ralston was prepared to resign on this matter.[73]

Mackenzie King could also get emotional about the fate of the thousands of men who were dying overseas, but his responsibility at this time was different. What would happen to the country if a conscription crisis erupted at this stage? Every time the army overseas had been increased in size, the Cabinet had been assured that sufficient men were available. Where were they now? And the war was almost over— why tear the nation apart at this late date for a few thousand men? ' ... I thought it would be much better if the necessity demanded to reduce the size of our army overseas.'[74]

The next day Ralston came before the Cabinet War Committee, stunning its members with his news. The lines, this day and the next, began to be drawn among the ministers, while at the same time the search for expedients began. King's staff began to suggest disbanding units, reducing the strength of infantry battalions from four to three companies, and a determined drive to 'comb out' General Service men in Canada.[75] But the military had their doubts of the efficacy of such efforts. The Chief of the General Staff, General J. C. Murchie, believed that there was substantial resistance among the NRMA to converting to overseas service, something that was certainly so, and Murchie feared that a new recruiting campaign among them might stiffen backs further. Murchie also was concerned about cutting down the number of companies. This was 'a matter of Government policy', he admitted, but before a decision was taken 'it would be essential' to consult the commanders in the field. The Acting Adjutant-General, Brigadier A. C.

Spencer, also prepared estimates that an additional 5,500 General Service men could be found in Canada by a series of tough measures, including a lowering of the minimum age from 19 to 18½. The key point, however, was Murchie's cautious comment that 'based purely on military considerations' the best course would be to use the NRMA.[76] Eight thousand NRMA infantry could be despatched almost at once, and a further 8,000 could be ready in a month or so. Fully 26,000 more could be re-mustered and trained as infantry in a longer period.[77]

This information was conveyed to the full Cabinet on 24 October. For most of the ministers this meeting was their introduction to the crisis, the first they had heard of it. Ralston told his colleagues that while he was willing to explore the situation further, 'I must say to Council that...I feel there is no alternative but for me to recommend the extension of service of N.R.M.A. personnel to overseas.' The Prime Minister took the floor next, setting out the case for those who did not believe matters had reached the crisis point that would necessitate conscription. The war was almost over, King said in a by now familiar refrain. It would be terrible to divide the country in the moment of victory, particularly as it was the army that had made the errors. In addition he had agreed in 1942 to impose conscription only if it was necessary to win the war; no one now claimed this.

For Ralston, weary after five years of immense burdens, this was the hardest point of the war thus far. In a long conversation with his friend Currie, he went over all the ground, worrying about the implications of the figures supplied by the military and about his duty:

> We discussed at great length his personal position as Minister [Currie recorded of this talk on 25 October]...He was prepared to sacrifice his personal reputation and position for the cause if that was the right thing to do. I said that I thought a man could sacrifice his personal position to a certain point but no further. In this case he had given his word of honour and his promise that he would take certain action if certain things happened. If he was completely satisfied that the condition had now actually arisen where he had to meet his promise, then he should go through with it, irrespective of the fact that his colleagues maintained that it would split the Cabinet, split the country and perhaps cause a revolution, etc. I suggested that he should be careful not to act in a manner unnecessarily provocative or belligerent, so that he could not be accused of opening a public controversy. I said that I thought he should, in putting in his recommendation to the Cabinet, make sure that they had all

the facts before them, that they were satisfied that nothing was withheld from them, and that they could form their own opinions. He should not be an advocate of any particular action, except to say that as a result of the situation, he must recommend to Cabinet that the Zombies be sent overseas.

It was pointed out that the danger would be that the Cabinet would delay action ... The Minister seemed determined that he would not permit procrastination and would bring the matter to a head as soon as possible. I suggested that as soon as the decision was arrived at, and obviously it was going to be against his recommendation, he should quietly hand in his resignation, which should be in very simple terms, and immediately retire to Montreal. He should make no statement other than to refer those asking for such a statement to the Prime Minister.[78]

This discussion clearly guided Ralston in his conduct over the next week.

At Cabinet on 25 October, as on the day before, the ministers tried to grapple with the problem. On the 25th, for the first time, the ministers became aware that there were 120,000 General Service men in Canada, and a further 90,000 in England, a revelation that led to Chubby Power's fervent expostulation, 'My God, if that is the case, what are you talking about getting more men under conscription?'[79] The result was that the three Ministers of National Defence were asked to study this question and to report back. Power recorded his impressions of the meeting of the Ministers with their staff officers:

Pulhems [the army system of rating physical fitness] were discussed at great length, and for the first time I realized, what possibly I should have realized before, that the standards for an infantry man had been made extremely high. I also ascertained that men of 38 and over, even though perfect from the standpoint of Pulhem, were not allowed to go overseas, and that there were a great many Pulhem 'S' [meaning instability and hence unsuitability for front-line service]. ...

We went over the figures as thoroughly as we could and had much discussion during which time Macdonald was most helpful in exploring every possibility of getting men from the pool of 120,000. Stuart, I thought, was a little uncooperative.

We also went over the question of the rate of casualties. I could not get Stuart to say that it was extremely likely that the Canadian troops would be withdrawn from the line after the Schelte [sic] Estuary show was over, and that there would be few if any casualties for some little time afterwards. ...

Stuart put up figures of 22,000 casualties between October 23rd to January. In fact he was inclined to raise them by stating that sickness had not been figured in these casualties which were those caused by direct enemy action.[80]

Nonetheless the Ministers had to report to the War Committee on 27 October that no more than 15,000 General Service men could be found among the 120,000 in Canada who would be suitable for infantry service.* Perhaps some more could be uncovered if the PULHEMS standards were lowered, but no one seemed to relish subjecting the unfit to the rigours of the front. Nor were there very many who could be found among the 90,000 in Britain. Thousands were on the staff, in training, recuperating, or employed in specialist units that could not readily be replaced.

This did seem an astonishing state of affairs. The army as a whole was so large, the number of infantry reinforcements needed so small. But the difficulty was that previous efforts to shake loose fit G.S. men had swept all but the most entrenched away. Those who remained were in the overwhelming majority of cases genuinely unfit or untrained for infantry duties or too young or too old. The problem was more a product of an inflexible system than it was a shortage of men, but that could scarcely be remedied in the atmosphere of crisis that characterized the last weeks of October. Once again the answer seemed to be that the necessary infantry reinforcements—necessary, that is if the estimates of casualties through to the end of the year were accurate —could be found only among the NRMA. About all that could be said was there were enough reinforcements under all circumstances to last into January, but after that time the reinforcement pool would be drained.[81] There did not seem anywhere to turn but to the NRMA.

---

*According to a Top Secret memorandum, 'Total Strength of Canadian Army', dated 30 October 1944, the army overseas consisted of 234,065 'effectives' on 31 August 1944, divided as follows: Western Europe, 104,751; Italy 67,325; and the U.K., 61,989. In addition, there were a further 26,263 'Non Effectives', being men in hospital, detention, on courses, etc. In Canada as of 27 September 1944 there were 16,146 officers and 120,604 other ranks, all General Service. According to the memo, 67,000 of the 120,000 G.S. men were over-age or under-age or of low-PULHEMS category; 31,000 were scheduled for embarkation between 23 September 1944 and 31 May 1945; and 10,600 were calculated as 'wastage'. A further 3,000 were either in officer training or medical and dental students, while 84,000 were listed as 'key personnel'. For the NRMA, the total strength was 68,489 on 27 September 1944 of which 8,743 were on extended leave; 16,000 were trained as infantry and a further 26,000 were of age and medical category suitable for infantry. (Copy in Ralston Papers, Vol. 66.)

Mackenzie King, however, was not yet ready to give up the fight. In the first place he and others doubted the army's figures. On 30 October, for example, General Stuart had to admit that some of the data he had presented to the War Committee were incorrect.[82] Others, even if they believed the figures, simply were not prepared to consider conscription at such a late date. Finally King knew that he could count on a good majority of the Cabinet to side with him. All the Quebec ministers opposed conscription, naturally enough, including Power who had been less than 100 per cent certain in 1942, and only Ilsley, the Minister of Finance, Colin Gibson, the Minister of National Revenue, and T. A. Crerar, the Minister of Mines, seemed willing to back Ralston and his faithful colleague, Angus Macdonald, at this stage.

Those who were in favour of conscription, King realized on 30 October, were the same Cabinet ministers who had opposed his program of social security when it had been discussed on several occasions earlier in 1944. 'It is not merely a question of conscription,' the Prime Minister wrote in his diary. 'The same men who are for conscription are the same identically as those who opposed most strongly the family allowances and other social reforms in the budget....' King's dark, brooding mood was made worse when he opened a telegram from George Fulford, a Liberal M.P. from Brockville, Ontario and one of the private members who had fought against the baby bonus in caucus. Fulford demanded conscription now, a further proof of the conspiracy of reactionaries King saw gathering around him. It was all clear to the Prime Minister now. Conscription was not the real intent; rather it was to divide the country for spurious reasons and thus drive him from office in order to stop the country from reaching towards the welfare state.[83]

There was a certain logic in King's somewhat paranoiac response to the strain of the last two weeks. There *was* a striking coincidence among those who supported conscription and those who had fought against the social-welfare platform.[84] But this did not mean that a conspiracy was afoot, not at all. Still, as King contemplated his next moves, only a conspiracy would suffice. For King, hitherto trying hard to retain Ralston in the government, was reaching the conclusion that the Minister of National Defence, the proponent of conscription, was expendable, and indeed would have to resign if the government was to live.

The Prime Minister's problem now was to find a successor for Ralston, and fortunately he had just the man in mind in General Andrew George Latta McNaughton. McNaughton had been the commander of the 1st Canadian Army overseas until the British had insisted on his relief at the end of 1943 on the grounds that he was unable effectively to command an army in the field. McNaughton had returned to Canada on sick leave—the public explanation of his relief was that ill-health was the cause—and he had been dabbling at the fringes of politics, talking seriously with the Progressive Conservatives, and less seriously with the CCF. He and the Prime Minister had also actively discussed the prospect of McNaughton's becoming the Governor General, the first Canadian-born vice-regal representative, and on 14 October McNaughton had agreed to accept the post. But the General had another qualification for office, at least in the Prime Minister's view. McNaughton and Colonel Ralston had strained their personal relations as long ago as the 1920s, and McNaughton felt that Ralston and certain senior officers in National Defence, especially General Stuart, had either conspired to drive him from his command or had certainly not resisted British efforts with the force they might have. This personal animus would probably make McNaughton amenable to vindicating himself by taking over from Ralston.[85] In addition, and equally important to the Prime Minister, McNaughton clearly did not feel that conscription was an effective way to fight the war. When he and King talked on 31 October, for example, the General said he was 'strongly of the belief that the conscription issue in Canada would work irreparable harm.'[86] This was exactly Mackenzie King's view, and McNaughton was his man.

The Prime Minister's ground was now prepared, and he went off to a meeting of the Cabinet on 31 October in a happier frame of mind. At the Council table the lines were clearly drawn, and King calculated that he had 13 ministers who would side with him while Ralston could count at the most on eight colleagues who might be considered pro-conscriptionists.[87] Ralston himself had reached an even more bleak conclusion. On 30 October he had told Currie 'that only one result could be expected and that *he was all alone.*' That night Currie and Ralston, as the former Deputy Minister of National Defence recorded, 'had a long and intimate talk, and took about two hours drafting his resignation. It was drawn up along exactly the lines that I had originally suggested. He mentioned the fact to me that if the Prime Minister did a clever thing, he would fire him before he could get his resignation.'[88] Exactly. Ralston's letter of resignation was dated 31 October.[89] Both sides were now firmly in place, and with a sense of finality, King informed his colleagues at the meeting on the last day of October that the matter would have to be settled one way or the other the next day.

When the Council met at 3 p.m. on 1 November Ralston made no move to press his resignation. Indeed, he seemed surprisingly accommodating, prepared to consider a further appeal to the NRMA, to make every effort to avoid a split in the government. For the Prime Minister, banking on Ralston's provoking a break, this seemed deeply suspicious. He wrote in his diary, 'here is a scheme to make the situation still more difficult for me. We will be met tomorrow by some condition of things which will mean going over the same ground again to no effect.' As soon as this realization hit him, the Prime Minister decided 'that the time had come to speak out', that he should force the break.

> I then said I thought we ought to, if possible, reach a conclusion without further delay.... After what had been said last night I realized some way would have to be found... to save the government and to save a terrible division at this time.... That I had been asking myself was there anyone who could do this.... If there was, I thought it was owing to the country that such a person's services should be secured. I said I believed I had the man who could undertake the task and carry it out. I then mentioned General McNaughton's name.... I said he believed he could get the reinforcements that were necessary....
>
> I then said that the people of Canada would say that McNaughton was the right man for the task, and since Ralston had clearly said that he himself did not believe we could get the men without conscription, while McNaughton believed we could, and that he, Ralston, would have to tender his resignation... that I thought if Ralston felt in that way he should make it possible for us to bring McNaughton into the Cabinet at once—the man who was prepared to see this situation through. I said that in regard to a resignation from Ralston, he had tendered his resignation to me some two years ago and had never withdrawn it.... [90]

The council chamber was quiet as Ralston, a gentleman and a soldier, rose, said he would hand in his resignation, shook hands, and left the room. The Cabinet sat in silence, stunned by the swift brutality with which King had applied the axe. None of Ralston's supporters moved a muscle or made to follow the departing Minister of National Defence. King's seizure of the psychological moment had been supremely calculated, a feat that was all the more impressive for his having reacted on the spur of the moment.*

*Professor C. P. Stacey disagrees that King acted on the spur of the moment in sacking

The first stage of the crisis had ended with Ralston's firing. The issues, however, had not been resolved in any way, and McNaughton, coming to the ministry as a new man, would still have to find the reinforcements needed—or persuade the General Staff that their figures were incorrect.

IV

Meanwhile public opinion, certain to be a critical factor in the continuing problem of reinforcements, was beginning to reach a fever point. The debate in the Cabinet and in the War Committee had been conducted in secret, and not until 26 October did leaks of the difficulty begin to filter out to the public.[91] Thereafter, although details were short, the stories of crisis were commonplace: 'the national crisis,' the Montreal *Gazette* said on 27 October, 'has at last become a Cabinet crisis also.' The problem now could 'no longer be solved by political manoeuvres', the Montreal morning newspaper argued again three days later, for now the government was 'under the pressure of battle-field realities'.*

Ralston's firing on 1 November heated the debate considerably. McNaughton's appointment, wrote Bruce Hutchison in the Vancouver *Sun* on 2 November, was 'the most astounding move in Mr. King's long

---

Ralston. In his view, a view for which there is no hard evidence, King had decided to fire Ralston on 30 or 31 October but had not confided this 'deadly secret' to the diary. ('Telling Sad Stories of the War and King', *Books in Canada*, March, 1975, p. 17.) The written evidence, all that one can confidently use to form a judgement, suggests that King was prepared by 30 or 31 October to let Ralston resign. Indeed this was the Prime Minister's intention, and as we have seen Ralston did indeed draft a letter of resignation and was expecting to resign. Only when he determined that Ralston was seemingly becoming more co-operative during the meeting of 1 November did King feel it necessary to precipitate matters. By this date, of course, McNaughton was waiting in the wings, and King could move with some confidence.

*One sign of the popular discontent was the flood of semi-scurrilous verse. One bit of doggerel in PAC, John Bracken Papers, Vol. 34, by an anonymous poet sums up the feeling:

Seventy thousand Zombies, isn't it a farce,
Seventy thousand Zombies, sitting on their————
Eating up the rations, morning, noon and night.
Squatting here in Canada while others go to fight.

Seventy thousand Zombies, hear the buzzards sing,
Here's our thanks to you Quebec and old Mackenzie King,
Never mind our comrades, let them be the goats,
As long as the politicians protect their slimy votes . . .

record of political manoeuvre ... The boldness of this stroke left the politicians of Canada reeling.' The McNaughton move also left the Opposition press fuming. The *Gazette* argued on the same day that it was 'hardly good enough for Mr. King to declare dogmatically that General McNaughton was chosen because the men overseas and their next-of-kin would have confidence in him.' In French-language news-papers, however, McNaughton's appointment was widely hailed as ending the ministerial crisis, as a logical step by the Prime Minister, as a defeat of the conscriptionists.[92] Reports from overseas were more confusing. Ross Munro, reporting for the Canadian Press, found the soldiers in North West Europe 'delighted' by Andy's return to active duty. His colleague, Lionel Shapiro, found the men 'shocked' that the General had thrown in his lot with the 'anti-conscriptionists'.[93] Clearly sentiment was in the eye of the beholder overseas—and in Canada too.

The result of the trend in press opinion was clear within a few days, and the Wartime Information Board could report to the government on 18 November that 'There are no English-language papers which oppose conscription on principle.' Such division as existed 'is between those who believe conscription is necessary now, and that the government is avoiding it in an unjustifiable attempt to placate Quebec, and those which believe that the government will introduce conscription when it becomes necessary.' The French-language press was equally united: 'all ... are opposed in principle to conscription.'[94]

But public opinion, as distinguished from editorial opinion, was not so unified. The Canadian Institute of Public Opinion had continued regularly to ask respondents for their opinions on manpower questions and related subjects. On 17 June 1944, just after the invasion of Nor-mandy, for example, Canadians were asked if they believed Canada was doing all it could in the war. Seventy-three per cent said the nation was, only 18 per cent arguing it was not.[95] And when people were asked how they would 'vote today on the question of conscription for overseas service', a regular question of the pollsters, the results were clear:[96]

	For	Against	Undecided
6 Dec. 41	53%	35%	12%
30 Dec. 41	57	34	9
31 Jan. 42	55	35	10
25 Feb. 42	52	37	11
13 Mar. 42	55	37	8
20 Apr. 42	55	36	9
30 May 42	59	33	8

29 Aug. 42	62	32	6
14 Aug. 43	61	32	7
13 Nov. 43	57	36	7
13 Nov. 44	57	36	7

That there was a substantial majority of the public favouring conscription was undeniable; but there was nothing approaching unanimity across the nation. Unfortunately, there are no data by region or by age for the 1944 figures, but such data do exist for the poll conducted on 13 November 1943. At that time Quebec responses showed that 17 per cent would vote for conscription and that 80 per cent would not. In the rest of the country 71 per cent would vote for conscription, 21 per cent would not. Among those between 21 and 29 years of age, only 44 per cent supported conscription while 50 per cent did not; of those between 30 and 49, the figures were 58 and 35 per cent; for those over 50 years of age, the percentages were 61 and 31.[97] In other words, conscription still divided the nation sharply, pitting most French Canadians against most English-speaking Canadians and sharply dividing the young against the old.*

Still the question was a difficult and sharp one. A typical response to the crisis was that of Donald Fleming, a Toronto alderman, who spoke to a Woman's Association meeting on 7 November. The Prime Minister, Fleming said flatly, is 'deliberately ruling according to the will of a minority'. Why, the young Tory asked, 'Why did he not tell us at the time of the plebiscite in 1942 that he would not use the conscript army for fighting overseas if the Province of Quebec opposed it?'[98] By contrast, the *Canadian Forum* argued that public opinion was being manipulated by a fanatic and unscrupulous press campaign.[99] Perhaps the most balanced view was that of the British *Economist*. 'It will really make very little difference to the course of the war, or to the magnitude of Canada's part in it, whether a handful of men are conscripted or not, while, on the other hand, the damage done to the relations between

---

*The government and the Prime Minister considered different methods of dealing with Quebec opinion. J. W. Pickersgill, King's closest political aide at this time, suggested on 13 November that Quebec Liberals could ease matters by not showing too much satisfaction about the government's unwillingness to adopt conscription. (King Papers, f. C244874.) On the other hand, a memo headed 'Appeasing Quebec', (*ibid.*, n.d., ff. C244016ff.) suggested that King should admit that he opposed conscription because Quebec opposed it. This was not the only reason but 'a very important reason'. The Quebec *nationalistes*, the memo urged, should be sharply attacked for trying to destroy Canada as a nation. The *Québécois* in the armed forces, King was urged to say, 'are all fighting as Canadians for *one Canada, not two*'. King did not act as suggested.

French-speaking Canadians might disturb the unity of the Dominion for decades to come.'[100] Distance lent perspective, and few in Canada could see so clearly.

V

Meanwhile General McNaughton was turning to the task at hand, assisted by a Cabinet Recruiting Committee, named on 3 November. The Committee's task was to pry converts out of the NRMA army in Canada, and as a first step all available data on the Zombies were gathered. Analysis of marital status and previous civilian occupation produced some interesting figures:[101]

Occupation	Married	Single	Widower	Separated	Total
Agriculture	1,236	9,870	5	3	11,114
Bldg. trades	1,084	3,184	3	5	4,276
Clerical	377	1,935	1	5	2,318
Manufacturing	3,163	9,178	6	13	12,360
Forestry	345	1,704	2	—	2,051
Mercantile	778	1,939	3	8	2,728
Mining	288	739	—	2	1,029
Professional	128	489	1	2	620
Transport	1,921	4,659	11	6	6,597
Misc. (chiefly unskilled)	2,867	13,692	16	11	16,586
	12,187	47,389	48	55	59,679

Of the 42,000 NRMA soldiers considered as possible infantry reinforcements, 10,250 were born in Ontario, 16,300 in Quebec, 2,600 in the Maritimes, 10,000 on the Prairies, and 2,850 in British Columbia. Not more than 37 per cent were of French-Canadian origin. Other data demonstrated that 6,000 of the men had been NRMA since 1941, 25,000 since 1942, and 17,000 since 1943.[102]

The Recruiting Committee agreed that the best approach to the NRMA would be simply to state the facts, rather than to continue 'skating around the problem'. Its members considered that the situation 'should and can be met by the voluntary co-operation of the Canadian people.' Radio appeals of a 'non-political' nature would be made by McNaughton and the Prime Minister, and Church dignitaries and other influential citizens would be urged to suggest that parents of NRMA soldiers put the pressure on their sons to volunteer. The goal was to create a favourable atmosphere for the government's policy, probably an impossible task in English Canada, and to persuade people to do their utmost to urge men to volunteer.[103]

In making the pitch directly to the NRMA men, the Committee determined that the platoon and unit officers should carry the burden. NRMA soldiers would not be harangued in large groups but canvassed individually; there would be no discrimination practised against the men, and they were to be made to feel that they had been well prepared for action and that they had been and were well treated.[104] At the same time, NRMA men were told that they would be the last soldiers to be demobilized.[105]

This campaign would have some minimal success; that there was no greater result was in part the fault of General McNaughton. On 5 November the new Minister went to Arnprior, Ontario to deliver a speech:

> I have read and studied the reports from our officers in the Field—I have read and studied the suggestions made by our officers here— and I am firmly convinced that the best hope lies in the maintenance of our long traditions of Voluntary Service.... The figures of the reinforcements now available show that we can safely count on some short period yet before there is danger of the situation becoming acute.[106]

His remarks were coolly received, and the next day in an address to a Canadian Legion gathering in Ottawa McNaughton was booed and jeered. Clearly the stormy reception shook the General, who had never dreamt that his comrades from the Great War would meet his requests for patience and assistance with catcalls.[107] The Minister of National Defence would not again venture out of Ottawa.

His efforts at pressing his officers to work at the task of converting the NRMA met with only marginally greater success. On 14 November the senior officers from across the country gathered in Ottawa to hear the General reaffirm the government policy of employing only volunteers overseas. It was, he added, the duty of all officers to employ 'every means ... to enlist the support of the public and to emphasize to NRMA personnel the opportunity and public responsibility which is theirs in this time of national emergency.' This said, McNaughton gathered his papers and prepared to leave, the officers, some having travelled 2,000 miles, sitting in stunned silence that this was all McNaughton had to say. As he left a few called out, including General George Pearkes, commanding on the Pacific coast, 'Don't you wish to hear the reports from the District Officers Commanding?' At this the Minister returned to his seat to be subjected to the gloomy story of all the difficulties the army in Canada had experienced in trying to persuade the NRMA to volunteer. McNaughton could have been left in no doubt that the chances of finding the needed reinforcements from among the NRMA were slim indeed.[108]

Nonetheless the General shortly told the representatives of the press that all was for the best, that the volunteers would be forthcoming, that his officers were sanguine. This provoked the military brass who had attended the meeting into wiring protests to the Chief of the General Staff.[109] On 20 November one of those protesting commanders, General Pearkes, let some of his staff officers talk freely to the press, with the predictable result that pent-up feelings were unloaded: 'Home defence soldiers,' one said, 'should not be expected at this stage of the game to make up their own minds. They are ready to go . . . but they are convinced the Government should tell them to go.'[110]

The problem was that the drive to get the NRMA to convert was going nowhere. There were lower casualties overseas since the beginning of November, McNaughton could tell his colleagues, but unfortunately the conversion rate was low too, ranging from 151 to 280 men in each of the weeks for which latest figures were available. The result as of 20 November was that all the General could promise was a surplus of reinforcements of 700 at the end of December, followed by deficits that he predicted would amount to 9,500 by the end of May 1945. Those figures were very close to the ones the Cabinet had had before Ralston's sacking.[111] In other words, McNaughton had been able to do nothing of significance to remedy the situation.

The brief flurry of optimism that had been generated in the Prime Minister's mind by McNaughton's appointment was once again replaced by worry, a condition complicated by the reconvening of Parliament, set for 22 November. For Mackenzie King, besieged by ministers and advisers offering conflicting advice, the need was to set down in clear form what had to be done. In a brief memorandum King did this. What were foremost, the Prime Minister wrote, were the needs of the men overseas. His power and authority came from the Liberal caucus and through them from the people, King reminded himself, and he did not want any election before the war's end. If others forced a general election then the responsibility would be theirs. But 'The King's Government must be carried on—do all possible to this end. . . . May mean turning over government to those who are most needed for that purpose . . . Be careful *who you take into government* and

about attempting to carry on without men needed in Defence Departments—Finance, munitions...'[112] The Prime Minister did not intend to
surrender easily, that was clear, but his goal was to avoid an election
on this issue, and he would give office to another before he would let
this divisive question go to the people at this stage of the war.

As King also had expected, his conscriptionist ministers were becoming increasingly restive, particularly after McNaughton's hopeless
report on 20 November. Macdonald, Ilsley, and T. A. Crerar, the
Minister of Mines, were becoming more and more aggressive, pressing
for a date to be fixed after which conscription would be imposed if the
men were not found among the NRMA. This led King to put his
thoughts down in a memorandum that he read to his colleagues on 21
November:

> I would ask the public appeal for the trained men for service over-
> seas to be continued until...(three weeks as a minimum). If at the
> end of that time, the requisite number of men are not available I will
> then make way for some other member of the Administration to
> take over, which will leave the Administration free to pass immedi-
> ately an order in council under amendment to the N.R.M.A. Act [sic]
> making its provisions applicable to men called up under provisions
> of the Act....
>
> I shall not take any step which will prevent the men who are
> fighting overseas from obtaining needed reinforcements....
>
> I have taken the only method that I believe possible.
>
> It is for those who believe in a different method to be given the
> opportunity.[113]

This was an honourable course, King believed, but he had certainly
calculated his words closely. For the Prime Minister to resign at this
stage of the war and on such an issue would precipitate a violent public
response from Quebec that could possibly wreck the Liberal Party for a
generation. Who would want to take over with such a prospect in store,
particularly if Mackenzie King stayed in the House of Commons with a
large and probably solid group of M.P.s behind him? No one but a fool
would take the post under those circumstances. As soon as King had
finished speaking, the Quebec ministers indicated they would resign
with King, as did James G. Gardiner, the Minister of Agriculture, and
others. This led Macdonald, probably the leading conscriptionist, to
remark that it was clear the Cabinet was against conscription and that
the best course might be for the conscriptionists to leave.[114] At this
point, with the Cabinet in something of an uproar, Gardiner remarked

that if King agreed to remain 'we would announce that if the voluntary system failed at the end of the test period, 8,000 Zombies would be sent over. The question would be reviewed with regard to the second 8,000, but we would send the rest home and would have no more conscription of any shape, no more call-up.'[115] There was a brief discussion about this suggestion but Power and St Laurent, the Minister of Justice and the leading *Québécois* in the ministry, objected. The discussion drifted away from the point and the Cabinet meeting ended inconclusively, with Macdonald, Ilsley, and some other ministers talking of leaving the government while King groaned about his difficulties in carrying on without men like Ilsley.[116]

Clearly the government faced collapse. King thus far had indicated that he would resign rather than move towards conscription; Power and St Laurent had rejected a potential compromise in the Gardiner offer; and the conscriptionist ministers, led by Ilsley, Macdonald, and Crerar, were talking of leaving rather than waiting indefinitely for conscription to be imposed. There seemed to be no room to manoeuvre, nowhere to go but into the House of Commons on 22 November with a ruined government.

At this point McNaughton provided Mackenzie King with the excuse he needed for action that would save the government. On the morning of 22 November the Minister of National Defence called King with news that, he said, had hit him like a blow in the stomach. 'The Headquarters Staff here had all advised him that the voluntary system would not get the men . . . it was the most serious advice that could be tendered and he wished to have it in writing.'*[117]

*The written advice was innocuous:

1. In my memorandum of 23 Oct. [General Murchie, the Chief of the General Staff, wrote McNaughton on 22 November], a copy attached, it was stated that the extension of the Terms of Service of NRMA personnel to permit their despatch overseas would most readily meet the immediate requirements of the Army Overseas and maintain its fighting efficiency.
2. On the 2 Nov. I placed before you a statement of the problem as it then existed, copy attached.
3. Careful examination of the problem has continued and every effort within our power has been made to meet this problem by the voluntary system.
4. After a careful review of all the factors including the latest expression of their views by the District Officers Commanding, I must now advise you that in my considered opinion the Voluntary system of recruiting through Army channels cannot meet the immediate problem.
5. The Military Members [of the Army Council] concur in this advice.
(Printed in C. P. Stacey, *Arms, Men and Governments: The War Policies of Canada 1939-1945* (Ottawa, 1970), p. 471.)

Conveyed to King by the upset and nervous McNaughton, a man who was probably aware for the first time of the extent of the difficulties and the stakes involved, this information hit the Prime Minister like a thunderbolt. 'Instantly,' he wrote in his diary. 'there came to mind the statement I had made to Parliament in June [1942] as to the action the government would necessarily take if we were agreed that the time had come when conscription was necessary.' Now whatever the causes, whatever the errors, conscription was necessary and the Minister of National Defence said it was. ' . . . it will be my clear duty to agree to the passing of the order in council and go to Parliament and ask for a vote of confidence . . . This really lifts an enormous burden from my mind,' the Prime Minister added in the truest words he had ever written, 'as after yesterday's council it was apparent to me that it was only a matter of days before there would be no Government . . . '[118]

King had decided to opt for conscription. In his mind, seeking desperately for a way out of his dilemma, the army advice provided the best of opportunities to justify a switch. The unrest among the senior commanders, the foolish action of General Pearkes a few days before, the near ultimatum presented by the Chief of the General Staff—all provided a screen of verisimilitude behind which King could cloak his political responses. This was vital to King, of course, because now he had to persuade Louis St Laurent, the key minister at this point, not to resign when the policy altered. At a meeting with the Justice Minister later that day, this task was apparently easily handled, St Laurent being concerned that this meant the 'surrender of the civil government to the military', a 'palace revolution'.[119] He would go along.

The other key Cabinet minister was Power. But as a Minister of National Defence, as one who knew most of the generals reasonably well, Power would not easily be persuaded by talk of a military revolt:

I went to his office at the appointed time [Power wrote]. Mr. King was late, and as soon as he came in said to me, 'I don't know what I would do without you Chubby'. He said he thought the day had gone well. . . . He then said he wanted my assistance, as he had never done before, and proceeded to tell me that McNaughton had gone to see him in the morning to tell him that it was impossible for him to obtain the men needed for reinforcements within any reasonable time. There were various reasons given . . . He then said he proposed to pass an order-in-council sending 16,000 Zombies overseas; not to impose Conscription; to stick to the Voluntary system . . .

I could not fully follow what he had in mind, but I told him that I thought St Laurent would follow him and my other colleagues from Quebec. I said the only thing I could do was to go out quietly and make no fuss about it.[120]

This was less satisfactory, but King continued to hope the Air Minister could be persuaded to reconsider.

Thus matters were prepared for the Cabinet meeting of 8 p.m. on 22 November. Only St Laurent and Power knew that King was prepared to make a *volte-face*, and in fact the conscriptionists had been meeting earlier in the day to co-ordinate their moves—the submission of letters of resignation by Crerar, Macdonald, Ilsley, Mulock, the Postmaster General, Gibson, the Minister of National Revenue, and C. D. Howe, the Minister of Munitions and Supply.[121] King's uncanny combination of luck, prescience, and adaptability had led him to change front in the nick of time to forestall the loss of most of his key English-speaking ministers. And the Prime Minister had not even known that the ministers were meeting, nor did he learn this until January 1945.[122]

King explained his new position to the Council, stunning the Quebec ministers with this sudden abandonment of his hitherto unalterable position, and taking the conscriptionists completely by surprise. Power repeated his private advice to the Prime Minister that he would resign, and Gardiner, the Agriculture Minister, talked of leaving too. But the main part of a desultory discussion concerned the ways in which conscription could be implemented, a discussion that closed without any firm conclusion.[123]

This would come the next day after a long series of prime ministerial telephone calls to Quebec notables explaining the shift, after a caucus, and after discussions again on methods in the Cabinet. The upshot was an order-in-council to send up to 16,000 NRMA men overseas. King was leaving his options open—if some miracle occurred and less NRMA soldiers could do the job, less would be sent; but up to 16,000 could be. Shortly afterwards Parliament was told and through Parliament the public. There was widespread shock among the Quebec members—Maxime Raymond, the one-time Liberal turned leader of the Bloc Populaire Canadien, wrote 'Trahison conscription directe' when he learned of the switch[124]—and there were some demonstrations in Quebec City. The Conservatives, however, once again came to the realization that the Prime Minister had forestalled them.

Public opinion on the government's course was a mixture of confusion, bitterness, and 'I told you so' attitudes. The Ottawa *Journal*, a Conservative sheet, said that 'All of us know what has happened. Mr. Mackenzie King has shown that he would rather be Premier than right

... abandoned on Thursday what he said was right on Wednesday. . . .'
More thoughtful responses came a week or two after the event. In the
Winnipeg Free Press, a conscriptionist paper but a Liberal one too, Grant
Dexter wrote on 7 December that the evidence indicated 'that there was
a breakdown or failure in the general staff in 1944. As a result . . . the
country was plunged without warning into the conscription crisis.' That
seemed a fair assessment of the events that had precipitated the crisis.
And Bruce Hutchison, again in the *Free Press*, on 9 December struck at
the racism he had found in British Columbia during the crisis: 'the issue
at Ottawa had ceased to be military. It had become racial . . . whether we
should put the French-Canadians in their place.' Too many influential
British Columbians, Hutchison said, wanted to seize the opportunity presented by the conscription crisis to establish domination over Quebec, to
repeal the Confederation bargains with Quebec, and to abolish the
French language in Canada.[125] That sort of attitude was not confined to
the west coast. The opinion polls, however, indicated fairly widespread
approval for the government's action. When asked if they supported the
sending of the NRMA men overseas or if more voluntary enlistment
should have been encouraged, 50 per cent approved the order while 33
per cent wanted further efforts at voluntary enlistment. The Canadian
Institute of Public Opinion broke the data down further, reporting that
66 per cent of those of British origin supported the government move, 8
per cent of French-Canadian origin, and 55 per cent of 'other'. By age
groups, those between 21 and 29 years were least enthusiastic, only 46
per cent approving the government policy, while of those over 50 years
of age 54 per cent did so approve.[126]

VI

All that remained now was to get the NRMA men overseas, a task that
proved more difficult than many of the conscriptionists might have
expected. In the House of Commons on 24 November General
McNaughton (present by special arrangement as he was not an elected
Member) indicated that 10,000 additional men would be despatched in
December and January, that the units concerned had been selected that
morning, and that they would shortly be moved east prior to despatch
overseas. The Minister added that 'The men who wish to volunteer will
be given every opportunity to do so. The others, the whole units
including those men, will be despatched on the dates which at the
present time are being arranged.'[127] The 10,000 would be made up of
7,500 fully trained infantry and 2,500 whose training was at an

advanced stage. The remaining 26,000 NRMA men considered suitable for infantry service were to be readied for such duties.

The bulk of the NRMA men were to be found among units of the 6th Division, stationed in British Columbia. Trouble had erupted there as soon as the soldiers realized that only partial conscription had been imposed on them, that only 16,000 were liable for overseas service. This, at least, was General George Pearkes' explanation. Whatever the cause there was trouble indeed. One thousand men marched through the streets of Vernon, B.C. shouting 'Down with Conscription' and 'Conscript Money as Well', and two officers were roughed up by the troops. Pearkes later reported on the effects of this incident:

> Indiscreet handling of news releases by the Press had decided contributory effect. The first news story of the Vernon demonstration stated that 1000 men took part, whereas less than 200 were actually involved. Such exaggeration was obvious encouragement to malcontents in other camps, who were led thereby to believe that the movement was much stronger than in reality.[128]

At Terrace events got completely out of hand on 24 November. French-speaking soldiers of Les Fusiliers du St Laurent, joined by some men of the Prince Edward Island Highlanders and the Prince Albert Volunteers, armed themselves and mounted anti-tank guns to command the approaches. The despatch of a unit to another camp was blocked, and by 28 November, rather a long time after the fact, senior officers decided they had a mutiny on their hands.[129]

In Ottawa the events out west caused consternation. McNaughton had long feared difficulties among the NRMA men and he knew there were no troops in the country that could restore order—except for other NRMA units. To King this revolt in the west was clear proof that all those officers who had told the government that the men would go overseas if ordered had lied.[130] And the consternation turned into near panic when word reached National Defence Headquarters, apparently as a result of someone's confusion, that General Pearkes had ordered the RCAF to make passes over the Terrace camp. Fortunately this did not take place, and the troubles gradually petered out.[131] Although the disturbances were fairly widespread throughout British Columbia camps, few men were apparently punished for their actions, in part at least because there was relatively little property damage. To General Pearkes, a few ringleaders only had caused the trouble, men who did not want to go overseas for any reason, and they had been joined by many others in a spirit of 'horse play'.[132]

The disturbances gradually ceased and the NRMA units began to be shipped east. In an effort to persuade more men to convert to General Service, French-speaking units went to camps in Quebec, and the NRMA men generally were delighted at the prospect of a return to their home area.[133] But in all units, English-speaking or French-speaking, there was a high degree of absenteeism, and there were recurring bouts of rioting, sit-down strikes, and a definite reluctance on the part of NRMA men to 'go active' even though that had advantages for them.[134] There was also one famous case of a soldier who threw his kitbags and rifle into the sea as he went on board ship for overseas. This incident, magnified by gossip, was turned into a campaign charge by the Conservatives that hundreds of NRMA soldiers had so acted. The one incident, allegedly by a soldier with psychiatric troubles, had major political repercussions,[135] and the Conservatives created the picture of an NRMA army that was riddled with dissension. Unfortunately that was not too far off the mark, and what some officers referred to as 'Atlantic fever' was fairly widespread.[136]

Word of the troubles with the NRMA men was largely kept from the public by censorship. The Toronto *Globe and Mail*, however, was convinced that the censorship was motivated by political reasons, not, as the Chief Censor maintained, for military security. The *Globe* and the Montreal *Gazette*, both Conservative papers, were tempted to burst the censorship bonds, but beyond an editorial by the Toronto paper denying that the security reasons were valid, an editorial that must have puzzled readers, the papers did nothing. Once the convoys had arrived in Britain, however, there was no longer any reason for censorship, and in late January there was a spate of articles that revealed, among other things, that over 200 of the 482 absentees in Pacific Command were G.S. volunteers! Nonetheless the state of affairs was bad enough among the NRMA, as the *Gazette* demonstrated in an editorial of 22 January:

> . . . It is now a matter of official admission that of the 15,600 Home Defence troops advised that they were to be sent overseas, 7,800 or precisely one half, were at one time overdue or absent without leave. To the present time only 1,500 of these have returned or have been returned by police action.

These reports led to widespread unfavourable publicity in the United States.[137]

They led as well to extensive efforts to crack down on deserters, to advertisements warning people that harbouring absentees was a criminal offense, and to raids on public places by RCMP and military police.

In Drummondville, Quebec on 24 February a 100-man raiding party was attacked by a mob, their vehicles overturned and smashed, while fighting lasted in the streets for three hours, and scores required hospital treatment.[138] There was no room for doubt that many of the NRMA men did not want to go overseas; nor was there any doubt that in Quebec at least, civilians too did not want them to go.

Curiously, once the NRMA soldiers did get overseas, they served very well indeed. The Loyal Edmonton Regiment's War Diary, for example, noted on 30 April 1945 that the NRMA reinforcements were treated the same as G.S. men and 'in the few small actions they have engaged in so far they have generally shown up as well as all new reinforcements do.' Other accounts stressed that once the men had been in action no one any longer cared who was or was not a 'Zombie'.[139]

In all, 12,908 NRMA men went overseas and 2,463 were posted to units of the First Canadian Army in North West Europe. Of these 69 were killed, 232 were wounded, and 13 became prisoners of war.[140] More important, the estimates of need that had provoked the crisis in October 1944, those guesses on the future course of events, proved to be in error. Action on the Canadian fronts was less heavy than the General Staff had expected; the corps in Italy was transferred to North West Europe and was out of action as a result, with a consequent saving of casualties; and the Germans collapsed rather more rapidly in the end than many had feared. Even without the reinforcements provided by the NRMA men, there would have been 8,500 men in the reinforcement pool overseas on 27 April 1945.

The NRMA crisis, then, fizzled out like a damp squib. Its importance was more symbolic than real, but that was importance enough.

VII

The political implications of the conscription crisis, similar to the actual military effects, tended to disappear more quickly than many had feared. The country was concerned and aroused in an intense fashion, but this lasted for a short time only.*

---

*Surveys of public opinion prepared for the Cabinet by the Wartime Information Board demonstrated the shift in opinion. On 27 November the WIB reported that for three weeks every report it had received from its opinion-sounders across the country had been preoccupied with the manpower question. A week later the Cabinet was told that *Québécois* had 'lost faith in everyone' while the predominant mood in English Canada was that 'it's about time' that NRMA men were sent overseas. On 11 December 'Excitement has disappeared

In the House of Commons, for example, the Quebec members were genuinely shocked, even stunned, by the way Mackenzie King had reversed his course. But although Chubby Power resigned from the ministry, and although many other ministers, parliamentary assistants, and backbenchers talked of imitating him, few moved, thanks in substantial part to the efforts of St Laurent. In the final vote in the House on a motion of confidence in the government, however, only 23 French-Canadian Liberals voted with the government, and the motion carried 143 to 70.[141] King had survived the shift in policy without too much loss of support in Quebec, at least not enough to topple the government.

Opinion in Quebec at large generally cooled down quickly, although many would feel betrayed for years. In the first days after the adoption of the order-in-council sending the NRMA overseas, feelings ran high. *Nationalistes* gathered to move resolutions, and the Quebec legislature passed a motion condemning Ottawa for its breach of faith with Quebec.[142] But somehow there did not seem to be too much heart left in the game. The war was almost over, and large numbers of *Québécois* were overseas helping to win it. In addition the political divisions among the people of the province were sharp, with Duplessis holding many conservative *nationalistes*, with André Laurendeau and Maxime Raymond leading the more liberal Bloc Populaire Canadien, and with many standing aloof because of dislike for the former or because of a clear fear that the latter would go no place, a feeling that had something behind it after the disappointing BPC showing in the August 1944 provincial election.

In Quebec, however, Chubby Power and P. J. A. Cardin, the minister who had resigned during the first conscription crisis, provided potential rallying points for dissident Liberals and others. Attempts in early 1945 to strike an alliance between the two failed, and both went their own way. Cardin in the spring even set up his own party, only to throw in the cards in May. Power tried to create an independent Liberal organization, but he too threw in his hand and linked up with King and St Laurent.[143] For better or worse Mackenzie King's Liberals seemed to be the best support Quebec had in Ottawa; certainly the Conservative Party, seemingly wanting to conscript everyone and seemingly full of people who had little if any commitment to the idea of a bilingual

---

everywhere,' the WIB said; on 18 December 'English-speaking reports agree that discussion has practically ceased,' although in Quebec the issue of the NRMA was still widely discussed. (PAC, Privy Council Office Records, Box 3, file W-34-10, Memoranda to Cabinet, 27 Nov. and 4, 11, 18 Dec. 1944.)

Canada, offered no home; the CCF had taken a saner position on the manpower question, but the party was unfortunately socialist and somewhat beyond the pale as a result. There was no other home possible but the Liberals.

Outside Quebec, feeling against the government could still become very strong. Ontario, in 1917, 1942, and 1944 pre-eminently the conscriptionist province, harboured its grudges, whipped along by the Conservative Party and by unleashed racism. The first test of sentiment in the province after the crisis was the Grey North by-election of 5 February 1945, where General McNaughton was seeking a seat in the House of Commons. McNaughton was a Protestant but his wife was a Roman Catholic, an opening that bigots seized on with eagerness. The links between McNaughton and the Pope, between McNaughton and the NRMA were deemed to be one and the same. Reverend T. T. Shields, the pillar of Toronto's Jarvis Street Baptist Church, even came to Owen Sound to urge the voters of staunchly Protestant and Orange Grey North to reject the Pope's candidate.[144]

All this would have been funny had people not believed it. McNaughton's role in the conscription crisis had been ambiguous enough to confuse people, and many looked on him as a man who had leaped at a chance to advance himself without much regard for principle. The General's own campaign style was also awkward, and he found it difficult, he said, to get away from Ottawa for long, something that inhibited his campaigning in a riding that he did not know and one that he naively announced he would not run in again at the general election.[145] Worse, he insisted on coming to the constituency in a radio-equipped railway car, a necessity if he was to stay in close touch with Defence headquarters, but a seeming show of extravagance in a frugal area.[146] All the omens were bad.

About all that the General and the Liberals had going for them was the Conservative candidate. Garfield Case had been the mayor of Owen Sound. He also was against conscription, or so private correspondence of his released during the election seemed to show.[147] Case was more buffoon than serious candidate, a man capitalizing on know-nothingism, and something of an embarrassment to his party. As a result John Bracken, the Progressive Conservative leader, had to come into the riding to unleash the big guns—a charge that Zombies had thrown their rifles and equipment overboard in an attempt to stop themselves being sent overseas. This charge was almost groundless, as we have seen, but it was effective nonetheless, and there was enough corroborative evidence in the shocking figures of NRMA men who had gone absent without leave. The question, Bracken said, was simple and clear: 'Do you or do you not approve as Minister of National Defence a man whose recent course of action is held in complete contempt by the men overseas?'[148] The voters' answer on 5 February was to elect Garfield Case to Parliament.

The McNaughton debacle was the nadir of government fortunes. The government began to get a good press again as the family-allowance scheme, scheduled for implementation on 1 July 1945, began to make well-publicized preparations for enrolling and registering children and parents. The United Nations Conference on International Organization at San Francisco gave Mackenzie King a chance to appear on the world stage, a forum that John Bracken was barred from. And the end of the war in Europe on V-E Day, 8 May 1945, turned public attention towards the peace. The Liberals, as the government, had the ball here, and they had been working for years on the preparation of effective legislation designed to cushion the transition from war to peace. There were very generous veterans' benefits, aid for housing, aid to businessmen and exporters, help for farmers, fishermen, the aged. It was a good program and much of it was in place, a far cry, naturally, from the promises of the Conservatives and CCF.[149]

The Conservatives also made the fundamental error of misjudging the impact and significance of Grey North. This by-election, they believed, had shown that conscription would be an effective electoral weapon. It might have been if the war was still on at election time, but Mackenzie King had gambled and fixed 11 June as polling day, a shrewd enough guess as it turned out. The only war still under way was that in the Pacific, and the Conservatives promised to finish that war with conscripts.[150] This probably appealed to some people, particularly in British Columbia,[151] but in Quebec, a province for which the Tories had had hopes, it killed them. Nor did it seem to make much impact elsewhere in the country, for the Japanese war had tended to be a subsidiary theatre to most Canadians and few servicemen had fought in the Pacific theatres.* What the Conservative pledge did was to

---

*A public-opinion survey conducted by the Wartime Information Board and forwarded to the Cabinet on 14 May 1945 found that 50 per cent of the people believed that the war against Japan should be carried on by volunteers while 39 per cent thought that all available men should be used. Eleven per cent thought Canada should have no role at all. From Ontario to the Pacific coast, the WIB survey found, Canadians thought Canada should do as much as against Germany; Quebec was heavily against a major effort and in the Maritimes more than half those surveyed thought Canada should do less than it had against the Nazis. (PAC, Privy Council Office Records, Box 3, file W-34-10, Memorandum to Cabinet, 14 May 1945.)

reinforce the impression that the Conservatives were bloodthirsty, that any war was better than no war, and that the Liberals were probably the party best able to handle the transition to peace.

The election results were a near thing for the Liberals, the King government returning with from 125 to 127 Members (depending on independents) in a House of 245. For Bracken's Tories, however, it was a disaster, with only 67 Conservatives elected, 48 of them coming from Ontario. The CCF had 28 seats, the Bloc Populaire 2. The key to the election was Quebec. There the government won over half the popular vote and returned 53 Members; the Conservatives, saddled with the conscriptionist label in an irredeemable fashion, won a mere 8 per cent of the vote and returned only two Members of Parliament.

Mackenzie King's course of action in handling the issue of conscription, then, was vindicated by the voters, and particularly by those in Quebec. Quebec was the province most affected by the crises of 1942 and 1944, and Quebec had again voted for King. This was an unenthusiastic vote, a vote that recognized King as the best of a bad lot, a vote that in effect represented a turning of the back on the events of the war. But to some extent Quebec's vote for the Liberals was a recognition that however his course had wavered and however tortured his reasoning became at times, Mackenzie King had tried to honour his promises to French Canada. If he had been driven away from his pledges of 1939 and 1940, it was only because the majority pressured him and threatened to destroy the Liberal Party, the one party that did attempt to combine French Canadians and English Canadians. There was more than an element of truth in this reasoning.

Certainly Mackenzie King had demonstrated that he had learned from 1917. There had been no coalition government with French Canada left on the outside. There had been no racist election campaign run by the government and employing a virtually solid English-language media. There had been no irreparable blows to French Canada. Certainly English Canadians had talked again in this war of 'equal sacrifice' when they meant that French Canadians were not enlisting in proportionate numbers; but Quebec did contribute a vastly greater share to the war effort in 1939-45, and the government fought vigorously against the racists. It was a different war, fought abroad with different weapons and tactics, and fought at home with greater intelligence, better leadership, and greater awareness of the difficulties of governing a divided country. There had been errors in plenty, but Mackenzie King's skill in dividing Canadians least had been supreme.

NOTES

1 *Report of the Labour Supply Investigation Committee to Labour Coordination Committee* (October, 1941), pp. 26, 158. For a summary, see Public Archives of Canada [PAC], J. L. Ralston Papers, Vol. 144.

2 *Report*, pp. 156-7.

3 Memorandum by Grant Dexter, 15 Dec. 1941, copy in PAC, J. W. Dafoe Papers, Vol. 12.

4 Ralston Papers, Vol. 144, Manpower Committee Minutes, 16, 23 Dec. 1941, 8, 9 Jan. 1942.

5 PAC, Privy Council Records, Cabinet War Committee Minutes, 4 Feb. 1942. See also Charles Stacey, *Arms, Men and Governments: The War Policies of Canada 1939-1945* (Ottawa, 1970), p. 404.

6 Cabinet War Committee Minutes, 26 Feb. 1942.

7 PAC, Department of External Affairs Records, Vol. 107, file 694, Robertson to King, 14 Nov. 1941.

8 Ralston Papers, Vol. 76, Adj.-Gen. to Ralston, 29 Apr. 1943. See documents on PAC, Department of National Defence Records, file HQS 6615-4-A. See also Ken Adachi, *The Enemy that Never Was* (Toronto, 1976), *passim*.

9 House of Commons *Debates*, 24 Mar. 1942, pp. 1563ff.

10 See C. C. Lingard and R. G. Trotter, *Canada in World Affairs 1941-1944* (Toronto, 1950), p. 103.

11 Cabinet War Committee Minutes, 8, 17 July 1942.

12 Queen's University, Grant Dexter Papers, Memorandum, 2 Aug. 1942.

13 Queen's University, T. A. Crerar Papers, Crerar to J. W. Dafoe, 1 Aug. 1942.

14 *Wartime Work of Department of Labour*, a supplement to the *Labour Gazette* (November, 1943), p. 17.

15 'Memorandum on Manpower submitted by Director of National Selective Service', in Cabinet War Committee, Documents.

16 *Ibid.*

17 Cabinet War Committee Minutes, 17 Sept. 1942; J. W. Pickersgill, *The Mackenzie King Record*, Vol. I: *1939-44* (Toronto, 1960), p. 446.

18 PAC, W. L. M. King Papers, Diary, 17 Sept. 1942.

19 Stacey, *op. cit.*, p. 407.

20 Dexter Papers, Memorandum, 29 Oct. 1942.

21 King Diary, 18 Nov. 1942.

22 See Raymond Ranger, *Report on the Operations of National Registration and Military Mobilization in Canada during World War II* (Ottawa, 1949), pp. 25, 57. Copy in Department of National Defence, Directorate of History.

23 King Diary, 10 Dec. 1942. P. C. 11326 of 15 Dec. 1942 implemented this decision.

24 Comparative Labour Force Distribution, copy in Ralston Papers, Vol. 144.

25 See Ralph Allen, *Ordeal By Fire* (Toronto, 1961), p. 394.

26 Department of National Defence Records, file HQS 650-99-7, Memo, K. Turner to Director of Special Services, 10 June 1943.

27 *Ibid.*, K. Harvie to Director of Special Services, 5 Feb. 1943.

28 Based on Cameron Macpherson, 'The Birth of a Minority: The Army System and the Zombie Myths', York University undergraduate paper, 41-2.

29 Stacey, *op. cit.*, p. 600.

30 Ralston Papers, Vol. 144, Memo, 3 May 1943.

31 Department of National Defence Records, file HQS 9011-9-1, Adj.-Gen. to Ralston, 22 June 1943; HQS 9011-0-2-2, de Lalanne to Vice Adj.-Gen., 26 Jan. 1943.

32 *Ibid.*, file HQS 9011-6-1-1, Ralston to Mitchell, 4 June 1943.

33 Queen's University, Donald Gordon Papers, Gordon to Ilsley, 26 Mar. 1943.

34 See Ralston Papers, Vol. 146, 'Notes for the Minister . . .', 1 May 1943.

35 Department of National Defence Records, file HQS 9011-6-1-1, Ralston to Mitchell, 19 May 1943; House of Commons *Debates*, 18 May 1943, p. 2779.

36 Department of National Defence Records, file HQS 9011-6-1-1, Mitchell to Ralston, 27 May 1943.

37 Stacey, *op. cit.*, p. 411.

38 Docs on Department of National Defence Records, file HQS 9011-0-1-5, Vols. 1-3.

39 Docs on *ibid.*, file HQS 9011-6-1, and especially Adj.-Gen. to Ralston, 29 May 1943.

40 Cabinet War Committee Minutes, 24 June 1943.

41 *Ibid.*, 26 June and 2 July 1943.

42 Department of National Defence Records, file HQS 9011-6-1, MacNamara to Mitchell, 5 July 1943; Cabinet War Committee Minutes, 7 July 1943.

43 Stacey, *op. cit.*, p. 410.

44 Cabinet War Committee Minutes, 21 July 1943.

45 Stacey, *op. cit.*, p. 411.

46 Ranger, *op. cit.*, p. 34.

47 *Wartime Work of the Department of Labour*, p. 17.

48 Department of National Defence Records, file HQS 9011-6-1-1, Mitchell to Ralston, 15 Mar. 1944.

49 *Ibid.*, Ralston to Mitchell, 1 Apr. 1944.

50 *Ibid.*, file HQS 9011-6-0, Mitchell to Ralston, 15 Apr. 1944.

51 Privy Council Office Records, Box 13, file M-5-1, MacNamara to Heeney, 2 Mar. 1944. The only detailed study of women in the war labour force is Ruth Pierson, 'Women's Emancipation and the Recruitment of Women into the Canadian Labour Force in WWII', a paper presented to the Canadian Historical Association, 1976.

52 Privy Council Office Records, file W-34-10, Memorandum to Cabinet, 7 Aug. 1944.

53 Dexter Papers, Memorandum, 23 June 1944.

54 Minutes, 21 June 1944, in Ralston Papers, file 614-11.

55 Queen's University, C. G. Power Papers, Vol. 78, 'Release of Aircrew' file; Ottawa *Citizen*, 21 Oct. 1944.

56 Public Archives Record Centre [PARC], National Defence Records, War Diary, Directorate of Army Recruiting, April 1944, Appendix 19.

57 Ottawa *Journal*, 24 Apr. 1944.

58 Ralston Papers, Vol. 50, 'Mobilization of 13 Brigade on an Active Basis', 2 May 1944. Printed in part in Stacey, *op. cit.*, pp. 591ff.

59 Power Papers, Staff Memo notes re War Committee Meetings, Oct.-Nov. 1944, 'Report of Cabinet Committee on Army Enlistments for G.S.', 6 Nov. 1944.

60 Macpherson, *op. cit.*, 51-2; Toronto *Star*, 8 July 1944.

61 J. L. Granatstein, *The Politics of Survival* (Toronto, 1967), p. 176.

62 PAC, Arthur Meighen Papers, Box 7, Meighen to Bracken, 7 July 1943; a different view is in Dafoe Papers, Dafoe to B. T. Richardson, 8 July 1943.

63 Ottawa *Journal*, 20 June 1944; Granatstein, *Politics of Survival*, p. 177.

64 Dexter Papers, Memorandum, 24 June 1944.

65 *Ibid.*, 23 June 1944.

66 Cabinet War Committee Minutes, 3 Aug. 1944. See Stacey's good account in *op. cit.*, pp 434ff.

67 See the detailed account in *ibid.*, pp. 424ff.

68 Dexter Papers, Memo by Currie, 4 Nov. 1944 enclosed with Currie to Dexter, 18 Jan. 1950; Stacey, *op. cit.*, pp. 432ff.

69 House of Commons *Debates*, 29 Nov. 1944, p. 6669.

70 Directorate of History, Department of National Defence, CMHQ file, 1/Manpower/2/3, Macklin to Chief of Staff, 16 Oct. 1944.

71 Ralston Papers, Vol. 43, Chief of Staff to Ralston, 15 Oct. 1944.

72 King Diary, 13 Oct. 1944.

73 *Ibid.*, 18 Oct. 1944.

74 *Ibid.*

75 J. L. Granatstein, *Canada's War: The Politics of the Mackenzie King Government 1939-1945* (Toronto, 1975), pp. 345-6.

76 Directorate of History, file 112.3S2009 (D36), Murchie to Ralston, 23 Oct. 1944; HQS 9011-9-1, Spencer to Ralston, 23 Oct. 1944.

77 Ralston in House of Commons *Debates*, 29 Nov. 1944, p. 6671.

78 Currie memo.

79 J. W. Pickersgill and D. Forster, eds, *The Mackenzie King Record*, Vol. II: *1944-45* (Toronto, 1968), 152; King Diary, 25 Oct. 1944; but Power Papers, Notes of Discussions on the Conscription Crisis, put this on 26 Oct. Power's Notes are a very full account of the ministers' positions. See also D. G. Creighton, *The Forked Road: Canada 1939-57* (Toronto, 1976), pp. 92ff.

80 Power Papers, Notes of Discussions on the Conscription Crisis, 26 Oct. 1944. Currie attended this meeting and his memo deals with it similarly.

81 Cabinet War Committee Minutes, 27 Oct. 1944; Directorate of History, file 112.3H1.009 (D10), Statement by McNaughton, 12 Feb. 1964.

82 Ralston Papers, Vol. 43, Chief of Staff to Ralston, 30 Oct. 1944.

83 King Diary, 30 Oct. 1944.

84 On the Cabinet splits over social welfare, see Granatstein, *Canada's War*, pp. 272ff.

85 See on McNaughton at this period, John Swettenham, *McNaughton*, Vol. III: *1944-1966* (Toronto, 1969), chapters 1-2; Granatstein, *Canada's War*, pp. 351-2.

86 Pickersgill and Forster, *op. cit.*, 177; PAC, A. G. L. McNaughton Papers, Vol. 267, Memorandum, 31 Oct. 1944.

87 King Diary, 31 Oct. 1944.

88 Currie memo.

89 Ralston Papers, Vol. 43, draft, 31 Oct. 1944.

90 King Diary, 1 Nov. 1944; Public Archives of Nova Scotia, Angus L. Macdonald Papers, Diary, 1 Nov. 1944. Cf. Macdonald's public account in *Halifax Chronicle-Herald*, 29 Dec. 1949.

91 Montreal *Gazette*, 26 Oct. 1944.

92 Survey of Quebec editorials in Toronto *Globe and Mail*, 6 Nov. 1944.

93 Noted in Ottawa *Journal*, 6 Nov. 1944.

94 King Papers, Notes and Memoranda, Conscription file No. 6, WIB Survey No. 50, 18 Nov. 1944; see also Public Record Office (London), Dominions Office Records, DO 35/ 1118, Review of the Dominions Press, 18 Jan. 1945.

95 *Public Opinion Quarterly*, VIII (Fall, 1944), 453.

96 *Ibid.*, VIII (Winter, 1944-5), 591.

97 *Ibid.*, VIII (Spring, 1944), 153.

98 Toronto *Globe and Mail*, 7 Nov. 1944.

99 *Canadian Forum*, XXIV (December, 1944), 196.

100 *Economist*, 2 Dec. 1944, 729.

101 Department of National Defence Records, file HQS 9011-15-0, 'Analysis of NRMA Soldiers . . .', 27 Nov. 1944.

102 McNaughton Papers, file 892-10, Heeney to Cabinet, 6 Nov. 1944.

103 *Ibid.*

104 *Ibid.*

105 PAC, C. D. Howe Papers, Vol. 53, Heeney to Howe, 25 Sept. 1944.

106 Copy in Dexter Papers, Vol. 13, file 70a.

107 McNaughton interview, 23 Mar. 1966; Cf. Swettenham, *McNaughton*, 521.

108 See R. H. Roy, 'Major-General G. R. Pearkes and the Conscription Crisis in British Columbia 1944', a paper presented to the Canadian Historical Association, 1975, pp. 16-17; King Papers, 'Minutes of a Conference of GOCs . . .', in Black Binders, Vol. 7, file 25.

109 *Ibid.*

110 Montreal *Gazette*, 21 Nov. 1944.

111 Macdonald Papers, Diary, 20 Nov. 1944.

112 King Papers, Memo, n.d., ff. C244028-9.

113 *Ibid.*, ff. C244030-2.

114 Macdonald Diary, 21 Nov. 1944; King Diary, 21 Nov. 1944.

115 Power Papers, Notes on Discussions on the Conscription Crisis, 21 Nov. 1944; Macdonald Diary, 21 Nov. 1944.

116 Power Notes, 21 Nov. 1944.

117 Pickersgill and Forster, *op. cit.*, 229; Swettenham, *McNaughton*, 59; Dexter Papers,

Memorandum, 9 Jan. 1945. See also Bruce Hutchison, *The Far Side of the Street* (Toronto, 1976), pp. 223-9.

118 Pickersgill and Forster, *op. cit.*, 229.

119 J. W. Pickersgill, *My Years with Louis St. Laurent* (Toronto, 1975), p. 24; Dale Thomson, *Louis St. Laurent, Canadian* (Toronto, 1967), p. 150; Dexter Papers, Memorandum, 9 Jan. 1945; for St Laurent's view see his article in *Globe and Mail*, 14 Oct. 1961.

120 Power Notes, 22 Nov. 1944. For Power's view on the 'revolt' see *ibid.*, Power to B. Hutchison, 27 Mar. 1952.

121 Macdonald Diary, 22 Nov. 1944; Ralston Papers, Vol. 85, (T. A. Crerar's) Notes for the Record; Dexter Papers, Memorandum, 23 Nov. 1944.

122 King Diary, 9 Jan. 1945.

123 Saskatchewan Provincial Archives, J. G. Gardiner Papers, Gardiner to King, 23 Nov. 1944; Macdonald Diary, 23 Nov. 1944; Power Notes, 22 Nov. 1944; Pickersgill and Forster, *op. cit.*, 233.

124 Fondation Lionel-Groulx, Fonds Maxime Raymond, 1945 election file, note, n.d.

125 Ottawa *Journal*, 27 Nov. 1944; *Winnipeg Free Press*, 7, 9 Dec. 1944. A good sampling of cartoons on the crisis is in *Saturday Night*, 2 Dec. 1944, 5.

126 *Public Opinion Quarterly*, VIII (Winter, 1944-5), 591.

127 House of Commons *Debates*, 24 Nov. 1944, p. 6589.

128 Department of National Defence, file HQS 20-6, Vol. 81, Pearkes to Secretary, Department of National Defence, 5 Dec. 1944; see also R. H. Roy, 'From the Darker Side of Canadian Military History: Mutiny in the Mountains—the Terrace Incident', *Canadian Defence Quarterly*, VI (Autumn, 1976), 42-55.

129 *Ibid.*

130 King Diary, 29 Nov. 1944.

131 *Ibid.* See Stacey, *op. cit.*, pp. 474ff.

132 Department of National Defence, file HQS 20-6, Vol. 81, Pearkes to Secretary, Department of National Defence, 5 Dec. 1944.

133 PARC, Department of National Defence Records, MD No. 4, file MS 2-93, Vol. 10, Langlois to DOC, 7 Dec. 1944.

134 *Ibid.*, War Diary, No. 1 District Depot, 31 Dec. 1944; War Diary, Fusiliers de Sherbrooke, 8-9 June 1945; War Diary, Prince Edward Island Highlanders, 5-7 Jan. 1945.

135 See Granatstein, *Politics of Survival*, p. 184.

136 PARC, Department of National Defence Records, War Diary, Dufferin and Haldimand Rifles, 15 Feb. 1945.

137 Directorate of History, file 314.0009 (D15), Tel., Pearson to Robertson, 22 Jan. 1945.

138 Ottawa *Journal*, 26 Feb. 1945; PARC, Department of National Defence Records, War Diary, 34 and 35 Companies, Canadian Provost Corps, 24 Feb. 1945.

139 Montreal *Gazette*, 14 Mar. 1945.

140 Stacey, *op. cit.*, pp. 481-2.

141 Robert Rumilly, *Histoire de la province de Québec* (Montréal, 1969), XLI, 168.

142 Quebec *Official Gazette*, Vol. 76, No. 47a, 30 Nov. 1944; Rumilly, *op. cit.*, 156-7; Michel Brunet quoted in Ottawa *Citizen*, 2 Sept. 1964.

143 See Granatstein, *Canada's War*, chapter X.

144 Paul Bennett, 'The Grey North By-Election of February 5, 1945', a York University undergraduate paper, 1971.

145 Granatstein, *op. cit.*, p. 390.

146 McNaughton Papers, Arthur Roebuck to McNaughton, 2 Jan. 1945; King Diary, 24-5 Jan. 1945.

147 Bennett, *op. cit.*, 35-6.

148 Toronto *Globe and Mail*, 1 Feb. 1945.

149 See Granatstein, *Canada's War*, chapter VII.

150 PAC, John Bracken Papers, Vol. 92, speech of 18 May 1945.

151 King Diary, 11, 12 June 1945.

Seven

THE COLD WAR YEARS

The events of the war years should have ended any consideration of conscription in Canada. The strains produced by the crises of 1942 and 1944, coming just a quarter-century after the first crisis in 1917, should have convinced every Canadian that one of the subjects about which one does not speak or even think was that of compulsory military service. Chubby Power apparently believed that this had occurred. In his memoirs the wartime Minister of National Defence for Air wrote that after 1945 conscription 'appeared to be completely dead, both as a political bogey and as a real issue. Under the conditions of modern warfare, I believe it is gone forever.'[1] Power was often an unusually astute observer, but he was wrong on this occasion.

Conscription did not disappear as an issue with the end of the Second World War. The subject was most often raised in private, in the Council chamber or in the conference rooms at National Defence Headquarters, but what is significant is that the subject was raised at all. For a time in the early 1950s indeed, it seemed that discussion might be turned to action and that the Liberal government of Louis St Laurent might introduce conscription. That unfortunate eventuality was averted, but even as late as 1966, at the height of the debate over the unification of the armed forces, conscription talk was still being bandied about. The issue would not die.

Why? After the political trauma of 1917, 1942, and 1944, why would any government consider any such step? In particular, why would the Liberal Party, led from 1948 to 1958 by a French Canadian, even talk of such a measure? This chapter, written with only partial access to the sources, attempts to consider these questions.

I

Throughout the war Canada's efforts to receive recognition commensurate with its contribution to the Allied war effort were regularly and almost routinely rebuffed by both the White House and Downing Street. The Canadian response was never completely consistent, mixing occasional tough talk and threats with the more normal compliance. But there was also an attempt to secure a special place for this country in the United Nations Organization. Where Canada had capacity, as in civil aviation, industrial and raw-material production, the statesmen and diplomats argued, then its special role should be conceded. There was no claim to be a great power. Canadians, however, did claim to be a middle power with the ability to function as a near-great power in certain areas. For example, Canada had demonstrated its capacity to mobilize large armies during the war, and when the United Nations conferences at Dumbarton Oaks and San Francisco decided to create a world army to put down aggression, Canada expected to be part of it. The great powers could not be permitted to demand that Canada provide troops for collective-security actions without Canadian participation in arriving at such a decision.[2]

What is noteworthy is that defence planning for the post-war years took into consideration the likelihood that Canada would be asked, as General Charles Foulkes put it, 'to provide . . . for the possibility of a U.N. commitment'.[3] But how much force would be required? The original plans developed at the United Nations by the Big Five representatives on the Military Staff Committee called for huge armies, fleets, and air forces. These original plans were never implemented, of course, and all too soon the world organization was bogged down in futility. As a result there was more than a little impatience in the remarks by the Secretary of State for External Affairs at the General Assembly in 1946: 'The Government and people of Canada are anxious to know what armed forces, in common with other members of the United Nations, Canada should maintain as our share of the burden of putting world force behind world law.'[4]

If the Department of External Affairs was worried about the delays, the Department of National Defence was not. The prospect of Canada's supplying troops to the UN must have come like manna from heaven to the military planners at Cartier Square in 1945. How else could senior officers retain their high ranks and their important commands? And what better way to raise this army than with conscription? After all, conscription was fair, equalizing the burden on the rich man's son and on the poor boy; conscription would bring physical fitness to a soft nation; and conscription would teach civic virtues to a generation that already was becoming addicted to zoot suits, bebop, and duck-tailed haircuts. Conscription, the generals believed with a political blindness that equalled that of their predecessors in 1918-19, was the best solution to the problems of Canadian defence and the only way that Canada could have in readiness enough men to meet the demands of the United Nations.[5]

Such, it may confidently be assumed, was the unstated rationale behind Plan 'G', a product of the Army's Directorate of Staff Duties. So called because it was the seventh version produced by the Directorate, Plan 'G' was first presented to the Ministers of National Defence at a meeting on 25 June 1945. The plan envisaged a peacetime army of 55,788, primarily organized into a self-contained brigade group but with additional men on coast-defence duties, research and development, administration and training. To find the necessary manpower, the planners contended, a form of universal military training would be necessary. Youths of 18½ to 19½ years of age would be inducted at four-month intervals for one year of training, and estimates were that 48,500 conscripts would be under training at any one time. The trained soldiers would then undergo a period of obligatory service in the militia, and a strength of 177,396 officers and men was envisaged here. The militia was to be organized into two corps of six infantry divisions and four armoured brigades, and this reserve force was to provide the manpower needed for future emergencies.[6]

The square pegs had all been wedged tightly and carefully into the round holes. Unfortunately for army headquarters, however, Plan 'G' neglected a few details. The Chiefs of the Air and Naval Staffs, for example. Neither officer was interested in any plan for compulsory service, particularly one that would increase the size and power of the army, and both senior officers insisted that their needs could be met by voluntary enlistment. The two Chiefs had their own demands (the navy wanted 20,000 men, two aircraft carriers, four cruisers, and two destroyer flotillas, while the RCAF envisaged a force of 30,000 men) and both were presumably shrewd enough to realize that the prospect of conscription or universal military training was not going to assist in the realization of their plans, whatever the needs of the UN might be. This proved to be the case. The Minister of National Defence (Naval Services), Douglas Abbott, and the Minister of National Defence (Air), Colin Gibson, were quick to note that any compulsory scheme was unlikely to be politically acceptable.[7] The Canadian Institute of Public

Opinion had demonstrated in 1944, when the war was still under way, that 60 per cent of the people approved of peacetime conscription,[8] but no government led by Mackenzie King would consider conscription in any form, and certainly not in peacetime.

King was interested in the UN, if not overly optimistic about its future, and he seemed willing to accept the advice of his bright young men in the East Block that Canada should be prepared to contribute military forces to the organization. But conscription was out of the question in peacetime. When he learned of the army proposals in early August 1945 the Prime Minister was furious, calling the plan 'perfectly outrageous'. King noted in his diary that he 'resented strongly the post-war proposals based on the needs of another major war and the necessity of being in readiness for it.' The Cabinet agreed with him and on 3 August 1945 'Council, the moment I was absent,' King observed, 'decided strongly against beginning any compulsory training. . . . '[9] That was that.

Inevitably Plan 'G' died a forlorn death, a victim of the past. With it temporarily died the dreams of the Chiefs of Staff for a large peacetime military. The Cabinet Defence Committee decided on 28 September 1945 that it was not yet possible adequately to assess Canada's defence needs and recommended that no final decisions on force levels be made. The Cabinet agreed and informed the service chiefs that they could begin planning for a navy of 10,000, an army of 20,000-25,000, and an air force of 15,000-20,000.[10] This was not as much as the military had hoped, but it was more than they might have expected, and provided for larger peacetime regular forces than ever before.[11] Whether or not the Prime Minister was involved in this decision is unclear, but certainly he subsequently devoted himself with his customary energy to cutting back the size of the forces. His philosophy was simple (and essentially correct)—'Canada simply could not do what was necessary to protect itself. Our country would be a mere pawn in the world conflict'[12]—and in these circumstances King did not believe he could justify large defence expenditures either to himself or to the nation. In January 1947, for example, he was delighted when Brooke Claxton, the Minister of National Defence, managed to cut $100,-000,000 from the military establishment. As he noted in his diary, 'I did not think there was any justification for having large numbers in the defence forces, where [sic] money was needed for a reduction of taxation and for social services.'[13] As a result of this pressure from the Prime Minister's Office, the strength of the armed forces in 1948 was well under the planning figures of 1945. The RCN was home to only

6,857 men, the army to 15,885, and the RCAF to only 12,017. The total was under 35,000.[14] Moreover the military efficiency of the services was dubious. The RCN was plagued with what were euphemistically described as 'work stoppages', but which we might call mutinies.[15] The army was understrength, untrained even to company level, and as even staff officers were forced to admit, neither well organized nor well disciplined.[16] The RCAF suffered under equipment shortages, was still flying wartime Mustangs, and did not have a single operational squadron of Vampire jets until December 1948. Clearly Canada was in no position to meet a military threat of any consequence, not even the modest demands of the UN. In December 1948, for example, the UN asked for observers to serve in Kashmir. The request could not be met by the regular force, and the reserves had to be canvassed until four volunteers stepped forward.[17]

II

By this time great events were in progress. The simmering conflict between the Soviet Union and the United States had brought on the Marshall Plan, the coup in Czechoslovakia, and the Berlin blockade. The atmosphere was 'apocalyptic,' and as early as August 1947 senior officers of the Department of External Affairs were pronouncing the failure of the United Nations and the necessity for western states to form a collective security organization of their own.[18] The result of similar reactions in London, Washington, and in the capitals of Western Europe was the creation of the North Atlantic Treaty Organization in 1949 and Canada's adherence to the Treaty.

But however much the atmosphere was apocalyptic, there was no major reversal in Canadian defence policy. Not so long as Mackenzie King was still in charge. After listening to President Harry Truman's radio address on 17 March 1948, in which he called for selective service, King was appalled at the thought of the situation this speech could create in Canada. If conscription were to be considered, he said, large numbers of Canadians would join the Communist Party. 'They will say if we are to risk our lives fighting Communism, we better save our heads by joining with them.' Not even the Minister of National Defence's assurances that the Chiefs of Staff did not want conscription could calm the Prime Minister, and King warned his Cabinet that even if Canada joined the then-mooted Atlantic Pact 'certainly there would be no commitment of any kind' for conscription.[19]

However King's lengthy tenure of office was drawing to its close, and in August 1948 a national Liberal convention selected Louis St

Laurent as his successor. St Laurent had supported King's manpower policy during the war, but as John Holmes, a former senior official in External Affairs, has noted, he was 'less inhibited by the phobias which had prevented both nationalists and imperialists in the past from seeing Canada's place in the world clearly and confidently.'[20] As a French Canadian, as a Canadian, St Laurent had no innate desire to see this country field large military forces. He had in fact made a clearly negative reference to conscription in a major foreign-policy address in 1947 when he stated 'the first general principle ... [is] that our external policy shall not destroy our unity. No policy can be ... wise which divides the people. ...'[21] But as a convinced internationalist and as a believer in the principle of collective security, St Laurent would probably be more susceptible to demands for increased defence expenditures and a more aggressive military posture than Mackenzie King had been. In March 1948, for example, St Laurent refused a request from a Quebec labour organization for a pledge against conscription in any future war. The time might come, he told the delegation, when the Russians would have to be shown that the limit had been reached. What Professor Denis Stairs has called the 'period of changing perceptions' was under way.[22]

Certainly many Canadians were becoming worried by the condition of Canada's defences in the late 1940s. Vincent Massey, for one, noted that 'the tiny size of our fighting services, even on a relative basis, does little to help us maintain a position of reasonable dignity in joint discussion between ourselves and Washington on the subject of defence.'[23] The Canadian Legion at its 1946 Convention demanded 'a national unified system of compulsory military training for defence purposes. ...'[24] And General H. D. G. Crerar, the wartime commander of the First Canadian Army, was worried by what he saw as the Soviet military threat. The only effective deterrent to aggression was organized power, Crerar said, and Canada had to accept

> while still at peace, the procedure of compulsory military training. We simply cannot afford to wait until a year has passed after the outbreak of war, before our reserve formations are brought up to operational efficiency and before reinforcements become available to replace the inevitable losses from battle and sickness. Our potential enemies are under no such handicap. With them mobilisation means imminent, full-scale and sustained action on land, on sea, and in the air. They have compulsory military training and service. They have their trained reserves and reinforcements in all three services ready

now. Whatever our traditional attitude against the acceptance of this national, and to me, fundamentally democratic policy, just how can we justify clinging to such an attitude in the face of this tremendous military advantage now possessed by our potential enemies? I say, quite definitely, that we cannot.[25]

The General's appeal fell on deaf ears, and there was probably good reason for this. Simply put, he and his supporters in the Legion halls failed to take into account the effect that American atomic weaponry had had on Soviet policy. Even after the Russians acquired the fission weapon they lacked a delivery system, and in these circumstances there seemed little prospect that Stalin would expose his country needlessly to the American nuclear superiority.[26] The outbreak of the Korean War on 25 June 1950, however, seen as a sign of expansionist Soviet policy, was to give the proponents of compulsory military service and military preparedness a terrific boost.

Despite the early commitment of three destroyers and an RCAF long-range transport squadron to the UN effort in Korea, the Canadian government soon came under intense pressure from Washington to do more. The Cabinet considered the question, and on 7 August Prime Minister St Laurent announced that a brigade would be raised 'specially trained and equipped to be available for use in carrying out Canada's obligations under the United Nations Charter or the North Atlantic Pact. Naturally,' the Prime Minister said, 'this brigade will, subject to the approval of Parliament, be available for service in Korea as part of United Nations forces, if it can be most effectively used in that way when it is ready for service.'[27] St Laurent's linking up the possibility of NATO service for the brigade with that of its use in Korea probably can be explained, first, by the government's implicit belief that the major Communist threat was in Europe, the Korean fighting notwithstanding, and secondly by the hope that manpower commitments could be minimized. As the Minister of National Defence, Brooke Claxton, noted in his unpublished memoirs, the Cabinet had supported raising the special force. But 'as I expected [I was] put on the spot about the manpower problem. "Can the Cabinet be given positive assurances that we could raise the men we needed to support the initial forces and maintain them at full strength in the field by ordinary voluntary means?" This was a tough one,' Claxton wrote. 'However, I was confident that we could handle the job barring unforeseen accidents.'[28]

In western capitals the Korean War was seen as part and parcel of a co-ordinated Moscow-directed scheme for world domination. The NATO partners reacted by launching plans in September 1950 for an integrated force adequate to resist Soviet land strength, and the prospect that Canadian troops might be required for European service, much as St Laurent had indicated in his August statement, quickly became a real possibility. The pressures on Canada were mounting, and when the Chinese armies intervened with enormous strength across the Yalu River in Korea at the end of 1950, the UN position in Korea was in danger of becoming untenable. Clearly the special force would be needed in Korea, and more men would have to be raised for NATO. The government thus authorized the despatch of a maximum of 12,000 servicemen to Europe on 18 April 1951,[29] and a further recruiting effort was launched. The demands for men were increasing.

Canadian public opinion was in a confused state throughout this period of increasing world tension. In Quebec a majority of the newspapers had accepted the sending of troops to Korea, although both the *nationaliste* Montreal papers, *Le Devoir* and *Montreal-Matin*, were adamant in their opposition. In the Gallup polls, however, only 21 per cent of the Quebec population indicated that they approved of Canada sending men to Korea, while a whopping 62 per cent were opposed. The polls showed similar results when French Canadians were asked about the despatch of Canadian troops to Europe: 37 per cent accepted such action and 52 per cent did not.[30] At the same time, however, such a usually astute anglophone observer as Blair Fraser of *Maclean's* could observe that 'evidence continues to mount that Quebec is not so firmly and deeply anti-war as it used to be. No one has suggested that Quebec would go for conscription but there are signs that the old hysterical fear of it has calmed down a bit.'[31]

Conscription talk was beginning in earnest, nonetheless. At its Dominion Convention in September 1950 the Canadian Legion had enthusiastically approved a resolution that proposed conscription for the reserve forces. But the influential Toronto periodical *Saturday Night* noted that regulars were more urgently needed than conscripts, and 'Until we have established these professional forces in adequate strength talk about universal military service is inapposite. . . . '[32] For the moment at least, the message from Toronto was 'not yet'. Blair Fraser sounded a similar note from Ottawa: 'Few people here have any hope, though many wish, that we shall actually have conscription, not for a while yet anyhow. The highest hope, in any reasonable quarter, is for an early attempt at national registration. Get everybody listed, identified, classified as to occupation, age and civil status.'[33] As a good

Liberal, Fraser's sources were of the very best, for on 15 January 1951 Defence Minister Claxton had written to an intimate that the armed forces would probably have to be expanded beyond their planned level of 100,000 by 1954, and manpower could be best used if it were directed to areas of greatest need. For the moment, however, Claxton still did not feel that selective service was needed.[34]

But clearly the government was interested in preparing public opinion. On 20 February 1951 the National Advisory Council on Manpower, a newly created body composed of provincial government representatives, labour and business leaders, and representatives of farmers', veterans', and women's groups, met in Ottawa. The Minister of Labour, Milton Gregg, assured the delegates in their *in camera* sessions that the Prime Minister had made clear that the government 'would take such compulsory steps as are necessary' to obtain men for the armed forces to serve anywhere in the world. And the next day the Council was informed that plans were in hand for a national registration.[35]

There were more public indications of a readiness to take extraordinary measures, too. Prime Minister St Laurent was at once conciliatory and frank in a House of Commons speech on 1 February. 'To some sincere, patriotic Canadians it would appear that the first and foremost thing to do would be to have in force some form of selective service, some form of conscription of manpower. . . . ' There are others, he continued, 'who believe with equal sincerity, that to resort, at the present time, to compulsory military service would be disastrous to the Canadian economy.' The Prime Minister shared neither view in totality. Nor did he feel that conscription was something that had to be avoided simply because French Canadians had traditionally opposed it. 'So far as I am concerned, this is not a matter which can or should be decided on sentimental grounds. It is one which should be decided on its merits, and strictly on its merits, and with regard to what will make for the efficiency and the effectiveness of our contribution to the joint efforts that have to be put forth. . . . '[36]

In fact the Cabinet had already considered the question of conscription on its merits and decided that compulsory service would be introduced in the event of war with the Soviet Union. Grant Dexter, the *Winnipeg Free Press* reporter and editor, had spoken to Brooke Claxton about this:

I asked Brooke about military manpower [he wrote in one of his famous private memoranda]. He said there would be no repeat on the conscription controversy. The cabinet has decided that there should and will be over-all conscription on the day that actual war breaks out. This statement surprised me and . . . he said he thought this decision largely a demonstration of confidence by Quebec in Mr. St. Laurent. 'With this Prime Minister,' he said, 'we can do anything in Quebec.'[37]

Blair Fraser had access to many of the same sources as Dexter, and his conclusion was precisely the same—and all the more important for being made public in a featured article in *Maclean's*. 'If and when Canada goes to war,' Fraser said, 'we shall have all-out conscription immediately. The Government is committed to that already.' And Fraser quoted un-named French-Canadian M.P.s to the effect that they could swallow compulsion. Even 'a former firebrand of the Bloc Populaire', the *nationaliste* and anti-conscriptionist party that had been formed in 1942, told Fraser that 'there'll be no fight against conscription this time. . . . The people are apathetic. They got accustomed to the idea under Mackenzie King, and now they tend to take it for granted. Also it's a different enemy this time. Our people are far more anti-Communist than they ever were anti-Fascist.'[38] Whether these optimistic forecasts that Quebec would fall obediently into line were correct or not is uncertain. One opinion poll in 1951 that questioned French Canadians on their feelings about conscription for the Korean War found only 10 per cent in favour and 83 per cent opposed,[39] and the position of provincial leaders was not clear. For Premier Maurice Duplessis, however, to oppose conscription for a war against Communism might have been awkward. His anti-Communism was firmly on record.

Whatever the feelings of the people of Quebec, the army wanted conscription now. For Lieutenant-General Guy Granville Simonds, the best soldier Canada had produced during the Second World War and in 1951 the testy and opinionated Chief of the General Staff, military considerations alone were sufficient to require the immediate implementation of national selective service. In a memorandum to Brooke Claxton, the Minister of National Defence, on 9 May 1951 Simonds claimed that Canada would be unable without such service to meet its commitments in case of war. He noted that there were already difficulties in getting needed manpower, and he complained that a national registration would take precious time to be implemented. The result would be a shortage of specialists at the very time they would be most needed—at the beginning of a war.[40] A commentary on Simonds' memo was prepared for Claxton by his Deputy Minister, Brigadier C.

M. Drury. The Deputy Minister was clearly an expert in balancing options and in playing the bureaucratic games that high office seems to require, for while his position virtually required his taking issue with the Chief of the General Staff, he managed to do so as gently as possible. Drury maintained that it was necessary to plan for national selective service but that this scheme did not need to be implemented until mobilization. Furthermore there was no shortage of army volunteers, and what Simonds really was seeking was a guarantee that he would continue to get all the men he wanted. On the question of national registration, Drury agreed flatly with General Simonds. This, he said, should not be impossible. The memorandum concluded with a listing of the negative and positive aspects of Simonds' demands. The positive factors, Drury claimed, were that from a military point of view the Simonds plan was sound, more orderly and efficient, likely to end the international criticism of Canada that was heard occasionally at military conferences, and likely to stimulate recruiting. The single disadvantage was that conscription was likely to cause a cleavage in public opinion. It was a nice question of judgement, Drury's memorandum ended, whether the advantages were greater than the disadvantages.[41]

The Minister was all too aware of the nice question of judgement involved. At a meeting with representatives of the Conference of Defence Associations in November 1951, he privately indicated that he would support compulsion if he believed the advantages outweighed the disadvantages. For the moment he did not believe that they did, but as he indicated in a telegram to J. W. Pickersgill, one of the Prime Minister's key advisers, it might be necessary to press for compulsory service in the near future.[42]

The simple fact was that Canada and Iceland alone were the only NATO members without some form of conscription.[43] The Deputy Minister of National Defence had referred to international criticism of Canada on this score, and certainly there was some. Emmanuel Shinwell, once Labour's Minister of Defence in Britain, had spoken darkly at Westminster about some Commonwealth countries 'not pulling their weight'. The Chicago Tribune, that very model of midwestern journalism, complained that Canada was not doing its share in NATO or in Korea, and Newsweek observed that Canada was 'stingy and foot-dragging'.[44] More important to the government was the domestic criticism. The Toronto Globe and Mail, for one, was once again edging towards supporting conscription,[45] and both George Drew, the Progressive Conservative party leader, and Davie Fulton, one of his bright young men, came close to endorsing a measure of compulsion in the House of Commons.[46] General H. D. G. Crerar, too, continued his efforts, writing long articles on 'The Case for Conscription' in academic journals and preaching to the converted at Legion meetings.[47] But clearly there was little sense of public urgency on the matter, or at least the election results of 1953, yet another comfortable Liberal victory, did not seem to indicate any. The international criticism, too, could easily be countered by maintaining, as Dr J. A. Corry suggested, that so long as Canada met its commitments 'our methods . . . are our own affair.'[48]

The inescapable fact for the hard-pressed Minister of National Defence (this was also the period when horses were discovered to be gracing the payrolls at Camp Petawawa), however, was that he was having trouble meeting the demands for reinforcements for Korea. Although the strength of the army on 31 March 1952 was 49,278 all ranks,[49] the official history of the Canadian Army in Korea notes that 'The shortage of trained manpower, particularly infantry, became increasingly serious as 1952 unrolled.' The Adjutant-General estimated that the 25th Brigade, the Canadian formation in Korea, would be 374 infantry understrength by September—and this despite heroic measures to comb out trained soldiers. All the remaining Special Force soldiers in Canada were sent to Korea in early 1952, a procedure that netted 300 men. More specifically there was a shortage of French-speaking infantry—'there were just not enough French-speaking recruits coming forward to enable the [Royal 22nd Regiment] battalions to be brought up to strength and still retain their French-Canadian character.'[50] In fact there was a general shortage of French Canadians throughout all three services. Data prepared for the Royal Commission on Bilingualism and Biculturalism noted that in December 1950 only 12.3 per cent of the army's strength was French-speaking. In technical corps in particular the percentage was strikingly low: in the Royal Canadian Engineers, only 5.1 per cent of the officers were French-speaking; in the Royal Canadian Electrical and Mechanical Engineers only 2.5 per cent. Only in the infantry, where 26.1 per cent of the officers and 20.2 per cent of the other ranks were French-Canadian, was there anything approaching even a proper proportion. The situation in the navy (2 per cent of the officers and 11 per cent of the ratings) and the air force (4 per cent of the officers and 16 per cent of the men) was even worse.[51] Despite some efforts by the government, French Canadians simply did not seem to relish the military life in an anglophone army, navy, or air force. Apparently it mattered little whether the enemy was Communism or Fascism.*

*Data collected in 1966 for the three services demonstrated that there had been relatively little improvement since 1950. The figures also showed that 'other' Canadians were sub-

The overall shortage of manpower did not ease in early 1953. The Adjutant-General reported on 25 March 1953 that 16,200 men were needed to fill establishments but that only 12,450 were expected over the next 14 months. 'We are facing a somewhat critical period in respect of manpower,' he warned, 'and if we cannot adopt measures to improve our intake and reduce our wastage it would seem that there will inevitably come a time when we will not be able to meet our commitments.'[52] With the armistice in Korea in July, however, the problems eased, and soon the pressure on the government ended.

After the Korean War the threat (or prospect) of conscription was virtually finished. The attack on the government's defence policies continued, however, coming this time from a different direction. General Simonds, apparently feeling freed of restraints now that the hostilities in Korea had ceased, told a 'private' army gathering in Saint John, New Brunswick in June 1954 that his view and that of the 'vast majority of Canadian officers' was that every Canadian youth should get two years' military training. Simonds received only a polite reprimand for this breach of policy, Brooke Claxton apparently accepting his explanation that the remarks that appeared in the press had been taken out of context. But early the following year Simonds again went public, telling a Montreal Canadian Club meeting that he 'would like to see every young man in Canada given two years' military training. . . . A system of compulsory military training would be good for the boy, for the army, and for the country.' This speech produced another reprimand, this time by Claxton's successor as Minister of National Defence, Ralph Campney, and soon after the General entered his retirement.[53] But he would be no less pugnacious in retirement and was soon in print, attacking the government's willingness to put all its defence eggs in the Americans' massive retaliation basket. By thinking in terms only of all-out nuclear war, by making air defence the major—and most expensive—plank in its defence platform, the government was deliberately acting so as to avoid even the possibility of having conscription considered.

---

stantially under-represented in the military, leaving those of British origin with most of the positions.

Ethnic Origin	National 1961	All Pers.	Offrs	Men
British	43.8%	64.6%	73.2%	63.1%
French	30.4	19.2	12.5	20.3
Other	25.8	16.2	14.3	16.6

(Pierre Coulombe, 'Social and Cultural Composition of the Canadian Armed Forces', in Hector Massey, ed., The Canadian Military (Toronto, 1972), p. 145.)

'Our views are so inhibited by a desire to avoid coming face to face with the issue of organizing our national manpower,' Simonds wrote in *Maclean's*,[54] 'that we have been ready to concur in proposals that seem to avoid that necessity.' How much of this beating of the tom-toms for conscription was just good old service pique at the unaccustomed power being wielded in Ottawa by the RCAF is unknown. What is clear now is that General Simonds was almost certainly correct in his assaults on the theory of massive retaliation that held sway in the 1950s. What choice Canada had, how we could have avoided concurrence in American proposals, the General did not discuss.

Conscription had one brief—and final—fling in the mid-1960s at the time of the debate over the unification of the armed forces. An organization calling itself the Tri-Services Identities Organization (TRIO) was formed by retired senior officers, a species whose number was growing rapidly in 1966 and 1967. TRIO claimed in August 1966 that unification would destroy the identities of the services, slow recruiting as a result, and inevitably lead to conscription if Canada were to meet all its commitments abroad.[55] By 1967 however many Canadians were beginning to wonder just why Canada should have so many overseas commitments in any case, and the TRIO agitation died as complete a death as did the RCN, the RCAF, and the Canadian Army. Nor were TRIO's fears realized. Recruiting did not seriously slow, and under the administration of Prime Minister Pierre Trudeau the strength of the armed forces was reduced drastically.

By 1974, then, when the Gallup Poll asked Canadians if they favoured one year of compulsory military training for 18-year-olds, the results were the least favourable to the idea since the end of the Second World War:[56]

National	Favour	Oppose	No Opinion
Today	44%	46%	10%
1956	60	32	8
1955	51	40	9
1946	66	27	7

A further breakdown of the 1974 results indicated, predictably (and as much as in wartime polls), that the oldest and least-well-educated were the supporters of compulsory military training:

Today	Favour	Oppose	No Opinion
18-29 yrs	24	68	8
30-49 yrs	45	46	9

50 yrs and over	58	31	11
Elementary educn	55	29	16
High School	42	50	8
University	26	68	6

III

Why did the demand for conscription not succeed in post-war Canada? There are a number of reasons, of which the most important is that unquestionably the international situation at no time justified such an extreme step from a small country like Canada. In retrospect, the Soviet pressures were by no means as great as they seemed in 1950 and 1951. Revisionist historians in the United States, if not yet in Canada, have changed our view of the early phases of the Cold War. Another and peculiarly Canadian reason was that no one knew how Quebec would react to conscription. Mr St Laurent was unquestionably a powerful figure, but he was probably *un peu trop anglifié* for most *Québécois*. The opinion polls lent little support to those who maintained that Quebec would follow wherever St Laurent led, and the difficulties in reinforcing the Royal 22e Régiment in Korea should have served as a caution.

Equally important perhaps were the military and fiscal reasons. In his memoirs Brooke Claxton dealt at some length with conscription, providing a host of justifications to explain his and the government's course. Conscription was expensive, he maintained. It took one regular soldier to train and maintain each two conscripts and it cost $10,000 to train one regular infantry soldier. In addition Claxton pointed to the United States to support his claim that conscription dried up voluntary enlistments. Canada's re-engagement rate was always over 70 per cent, while in the United States it was under 20 per cent. In addition, Claxton maintained, conscription was unfair, being contrary to Canada's sense of freedom and liberty. Besides, Canada had met its commitments with the voluntary system. 'Why think of scrapping something that has worked so well?'

Claxton was fair enough to note that 'If I were a professional soldier concerned only with the end result of having the strongest possible forces, of course I would be for conscription. . . . As a soldier I might even be remiss if I did not take this view.' But as a politician he had to consider other factors and these, he believed, outweighed the military arguments. In case of war, however, 'we would have to take whatever means were necessary to get people to do the best job the soonest . . . there would be no difficulty in setting the machinery underway without delay.' Concluding his case, Claxton noted that 'There is no advantage in conscription as such. All experience shows that it is a thoroughly wasteful and unfair way of getting men to do what they do not want to do. The suggestion that it would give men who have passed through the ranks a sense of "dedication to the service of the country" could not be further from the truth.' Claxton was writing long before the Viet Nam War had demonstrated to Americans and others that conscription can impose burdens that may be too heavy for a free society to bear, and his prescience was impressive. So too were his last words: 'Conscription is not the right way to man a modern army.'[57] For Canadians, in fact, conscription has never been the right way.

NOTES

1 Norman Ward, ed., *A Party Politician: The Memoirs of Chubby Power* (Toronto, 1966), p. 178.

2 Similar views seem to have been shared by the public. According to CIPO data, 76 per cent of the public believed that Canada should contribute to an international police force (10 Jan. 1945). When asked if Canada should contribute without a say in the decision, however, this figure dropped to 52 per cent. Quebec figures were 51 per cent and 25 per cent respectively. *Public Opinion Quarterly*, IX (Spring, 1945), 106.

3 Gen. Charles Foulkes, 'Canadian Defence Policy in the Nuclear Age', *Behind the Headlines*, XXI (May, 1961), 2. Cf. Capt. J. P. Brennan, 'Do we need peacetime armed forces?', *Canadian Army Journal*, I (January, 1948), 25.

4 L. S. St Laurent, 29 Oct. 1946 in Department of External Affairs, *Conference Series 1946, The United Nations* (Ottawa, 1946), pp. 105-6.

5 This was also the reluctant conclusion of one Liberal M.P., René Beaudoin. House of Commons *Debates*, 18 Oct. 1945, pp. 1275ff. See H. D. G. Crerar, 'The Need for Canadian Military Preparation', *Empire Club Addresses 1945-46* (Toronto, 1947), p. 380.

6 Public Archives of Canada [PAC], Privy Council Office Records, Box 18, file D-19-D, 'Minutes of Special Meeting of Ministers of National Defence and Chiefs of Staff', 25 June 1945; *ibid.*, Vol. 3985, file N-2-13-9, 'Strategic Factors Affecting Canada's Post War Military Requirements', 5 July 1945; Department of External Affairs, External Affairs Records, file 1-AB (s), Memo, Ignatieff to Wrong, 28 June 1945; Lt-Col H. F. Wood, *Strange Battleground: Official History of the Canadian Army in Korea* (Ottawa, 1966), p. 17. As late as January 1946, J. S. Thompson, President of the National Conference of Canadian Universities and a member of the Joint Services Universities Training Board, was considering the implications of conscription on university officer training programs. Queen's University, W. A. Mackintosh Papers, 'Memorandum on Service Training at the Canadian Universities', 2 Jan. 1946.

7 Wood, *loc. cit.*

8 CIPO polls, 29 Nov. 1944 and 3 Mar. 1945 in *Public Opinion Quarterly*, IX (Winter, 1944-5), 603 and X (Spring, 1945), 107.

9 PAC, W.L.M. King Papers, Diary 2, 3 Aug. 1945. See also Privy Council Office Records, Box 35, file C-10-9 for minutes of a Special Cabinet Committee on the postwar programs in defence, 13 Aug. 1945; and *ibid.*, Box 18, file D-19-P, Gen. Pope to A.D.P. Heeney, 21 Aug. 1945.

10 Wood, *loc. cit.*

11 C. P. Stacey, 'The Development of the Canadian Army', Part IV, *Canadian Army Journal*, VI (July, 1952), 20.

12 J. W. Pickersgill and D. F. Forster, eds, *The Mackenzie King Record*, Vol. III: *1945-46* (Toronto, 1970), 266.

13 *Ibid.*, Vol. IV: *1947-48*, 9-10.

14 *Report of the Department of National Defence . . . 1948* (Ottawa, 1949), pp. 14, 21, 33.

15 John Harbron, 'Royal Canadian Navy at Peace, 1945-55: The Uncertain Heritage', *Queen's Quarterly*, LXXIII (Autumn, 1966), 320.

16 A. W. Taylor, *et al.*, *Peacekeeping: International Challenge and Canadian Response* (Toronto, 1968), pp. 101-2.

17 *Ibid.*

18 Escott Reid, 'The Birth of the North Atlantic Alliance', *International Journal*, XXII (Summer, 1967), 434; E. Reid, 'Canada's Role in the United Nations', 13 Aug. 1947, Department of External Affairs, *Statements and Speeches*, 47/12.

19 Pickersgill and Forster, IV, 170-1, 173. According to Brooke Claxton, by 1948 the army had become opposed to conscription on the grounds that compulsion required the mis-employment of too many professional soldiers and that it cost too much. Queen's University, Grant Dexter Papers, Max Freedman to Dexter, 15 Apr. 1948.

20 John W. Holmes, 'Canadian External Policies Since 1945', *International Journal*, XVIII (Spring, 1963), 137.

21 L. S. St Laurent, *The Foundations of Canadian Policy in World Affairs*, (Toronto, 1947), p. 19.

22 J. W. Warnock, *Partner to Behemoth* (Toronto, 1970), p. 42; Denis Stairs, 'The Military as an Instrument of Canadian Foreign Policy', unpublished paper, 19.

23 Vincent Massey, *On Being Canadian* (Toronto, 1948), p. 122.

24 C. B. Price to W. L. M. King, 28 Mar. 1947 in *The Legionary*, XXII (May, 1947), 5.

25 Address, 10 Feb. 1949, cited in Eric Harrison, 'Strategy and Policy in the Defence of Canada', *International Journal*, IV (Summer, 1949), 227.

26 Gen. E. L. M. Burns, cited in Warnock, *op. cit.*, p. 49.

27 Printed in Department of External Affairs, *Canada and the Korean Crisis* (Ottawa, 1950), p. 34. There is some evidence that the decision to raise a brigade for Korea was not easily reached and that the Cabinet split sharply on the question. Leading the opposition were J. G. Gardiner and Paul Martin, with C. D. Howe, concerned about interference with industrial growth, also lukewarm. Lester Pearson, the Secretary of State for External Affairs, apparently came close to resignation on this question, but when the Prime Minister, after some hesitation, supported him, the question was resolved by the decision to raise the men. Dexter Papers, Memo by Ken Wilson, 12 Aug. 1950;

Memoranda by Bruce Hutchison, 24, 25 Oct. 1950. The best published study of Canada and Korea is Denis Stairs, *The Diplomacy of Constraint* (Toronto, 1974).

28 PAC, Brooke Claxton Papers, Draft Memoirs, Vol. 6, 1143. On recruiting, see Stairs, *op. cit.*, pp. 185ff; Dexter Papers, Chester Bloom to Frank, 8 Aug. 1950; and H. F. Wood, *The Private War of Jacket Coates* (Toronto, 1966), a very funny novel by the official historian that says what he could not in *Strange Battleground*.

29 P.C. 5598.

30 J. I. Gow, 'Les Québécois, la guerre et la paix, 1945-60', *Canadian Journal of Political Science*, III (March, 1970), 98, 107. Cf. Dale Thomson, *Louis St. Laurent, Canadian* (Toronto, 1967), p. 299. Cf. Dexter Papers, Memo by B. Hutchison, n.d. [1949].

31 'Backstage at Ottawa', *Maclean's* (1 Nov. 1950), 53. Cf. *The Financial Post*, 20 Jan. 1951, 1. See also House of Commons *Debates*, 2 Sept. 1950, pp. 177-80 (M. Poulin).

32 'The Front Page', *Saturday Night*, 24 Oct. 1950, 6. Cf. M. Barkway, 'Constructive Criticism Called For', *ibid.*, 30 Jan. 1951, 7; 'Compulsory Service', *ibid.*, 23 Jan. 1951, 5.

33 *Maclean's*, 1 Nov. 1950, 52.

34 Claxton Papers, Memo, B.C. to J. W. Pickersgill, 15 Jan. 1951.

35 Mackintosh Papers, Box 4, file III, Minutes, 20-1 Feb. 1951. Cf. Gregg's comment in Toronto *Globe and Mail*, 2 Apr. 1951.

36 House of Commons *Debates*, 1 Feb. 1951, p. 27. Cf. Thomson, *op. cit.*, pp. 308-9; M. Barkway, 'Taking the Curse off Conscription', *Saturday Night*, 13 Feb. 1951, 9; *Canadian Business*, XXIV (March, 1951), 18. For further press response, see Montreal *Star*, 2 Feb. 1951 and Ottawa *Journal*, 3 Feb. 1951.

37 Queen's University, T. A. Crerar Papers, Dexter to Crerar, n.d., encl. memo, 22 Feb. 1951. Whether there was still any difficulty with this question in Cabinet is unclear. Only three anti-conscription ministers from 1944 were still in the government, J. G. Gardiner, A. Fournier, and E. Bertrand.

38 'Conscription', *Maclean's*, 15 Mar. 1951, 14, 61. But see, for example, comments in Parliament by Quebec M.P.s: House of Commons *Debates*, 6 Feb. 1951, p. 133; 7 Feb. 1951, p. 170.

39 Gow, *op. cit.*, 107, 109.

40 Claxton Papers, Simonds to Claxton, 9 May 1951.

41 *Ibid.*, Memo, C. M. D. to Claxton, 19 June 1951.

42 *Ibid.*, tel. B.C. to Pickersgill, 11 Nov. 1951.

43 R. S. Ritchie, *NATO: The Economics of an Alliance* (Toronto, 1956), pp. 87-9.

44 *Newsweek*, 15 Oct. 1952. Cited by B. S. Kierstead, *Canada in World Affairs 1951-3* (Toronto, 1956), pp. 155-6. Cf. PAC, Department of External Affairs Records, Vol. 2131, file Defence-U.S., part VIII, Minute, Wrong to Ignatieff, 7 Sept. 1950.

45 Editorials, 3 Feb. 1951 and 23 May 1952.

46 House of Commons *Debates*, 1 Feb. 1951, p. 24; 16 Feb. 1951, p. 424; 6 Sept. 1950, p. 343. But cf. Drew in *ibid.*, 16 Feb. 1951, p. 425.

47 Gen. H. D. G. Crerar, 'The Case for Conscription', *Queen's Quarterly*, LVIII (Winter, 1951-2); T. A. Crerar Papers, 'Address by Gen. H. D. G. Crerar to Dominion Convention, Canadian Legion, Aug. 11, 1954'.

48 J. A. Corry, 'Canada, the North Atlantic Community and NATO; Domestic Political Implications', *Transactions of the Royal Society of Canada*, XLVI (June, 1952), 29.

49 *Report of the Department of National Defence . . . 1952* (Ottawa, 1953), p. 55.

50 Wood, *Strange Battleground*, pp. 162-3. But cf. James Eayrs, 'Canadian Defence Policies Since 1867', in House of Commons, *Special Studies Prepared for the Special Committee of the House of Commons on Matters Relating to Defence* (Ottawa; Queen's Printer, 1965), p. 17, who notes that 3,134 of the 10,587 men recruited for the Special Force were from Quebec, almost the exact percentage of French Canadians in the general population. Presumably *Québécois* avoided the infantry.

51 Royal Commission on Bilingualism and Biculturalism, 'Armed Forces Historical Study', (n.d., mimeo), part II, p. 58; R. A. Preston, *Canada's R.M.C.* (Toronto, 1969), p. 344; see J.-Y. Gravel, 'La Fondation du Collège Militaire Royal de Saint-Jean', *Revue d'Histoire de l'Amérique Française*, XXVII (septembre, 1973), 257-80 and James Eayrs, *In Defence of Canada* (Toronto, 1972), III, 130ff. for further detail.

52 Claxton Papers, Memo, Adj.-Gen. to Chief of General Staff, 25 Mar. 1953.

53 Eayrs, *op. cit.*, 65-6.

54 4 Aug. 1956. See also Simonds' article 'Canada's Survival' in *The Legionary*, XXXI (May, 1956).

55 Based on press clippings and TRIO mailings in the author's possession.

56 In *Toronto Star*, 7 Sept. 1974.

57 Claxton Papers, Memoirs, Vol. 5, 1009-22.

Eight

CONCLUSION:
THE END OF AN ISSUE?

Conscription has plagued Canadians for more than 65 years. From its first effective use as a political weapon in the Quebec constituency of Drummond-Arthabaska in 1910, through its implementation in the two world wars, and in the political and press discussions of compulsory service at various times after 1945, conscription has done yeoman service in fostering suspicion and mistrust among Canadians. No single issue has done more to muddy the political waters or to destroy the unity of the nation.

Lamentably, inescapably, one must conclude from Canada's experience with conscription that history repeats itself. Always when conscription has been seriously mooted or implemented, military necessity has been cited as the overriding reason; and yet conscription has never produced any military results of significance. In each case compulsion has been introduced to the accompaniment of broken promises and broken pledges that instantly alienated a large part of the population. In each case, except one, English Canada's pressures for a greater military effort, occasionally carefully thought out but often little more than gut responses to sometimes misperceived needs, ran headlong into the resistance of French Canada, into the refusal of Quebec to be bullied into fighting someone else's war. The solitary exception is the consideration given compulsory service in peacetime by the St Laurent government in 1950-1, but here too it seems probable that the government had underestimated the resistance that might be offered by the *Québécois*. Truly Canadians seemed condemned to re-live the mistakes of the past.

Why? No one could seriously claim that conscription in Canada was necessary to win a war. However great the Canadian effort, the nation was never and could never be more than a small part of the Allied war machine. The role was important but subsidiary, and the result in two world wars would have been the same even if there had never been a Canadian at the front. And yet military necessity was the primary reason, the only reason, cited by Borden in 1917 and King in 1944 for the imposition of conscription.

How real was the need? The Great War was a charnel house that could swallow armies whole, and men were required in huge numbers to sustain the divisions at the front. Whether Canadians were needed, however, is another question. The United States, fresh, untouched, and more than ten times Canada's size, had entered the war in April 1917 with conscription and with the capacity to raise an army of millions in months. These doughboys would win the war, not the few thousand conscripts from the Dominion.

The Canadians were needed, therefore, only within a specific definition of necessity. For domestic and imperial political reasons the Corps had to be maintained at strength, or so Borden decided. English Canadians wanted this and insisted upon it. The British wanted it so that the Empire's side would be kept up preparatory to the peace settlement. And Borden wanted it because he believed it was both right in its own terms and politically expedient. Only General Currie, commanding the Canadian Corps, was less certain. The General had become convinced by the election of 1917 that conscription would be no panacea, that compulsory service would produce too little too late to help his men. Far more important to Currie were the 21,000 men of the 5th Division, sitting idly in England. If he could pry loose these men, he believed, many of the Corps' problems would be resolved, and certainly the men of the 5th reached the front well before any conscripts did and in almost the same numbers.

No one can deny that there was a shortage of reinforcements in 1917, a shortage created by the casualties sustained over years of fighting. But contributing to the problem was an inefficient military organization, a dreadful recruiting mess, and more than a fair share of political interference. Conscription probably could have provided enough men to meet the needs of the front had the war continued long enough; fortunately the sudden collapse of the German army ended the war sooner than everyone had expected.

Much the same kind of arguments can be raised about the 1944 crisis. Again nothing Canada did would affect the outcome, and in

November 1944 no one had any doubts that Nazi Germany's capacity to wage war was nearing its end. The crisis sprang primarily from military reasons. Canada had two corps operating in Italy and North West Europe, huge establishments in the United Kingdom, and a substantial base and training operation in Canada. Almost half a million men and women were on the strength of the Canadian Army at the end of 1944, but out of this huge force 15,000 trained infantry reinforcements could not be produced when the planners began to see a need for them. Because of this expected shortfall the Cabinet was shattered and a splendid war effort jeopardized. And for what? In the end, in part through fortuitous accidents, the projected infantry shortage turned out to be largely illusory, and fewer than 2,500 NRMA men had reached the front by the time the war ended. Once again the military need turned out to be much less than had been feared.

What if the need had been pressing? Should military needs override political requirements? Is it worthwhile to impose conscription if by so doing you threaten to destroy the nation and the national unity that the men at the front are presumably fighting to preserve? Those are difficult questions to answer, particularly in Canada where we have relatively little experience with war and no military tradition to speak of. These lacks, fortunate as they may be, make Canadian politicians harsh on the military in peacetime and uncommonly receptive to its advice in war. Older, wiser societies produce statesmen who are more skeptical, who recognize that generals always want more men, who understand that the military know nothing of political realities. Certainly this last is true of Canada's generals. Who else would have suggested universal military training one year after conscription had been imposed in each of two world wars?

But should the blame for the conscription crises be fixed upon the military? We can easily rail against the stupidity and insensitivity of the British generals who ordered Dominion troops—and British troops, too —to attack uncut wire and entrenched machine guns in the Great War. We can weep at the failure of the General Staff to adjust its reinforcement planning to accord with the reality of conditions in Europe in late 1944. Some of the blame can and should be fixed on the generals. But most must be fixed on their political masters. It was Sir Robert Borden who permitted Sam Hughes to have free rein and to create an unholy mess out of recruiting. It was Borden, in an uncommon excess of zeal and apparently after only cursory consultation, who announced that the Canadian Expeditionary Force would be authorized to recruit to a strength of 500,000 men. These decisions, made and unmade, were the root causes of the conscription crisis of 1917. Borden's almost casually taken and widely publicized pledge became a debt of honour that Canada had to redeem, even if the country was torn to pieces in the process. For Mackenzie King the crucial decision came in January 1942 when, against his better judgement, he acceded to the demands of his generals, expressed through Colonel Ralston, for a large army. For Canada to sustain two corps, a huge air force, and a substantial navy, alongside a vast industrial and agricultural effort would have required a population half as large again. King knew this, but he agreed to a large army because he accepted the advice of the military that this could be raised without conscription. Despite much better management than in 1914-18, that error in judgement led inexorably to November 1944 and the crisis that saw his government nearly collapse.

The political leaders in both wars also had to break promises. Again and again through the first two years of the war, Sir Robert Borden expressed his faith in the voluntary system and his assurances that conscription would not be implemented. Those promises were broken in May 1917. And such was the impact of the Military Service Act on Canadian politics that Mackenzie King made his first promise against conscription five months before war broke out. He and his leading ministers repeated the pledges time and again in the months that followed. When in 1942 King called a plebiscite and then moved to pass Bill 80, Quebec came to the realization that King's promises had little more value than those Borden had made 25 years before. The 1944 crisis merely confirmed the inevitable, simply demonstrating that English Canada, no matter who led it, would insist on its way.

And to get its way the majority exercised its power with scant consideration for its compatriots. In both wars English Canadians demonstrated quite clearly that they wanted conscription so that Canada would have the largest possible military effort. There were qualifications to this support. In 1917, it seems clear, farmers and men of military age were somewhat limited in their enthusiasm for compulsion; in 1942 opinion polls showed substantial variations in support for conscription among those of different ages, education, social class, and place of residence. But certainly heavy majorities among English-speaking Canadians wanted conscription in both wars.

Why? Part of the reason was simple patriotism. But much of it was less attractive. Conscription would ensure that others did their duty and assumed a fair share of the burden of sacrifice. The others might be the aliens in the ghetto, the French Canadians in Quebec, or the slacker down the street, but whoever they were they had to do their duty. Britain's war was by definition Canada's war, and all who lived in this fair land had to share equally in the fighting. Equity is not a bad principle on its own, to be sure, but the zealots who preached for equality of sacrifice were probably the same people who let the war bring out their visceral and racist responses, who let their latent hostilities emerge into the open under the tensions of the war. Those attitudes helped persuade other Canadians that this war was not theirs at all, and this natural response served only to feed the majoritarian fires.

To be fair, by the Second World War many Canadians had learned something from the experience of 1917-18. Men such as Dr Manion took their political lives in their hands and opposed conscription; some, like Manion, paid a heavy price. Few politicians wanted another race war in Canada, and until the crisis of 1944, except for the brief Meighen interlude, the Conservative Party behaved cautiously. Indeed much of its effort was devoted to manoeuvering so that the Liberals this time would have to assume responsibility for imposing conscription. Mackenzie King's great skill at squaring the circle helped him avoid that burden and its costs until late 1944, and when he was finally forced to assume it in a partial way, it was to the cheers of the Tories and with their cries for more draconian measures loud in the air. King had broken his promises, but he had done so in a fashion that did not completely alienate French Canada. That was the difference between King and Borden, between conscription 1917 and conscription 1944.

Certainly French Canada had changed too. The hostility of 1917 had no parallel in the Second World War, and neither Maxime Raymond nor André Laurendeau was the equivalent of Henri Bourassa. Part of this sprang from the different nature of the war and the different way it was perceived in Quebec. Many could believe, and rightly so, that the Great War was only a struggle between rival empires; but Hitler was different than the Kaiser and Nazism was a particularly virulent form of imperialism. Then, too, the 1939 war came closer to Canadian shores than had the earlier one, something that had to affect Quebec opinion. Most important, perhaps, the Liberals were in power in 1939, a party that had pledged itself against compulsory service and that had seemed to mean it. Mackenzie King was trusted far more than Borden had ever been, and Ernest Lapointe was a presence whose like had not even existed in Borden's Conservative government.

Above all, the government of King had learned something from the mistakes of 1917. The propaganda was different in tone, far more nationalist than in 1914-18. The organization of the economy and of the war effort was infinitely better, and even the army was marginally more sympathetic to French Canada and aware of the problems than had been the case in the Great War. And King himself, fully aware that Canada could founder on the rock of conscription, paid full attention to the situation. All those factors mattered, and Quebec was never alienated in the Second World War. After Lapointe's death, for example, King could go to the Quebec élite and draw Louis St Laurent from the boardrooms to the Cabinet without difficulty; Borden never had that capacity.

Significantly, when St Laurent became Prime Minister in the midst of the Cold War, he was apparently willing to implement conscription. Perhaps a Quebec Prime Minister could have got his way without creating a new national trauma over compulsion; perhaps the fear of Communism could have been made into a powerful weapon to bring Quebec along. But the opinion polls provide no support for such a view, and Canada is probably fortunate that St Laurent did not find it necessary to imitate Borden and King on this issue.

The evidence then seems clear. Conscription may theoretically be the best, the fairest, and the most expeditious way to raise an army; it may equalize the demands and equalize the suffering far better than the hazards of voluntarism. All this may be so, but not in Canada. Here conscription has divided French-speaking Canadians from their compatriots. Here conscription has created chaos, shattering the political system and fostering mistrust and division in the country. And here conscription has had scant military impact, certainly not enough to provide a *post facto* justification for it. Conscription has simply not worked in Canada, and there seems no reason to believe that it ever will.

Select Bibliography

This listing is not intended to be all-inclusive. Cited are the major primary and secondary sources that were useful in the preparation of this work.

PRIMARY SOURCES

Directorate of History, Department of National Defence
    H. D. G. Crerar Papers
    Historical Records
Fondation Lionel-Groulx, Montréal
    Fonds de la Ligue pour la défense du Canada
    Fonds Georges Pelletier
    Fonds Maxime Raymond
Harvard University
    J. Pierrepont Moffat Papers
London, England
    Beaverbrook Papers
Public Archives of Canada
    R. B. Bennett Papers
    Robert Borden Papers
    Henri Bourassa Papers
    John Bracken Papers
    A. K. Cameron Papers
    Loring Christie Papers
    Brooke Claxton Papers
    M. J. Coldwell Papers
    Colonial Office Records
    Arthur Currie Papers
    J. W. Dafoe Papers
    Department of External Affairs Records

Department of Finance Records
Department of Militia and Defence Records
Department of National Defence Records
Devonshire Diaries
Charles Fitzpatrick Papers
George Foster Papers
J. T. Fotheringham Papers
G. S. Gibbons Papers
J. M. Godfrey Papers
Lomer Gouin Papers
W. L. Grant Papers
W. G. Gwatkin Papers
R. B. Hanson Papers
C. D. Howe Papers
Edward Kemp Papers
W. L. M. King Papers
Ernest Lapointe Papers
Wilfrid Laurier Papers
A. G. L. McNaughton Papers
R. J. Manion Papers
Arthur Meighen Papers
Talbot Papineau Papers
George Perley Papers
L. -P. Picard Papers
W. M. Ponton Papers
Privy Council Office Records
Privy Council Records, Cabinet War Committee Minutes & Documents
J. L. Ralston Papers
Escott Reid Papers
Newton Rowell Papers
Clifford Sifton Papers
R. E. W. Turner Papers
David Watson Diary
War Office Records
J. S. Willison Papers
J. S. Woodsworth Papers
Public Archives of Manitoba
J. S. Ewart Papers
Public Archives of Nova Scotia
F. W. Borden Papers

A. L. Macdonald Papers
E. N. Rhodes Papers
Public Archives of Ontario
    A. E. Belcher Papers
    H. J. Cody Papers
    Mitchell Hepburn Papers
    James Whitney Papers
Public Record Office, London
    Cabinet Records
    Colonial Office Records
    Dominions Office Records
Quebec Archives
    Conscription Scrapbooks
    F. -X. Lemieux Papers
Queen's University Archives
    Herbert Bruce Papers
    T. A. Crerar Papers
    Grant Dexter Papers
    W. A. Mackintosh Papers
    C. G. Power Papers
Saskatchewan Provincial Archives
    J. G. Gardiner Papers
Toronto Public Library
    Main Johnson Papers
University of New Brunswick
    J. D. Hazen Papers
University of Toronto Archives
    Edmund Walker Papers

SECONDARY SOURCES

Armstrong, Elizabeth. *The Crisis of Quebec* 1914-18. New York, 1937.

Berger, Carl. *The Sense of Power*. Toronto, 1970.

Borden, Henry, ed. *Robert Laird Borden, His Memoirs*. Toronto, 1938.

Brown, R. C. and Ramsay Cook. *Canada 1896-1921*. Toronto, 1974.

Bruchési, J. 'Service National et Conscription 1914-1917', *Transactions of the Royal Society of Canada* (1950).

Crerar, H. D. G. 'The Case for Conscription', *Queen's Quarterly*, LVIII (Winter, 1951-2).

Dafoe, J. W. *Clifford Sifton in Relation to His Times*. Toronto, 1931.

Dawson, R. M. *William Lyon Mackenzie King*, Vol. I: *1874-1923*. Toronto, 1958.

Duguid, A. F. *Official History of the Canadian Forces in the Great War 1914-1919*. Ottawa, 1938.

Durocher, René, 'Henri Bourassa, Les Evêques et la guerre de 1914-1918', Canadian Historical Association, *Historical Papers 1971*.

Eayrs, James. *In Defence of Canada*. 3 vols to date. Toronto, 1964-72.

Frost, Leslie M. *Fighting Men*. Toronto, 1967.

Gow, J. I. 'Les Québécois, la guerre et la paix, 1945-1960', *Canadian Journal of Political Science*, III (March, 1970).

Granatstein, J. L. *Canada's War: The Politics of the Mackenzie King Government, 1939-1945*. Toronto, 1975.

————. *The Politics of Survival: The Conservative Party of Canada, 1939-1945*. Toronto, 1967.

Hitsman, J. M. *The Incredible War of 1812*. Toronto, 1965.

————. *Safeguarding Canada, 1763-1871*. Toronto, 1968.

Hopkins, J. C. *The Book of the Union Government*. Toronto, 1918.

Hyatt, A. M. J. 'Sir Arthur Currie and Conscription', *Canadian Historical Review*, L (September, 1969).

La Terreur, Marc. *Les Tribulations des conservateurs au Québec*. Québec, 1973.

Merritt, W. H. *Canada and National Service*. Toronto, 1917.

Michel, Jacques. *La Participation des Canadiens Français à la Grande Guerre*. Montréal, 1938.

Morton, D. P. *The Canadian General: Sir William Otter*. Toronto, 1974.

————. 'French Canada and the Canadian Militia, 1868-1914', *Social History*, no. 3 (April, 1969).

————. 'French Canada and War: The Military Background to the Conscription Crisis of 1917', in J. L. Granatstein and R. D. Cuff, eds, *War and Society in North America*. Toronto, 1971.

————. 'Polling the Soldier Vote', *Journal of Canadian Studies*, X (November, 1975).

Neatby, H. B. *William Lyon Mackenzie King*, Vol. II: *1924-1932*, Vol. III: *1932-1939*. Toronto, 1963.

Nicholson, G. W. L. *Canadian Expeditionary Force, 1914-1919*. Ottawa, 1962.

Pearson, L. B. *Mike: The Memoirs of the Rt. Hon. Lester B. Pearson*, Vol. I: *1897-1948*. Toronto, 1972.

Pickersgill, J. W. *The Mackenzie King Record*. 4 vols. Toronto, 1960-70.

Prang, Margaret. *N.W. Rowell: Ontario Nationalist*. Toronto, 1975.

Report of the Director of the Military Service Branch to the Minister of Justice, 1 Mar. 1919. House of Commons, Sessional Paper 246.

Robin, Martin. *Radical Politics and Canadian Labour*. Kingston, 1968.

Roy, R. H. 'Major General G. R. Pearkes and the Conscription Crisis in British Columbia', *BC Studies*, no. 28 (Winter, 1975-6).

Rumilly, Robert. *Maurice Duplessis et son temps*. Montréal, 1973.

———. *Henri Bourassa*. Montréal, 1953.

———. *Histoire de la province de Québec*. 41 vols. Montréal.

Skelton, O. D. *Life and Letters of Sir Wilfrid Laurier*. Toronto, 1921.

Stacey, C. P. *Arms, Men and Governments: The War Policies of Canada, 1939-1945*. Ottawa, 1970.

———. *The Military Problems of Canada*. Toronto, 1940.

———. 'Nationality: The Experience of Canada', *Canadian Historical Association Report, 1967*.

———. *Six Years of War*. Ottawa, 1955.

Stairs, Denis. *The Diplomacy of Constraint*. Toronto, 1974.

Stratford, Philip, ed. *André Laurendeau: Witness for Quebec*. Toronto, 1973.

Swettenham, John. *McNaughton*. 3 vols. Toronto, 1968-9.

Thomson, Dale. *Louis St. Laurent, Canadian*. Toronto, 1967.

Urquhart, H. M. *Arthur Currie*. Toronto, 1950.

Ward, Norman. *A Party Politician: The Memoirs of Chubby Power*. Toronto, 1966.

Willms, A. M. 'Conscription 1917: A Brief for the Defence', *Canadian Historical Review*, XXXVII (December, 1956).

Wood, H. F. *Strange Battleground: Official History of the Canadian Army in Korea*. Ottawa, 1966.

Young, W. R. 'Conscription, Rural Depopulation and the Farmers of Ontario, 1917-1919', *Canadian Historical Review*, LIII (September, 1972).

Index

3 1221 05885 1051